DINING
with the
DEAD

A Feast for the Souls on Day of the Dead

M E X I C O

Traditional Mexican Recipes for Beloved Celebrations

Mariana Nuño Ruiz & Ian McEnroe

Rio Nuevo Publishers®
P. O. Box 5250
Tucson, AZ 85703-0250
(520) 623-9558, www.rionuevo.com

Text © 2022 by Mariana Nuño Ruiz McEnroe and Ian McEnroe.
Photographs © 2022 by Ian McEnroe, except where noted.
Photos © 2022 by Mariana Nuño Ruiz McEnroe: pages ii–iii, vi, 4 bottom right, 5, 6 bottom left and right, 12, 13, 17, 19, 26 all, 35 top, 43 bottom right, 67, 158 left, 240.

Collage pages 10–11 © 2022 by Mariana McEnroe.

All Rights Reserved. No part of this publication may be reproduced, stored in or introduced into a retrieval system, or likewise copied in any form without the prior written permission of the publisher, excepting quotes for review or citation.

Library of Congress Cataloging-in-Publication Data

Names: Ruiz McEnroe, Mariana Nuño, 1977- author. | McEnroe, Ian, 1974- author.
Title: Dining with the dead : a feast for the souls on the day of the dead / Mariana Nuño Ruiz McEnroe and Ian McEnroe.
Description: Tucson, AZ : Rio Nuevo Publishers, [2020] | Includes bibliographical references and index.
Identifiers: LCCN 2017040957 | ISBN 9781940322384 (hardcover) | ISBN 1940322154 (hardcover)
Subjects: LCSH: Cooking, Mexican. | Mourning etiquette. | All Souls' Day—Mexico. | LCGFT: Cookbooks.
Classification: LCC TX716.M4 R85 2020 | DDC 641.5972—dc23
LC record available at https://lccn.loc.gov/2017040957

Managing Editor: Aaron Downey
Associate Editor: Caroline Cook
Recipes and food styling: Mariana Nuño Ruiz McEnroe
Photo Editing and illustrations: Mariana Nuño Ruiz McEnroe and Ian McEnroe
Book design: Mariana Nuño Ruiz McEnroe and Preston Thomas, Cadence Design Studio
Cover design: Mariana Nuño Ruiz McEnroe and Ian McEnroe

Printed in China.

13 12 11 10 9 8 7 6 5 4

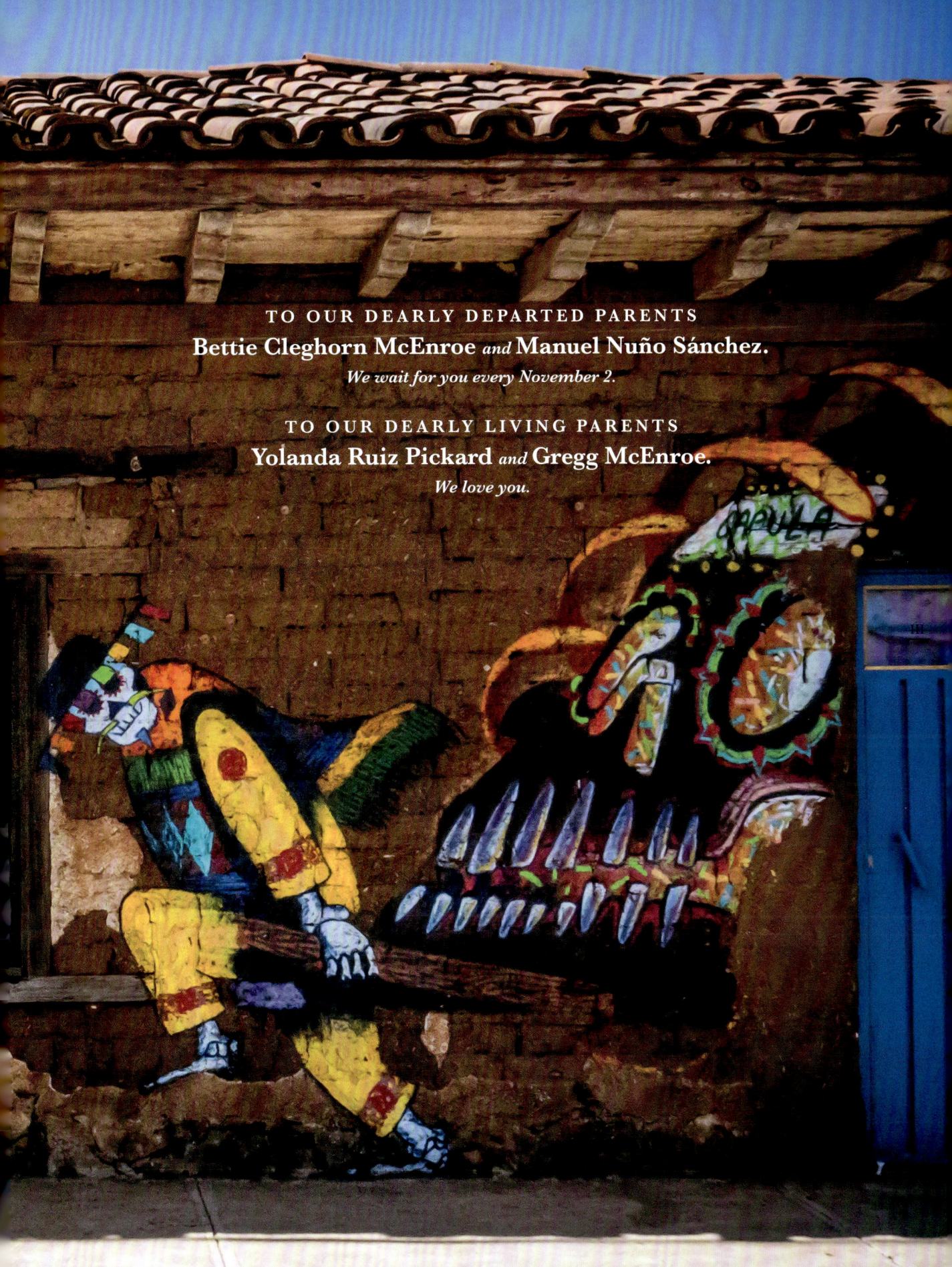

TO OUR DEARLY DEPARTED PARENTS
Bettie Cleghorn McEnroe *and* **Manuel Nuño Sánchez.**
We wait for you every November 2.

TO OUR DEARLY LIVING PARENTS
Yolanda Ruiz Pickard *and* **Gregg McEnroe.**
We love you.

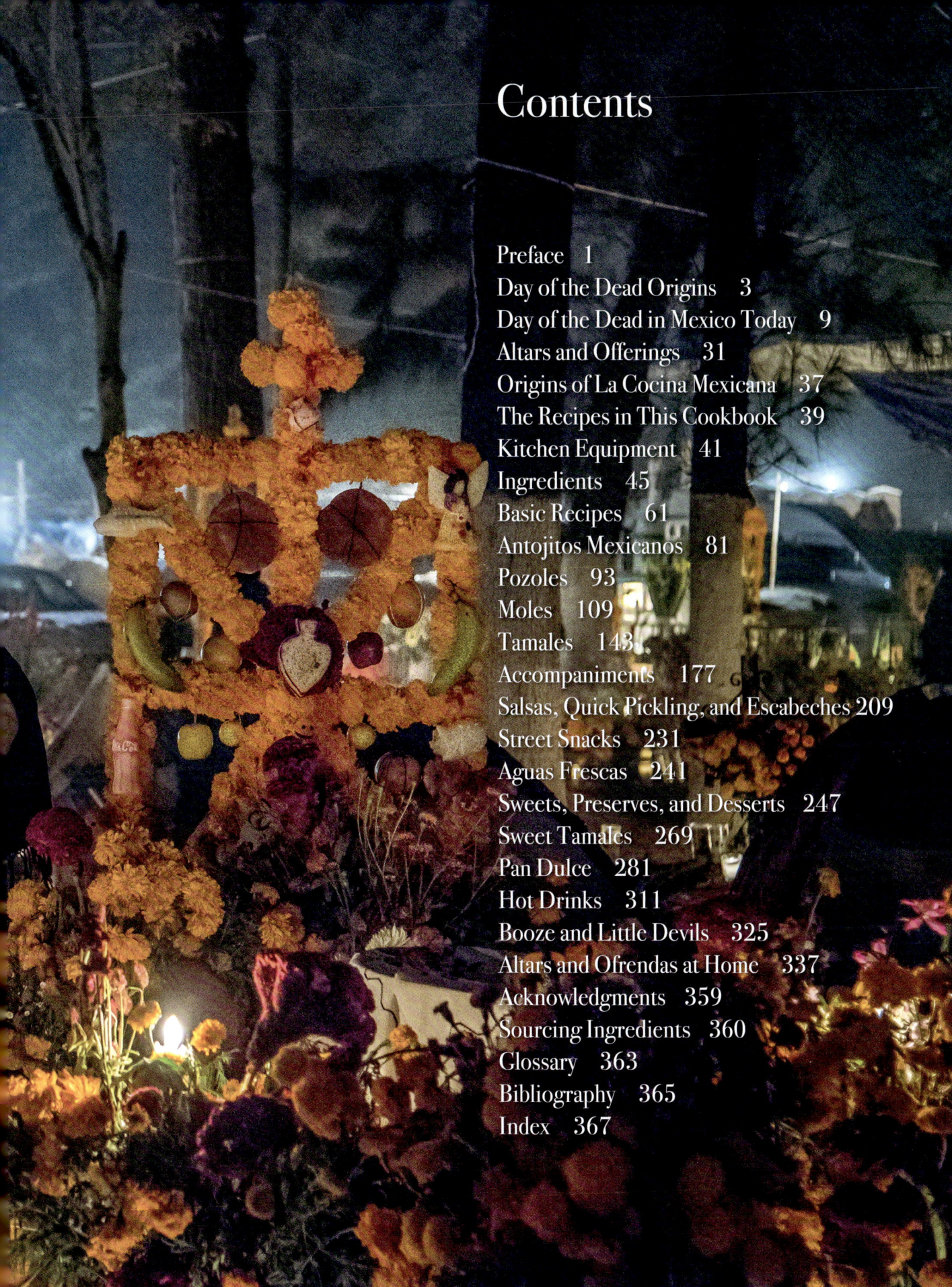

Contents

Preface 1
Day of the Dead Origins 3
Day of the Dead in Mexico Today 9
Altars and Offerings 31
Origins of La Cocina Mexicana 37
The Recipes in This Cookbook 39
Kitchen Equipment 41
Ingredients 45
Basic Recipes 61
Antojitos Mexicanos 81
Pozoles 93
Moles 109
Tamales 143
Accompaniments 177
Salsas, Quick Pickling, and Escabeches 209
Street Snacks 231
Aguas Frescas 241
Sweets, Preserves, and Desserts 247
Sweet Tamales 269
Pan Dulce 281
Hot Drinks 311
Booze and Little Devils 325
Altars and Ofrendas at Home 337
Acknowledgments 359
Sourcing Ingredients 360
Glossary 363
Bibliography 365
Index 367

Night vigil ofrenda at the Pacanda Isle cemetery at Lake Pátzcuaro, Michoacán, México.

Preface

The souls of Mexico are always hungry. At one time, Aztecs prepared masa dough from corn, which fed the creation of an empire. Today, chefs continue to use masa as the backbone of a cuisine that feeds the living and honors the dead. Culture and tradition pervade Mexico. Through centuries of change in culture, politics, religion, and economy, Mexico's food connects the past and present, as in the celebration of the Day of the Dead. Named by the United Nations Educational, Scientific and Cultural Organization (UNESCO) as an Intangible Cultural Heritage of Humanity in 2008, the Day of the Dead tradition has been recognized for its unique celebration of death and life, reuniting families every year through food, reinforcing tradition, and celebrating the beautiful aspects of Mexican heritage and culture that have become known around the world.

This book is a journey through the modern and historically rich culture at the core of Mexico and its offerings on the table, in the home, and in the plaza and market. It will introduce you to warm atole sipped by the graveside and tamales for beating hunger during night-long vigils. You will learn the secrets to the rich moles families eat when gathered in celebration and how to bake the pan de muerto left on the family altar to feed the visiting spirits on Día de Muertos.

The recipes in this book are celebratory dishes traditionally prepared during this holiday. We will show methods, such as the preparation of dried chiles for salsas and the nixtamalization of corn for masa, used in many of the recipes. And we describe how to create crafts, such as sugar skulls and paper flowers, as well as methods for building a family altar for your home.

The time we spent in Mexico researching and gathering content for this book was intense, exciting, and full of learning adventures. We chose the state of Michoacán for our Day of the Dead research, particularly the region of the Laguna de Pátzcuaro. There we met the indigenous people, the Purépechas, some of the kindest people of Mexico. Their traditions have carried on for ages, and some of their towns seem unchanged by time. Michoacán is known as the heart of Mexico, in part because of its robust indigenous and traditional identity. It is also known for its local artisans and rich gastronomy, so we knew we would taste food with traditionally rooted flavors there.

In 2004, a group of women called Cocineras Tradicionales—Traditional Cooks of Michoacán—was created. Their first event, *Encuentros de Cocina Tradicional Michoacána*, "Traditional Michoacán Gastronomy Encounters," was created to promote and pay tribute to the cooking of Michoacán. These women's love, knowledge, and techniques combined to express community identity, reinforce social bonds, and build stronger local, regional, and national culinary pride. These amazing cooks have since gained a worldwide reputation, and some have been sent abroad as culinary ambassadors of traditional Mexican cooking. In 2010, UNESCO added traditional Mexican cuisine to the Representative List of the Intangible Cultural Heritage of Humanity, a list of cultural riches worthy of preservation. The opportunity to learn from one of the best Cocineras Tradicionales in Mexico had a profound affect on my cooking. Reconnecting with the traditional flavors in the Mexican kitchen touched off memories of cooking with my Grandma in her humble little kitchen. You will "meet" my Grandma Margarita throughout these pages as well.

Many years of effort and care have gone into assembling the content of these recipes, some of which were first seen on our blog, *Yes, More Please!* We are grateful to our many friends and family in our hometown of Austin, Texas, and elsewhere around the world, and any and all who have stimulated and supported our enthusiasm and love for Mexico's cuisine and culture. And to those many who shared with us their home, their food, places of worship, hospitality, and heritage, we owe a great debt of gratitude. We offer an enormous *Muchas Gracias* to all the citizens of Pátzcuaro, the people of Michoacán, and to all of Mexico.

We hope you enjoy exploring *Dining with the Dead* and that it inspires an appreciation for a wonderful people and their colorful culture and exciting traditional cuisine.

Artisanal clay Catrinas at the Catrina Festival in Capula, Michoacán, México.

Day of the Dead Origins

On the first and second days of November, Mexicans celebrate and remember their dead by welcoming their traveling souls. This social tradition is an important part of family life, identity, religion, history, and culture. The evolution of Día de Muertos into the cultural folk tradition of today has deep roots in Mexico's past.

Día de Muertos origins are uncertain, as descriptions of its history either did not survive or, more likely, were never recorded. What we do know is that a western religious holiday supplanted a native harvest festival with corresponding dates and similar agendas. Western colonial control and beliefs overwrote those of the natives and virtually erased their culture. It was only centuries later, after the Mexican Revolution, that an indigenous cultural identity was rekindled and reclaimed, and reminiscent indigenous ritual elements became incorporated into the Día de Muertos celebration.

Aztecs and Death

Día de Muertos shares some similarities with pre-colonial Mesoamerican beliefs. Venerating the dead was well established in Mexico's native world, especially among the Aztecs. To them, death was part of the natural cycle, mirroring life. Their calendar followed nature cycles that marked each celebration and ritual. At the end of summer when the agricultural cycle came to a close, the Aztecs gave thanks and paid tribute to their gods and ancestors with a harvest and abundance festival.

As native beliefs were dictated by supernatural forces, a part of this festival was the presentation of offerings and human sacrifices to the gods. A ceremonial sacrificial death was an honorable and necessary appeasement to the many gods who controlled the natural world, and each ritual sacrifice also served as a renewal of the cycles of the sun, moon, rain, and harvest. Consumption of the victim's flesh and blood was part of these rituals, as was a belief in the afterlife. These beliefs, though pagan in the eyes of the Spanish conquerors, would provide a way to introduce notions of Roman Catholic faith to the Native population.

Spanish Conquest in Mexico

European discovery of the New World changed the fate of the native population. Spain began to take control of Mexico and its people in 1518 with the arrival of conquistador Hernán Cortés and his military. Spain's interest was in the land and its resources, not the people. Soon the native population was decimated by disease brought from Europe and Native leaders suffered the near total loss of their social and political power.

In 1524, twelve Franciscan friars arrived at Tenochtitlan to convert the indigenous population. The friars worked to prevent the violent abuses by the conquistadors and to learn the native language and traditions to more effectively establish grounds for the new faith. One obstacle to proselytizing in the New World was the differences between Roman Catholic beliefs and those held by the native cultures. An effective conversion technique was to replace native supernatural beliefs with similar Catholic theology by exploiting commonalities. For example, belief in the divine nature of Jesus could be strengthened by adapting the Aztec's voluntary ritual blood sacrifice to the Catholics' belief in Christ's willing sacrifice of himself. The Aztec consumption of their victim would be replaced by the ritual consumption of Christ's body and blood as a sacrament in the Holy Eucharist.

All Saints' Day and All Souls' Day

Church and native festivals also had similarities that encouraged Christianization. From the middle of July through the middle of October, the ninth through the twelfth months according to the Aztec monthly calendar, Aztecs held four major festivals—the first two dedicated to the dead and the later two dedicated to the harvest. These festivals were adapted by the friars to correspond to the Church celebrations of All Saints' Day and All Souls' Day (Día de Fieles Difuntos). All Saints' Day memorializes saints, the intermediaries to God. The following day, All Souls' Day, was a day to

Top: Virgen María y San José dressed in Purépecha indigenous attire at Templo de la Compañía, Pátzcuaro, Michoacán, México.
Bottom left: Juan O'Gorman's mural, "The History of Michoacán," inside the Biblioteca Pública Gertrudis Bocanegra in Pátzcuaro, Michoacán, México.
Bottom right: Altar for Día de Fieles Difuntos, Parroquia de San Diego de Alcalá, Quiroga, Michoacán, México.

pray for the departed at churches and cemeteries. Similarities between the content and dates of the two cultures' celebrations allowed the Church holiday to more smoothly replace the death and harvest festivals of the natives.

In the Spanish tradition of the sixteenth century, the Church held that All Saints' celebrations offered the souls of the deceased a means to redeem themselves from Purgatory. During All Saints' Day celebrations, saints' bones were exhibited in ornate boxes called reliquaries or on special altars where people prayed and devotees could buy favors from the saints. These rituals are still practiced in rural Spain and in Mexico City.

In Spain at that time, a *verbena* (modest festival) was held in the atriums of the churches, at which a number of handmade pastries and confections were sold. Among the market offerings were breads shaped like saints' bones called *pan de muerto*, skulls made of sugar, almond paste candies with different fruit fillings called *huesos de santo* (bones of the saint), and replicas of relics. For a small fee, the priest would bless the confections, and people would take them home, pray to them, and eat them as an act of communion with the saints.

Today's conventions of Día de Muertos originate from these Spanish verbenas and smoothly replace the Aztec rituals. Pan de muerto, now commonly placed on the altars, easily substituted for the beating heart of a warrior or a virgin maiden. Sugar skulls replaced the skulls of the warriors, war captives, or other sacrificial victims on the *tzompantli*, a Mesoamerican wooden rack used for displaying human skulls. The Catholic use of flowers and candles during rituals was another element that fit neatly with the native practice of celebrating the emergence of flowers in the ninth month of their calendar.

Nineteenth Century Mexico

The Independence of Mexico in 1810 marked the end of almost 350 years of Spanish oppression over the indigenous people. Dramatic changes in Mexico affected national identity and attitudes toward the Church. At this time the Catholic Church controlled birth and death records and funeral services. People were buried under the wood floors of the churches, where stacked coffins were housed, organized in height and proximity to the altar by prominence and nobility—the wealthier the person, the closer to God. Working class and indigenous people were buried outside in the courtyards, or at their home patios, unless they were Caciques or prominent merchants.

But frequently opening the floors for new burials released airborne bacteria, which was believed to be the cause of the deadliest cholera morbus epidemic in Mexico in 1833. Consequently, new sanitary ordinances to control disease compelled the Church to move burials from the churches to the countryside. Clandestine burials in churches finally ended after the second largest outbreak in 1855, and cemeteries were officially established for everyone regardless of economic status. Small chapels were built at the cemeteries for funerary services for all, and prominent families had shrines for private ceremonies.

The veneration of the souls in their new resting places required families to travel outside the cities for the Day of the Faithful Departed, giving rise to vendors along the road who supplied food, drinks, flowers, candles, and all that was needed to celebrate the day and to spend the night at the cemeteries, leading to some of our modern Día de Muertos traditions.

After these changes, the Mexican Constitution of 1857 implemented liberal ideas, freedom of expression, and the separation of church and state, debilitating the Catholic Church and giving space for new ideologies and religions.

In 1877, Porfirio Díaz, a Mexican general, became the 35th president of Mexico. He remained in power until 1911 after the start of the Mexican Revolution. During the long years of the Porfiriato, (the name given to this era), Mexico experienced profound political, economic, social, and cultural changes. This modernization of Mexico came at the cost of loss of political freedom and a watered-down Mexican identity, as during the Porfiriato, a heavy French influence shaped Mexican society and culture.

Mass for Fieles Difuntos at cemetery chapel in Arocutín, Michoacán, México.

Top left: La Calavera Garbancera (Dapper Skeleton), zinc etching 1910–1913 by J. G. Posadas.
Translation: "Happy Skeleton Auction. Those who today are powdery aloof chickpea ladies will end up as deformed skeletons."
Top right: Close-up of Catrina in Diego Rivera's mural, "Sueño de una Tarde Dominical en la Alameda Central" (Dream of a Sunday Afternoon in the Alameda Central), 1946–1947, Mexico City, Mexico.

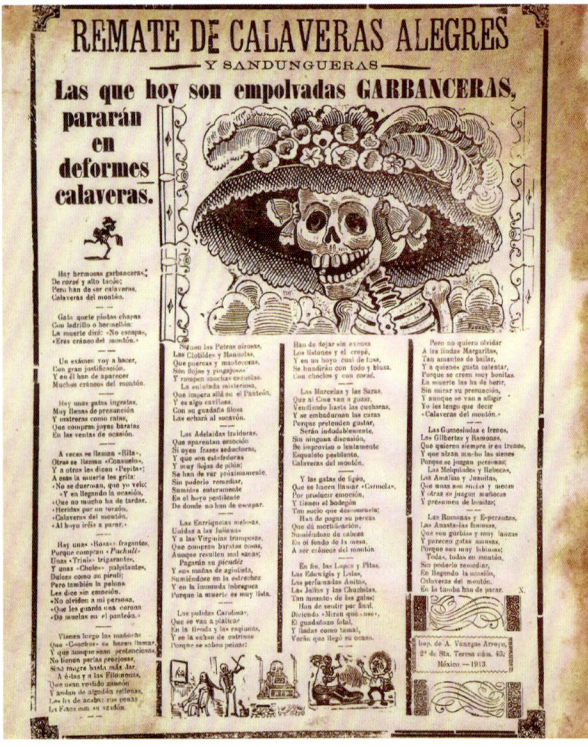

Bottom left: Clay Catrinas made by the artisans of Capula, Michoacán, México.
Bottom right: Folksy Catrinas in San Antonio, Texas, 2017.

José Guadalupe Posada and "La Calavera Garbancera"

At the same time that political and economic power were being consolidated in the elite surrounding Porfirio Díaz, a class of journalists developed that criticized politicians and upper-class society and denounced Mexico's economic, social, and cultural inequalities. Writers and journalists created characters as a form of social and political criticism, and their work spread the revolutionary ideas that ignited change.

One of the most important figures in this field was an illustrator named José Guadalupe Posada. Posada used cartoon skeletons to represent Mexican life, and humor and satire to address inequality, injustice, and the scarcity of economic resources. His cartoons also illustrated *corridos*, stories told in song, that often had political themes or narratives of historical events or romantic stories. Corridos also satirized criminals, politicians, ladies of society, bullfighters, and revolutionary figures.

Posadas's most noteworthy creation was an editorial cartoon known as "La Garbancera," which translates as "the chickpea lady." The famous skeleton was depicted wearing a pompous Victorian hat adorned with lace, flowers, and fruits. La Garbancera poked fun at the Mexicans who impersonated French aristocrats in pompous clothing and powdery faces in order to be accepted by the very society that rejected their indigenous roots. Why La Garbancera? At that time garbanzo beans, or chickpeas, were the cheapest food. La Garbancera highlighted the absurdity of those who can afford only garbanzo beans putting on fashionable European airs.

The Mexican Revolution, Vasconcelos, and Post-Revolution Nationalism

The Mexican Revolution broke out in 1910, causing Porfirio Díaz to flee the country one year later. For the next ten years, peasant leaders like Emiliano Zapata in the south and Pancho Villa in the north rose to power and brought with them notions of popular democracy and indigenous equality.

After nine years of revolutionary unrest, General Álvaro Obregón was overwhelmingly elected president in 1920. In 1921 he appointed José Vasconcelos as head of the Secretary of Education. From 1921 to 1924, Vasconcelos made extraordinary contributions. He organized rural indigenous communities by giving them public education, creating libraries, stimulating art, creating a publication program, and importing educators. These actions changed Mexico's national identity.

Vasconcelos is the father of "Indigenism," a nationalist political ideology that promoted heritage and identity for the nation by reclaiming its indigenous ancestral roots. In 1925, he wrote *La Raza Cósmica* (*The Cosmic Race*), an essay promoting the idea of Mestizos (half-indigenous and half-Spanish) as the new and only valid race, assimilating all of Mexico's indigenous cultures as one. Unfortunately, this Mestizo concept made a composite of dozens of different peoples, which masked their diversity, and was more propaganda than geneology. Cultural identity is more complex than that, and each individual's heritage is not accounted for in this otherwise well-intentioned philosophy.

To spread his ideas and unify the people, Vasconcelos commissioned artists and writers to create work that reflected the new national identity (mestizo). These works were paintings of working-class Mexicans in plain clothes, sombreros, and sarapes farming the land or in domestic scenes, or colorful scenes of robust Aztecs in romanticized pre-Columbian landscapes wearing ceremonial garb. This imagery emphasized a folksy Mexican heritage over the predominantly European identity adopted over the previous three centuries. This propaganda was spread in calendars, prints, movies, art, photography, music, and traditional crafts. Nationalistic classical composers emerged and popular folk music like mariachi and ranchero music now defined Mexico's musical identity. And the new ideology also influenced culinary traditions, giving birth to today's *antojitos Mexicanos*, a mix of Spanish, French, and indigenous food, which became the typical foods of Mexico.

The Muralists' Influence

Vasconcelos commissioned some of the most talented artists in Mexico to spread his ideology. They painted murals in public buildings that told the story of Mexico's indigenous ancestral rituals, colonial and religious oppression, and revolutionary leaders. They depicted the faces of the indigenous oppressed. Diego Rivera was one of the greatest of Mexico's muralists. Examples of indigenous elements can be found in his frescos in Mexico City, and many of his frescos portray the Día de Muertos celebration. Examples include murals entitled *The Maize Festival, The Sacrificial Offering—Day of the Dead, The Day of the Dead—the Dinner,* and *Day of the Dead—Party in the City.* They depict ordinary people wearing plain indigenous attire and paying respects to the dead in the cemeteries decorated in marigolds, making crosses of corn stalks, celebrating with street parties, and other religious funerary rituals.

In 1946, Diego Rivera painted a mural called *Sueño de una Tarde Dominical en la Alameda Central,* or "Dream of a Sunday Afternoon in the Alameda Central Park." In it, Rivera depicts an eclectic crowd of politicians, caudillos, writers, and artists from Mexico's history, as well as his wife, the well-known painter Frida Kahlo. The mural portrays bourgeoisie complacency and the events that led to the Mexican Revolution. The elegantly dressed central figures in this mural are walking in a parade under the protection of Porfirio Díaz, while an indigenous family is forced back by the police. The painting represents the story of Mexico and the dream of justice in which all fit together in one democratic place, la Alameda Central.

La Catrina

Along with the crowd in this mural, Rivera incorporated Posada's La Garbancera. He adapted the "garbanzo bean skull lady" and gave her a new name, "La Catrina." *Catrina* was slang for someone who dressed in fine clothing but was unaccustomed to it. Rivera also transformed her from just a skull to a full skeleton with attire.

Rivera placed La Catrina near the center of the mural, where she holds the arm of her creator, Posada, on one side, and the hand of a childlike version of himself in the other. He also gives her a strong identity, playing with fashion and elements from the Aztec Dame of Death, the Earth Mother Coatlicue, who is often shown as a skeletal figure wearing a feathered serpent around her neck. The serpent represents her son, the deity Quetzalcoatl, the Aztec feathered serpent god of wind and learning and the creator of humankind. The buckle on her dress is engraved with the Aztec astrological sign of Ollin, symbolizing perpetual motion. Rivera also gives her a set of reading glasses, as a symbol of educational reform. In this mural, La Catrina is also a political figure, the Lady Death, and the embodiment of the end of an era.

Over time, Catrina and her skeletal brethren have moved off the engraver's plate to many other media, including papier-mâché, giant statuary, wood, food, clothing, ceramic, and, most recently, animated feature films. In the little town of Capula, Michoacán, La Catrina has kept artisans busy for years. Capula is one of the biggest producers of decorative terra-cotta Catrinas, and much of its economy relies on these figurines. Each artist depicts her as different personalities, such as in typical indigenous attire or pompous French Victorian garb, or as Spanish folks, Mariachi bands, or even as Frida Kahlo.

Catrina is a modern mascot of Día de Muertos. She is a caricature who pokes fun at death and beckons us to embrace the absurdity of life's posturing and ambition. She is Death in cartoon form, and unlike the European Grim Reaper's dark, threatening embodiment of final doom, she reflects instead the Mexican outlook: Take death and your Earthly struggles with a dose of levity. Eternity is your fate, no matter what you think or do.

Day of the Dead in México Today

The Día de Muertos celebration has become one of Mexico's most cherished and iconic traditions and a holiday that celebrates our Mexican roots through our ancestors. The holiday has become secularized in some areas, while in others it remains deeply rooted in Catholicism, but it is still All Saints' Day and All Souls' Day in Mexico. Regardless of its complex origins, it is ultimately a holiday that simultaneously provides a sobering reminder of mortality while joyfully comforting the living as they memorialize the dead.

During the celebration, which starts on October 31 and spans November 1 and 2, people honor their dead with music, food, and religious folk rituals. Once a year on these nights, the souls or "ánimas" of our beloved departed ones—those who, as we say in Mexico, are "ahead of us"—return to commune with the living relatives and to enjoy the pleasures that made them happy in life: food, drinks, music, laughter, stories, and the warm company of family and friends. The living gather in cemeteries, churches, and at home to prepare welcoming feasts and celebrations to make the souls' long journeys worthwhile.

Despite sharing almost the same date as Halloween, Mexico's Day of the Dead shares little meaning with that commercial, sometimes macabre holiday. Celebrating with the dead in Mexico is not a morbid affair; the welcoming of their souls is always joyful!

Left background: La Leyenda de Popocatépetl e Iztaccíhuatl. Left to right: Benito Juarez; 1940s girl and charro boy; agent 007 and girlfriend; Mexican icon Abuelita; Frida Kahlo; Diego Rivera, creator of la Catrina; Jose Vasconcelos, father of the Mexican renaissance; Coatlicue earth mother Tonanzin, the mother of all origins for the Aztecs; La Catrina; Lázaro Cárdenas; Jose Guadalupe Posadas, creator of la calavera garbancera skull; Malinche and Hernán Cortés; Fray Bernardino de Sahagun, PH; Elsa Malvido, INHA investigator of studies about the Dead and Death in Mexico. Right window background Mexico City Cathedral, parade for Día de Muertos in Mexico City.

"Flores para el altar del tío Paco" (Flowers for Uncle Paco's altar).
Opposite page: Flower fields for Día de Muertos. Left to right: corn milpa, cresta de gallo, nubecita, marigolds.

The Celebratory Preparations in Mexico

The week before the celebration, you can feel the excitement building. Signs for Día de Muertos festivities appear. Special events and activities are scheduled at plazas, churches, schools, and museums. Communities hold fairs and colorful musical parades.

Markets and street vendors provide everything you need for the festivities. Artisans go to cities and larger towns to sell handicrafts, traditional pottery, woven baskets, wooden toys and kitchen utensils, textiles, embroidery work, and folk art. Markets overflow with seasonal fruits, vegetables, and flowers. Decorations used on the altars are sold from elaborate table displays. And one can find traditional ingredients to be used in special dishes like moles, tamales, and other homemade recipes. Talented cooks prepare traditional sweet treats for the ofrendas (offerings) at home and in the cemetery. Special artisanal decorations sold in the market for the churches and cemeteries include wood or palm-fiber items like archways, funerary wreaths, and crosses. And other indispensible elements for the celebration, like candles, ceramic sahumerios, copal, incense, images of saints, toys, ribbons, and papel picado, are readily available.

Handmade papel picado is prominent everywhere. This colorful tissue paper features artfully cut-out designs of skulls, skeletons, and other Day of the Dead motifs. It decorates the altars and the streets. Vendors also offer corn husks and tissue paper crafted into beautiful flowers and garlands, providing a festive atmosphere around towns, plazas, and churches.

To experience the market during this season is an adventure in colors, aromas, and flavors.

Flowers in the Market

Bright-orange, deep-burgundy, magenta, and white flowers also elevate the mood in the markets. These colorful flowers are harvested a few days before the holiday. Trucks filled with freshly cut blooms park around the markets and sell flowers to the townsfolk by the bushel.

Cempasúchil (Mexican marigolds), also known as "flores de muerto," are the iconic flowers used on altars and ofrendas because their scent and brilliant orange and yellow colors are said to be alluring to the souls and help illuminate the path in their journey back home. Other important flowers are the intense red-purple velvety cockscomb, which are usually chosen to decorate adult ofrendas. Other seasonal flowers used to decorate altars include baby's breath, white gladiolas, white carnations, calla lilies, and Casa Blanca lilies.

Top: Family of workers in flower fields in Tarímbaro, Michoacán.
Bottom: Entrance to municipal cemetery in Tzintzuntzan, Michoacán.

Top: Grandmas and grandchild getting candles, flowers, and papel picado to decorate their altar.
Bottom: Flower truck outside of the Basílica de Nuestra Señora de la Salud in Pátzcuaro, Michoacán.

Traditional Food at the Markets

Around the plazas, church atriums, and markets, street vendors set up long tables to display sweets and confections. Artisans sell decorated edible figurines made of sugar, chocolate, amaranth, and honey. A special sugar paste is made into figurines called *alfeñiques*, which are often shaped like lambs, chickens, rabbits, dogs, skeletons, miniature coffins, and angelitos (little angels). Edible skulls can be customized with the names of the departed or members of the family and friends to exchange as little gifts.

Traditional Mexican candies and candied seasonal fruits are sold as well. You'll find *calabaza en tacha* (pumpkin in sweet syrup), candied *camote* (sweet potatoes), *biznaga and acitrón* (sugary crystallized cacti), quince candies, *ates* (fruit pastes), *cajeta quemada* (caramels), and more, depending on the region.

One of the most iconic and beloved elements of Día de Muertos is pan de muerto, sweet bread of the dead. The smell of baking pan de muerto is the early announcement of the holiday. Pan de muerto and pan de yema (yolk bread typical of Oaxaca) are sold in large baskets in every town square and bakery. A slice of soft, delicious pan de muerto and a cup of hot cocoa is a delightful treat among the living before and during the holiday.

The invigorating smells of antojitos Mexicanos are everywhere. Options include an endless variety of street foods like tacos, tacos dorados, sopes, tostadas, flautas, tamales, atoles, aguas frescas, and seasonal fruits. Mexican corn is eaten on the cob, and as *esquites* (corn in a cup). Each town has their own food specialties and seasonal foods. Eating at the market is a festivity of its own and part of the wonderful experience before the holiday.

Sugar skulls and vendors at the Portales Plaza Vasco de Quiroga, Pátzcuaro.

Purépecha family cleaning and decorating tombs at the cemetery, Lake Pátzcuaro.

At the Cemetery

Mexican cemeteries are filled with gravesites of concrete or stone ranging from simple box-shaped structures to elaborate baroque shrines. A grave can be for one person or it can house an entire family. In the days leading up to Día de Muertos, families visit the cemeteries to clean, perform maintenance, and plan the decoration of these tombs.

Tasks are divided among family members, but everyone pitches in. Women clean the tombs and gravesites while men build or repair wood structures and hang decorations. Everyone gathers memorabilia to be placed on the altar at the gravesite. Women prepare food, and men are in charge of the drinks, chairs, blankets, and wood for the bonfire during the night vigil.

The Day of the Dead starts on October 31. The souls of babies, children, and people who have died in accidents arrive at midnight on November 1. Catholic mass is performed at the town's main church and at little chapels inside the cemeteries. A lit candle commemorates each departed family member. Celebrants pray to their saints for the absolution of the souls in transit. Afterward, family and friends take toys, sweet treats, and warm drinks to the cemetery where they play music and commune with *las almas chiquitas*, the "little souls."

Adult souls arrive at midnight on November 2. On the morning of November 1, friends and family gather at the cemeteries to finish decorating the tombs of adult souls. People take care of the tombs and graves other families have forgotten or of those who no longer have living relatives. Not a single tomb is left without a candle or a flower. Flowers are arranged in creative shapes like hearts, guitars, bicycles, or anything meaningful to the deceased. Portraits of the deceased and crucifixes, rosaries, small vessels filled with holy water, incense, and pictures of saints are placed on the stone tombs. Personal favorite objects of the deceased like cigars, candy, drinks, and alcoholic beverages are also part of the set up. In the late afternoon, families, friends, and visitors arrive to the cemeteries.

In the early evening of November 1, all is ready at the cemetery. The mood is festive as relatives and friends await the adult souls' midnight arrival. The tombs are brimming with fresh marigold flowers that shimmer in candlelight. White incense fog envelops the memorabilia of the deceased. The smells, colors, and sounds form a magical atmosphere. Just prior to midnight, another Catholic mass is celebrated for the souls of the *fieles difuntos* (faithful departed). A murmur of prayers can be heard. At the stroke of midnight, fireworks explode in the night sky above the small towns. Relatives, hired musical trios, and mariachis play the souls' preferred music. The welcoming celebration has begun! To be present for this beautiful night's splendor is a moving and contemplative experience.

After the fireworks and music, families and friends surround the gravesites to admire the decorations and to enjoy a warm drink and something to eat while communing with their dead. They express to them how much they have been missed and their hope for well being in the beyond. Family members present offerings to the souls. Baskets filled with fruits and pan de muerto, and small pots and plates with favorite foods and drinks are placed on the tombs. It is believed that no living person can eat these foods because the essence is consumed by the souls in transit.

Provisions are as important for the living as for the dead. So baskets with tamales, pan dulce (sweet bread), fruit, candy, and warm drinks like atoles, warm punch, pulque, and even tequila and mezcal are taken for the living folks spending the night at the cemetery. On this chilly night, celebrants wrapped in sarapes and blankets sit in folding chairs or lie on the ground. Families gather around small graveside bonfires to keep warm.

During the vigil, families play music and reminisce about their dead relatives and the good times they shared. Some people even settle grudges with the deceased. They pray, sing, drink, or talk all night. It's a time for reflection and appreciation, rejoicing and mourning.

At dawn a prayer is offered for the safe return journey of the souls. As they say goodbye to the traveling souls, loving family are left with good memories, content feelings, and the assurance they will be reunited again next year.

During the midday of November 2, people gather their belongings and clean up. The rest of the decorations and non-perishable offerings are left on the tombs. Families go back to their houses to rest and return to the cemeteries in the late afternoon to say goodbye to the souls.

One last mass is held at the churches to close the celebration cycle. At the cemetery, a priest gives the final blessing for the departed souls. For the rest of the week the cemeteries look bright and beautiful filled with the remaining flowers. After a week or so, people return to the cemeteries to do the final clean up, and the celebrations are over.

The day before Día de Muertos, Lake Pátzcuaro.

El abuelo telling family stories at the night vigil at Panteon de Cucuchucho, Lake Pátzcuaro.

Family gathers around the tomb; kids make bonfires and light candles for their abuelos.

Family gathering, ofrendas, and festive marigold arches at the cemetery for the night vigil.

Multi-family tomb with ofrendas for all.

Family altar at Museo de Artes e Industrias Populares, Pátzcuaro.

Altars and Offerings—*Altares y Ofrendas*

In Mexico during the week of Día de Muertos, many families assemble beautiful altars as the tangible legacies of previous generations. A Day of the Dead altar is the soul's shrine. It can take many forms but is usually a multileveled structure that displays several offerings. These altars and offerings represent the cultural, religious, and spiritual connection with our Mexican ancestors. But altars can memorialize anyone, from relatives and friends to historical or cultural heroes, and even pets.

The offerings placed on the altar are called *ofrendas*. Sometimes people use the terms *altar* and *ofrenda* interchangeably, but we will refer to the structure as an altar and the offerings as ofrendas.

There are three parts to an altar and its ofrendas. The first part is the structure, whether tables, wooden or cardboard boxes, or shelves. The second part typically consists of a portrait of the departed, marigolds, candles, incense, religious and sanctifying objects, as well as memorabilia. The third and most important part is all the earthly things the departed enjoyed most in this world.

Altar Origins

Although family altars are not built for worship, the concept originates in the Catholic Church. Altars and offerings were created by Spanish friars as a way to synthesize and sanctify the pagan rituals of the indigenous people in Mexico. The friars compared the meanings and similarities between the rituals dedicated to the veneration of the dead in both Catholic and indigenous faiths. Altars were a commonality that became a tool used to more easily establish All Saints' Day celebrations in Mexico.

These early altars were created as informal shrines in church atriums, at the tombs, in the cemeteries, and on tabletops in homes to sanctify the rituals of remembering the dead. Altars with staggered levels were built to mimic the niches in small chapels inside Spanish churches made for the veneration of saints and the exposure of relics on All Saints' Day. Altars were often constructed outdoors as a reference to the indigenous rituals performed on the stepped pyramids and were decorated with some of the same elements used for native sacrificial rituals. In churches, figurines of saints were dressed in indigenous attire to mirror the native culture.

Superimposing and swapping indigenous ritual elements with Catholic ritual elements was part of the evangelization process. One of the best examples of this is pan de muerto, the bone-shaped bread. Friars created the bread as a substitution for the skeletal remains of human sacrifices in Aztec rituals, just as confections sold in Spain on All Saint's Day mimic relics.

Other elements meaningful to both rituals were copal and incense, flowers, fruit, torches (replaced by candles), and memorabilia. Meaningful Catholic objects added to the altars included crucifixes, images of saints, rosaries, holy water, and, in modern times, the photo of the deceased. A few components of the harvest and abundance festival of the Aztecs, such as marigolds, fresh fruits, and vegetables like corn and calabaza, managed to stay as part of the offerings.

Some traditional indigenous food has endured and is vital to today's altars. Corn is the symbol of sustenance and the origin of the culture. It was the central ingredient in ancient recipes like tamales, tortillas, pozoles, and atoles. Other ingredients like chiles, herbs, and seeds were used in pre-Hispanic preparations, ground in stone mortars to make salsas and simple moles. Toasted cacao seeds were ground to prepare ceremonial drinks mixed with chiles and corn and sweetened with honey. These cacao beverages were dedicated to the ancestors and consumed during the rituals.

Teacher and students at the atrio de los olivos, a 500-year-old olive grove outside the Antiguo Convento Franciscano de Santa Ana, decorate one of the first outdoor chapels (from 1597) for Día de Fieles Difuntos. Today this convent is the Museum of the Old Franciscan Convent of Santa Ana in Tzintzuntzan, Michoacán.

Primary Altar Elements

Each part of the altar and the items placed on it has a particular significance.

Portrait of the beloved: Pictures and portraits are the portals for the souls to arrive and visit. They should be placed in the most important and visible place on the altar. Often a sugar skull with the name of the deceased is placed beside or underneath the photo. Some altars have multiple photos of family members, each on different levels.

Arch gateway or entrance: Arches symbolize the doorways to this world through which the departed souls return. They are placed as doorframes at the entrance of the house and are also situated at the top level of the altar, often framing the photo of the person. Arches are traditionally made with local materials leftover from the harvest, such as cornhusks, milpa, reed grass, palm, wood, or metal, and are usually covered with marigolds, fruit, ribbons, bells, sugar alfeñiques, and pan de muerto. If the altar is set up outside the house in a patio or terrace, a path made of bright-orange marigold petals is created to lead souls to the altar. These pathways and arches are also set up on tombs and gravesites.

The four cardinal directions: The cardinal directions—north, south, east, and west—are often represented by a cross made of salt, ashes, sand, flowers, or flower petals placed on the floor at the beginning of the path or at the foot of the altar. A candle is placed on each cardinal point. This is the compass that guides the soul on its trip to Earth and back home again.

The four elements:
Fire: Candles represent light, faith, and hope.

Water: A glass or bowl of water on the altar represents the "life source." It is offered to souls as refreshment and purification after their long trip.

Earth: Flowers and fruit are usually placed on the third level of the altar with a small bowl of sea salt. The salt is meant to purify and cleanse the souls for a safe return. Salt, ashes, and dirt on the floor in the shape of a cross can also represent the Earth element.

Wind: Symbolized by fruit hung from the arches and decorative paper hung on the entrance or at the top of the altar. Wind is also the vehicle for transmitting alluring scents from the flowers, fruits, copal, incense, and prepared foods.

Flowers:

Yellow-Orange: Cempasúchil flowers, known in the United States as Mexican marigolds, are the most iconic flowers of Día de Muertos. Their vibrant yellow-orange color and distinct scent is known to guide and welcome the souls. Their name comes from two Nahuatl words, *cemphalli* (twenty) and *xchitl* (flower) that makes *cempohualxochitl*, twenty-petaled flower. It is commonly known in Mexico as *flor de muerto*, or "flower of the dead." Every tomb, altar, basket, archway, path, and doorframe is decorated with marigolds. Their petals are used in spiritual pathways to lead the souls to the altars and tombs.

Red: Red flowers decorate altars and tombs and are part of the ofrendas dedicated to adults. Some examples are *cresta de gallo* (cockscomb), *flor de terciopelo* (velvet flower), *garra de tigre* (tiger's hand or tiger paw), and, as it's commonly known in Mexico, *flor de obispo* (bishop's flower) for its distinctive intense purple or reddish color. In Catholic symbolism, this flower represents the blood of Christ.

White: White flowers represent peace and purity. White baby's breath, gladioli, and wallflowers decorate altars and tombs and are used in ofrendas dedicated to babies, children, and innocent souls. White carnations, calla lilies, dahlias, and gladioli commemorate the elderly who recently passed.

Papel picado: Papel picado is colorful tissue paper or plastic cut into beautiful designs. Entire families in Mexico are dedicated to the art of designing and making this decorative paper depicting stories, skulls, skeletons, funerals, altars, Catrinas, and other motifs. Some of them are personalized with the name of the family or loved one.

Ancient Mexicans used ficus, fig, or mulberry tree bark to make amate paper (*amatl* in the Nahuatl language). It was also made out of the alkaline liquid from the corn nixtamalization process. This water, known as *nejayote*, contained dissolved hull, starch, and corn matter that was sieved and made into paper. The paper was then made into banners with cut-out figures or painted with decorative designs. Papel picado represents happiness, adds color, and reflects the festive mood of the celebration.

Candles: The warm glow produced by wax candles and *veladoras* (votives) is believed to sanctify the altars and tombs and to provide a peaceful atmosphere for the night vigil. Candles are placed on each level of the altars to illuminate the offerings and light the way for traveling souls.

Sahumerio and copal: A *sahumerio* is a clay incense burner. Burning copal is believed to purify the soul. A large ceramic goblet with burning copal placed on the gravesite creates columns of white smoke along with a rich and enchanting aroma that is believed to signal the souls. For home altars, a smaller ceramic sahumerio or copal incense stick is used instead.

Herb bundles: Herb bundles are used to cleanse the energy and make a peaceful place for the arrival of the dead. They are usually made of a combination of dry herbs like laurel, rosemary, mint, and sage.

Religious objects: These are usually placed on the top level along with the picture of the deceased.

Crucifix: The symbol of Christianity and sanctification.

Images of saints: The departed's favorite saint, the Virgin Mary, or other religious image to whom the living can pray and sanctify the journey of the dead.

Psychopomp symbols: Angels, pets, or any other symbols that were meaningful to the deceased and that will act as companionship on their journey to this realm.

Holy water: A cup of holy water is used to bless the altar. A marigold is usually placed upside down in the cup or beside it. The flower is dunked in the water and shaken to scatter the holy water to sanctify the offerings and the path to the altar.

Rosaries: Beads used to pray for the souls to help redeem their sorrows and to resolve feelings, problems, or sins the soul might want to address during their visit.

Paschal candle: A candle emblazoned with the cross, representing Christ's light entering the world.

Cross of ashes: A cross made with ashes saved from burnt palm leaves from Palm Sunday. It reminds us we are one with the Earth.

La Santa Muerte: "The Holy Death," is a controversial new saint in Mexico and a female personification of death. Prayer to La Santa Muerte has become widespread recently as worshipers frustrated by old, tyrannical, and rigid Catholic ideas have sought justice in faith. They have turned to "La Santa Muerte," concluding that "Death" is always impartial. She takes everyone equally: rich and poor, ugly and beautiful, good and bad. The Catholic Church disapproves of and prohibits the validity of La Santa Muerte in Mexico, regardless of her Spanish origins as the Grim Reaper.

Memorabilia of the departed: Returning souls rejoice in objects that once belonged to them—clothing, shoes, tools, musical instruments, toys, money, family heirlooms, music, or anything that reflects the departed's personality and that the soul might appreciate or that might be useful in their journey back from the afterlife. Letters to the departed are written for emotional relief and closure and displayed either sealed or for all to see. Some families even play jokes on their departed by placing their least favorite things on the altar.

Music at the celebration: Musical instruments, sheet music, recorded music, and live performance are common ofrendas. Performances come large and small, from mariachis, trios, and *bandas* (groups with horns and percussion) to a solo family musician. The music offered is the favorite of the deceased or a special dedication from a loved one.

"Calaveritas" (literary verses): Family and friends may write these short verses, either about the departed or one another. Then on the night of Día de Muertos these verses are exchanged. The simple verses are often funny, witty, or sarcastic. They poke fun and celebrate the living (with the notion of "what if you were dead") and the dead with laughter. Posada popularized these verses in his newspapers, accompanied by skeletal cartoons. Mexicans maintain a great sense of humor by not taking themselves too seriously about the afterlife journey.

Food offerings: Food offerings are placed in the lowest level of the altar on the table and should include the favorites of the deceased. The smells of the food represent nourishment to the soul and awaken memories of the family kitchen, favorite dishes prepared by mothers and grandmothers, and the comfort and happiness of home.

Meals are plated as if you were serving a dinner guest and are left on the altar all night. It is believed that the essence of the food is absorbed by the souls, leaving it flavorless, and therefore only the souls can enjoy the food on the altar.

The foods most often chosen for the altars are traditional Mexican celebration dishes. These elaborate seasonal dishes are usually prepared only for special occasions. Favorites include tamales, pozoles, moles, calientitos (warm fruit punch), pan dulce con chocolate caliente (sweet bread with hot cocoa), and seasonal desserts made with candied fruits. Nearly all of the recipes in this book are traditionally made for Día de Muertos.

Top: Night vigil at cemetery in Pacanda Island, Lake Pátzcuaro. Bottom left: La Santa Muerte, family altar and ofrenda. Bottom right: Ritual of ofrendas at 12 a.m. at the cemetery of Pacanda Island.

Origins of La Cocina Mexicana

Pre-Hispanic Cuisine

The seasons were very important to the ancient Mexicans, who understood what their Mother Earth offered during the annual planting and harvest cycle. They cooked with respect for their ingredients and used every part of them.

Corn was the main source of nourishment for the pre-Hispanic peoples. Some civilizations, like the Mayas, believed humans were made of corn. They worshipped their gods and ancestors to receive a good crop and to give thanks for the harvest. Corn was used in tortillas, masa, tamales, pozole, pinole, drinks, and porridges. They used every part of the corn, eating or drinking it fresh, dry, steamed, roasted, and pulverized into powder. In addition, the Aztec and Maya civilizations used nixtamalization, the process of precooking corn with limestone powder. This process significantly increases the nutritional value of the corn, unlocking niacin and protein, and gives it the right texture and flavor for the masa.

Other essential crops in their diet included beans, dry and fresh chiles, tomatoes, zucchini, pumpkin, potatoes, sweet potatoes, avocados, jicama, seeds, peanuts, cashews, amaranth, cacao, and honey. Ancient Mexicans also grew many types of fruit, including guavas, papayas, mangoes, avocados, mamey, sapote, cherimoyas, and various cacti. They ate popcorn and puffed amaranth. They drank *pulque* (*octli* in Nahuatl), a sweet fermented beverage made from the heart of the maguey plant, and prepared sweet and savory and hot and cold Cacao-based drinks. Ground cacao was combined with water and ingredients like masa, chiles, and herbs and occasionally sweetened with honey.

Natives hunted deer, rabbit, duck, and the native bird of the Americas, wild turkey (*guajolote*). They ate turkey eggs and occasionally the whole bird, but turkey was mostly used for special festivities and celebrations. Ants, grasshoppers, snails, frogs, and axolotls (salamanders) were consumed with salsas, chiles, herbs, mollis, and in tamales.

Fish, shrimp, lobster, and freshwater acocil crayfish were delicious dishes seasoned with chile paste, herbs, mollis, or sauces, then wrapped in plantain leaves, or incorporated into soups. They also consumed large amounts of nutritious, protein-packed algae called *tecuitlatl*, collected from Lake Texcoco.

Pre-Hispanic cooking preparations were based on simple methods like toasting, roasting, grilling, or steaming. The natives used a *comal* (ceramic flat grill), clay pots for boiling water, food wrapped in corn or banana leaves and then steamed, pits in the ground, and hot stones for cooking.

Their condiments were sauces made with chiles, onions, and seeds. These sauces were known as *molli*, the word from which we derive mole. These *mollis* were ground in stone mortars (*metates*) and then added to the rest of the food, from tamales to atoles and pozoles. Along with chiles, they also used aromatic vanilla orchids and honey to perfume sauces and drinks.

Today, some indigenous ingredients and pre-Hispanic preparations like corn nixtamalization, are still used for pozole and when making masa. Along with chiles and salsas, they remain an essential part of our cuisine.

Merging Cultures in the Kitchen

When Hernán Cortés arrived in America, he had only two kinds of food in the boat, cassava bread and bacon. Once established on the American continent, Spain sent provisions, including different types of cattle, nuts, spices, cereals, and seeds. They introduced wheat and sugarcane, and with it the production of refined sugar.

The Spanish people who arrived on the American continent became the dominant class. They brought a new faith, built churches and convents, grew new cultivars, and taught their techniques for preservation and food preparation. The convents' barns, gardens, and orchards became agricultural research centers, and their kitchens became the food laboratories of the colony. By the end of the seventeenth century, these convents contributed refined flavors and the most delicious sweet confections.

Native food changed with the introduction of Spanish ingredients. Animal lard made tamales moister and beans were prepared "refried." Carrots, lettuce, and dairy products were combined with native ingredients to create antojitos Mexicanos. Milk and sugar changed the flavor of atole and cacao drinks. The addition of pork, beef, and chicken enriched soups like pozole, and complemented guisos and sauces. Nuts, seeds, spices, tomatoes, chiles, and turkey combined by Spanish cooks

in a convent gave birth to one of the most iconic and representative Mexican traditional dishes: mole.

The colonial influence manifested in every aspect of Mexican life, including language, architecture, religion, ritual, and the racial identity of the people. Spanish blood mixed with native, producing mestizos. The interchange of Spanish and indigenous cultures produced a new cuisine in the kitchen, where it came to be practiced every day and where every ingredient, flavor, and technique mingled, creating a delicious culinary amalgamation. Over the centuries, Spanish, indigenous, criollos, and slave women brought to America from Africa and the Caribbean worked and cooked together and connected their knowledge of ingredients, flavors, and cooking heritage. These collaborations became what we know today as *la cocina Mexicana*, Mexican cuisine.

Traditional cuisine is rooted in history, culture, and the knowledge and techniques passed from one generation to another. It may change as it is passed along, but it always retains that connection. Passing along these recipes celebrates their origins and preserves Mexican heritage and identity.

The majority of this book's recipes have been written with consideration of traditional origins, history, and regionality, with some adaptations for today's home cook. Ingredient substitutions are carefully suggested in certain cases where traditional ingredients may not be available, as long as they don't compromise quality or flavor. I hope you enjoy these recipes and that in making them, they become celebrated family favorites to refresh old traditions and embrace new ones.

The Recipes in This Cookbook

The challenge in writing recipes lies in capturing the spirit, flavor, technique, and nuances of a dish. To translate aromas, sounds, and a sensibility for doneness is even more challenging. We cooks work with all our senses in the kitchen, the accumulation of experience, and love for the food we cook. How does one record in a recipe that which best describes my own process to instruct a person I have never met, to deliver victorious results? The best I can do is give you the most detailed steps and description of flavors, aromas, and a road map, in the hope they will bring you the same results.

With this in mind I have written detailed instructions and specific notes for each recipe. Along with these instructions, key step-by-step photos illustrate recipes, from textures to cooking process and techniques. Notes in each recipe describe how the dish is served and how long it will keep. To cook a recipe for the first time is challenging. I hope the following "recipe" helps you follow the recipes in this cookbook.

Recipe to Follow a Recipe
Makes an enjoyable recipe process and delicious results

1. **Read recipe:** Read the entire recipe before you make it. This will help familiarize you with the ingredients and techniques required. A few recipes call for pre-made elements. The basic recipes section (page 61) provides simple, easy-to-follow instructions on how to prepare these basic components and treat specific ingredients. Most of these basic recipes can be made days in advance.

2. **Know your ingredients and equipment:** Buy the best quality ingredients that you can. Pay attention to the kind of chiles, herbs, and spices required. The wrong ingredients can ruin a recipe. Please refer to the illustrated guide of ingredients and cooking equipment on pages 41 and 46 to help familiarize you with the essentials used in these recipes.

3. **Shop in advance:** Having everything you need at home will make the cooking process smooth and enjoyable. Mexican ingredients are now more commonly available at many supermarkets in the international or Hispanic food aisles. Shopping online for certain pantry items may save time and effort. See the ingredient sourcing list of supermarkets, specialty stores, and online providers on page 360.

4. **Time:** Many of these recipes require plenty of time to prepare. Some take a few hours, some all day. For this reason, Mexicans often prepare special dishes with family and friends and only for celebrations like birthdays, baptisms, weddings, anniversaries, and, in this case, Día de Muertos. Making time to cook is often challenging, but will ensure you enjoy the cooking process as much as the results.

5. **Season and taste:** Always season, taste, and reseason if needed. Differences in ingredients, vegetable size, and quality change flavors. Taste the food as you cook and adjust the recipes to your liking. Sample before serving, when you still have time to correct the recipe. When making salsa, evaluate chiles for the spiciness level; you might need to use fewer or add more than instructed. When using fresh fruits to make preserves or agua fresca, taste the fruits to check ripeness; you might need to adjust the sugar.

6. **Baking:** For the baking recipes in this book, all measurements of flour are also given in metric weight because measuring by volume is not accurate. An affordable digital kitchen scale might become your best baking tool. Using a scale when baking is easier than measuring ingredients by volume and will give you more accurate results. When baking, use farm fresh eggs if possible and whole milk, both at room temperature, and unbleached all-purpose flour. Use European style butter because it has the least amount of water and the best color and flavor. And check your oven's internal temperature with an extra thermometer for best baking times and results.

7. **Serving:** Presentation is the sum of your efforts. Serving the dish on a special platter will make it more special. Serve the food you prepare with love and take pride in what you made. Your family will notice and the food will taste and look its best.

Note: Cook boldly and embrace curiosity. Take ownership of the dishes you prepare. Results will vary. Share the food with your loved ones and taste Mexico. Enjoy!

Kitchen Equipment

This section explains the gear that I regularly use in my kitchen. Handmade Mexican utensils have a humble and artisanal quality. Artisans from different parts of the country specialize in wood, volcanic stone, clay, and metal kitchen equipment. Many of these are considered family heirlooms and are passed down through generations to the best cooks in the family.

Home Appliances

Blender: A good, powerful blender is useful in Mexican kitchens because grinding and pureeing sauces, chiles, and nuts is the base for almost every recipe.

Hand blender: I prefer this type of blender for small jobs or when preparing salsas or soups right in the cooking pot. Not as critical to own. Get a powerful one for best results.

Food processor: Ideal for chunky sauces and grinding nuts, but not as crucial to have as a great blender.

Slow cooker: A great alternative for cooking beans, hominy, and pork shoulder.

Spice grinder: Ideal for grinding cinnamon sticks, seeds, nuts, and spices.

Pots and Pans

Comal: A comal is a type of griddle that is wonderful for toasting chiles and cooking fresh corn and flour tortillas. A **large clay comal** gives the best flavor to fresh-made corn tortillas. The clay ones are harder to find in the States, highly breakable, and best used over wood stoves for best heat distribution. A cast-iron griddle is the next best option, and a durable substitute.

Clay pots: When purchasing any pot made of clay, make sure it is made of food-safe materials and glazes. Many pots with pretty designs have an enamel coating that makes them only suitable for serving food, not for cooking. With clay pots, Mexican foods cook evenly and taste even better. Beans cooked in a clay pot are flavorful, traditional, hearty, and delicious. Once you try clay pots, I think you will fall in love with them. If you have the opportunity, invest in a set of clay *cazuelas*—shallow pots with lids for cooking and serving. They keep food warm when serving family style or arranging a Mexican buffet for a party. Clay cazuelas and pots are generally hard to find in retail stores in the United States. There are a few online options in the sourcing section (page 360), but ship them at your own risk since they are fragile. Perhaps the best source for clay pots is your next trip to Mexico!

Steamer pot (tamalera): A must-have for making tamales. The size you want will depend on the size of your tamale mission. I own a 20-quart steamer and I can fit 3 to 4 dozen tamales in it, depending on their size. A 24-quart will fit 4 to 6 dozen, a 32-quart 6 to 8 dozen, and a 50-quart 8 to 12 dozen. Take into consideration the size of your stove burners when buying a large pot. For instance, a 50-quart pot requires a commercial-sized burner; for smaller sizes you want the pot to be centered on the burner for even heat.

Large stainless steel or enamelware pot: It is vital to own a large, tall pot, especially when making moles and pozoles. Make sure your pot is made of a combination of steel and aluminum for best heat distribution. Cast-iron enamelware (e.g., Dutch oven) is a great option. They hold heat at a steady range and are safe to cook tomato- and chile-based recipes.

Nice to Have

Clay dishes: There are many traditional designs and styles of clay pottery made in Mexico. Some of the most remarkable work is made in little communities where the craft has been passed down through generations. The most iconic styles and the states they come from are: *Burnished clay,* from Michoacán; *Red clay* from Jalisco; *Majolica* from Guanajuato; *Talavera* from Puebla; the *Tree of life* original from Metepec Estado de México; *Black clay* from Oaxaca; and *Pakime* from Chihuahua. Serving food in clayware brings food to life and is part of the everyday Mexican table. On holidays like Día de Muertos, families use their best dinnerware to set the table and present the food in a special and festive way. Many online stores sell this kind of pottery. Prices depend on how elaborately they are painted and if the pieces are high-fired. High-fired ceramics are denser and more durable.

Corn mill: If you are going to make nixtamal at home and process it into masa, you will need a corn mill that can grind corn kernels when they are soft and wet. Food processors and mixer attachments don't work well. Your best bets are:

Victoria Professional Manual Grain Grinder and Table Clamp Corn Mill: These mills run on arm power. You will build up some good biceps while you're at it. They are different sizes and can be attached to counters or tables. They cost about $50.

Nixtamatic: This household electric mill is made in Mexico and is hard to get in the United States. I have seen these on eBay for about $300.

Masienda Molinito: The only electric molino available in the United States that uses volcanic stones to grind nixtamal. Small enough for household use and great for a large familia. It comes with a pro pricetag of $1,800, but if you dream of perfect masa, look no further.

Metate: Probably one of the oldest cooking tools, this item for grinding grains, dry and fresh corn, herbs, nuts, and cacao was the workhorse of Aztec and Mayan cuisine. The surface is flat and provides a different surface for grinding compared to the bowl-shaped molcajete. Metates are still used by traditional cooks and there is a special technique to master when using one. *Metateras*, ladies who have learned how to use one at an early age, still say they learn from it every day.

Molcajete: This grinding tool that looks like a mortar and pestle is typically carved from a solid block of volcanic stone. The stone provides friction while retaining moisture when making salsas and sauces or grinding seeds, and the minerals in the stone impart flavor into salsa as it's ground. As with the clay pots, make sure to buy from the right source; some imitation molcajetes are made of softer stone, which can lead to bits of the stone getting in your food. It takes a long time to cure a molcajete. Before using it, submerge the molcajete in hot water overnight to hydrate the stone. The next day use a natural fiber brush to scrub it inside and outside, and rinse well. Add about half a cup of uncooked rice with some sea salt and a few garlic cloves and grind it using the pestle (*tejolote*). Use the weight of the pestle in combination with a circular wrist movement to grind the rice against the stone. Rice and sea salt together make a gentle abrasive paste that as you grind will get into the nooks and crannies of the stone and trap any loose stones and dust. Discard the paste and rinse thoroughly a few times until it rinses out clear water. Repeat this process as needed until the rice paste comes out as clean as possible. This process cleans, seals, and seasons the stone surface. Then mash half of a cooked tomato in the molcajete. Rub the tomato puree between your fingers to feel for any stone dust. If it feels grainy, you might have to repeat the rice process again. Curing a molcajete is a labor of love, and as everything that comes from love, it is worth it.

Tortilla press: If you want to make fresh corn tortillas at home, this is a must. Presses are typically made of wood or metal. Buy a medium size, about 7 to 8 inches in diameter to make a standard-size tortilla.

Utensils

Bean smasher or machacadora: Bean smashers are made of steel or metal and resemble potato mashers. Bean smashers have small holes on the bottom, whereas a machacadora is a solid block of wood with a long handle. When making refried beans, you want some texture in the beans, and either of these tools will yield the desired results.

Fine-mesh strainer: Most of the sauces and chile pastes blend into a fine puree if chiles are properly hydrated and not too much water is added. However, sometimes we can end up with a sauce that is not smooth. A fine-mesh strainer will save the day.

Long stainless steel ladle: Perfect for serving pozole, soups, and moles.

Molinillo: The molinillo is a pre-Hispanic tool for frothing hot chocolate that was carved out of a single piece of wood. It is a long straight handle with a round head at the end. Surrounding the wood stick, two or three loose rings are carved around it. To use, place the wood stick between the palms of your hands and rub your hands together to make it spin. This motion creates a smooth froth. It is also used to stir champurrados and atoles. The sound it makes announces that the cocoa is ready! Some molinillos are built right into chocolate pitchers.

Tongs: Aluminum tongs, long or short, are great when charring tomatoes in a direct flame or on the comal. They are also helpful in transferring soaked chiles to the blender.

Wood paddles and spoons: Ideal for stirring and serving moles, sauces, and salsas. A good selection of different size wood spoons will come in handy.

Ingredients

I want you to feel confident while shopping for ingredients and to recognize what you are buying. This guide will familiarize you with the ingredients I used in this book. Many of these are specialty items that are not found in your ordinary pantry and you will need to reliably identify and select the best components to get the best results in the recipes. You will find most of these ingredients in the international food aisle of your local supermarket, Hispanic markets, or specialty stores. For your convenience, I have also included a list of online suppliers on page 360 who are currently reliable sources of ingredients.

✳ ✳ ✳

Essential Mexican Ingredients, Spices, and Aromatics   46

Fresh and Dried Herbs   50

Fresh Chiles — *Chiles Frescos*   53

Dried Chiles — *Chiles Secos*   55

Preparing Dried and Fresh Chiles   57

Essential Mexican Ingredients, Spices, and Aromatics

Achiote paste: This is a concoction of annatto seed powder, salt, black pepper, allspice, garlic, onion, and corn masa. It is usually sold as small bars that are dissolved in vinegar and orange juice to make marinades or stews. When buying achiote paste, look for brands that have all-natural ingredients. Some brands have artificial colors that can ruin the flavor and quality of the dish. I prefer to get the annatto seeds and make my own powder using a spice grinder. I think it works best, and the flavors are more alive and vibrant. Specialty stores or spice shops will carry annatto seeds.

Allspice (pimienta gorda): This is known as "fat pepper" in Mexico because of its bigger size in relation to regular black peppercorns. These dried round berries have a complex flavor—a combination of cloves, cinnamon, and black pepper. Allspice peppercorns can be sold together in slightly different sizes, so when using them whole, use the average-size corns (about ¼ inch in diameter). Allspice is used in moles, stew meats, adobos, and cochinita pibil. Buy it whole since it will keep its natural oils and flavor longer.

Annatto seeds (achiote): These small red seeds are found inside the fruit pods of the achiote tree. Achiote was used in pre-Colombian times for body painting, textiles, and as a pigment for writing and coloring codices and murals. Today, the powder is still commonly used in the Yucatán Peninsula as textile dye. Achiote powder is combined with other spices and aromatics to make achiote paste. Peppery, floral, slightly lemony and fragrant, annatto seeds are pulverized and used in classic adobos and marinades like the iconic Yucatecán dish cochinita pibil (page 138).

Bitter orange (naranja agria): Brought from China to Mexico in the sixteenth century, the juice of this green gnarly-textured, highly acidic orange is so particular that it almost tastes like vinegar. Floral and sharp, these oranges are used unripened and are essential to cochinita pibil and other marinades for fish, bison, and armadillo dishes from southeast Mexico. Though often found in Mexican supermarkets here in the States, it can be replaced with a combination of equal parts vinegar, fresh orange juice, and lime juice.

Cooking oil: The oils used in Mexico are primarily canola, sunflower, safflower, and corn, or a combination of these sold simply as cooking vegetable oil. Olive oil is seldom used in Mexican cooking and appears mostly in recipes with strong Spanish influences. I like to use extra virgin olive oil in my green mole pipian because it pairs well with the herbs in it and lightens the flavor. For the rest, unless noted in the recipe, a vegetable oil will do.

Crema: Mexican crema is like French crème fraîche. It is sweet, slightly tangy, salty, and has a thick, smooth consistency. Due to its 45% fat content, its color is slightly off-white. Mexican crema is used as a topping, and it complements the flavors of spicy sauces as in enchiladas and antojitos Mexicanos. It can usually be found beside the fresh cheeses or heavy creams. Sour cream, although not the ideal substitute due to flavor and consistency, can be used if Mexican crema is unavailable. Loosen it with a dash of milk to get closer to a semi-liquid consistency.

Garlic: A variety of reddish-purple garlic called *ajo criollo* is one of the best kinds to use in Mexican cooking. It is not as sharp as white garlic and it has a bite with a sweet, mild flavor. Although somewhat harder to source, you will appreciate the subtle difference it makes when you cook with it. Look for it in Hispanic or specialty markets.

Lard: Pork fat was a flavorful inheritance from Spain. Lard that is naturally rendered tends to have a golden brown color. This kind of lard will give the best flavor to tamales and refried beans. If you are not too keen on the nutty pork flavor profile of this lard, use leaf lard, which has a cleaner flavor and less pronounced aroma but the same great properties of natural pork fat. Do not try to substitute other fats, especially when making savory tamales; the flavor and texture will not be the same. Avoid at all cost any logs of hydrogenated fat and processed pork fat in the supermarket.

Mexican cinnamon (canela): *Canela* means "cinnamon" in Spanish. Canela, the Mexican cinnamon (*Cinnamomum verum*), is different than the cinnamon commonly found in the United States (*Cinnamomum cassia*); it is flakier, softer, more aromatic, and has a subtler flavor. Other kinds of cinnamon are not good substitutes in Mexican baking and cooking.

Mexican cinnamon (also known as Ceylon cinnamon and "true" cinnamon) is grown mainly in Sri Lanka and about three-quarters of it is exported to Mexico. Canela is commonly sold in supermarkets, Mexican markets, spice shops, and online. The trick is to find canela that is actual Mexican cinnamon and not just cassia that has been translated as canela. One way to know the difference is that canela only comes in long or short sticks. These sticks are made of the tender trunk of the Ceylon tree, which is peeled into thin layers that are rolled into multilayered sticks, sort of resembling how tobacco leaves are rolled to make cigars. (*Cassia and Saigon cinnamon sticks are made of one hard layer.*) The reason I make such an emphasis on the types of canela is because it is the only type of cinnamon to be used in Mexican cuisine. No substitutions will work for these recipes. The aromatic qualities and flavor profile of canela is essential in moles, sauces, salsas, atoles, pan dulce, and pan de muerto. The most common ways to use canela in Mexican recipes are:

Canela sticks are used to make tea and flavor drinks and atoles. The whole stick can infuse a drink and then be easily removed. I keep my canela sticks in an airtight glass container to better preserve the natural oils. The sticks look like thin cigars with many flaky layers.

Crushed canela is often used toasted or fried along with other spices, such as in mole sauce. Crushing releases more flavor and aroma, and the small fragments are easier to grind up. Coarsely crushed canela is often added to candies, candied fruit, and baked goods. Use your fingers to break the stick lengthwise and separate the long thin layers, and then crush into smaller pieces.

Ground canela is used to flavor salsas, sauces, guisos, baked goods, and is sprinkled on hot cocoa, buñuelos, cookies, or pan dulce. For best results, crush first and then grind using a coffee or spice grinder. I only grind enough canela as needed to obtain the best flavor and aroma in each recipe.

Orange blossom water: This essential water, inherited from Mediterranean cuisine, comes from the flowers of bitter orange trees. I use it in pan de muerto, along with canela and orange zest. The floral aroma is so alluring that I always

have a bottle of this in my pantry. I add a few drops to cakes, arroz con leche, tea, or a cup of warm milk and honey before going to bed. You can find orange blossom water in specialty stores, Middle Eastern food markets, or online.

Piloncillo: Also known as panela or panocha, these dark, unrefined sugarcane cones have a very distinctive flavor, almost like caramel. Sugar cane juice is cooked in copper pots for several hours into thick syrup, which is then poured into wood or clay molds. When cooled, the cones are unmolded and then wrapped in banana leaf or paper to sell. The darker the cones, the better the flavor. Piloncillo is used in all sorts of Mexican desserts. It's the key flavor in sweet braised pumpkin and is used to sweeten atoles and hot drinks. Look for piloncillo cones at specialty or Hispanic markets, and make sure the label says "unrefined" sugarcane. Some of the best piloncillo comes from Veracruz, Mexico.

Queso cotija: Cotija cheese has been made in Mexico for more than 400 years. Made of skimmed cow or goat milk, and aged for 3 to 12 months, this is like the "Mexican Parmesan." It is salty, dry, and crumbly, with a distinctive acidic, nutty smell and flavor. Depending on maturity, cotija aquires different intensity of flavor and texture, so different styles of cotija are best used in particular dishes and preparations.

Cotija is used to top all sorts of antojitos Mexicanos, from sopes, tacos dorados, enchiladas, gorditas, huaraches, and tlacoyos. Because of its distinctive flavor, it also provides a great accent in frijoles de la olla or refried beans.

Queso fresco: Also known as *queso blanco* (white cheese), this is fresh cheese made of cow's milk or a combination of cow and goat milk. This soft cheese with a mild, salty, fresh milk flavor is easy to crumble, making it an ideal topping for antojitos Mexicanos or to fill some gorditas, sopes, or bean tacos, and to serve as garnish for certain types of tamales like uchepos and corundas tamales.

Sea salt: All the savory recipes in this book call for sea salt, which is what I always use. The flavor of sea salt brightens up the food without imparting an acidic flavor. To be specific, I use Sal Marina de Cuyutlán, which is extracted from the Lagoon of Cuyutlán near the Manzanillo Bay in the state of Colima, Mexico. The only way you can get this sea salt is online, and it is 100% worth it. You can use other sea salts or kosher salt, but be aware of the saltiness level. If using other types of sea salt, start with a little less than the recipe calls for and add a little at a time to move toward your desired saltiness.

Tomatillos: Tomatillos are native to Mexico and related to the gooseberry family. They are the base for many sauces, stews, moles, and pozole verde. They make excellent tangy and colorful salsas. Tomatillo husks are used when cooking nopalitos to tame the slimy nature of the cactus. And when boiled, the leftover water is used in the preparation of buñuelos; because of the acidity content, the water works as a leavening agent. Tomatillos are easy to find at regular and Hispanic supermarkets. For best flavor, choose the smallest ones with the greenest, freshest husks.

Tomatillo milpero: This is a smaller variety of tomatillo, the size of a small marble, with a large purple patch on their bright-green skin. These little tomatillos are best used in salsa verde cocida and salsa de molcajete because of their concentrated tangy, sharp, and fruity flavor. They are also less bitter than the medium-size tomatillos. This variety is not easy to find in the United States.

Tomatoes (jitomates): From the Nahuatl word *xitomatl* (xictli = navel, *tomatl* = tomato), tomatoes are a native fruit of Mexico and South America. Today, heirloom tomatoes are cultivated in just a few areas of Mexico. Commercially grown tomatoes farmed year-round have limited varieties available for cooking and pushed most of the heirloom varieties into obscurity. Today the most common tomatoes found in markets and used in home cooking in Mexico are *jitomate Roma* and *jitomate bola*. Heirloom varieties can be found in small amounts and sold locally. After decades of loss of variety, there is finally a movement in Mexico to promote and preserve ancient ingredients including heirloom tomatoes, chiles, corn, and beans. With the help of older farmers, younger generations are working to preserve these important varieties, thereby guarding the traditional flavors of Mexico.

Vanilla: Called the "black flower of the Aztecs," one of the best vanilla beans in the world grows in Papantla, Veracruz, Mexico. The tropical weather and altitude near the coast create a climate that yields a vanilla bean with a delicate floral flavor. When buying Mexican vanilla extract, look for a brand that contains less than 30% alcohol and less than 2% Vanillin. Mexican vanilla pods are a real treasure if you can get them. Check the sourcing list at the back of the book for a good source of authentic Mexican vanilla in the United States.

White onion: Mexican recipes that require onion call for the white variety. Less sweet than yellow and less sharp than red, white onions are juicy, crisp, and have a clean flavor. They are often used to flavor sauces and salsas, diced in tacos, and as a garnish for pozoles and soups. When used raw as garnish, consider giving them a quick rinse; this will help tame the sharpness. Choose medium-size onions for best flavor.

Fresh and Dried Herbs

The flavors of fresh and dry herbs are essential to Mexican cooking. They add aromatic qualities to stocks and soups, and complement the flavor of fresh and dry chiles in salsas and sauces. Most recipes in this book use dry herbs because they are easy to source. For the recipes that call for fresh herbs, however, fresh is a must. If you cannot find fresh herbs, it is better to omit them, because the flavor will change considerably.

Avocado leaf (hoja de aguacate): Avocado leaves have a unique, herbaceous, licorice flavor between a laurel leaf and fresh hoja santa with a hint of mint. I have found dry avocado leaves in some specialty supermarkets, usually near the holidays when people use them more frequently for moles and celebration dishes. Since they are sometimes used dried, you can find them in small amounts online. This is only necessary for a couple of recipes, so you can plan ahead and order them in time to make the recipe. *Fresh:* Best if you can find them.

Usually, avocado leaves are toasted or fried before adding to moles, sauces, or refried beans. *Dried:* Commonly used to flavor a pot of beans (frijoles de la olla), refried beans (refritos), sauces, and moles.

Cilantro: In Mexican cooking, cilantro is almost always used fresh; the greener, the better. For better salsas, include part of the stems, finely chopped. How to differentiate from parsley? Look for bright-green paper-thin leaves with scalloped instead of serrated edges and, of course, the unique smell. If you grow cilantro at home, add the flowers to salsas and soups for more fragrant and pleasant flavor.

Epazote: Epazote is recognized by its herbaceous, licorice, and woodsy, pungent flavor. Mostly used in central and south-central Mexico, epazote is an essential herb for flavoring beans, tortilla soup, pipian, and mole verde, among others. The most commonly used varieties are red Oaxacan and green epazote, which are easily found, and have intense, pungent flavor and aroma. *Fresh:* Use fresh epazote for better flavor, depending on the recipe. It is easy to grow your own epazote in pots. *Dried:* It holds its flavor well and is an adequate substitute in soups, stews, and beans de la olla.

Hoja santa: Also known as piper auritum, sacred leaf, or root beer plant, this is one of the most treasured aromatic flavors in central Mexico gastronomy. Hoja santa has an herbaceous, licorice, floral flavor unlike any other herb. There is no substitution for its flavor in moles and sauces. It's better to omit it than try substitutions.

Hoja santa likes warm, humid weather. In Mexico it can be found growing wild in the states of Veracruz, Oaxaca, Chiapas, and Tabasco, and it happily grows in Texas and California.

Since there are no easy substitutions and it's hard to find even at specialty supermarkets, I recommend finding seeds or a small plant at a specialty nursery and growing it in your garden or in a large pot. The plant has beautiful, large, heart-shaped, dark-green leaves with a long green-bean-like flower. *Fresh:* Always tastes best fresh, and nearly all recipes that need hoja santa will ask for fresh. *Dried:* Not my favorite option, but could work in an emergency scenario. I have seen dried hoja santa in the tea section in Mexican supermarkets, but haven't dared to try it as a substitute.

Marjoram: Sweeter than oregano, this herb has subtle mint-basil notes that complement some salsas and also works as a condiment and garnish for soups and pozoles. *Fresh:* Not very easy to find fresh, but if you do, it adds a fragrant herb note to soups and mild tomato salsas *Dried:* Most commonly found dry and works in every case. Before adding to food, rub it between your fingers to activate its oils and awaken its aromas.

Mexican bay leaf (laurel): I learned from author Diana Kennedy that the fragrant laurel leaf used in Mexico, *Litsea glaucescens*, comes from a different species of laurel than the European and U.S. varieties. It is grown in Oaxaca, Michoacán, and Veracruz, Mexico. Laurel leaves are most commonly used dried. Their woodsy, herbaceous notes add wonderful flavor to stocks, sauces, pork, chicken, and fish, and are essential to the characteristic flavor of escabeche-pickled vegetables (page 226). *Fresh:* If using fresh, double the amount because the flavor is milder. *Dried:* Commonly found.

Note: Thyme, oregano, marjoram, and bay leaves are known as Hierbas de Olor, meaning "aromatic herbs." They are commonly used to flavor soups, broths, stews, escabeches, and adobos.

Mexican spearmint (hierbabuena): Mexican spearmint is known for its fragrance and refreshing flavor. It is used sparingly in savory salsas and stocks as a heavenly addition. In contrast, it is used with abandon in aguas frescas, teas, and as digestives and stomach remedies. Two or three fresh sprigs can make a big difference in flavor. *Fresh:* Always use fresh for cooking. *Dried:* Not commonly used for cooking, but used to make teas and add infusions to agua frescas.

Oregano: If you can find "Mexican Oregano" on the label, you have a winner. Mexican oregano is more fragrant, slightly sweeter, and has more depth of flavor than other varieties. It is worth the hunt. *Fresh:* It grows easily in a pot, so if you can find seeds or a little plant, get it! It is not only tasty but also blooms beautiful little white flowers that can be added to salads and soups. *Dried:* Found in the spice aisle at your supermarket. Make sure the label says "Mexican Oregano." Before adding to food, rub it between your fingers to activate its oils and awaken its aroma.

Thyme (tomillo): In Mexican cooking, thyme is mostly used dried to season broths and soups. Adding thyme is a must for great flavor in stocks, broths, and chicken consommé, especially when these stocks are going to be part of moles, tamales, masa, and soups. *Fresh* or *dried* will work for soups and broths. Use dry in simple tomato salsa (page 220) or in tomato, oregano, and cinnamon salsa (page 220).

Fresh Chiles—*Chiles Frescos*

Chiles are the spicy soul of Mexican cooking. Despite their popular reputation of being merely hot, chiles have an impressive range of flavors, colors, and textures, and have much to offer. Chiles can be used either fresh or dry. Each kind of chile, whether fresh or dry, adds different levels of heat, flavor, color, and sweetness.

When buying fresh chiles, look for ones with pleasing color and shape that are shiny and smooth. Skip those that have leathery skin, bruises, brown spots, or that show dry or moldy spots at the base of the stem, or have no stem at all. Ask the produce manager, and they will help you find a fresher batch.

Chiltepín or Pequin: Chiltepíns are most commonly used in the north of Mexico where the plants grow wild. They are easy to grow in pots and will grow year-round. Chiltepíns are also known as bird peppers because birds love to eat them and it's said that their fiery flavor makes the birds sing. When fresh they can be found in red, green, or in between, or green and yellowish. In every color, these little chiles are fireworks in your mouth. They produce a burst of heat, and may make you sweat and cry, although the heat dissipates fast. Fresh chiltepíns are especially delicious when pickled because the vinegar tames their fire and makes them friendlier. They say good things come in small packages, and these little chiles are proof of that.

Green jalapeño: This is perhaps the most internationally known chile. (Jalapeños are so popular, they were used as the mascot of the 1986 FIFA World Cup in Mexico.) Green jalapeños' shape and bright, sharp, spicy flavor epitomize chiles. Look for deep-green color and pointy ends. For best flavor, choose jalapeños that are 3 to 4 inches long.

Habanero: These beautiful chiles were brought from South America to the Yucatán Peninsula, where they have flourished due to weather and soil conditions. It is said that if you want to try a real habanero, you have to go to Yucatán. Habaneros are high-pitch spicy, with a fruity aroma and a painfully addictive flavor; your mouth can be on fire and you will still be craving more. These little chiles help with digestion. They are best used charred, freshly chopped in a quick-pickled vinegar-lime salsa, or pureed into hot sauces. These chiles are the best companion to cochinita pibil (page 138), mucbil pibipollo (page 168), salbutes, and pan de cazon, and are an essential part of the Yucatán Peninsula cuisine. Habaneros can be light lime-green, yellow, light peachy-orange, or deep orange. Choose the smallest ones; the best specimens are roughly an inch and a half in diameter.

Manzano or Perón: These beautiful chiles are named for their apple-pear shape and egg-yolk color. Manzano peppers are not only beautiful but also fleshy, fruity, slightly sweet, and have a spicy kick. Boiled or charred, manzanos are a great addition to salsas de molcajete, and they make the best pickle concoction with carrots and onions. When buying, look for a bright yellow-orange hue and firm texture, and be sure the stems are still attached.

Poblano: Dark hunter green, waxy and shiny-looking, poblanos have a smoky flavor and a mild spice. Buy the ones that have smooth, firm skin. Poblanos with pointy ends that look like Aladdin shoes are usually tastier than the ones that have flat ends.

Red jalapeño: Less common than their green counterparts, red jalapeños have been left to mature a little longer on the plant. They tend to be hotter and have a slightly sweet flavor if roasted. Other than color, choose them using the same criteria as green jalapeños. They are a great color addition to escabeche and they make fiery salsas de molcajete.

Serrano: Long and skinny, dark hunter green, with sharp ends, these chiles can have the devil inside. Bright with a sharp spiciness, they are commonly used in roasted salsas and in the company of green tomatillos to make salsa verde. If used carefully, they mimic black pepper in sauces or moles instead of displaying their fiery heat. One of my favorite ways to eat serranos is toreados, blistering them in some cooking oil and serving them with a squeeze of lime and sea salt (page 218). When shopping for serranos, look for dark-green, skinny chiles about 3 to 4 inches long for the best flavor profile.

Dried Chiles—*Chiles Secos*

Dried chiles can perform miracles in the kitchen. They can resuscitate any stew or guisado, have long shelf life in airtight containers, and can make sauces with rich, complex flavors in minutes. Dried chiles are the base for most of the best moles, sauces, and stews. For a guide to cleaning, toasting, and preparing dry chiles, see the section on page 57.

Knowing your dried chiles and how to differentiate them is a priority. Many companies incorrectly label their chiles, and I have found bad labeling mistakes that, if not for double-checking the contents of the packages, would have made for culinary disasters.

Ancho: Anchos are plant-ripened, sun-dried poblano chiles. Anchos look and taste like a fruity prune with a mild, spicy flavor and a pleasant heat. They have a reddish-black hue and a thick stem, and are shaped like a wide, long triangle with a pointy end. Sometimes it is hard to tell the difference between an ancho and a mulato pepper. If you are unsure, gently pull up the stem a bit without removing it; anchos will have a deep cherry-red color at the base of the stem. Anchos, like guajillos, are one of the most prevalent chiles often used as a base in moles, sauces, and adobos.

Cascabel: These round cherry-shaped chiles are one of my favorites. They are small and have a complex character: smoky, cherry, woodsy, with a pleasant, piquant, intense spice. Cascabel means "jingle bell"—you can shake the dried chile and hear the seeds inside. These chiles are also commonly mislabeled, so check shape and size before buying. One of my favorite salsas, salsa roja asada (page 210), is made using toasted cascabel and their seeds, which are also toasted, giving the salsa a nutty, smoky, spicy note. Cascabels are great in carne guisados, salsas, and adobos.

Chile catarina: These are similar to cascabel chiles but with a distinctive oval pointy shape that looks like a 1950s Christmas tree lightbulb. These little chiles are very spicy, with a pronounced tangy pep, and they make vibrant vinegar-based hot sauces. These sauces are great complements to soups and pozoles.

Chile de árbol (árbol Yahualica): My number one dried chile. These long, deep-red, pointy-looking chiles have a sharp, intense flavor and are a notch above spicy. Originally from Yahualica, Jalisco, Mexico, they grow in a small plant that looks like a little tree, hence the name árbol. Their bright, piquant flavor is very distinctive when toasted or boiled for hot sauces and condiments. Adding one chile to the oil when preparing refried beans adds a huge punch of flavor. Combine with charred tomatillos for the best salsa taquera, or along with tomatoes to make a smoky salsa (page 210). Use as the base for salsa mucha muchacha (page 216), the ultimate condiment to have in your refrigerator.

Pay close attention when buying these chiles. I have often found Japanese red chiles labeled chile de árbol. They do not have the same flavor profile. Real chiles de árbol are long and skinny, deep red, and their stems are always attached. Mistakes like these are changing the flavor profiles in Mexican gastronomy. Last year I grew my own chile de árbol plants, which yielded more than 1,200 chiles each. (Every time I went to the garden to get some, I kept count in a notebook.) I dried them, stored them in airtight jars, and shared with my friends.

Chilhuacle negro: Chilhuacle chiles are an endangered species of chiles, still cultivated in only two communities around Cuicatlán, Oaxaca. Their short and wide shape is very distinct, and they are mostly found dried. There are three varieties of chilhuacles: black, red, and yellow. All three have a sharp, spicy flavor with a fruity flavor when hydrated, making them ideal for moles and sauces. They are pricey and hard to source, even in the state of Oaxaca. Some cooks substitute guajillos and increase the amount of other spicier chiles in recipes for moles to balance the recipe flavors. Unfortunately, there is not a more accurate substitution for flavor. If you want to go the extra mile, I found a seasonal online source for them; see the sourcing ingredients section on page 360.

Chiltepín seco (dried chiltepíns): They are most commonly sold dry in the United States. If you grow them in a pot, pick them from the plant and place them in a single layer on a tray to dry in the sun. Beware, these little chiles keep all their fiery bite when dried. Because of their intense heat, dried chiltepíns are added to soups and stews with hearty, meaty flavors (like pozoles and menudos). Used in modest amounts, it mimics a fresh cracked black pepper.

Chipotle meco: These are basically ripened red jalapeños that have been smoke-dried. They have a tobacco-like color and appearance. The popular chipotles en adobo are made from hydrated mecos, and because of their intense flavor, two or three are essential in mole poblano. When buying, look for a tobacco-leaf skin texture and color and a well-sealed package. Their smoky smell is unmistakable. When storing them, make sure they are kept in an airtight container to prevent them from overtaking your pantry.

Costeño: These chiles are grown in the coastal areas of Guerrero and Oaxaca. They are most commonly used dried, which gives them a beautiful bronze color—hence their name costeño, which refers to the coastal people and their beautiful tan skin. These chiles are used toasted in salsas and sauces for tamales and lighter moles. Costeños in combination with guajillos can be substituted for chilcostle chiles in mole Amarillo (page 123).

Guajillo: These are dried mirasol chiles. One of the oldest-known chiles, guajillos are long and skinny with leathery skin, and are the most-used chile in Mexican cooking. Their slightly fruity flavor and mild spiciness and acidity make them an ideal base for many sauces, moles, adobos, and salsas. When buying, look for pointy ends, thinner skin, and a deep brick-red color.

Mora & Morita: Both are small jalapeños. They come from the same plant but differ in ripeness and size. They are both smoke-dried and are powerhouses of flavor. Sweet and fleshy, intense and pruney, they display a complex pungency. Add one morita to a sauce, stew, or pot of beans for a pleasant smoky and spicy flavor. These chiles can be hydrated for adobos or fried to make intensely flavored chile oils and condiments, like my salsa mucha muchacha (page 216). Keep them in an airtight container to best preserve their smoky, highly addictive flavor.

Mulato: These chiles are the cousins of anchos. They have the same shape as poblanos, but when ripening on the plant, they turn purple instead of red. When sun-dried, they turn a rich, dark brown. Mulatos have a distinctive chocolaty flavor that is slightly sweet and spicier than anchos. At first sight they look just like anchos; the best way to distinguish them is to gently pull the stem up a bit and look for a deep-brown color on the chile skin underneath. Mulatos are used in traditional moles because of their pleasant spice and deep chocolaty flavor.

Pasilla: These are the dried version of chilaca peppers, a dark-green, narrow chile. Pasillas have a dark cherry-red hue. Their raisin-like flavor is what gives them their name; pasilla means "little raisin." Despite their fruitiness, they can be fairly hot with a sharp and rich flavor. Pasillas make good sauces and condiments, can be stuffed with cheese when hydrated, and are used as garnishes for tortilla soup, moles, and sauces. In the United States, some fresh chiles are incorrectly labeled as pasillas; remember, pasillas are dried.

Pasilla negro: The cousin of pasillas, pasilla negro peppers ripen to a dark-purple color. Pasilla negros are usually spicier than pasillas, and are often made into a chile powder, which combined with lime and sea salt is sprinkled on jicamas, oranges, and cucumbers. They are one of the chiles used in mole negro, the king of moles.

Preparing Dried and Fresh Chiles

Dried chiles are part of the backbone of Mexican cooking. They are available all year round and can be combined and treated in different ways. Toasted, fried, or hydrated, they will give different results and different flavor profiles to the sauces. They last for a long time in airtight containers, and in less than thirty minutes you can hydrate them and make a sauce that your grandma would be proud of. Almost every sauce, mole, adobo, or stew starts with this process.

Dry chiles can range from mild to hot and have intense chocolaty or fruity flavor and add color. So get familiar with them, and learn the differences and how to recognize them. See the flavor descriptions and photos on pages 54–56. If this is your first time cooking with dry chiles, it might be intimidating at first, but I assure you the process is very simple.

Cleaning chiles:

Always wipe your chiles with a damp towel to remove any dust. With scissors, remove the stems and cut the chiles along the side to open them up. In a small bowl, collect all the seeds and veins. The seeds and veins of the chiles carry the capsicum substance that makes the chile spicy, so you will want to remove them if you want a milder sauce. Also, adding too many seeds can add bitterness to the sauce.

In some recipes, like moles, some seeds are specially reserved, toasted, and ground as part of the sauce preparation. They add flavor, help with the consistency, and add the right level of heat. I usually leave the veins in half of the chiles, because I enjoy their piquancy and flavor.

Note: After handling chiles, avoid hand to eye contact and always wash your hands immediately to avoid any tears in the kitchen.
Tip: Keep some chile seeds to plant some chiles in your garden!

Toasting chiles:

Toasting chiles is the beginning of almost all recipes that use dried chiles. Toasting awakens the oils in the chiles, makes them pliable, and draws out the flavor.

Once the chiles are cleaned, on a medium heat comal or cast-iron pan, toast for about 30 to 40 seconds at a time on each side. Once the aromas are released and they look a bit shiny and have slightly different color, they are done. Avoid blistering them, because they will become bitter.)

After toasting, hydrate or fry them, depending on what the recipe calls for.

Note: Depending on the kind of chiles and their heat level, when toasting chiles, a warm spicy cloud in your kitchen can make you sneeze and cough. If this is your first time toasting chiles, before even starting, make sure to open any kitchen window, and turn on the stove exhaust fan. Also cover your nose with a bandana or handkerchief.

Roasting fresh chiles:

This is the easiest method for cooking fresh chiles. You can roast them on a tray in the oven by themselves or along with other salsa or sauce ingredients. Place them on the middle rack in your oven, start at a temperature above 400°F, and once they have changed color, place them briefly under the oven broiler to blister them. Another great way to cook fresh chiles is by grilling them. The charred skins and charcoal smoke give chiles extra flavor that makes some of the best salsas.

Hydrating chiles:

1. With a damp towel, wipe the dry chiles to remove any dust or dirt.

2. On a comal or griddle, toast the chiles for about 15 to 20 seconds per side, until they are pliable, the aromas and oils on their skins are awakened, and they start to slightly change color.

3. Use scissors to remove stems and seeds. Depending on the recipe, save some of the seeds and toast them to add to the sauce when it is time to puree.

4. Place toasted chiles in a bowl and cover them with boiling water. Let them soak for 20 to 30 minutes until they are soft, plump, and hydrated. Drain the leftover water. Always discard the water in which the chiles were soaked to avoid adding bitterness to the sauce.

5. Once chiles are hydrated, transfer with tongs to a blender and puree them. Use as little water as possible—just enough to get your blender going to obtain the smoothest puree.

6. You will need to strain the puree if you see chile skins in it; this will make for a smooth sauce. If you have a powerful blender, there's no need to strain. Once you have this chile puree, you can season it with any condiments you want, fry the sauce, or add it to adobos, soups, stews, tamales, pozoles, etcetera, according to the specific recipe you're using.

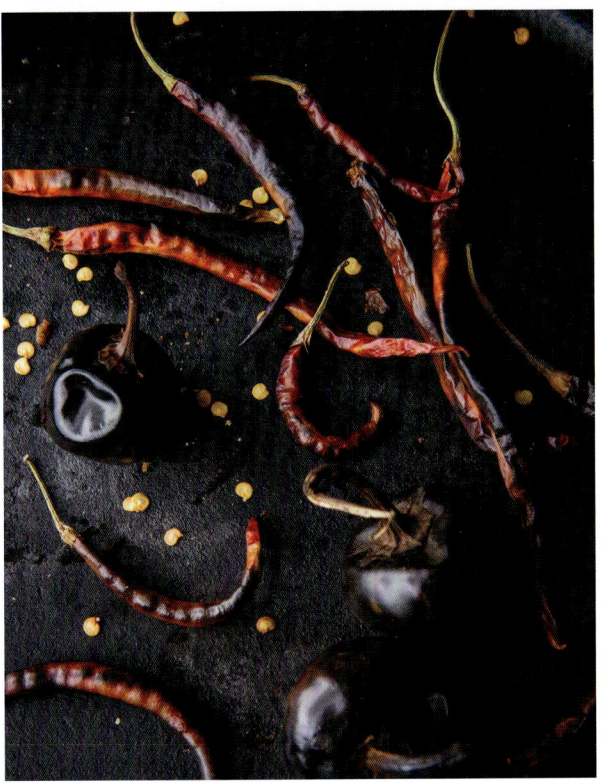

Charring dried or fresh chiles:

This is the most common method for starting any salsa de molcajete. Dried or fresh chiles are cooked on a comal, cast-iron pan, or griddle over medium temperature. Fresh chiles are cooked whole until large black blisters show all around but they still have some bright green color patches. This will give better texture and flavor to the salsa or other preparations. I especially like to char serranos, jalapeños, and habaneros for salsas de molcajete. When charring dried chiles, toss them constantly until they turn dark red-black. When charring chiles, I always leave the stems on so I can turn them by hand on the comal. For larger chiles I use tongs.

Basic Recipes

These basic recipes are often the starting components in recipes like moles, tamales, and chile-based sauces. Many of these recipes can be made in advance and kept in the refrigerator one or two days before cooking the main dish, or can be frozen for future preparations. For instance, with moles, having the chicken stock ready the day before is a great help. And when making tamales, making the filling is often a task in itself, so making it two or three days ahead can save you time and effort on the day that you prepare the masa and assemble and steam the tamales. Also, it's well known that broths, stocks, guisos, and sauces, including moles, taste better the following days after flavors settle. Read the recipes ahead of time to see what can be made early and plan accordingly.

❉ ❉ ❉

Caldo de Pollo para Deshebrar — *Shredded Chicken and Stock*   62

Carne de Pavo para Deshebrar — *Shredded Turkey*   62

Carne de Cerdo para Deshebrar — *Shredded Pork*   63

Caldo de Pollo Casero — *Mexican Homestyle Chicken Stock*   65

Corn (Maíz)   66

Nixtamalization   67

How to Make Nixtamal   69

How to Make Hominy   72

How to Make Corn Masa   75

Tortillas de Maíz — *Corn Tortillas*   77

Caldo de Pollo para Deshebrar
Ideal para Relleno de Tamales
Shredded Chicken and Stock
Ideal for Tamale Filling

This basic recipe yields moist and flavorful chicken meat to be used for tamale fillings, sopes de pollo, tostadas, tacos dorados, flautas, and enchiladas where the shredded chicken is going to be complemented and enhanced by other ingredients. Always save the stock to make sauces, moles, and rice, like *arroz a la Mexicana*.

Yields about 5 cups of shredded chicken and at least 1 to 1½ quarts of chicken stock

- 8 cups water, enough to cover chicken
- 1 whole chicken, about 4 to 4½ pounds
- 1 medium white onion, quartered
- ½ teaspoon dry thyme
- 1 bay leaf
- 6 black peppercorns
- 1 teaspoon sea salt

1. Bring 8 cups water to a boil in a medium-large pot.
2. Add chicken and onion. Bring to a rapid boil and immediately turn down the heat to a slow simmer. During the first 10 minutes, using a metal spoon, remove any foam that might form on the top of the stock and discard. Once stock is foam free, add thyme, bay leaf, black peppercorns, and salt.
3. Cook chicken for another 30 minutes. Check for doneness; carefully taste the stock and adjust salt if necessary. Turn off the heat, remove pot from hot burner and let it cool, about 45 minutes. Once the chicken is cool enough to handle, take out the pieces of chicken from the stock, place them in a bowl, and save the stock. Remove chicken from the bone and discard chicken skin and bone. Shred the chicken with two forks. As you shred the chicken, pour a couple of tablespoons of the stock over the shredded chicken to keep it moist.
4. Strain leftover stock and save it for future use.

Notes: If making tamales, shredded chicken can be made a few days in advance. It freezes well, as long it has some of the stock added to avoid the chicken from drying out. Always save and freeze leftover stock in batches of 2 to 4 cups to use in future recipes. Stock lasts for 4 to 6 months in the freezer.

Carne de Pavo para Deshebrar
Ideal para Mole o Relleno de Tamales
Shredded Turkey
Ideal for Tamale Filling

In Mexican cooking, using turkey for moles and tamales is a common practice. This is a basic recipe that yields an enhanced turkey stock and flavorful turkey meat. It is common to make *caldo* (stock) and simultaneously cook the turkey using a wet method to keep the turkey meat moist. Always save the stock and keep the fat of the stock to add flavor when making other preparations like tamale fillings, tamale masa, and mole.

Yields about 6 to 8 cups of shredded turkey and at least 1½ to 2 quarts of turkey stock

- 10 cups (2½ quarts) water, enough to cover the turkey
- 1 whole turkey, about 8 to 10 pounds, cut into pieces
- 4 celery stalks, cut in half
- 1 large white onion, quartered
- 1 head garlic
- ½ teaspoon dry thyme
- 3 bay leaves
- 8 black peppercorns
- 2 teaspoons sea salt

1. Bring 10 cups water to a boil in a medium-large pot.
2. Add turkey, celery, onion, and garlic. Bring to a rapid boil and immediately turn down the heat to a slow simmer. During the first 15 minutes, using a large metal spoon, remove any foam that might form on the top of the stock and discard. Add thyme, bay leaves, black peppercorns, and sea salt.
3. Cook turkey for another 35 to 40 minutes. Check for doneness; carefully taste the stock and adjust salt if necessary. Turn off the heat, remove pot from hot burner, and let it cool about 1 hour. Once the turkey is cool enough to handle, transfer turkey to a bowl, remove and discard skin and bones, and save the stock. Shred the turkey meat using two forks. Pour a couple tablespoons of the stock over the shredded turkey to keep it moist.
4. Strain leftover stock, and save it for future use.

Notes: If making tamales, prepare turkey 1 to 2 days in advance. Stock and shredded turkey both freeze well, as long it has some of the stock added to keep the turkey from drying out. Freeze leftover stock in batches of 2 to 4 cups and label with date and amount. Stock lasts for 4 to 6 months in the freezer.

Carne de Cerdo para Deshebrar, Ideal para Relleno de Tamales
Shredded Pork, Ideal for Tamale Filling

In Mexican cooking, pork is often cooked using a wet method, rather than braising or roasting, because the remaining broth is used to flavor stews, sauces, moles, and, most important, the masa for tamales. Using this broth makes a huge difference when preparing any of the traditional recipes in this book.

This is a basic recipe to use for pork shoulder, leg, or butt that will be used as shredded pork to make fillings for tamales, tostadas, tacos, sopes or tortas. The recipe is simple and flavorful and it brings out the best pork flavor.

Yields about 5 to 6 cups (about 3 pounds) cooked, shredded pork

6 pounds boneless pork shoulder or butt, or 8 pounds for bone-in pork
1 medium white onion, quartered
½ teaspoon dry thyme
¼ teaspoon oregano
1 bay leaf
6 to 8 black peppercorns
1 teaspoon sea salt

1. Cut the pork into 2 to 3 large pieces. Always cut along with the grain of the meat. This will allow you to have beautiful, long shreds of pork.

2. Fill a heavy-bottomed pot with enough water to cover the pork meat. Add the onion.

3. Bring pot to a rapid boil, and immediately reduce the heat to a slow simmer. During the first 10 minutes, using a metal spoon, remove any foam that might form on the top of the broth and discard. Once stock is foam free, add thyme, oregano, bay leaf, black peppercorns, and sea salt. Cover with a lid ajar and cook over a slow simmer for 1½ to 2 hours.

4. When pork is cooked, taste the stock and adjust salt if necessary. Turn off the heat and let the pork cool down and rest in the broth. (One of the biggest mistakes people make is to remove the pork from the pot while it's hot. Hot pork in the open air will lose its moisture through evaporation, making it dry with no chance to reabsorb some of its juices. So always rest pork in the pot with the lid half way on, to cool off.)

5. Once the pork is cool enough to handle, transfer it into a metal bowl. With the help of two forks, or using your fingers, start shredding the meat into long strips. As you shred the meat, baste it with a couple tablespoons of the stock to keep it moist.

6. Strain the stock, and save.

Notes: If making tamales or other preparations, shredded pork can be made a few days in advance. It freezes well, as long as it has some of the stock added to avoid drying out. Always save and freeze leftover stock in batches of 2 to 4 cups to use in future recipes like pozole, mole, or tamales. Stock lasts for 4 to 6 months in the freezer.

When cooking any protein, especially bone-in chicken or turkey, try to remember to pull it out from the refrigerator for at least 30 minutes before cooking. This will yield more tender meat and it will keep the cooking times accurate. If using a slow cooker, adjust the cooking time to the manufacturer's instructions.

Caldo de Pollo Casero
Mexican Homestyle Chicken Stock

The trick to a great stock is simple: Bring the pot to a boil and then immediately turn down to low to allow the stock to develop its flavors slowly while barely simmering, and adding the vegetables according to their hardness. In stocks I prefer to use fresh herbs, which give an aromatic flavor to the stock. Chicken stock is the base of many Mexican dishes like moles, soups, rice, and sauces. In Mexico, this kind of soup is referred to as *caldo de pollo*. It is served along with a piece of chicken, lots of vegetables, and a scoop of rice for 100% homestyle comfort. A caldo de pollo made by your grandma, your mom, or your aunt is the best medicine for anything that ails, and it's also the best warm supper on a rainy or cold day. Usually, we have caldo de pollo as a meal on the day it's prepared, and then save the rest of the chicken for another meal preparation. I sieve the rest of the stock and reserve it for use in my favorite dishes, or to cook arroz a la Mexicana, soups, or sauces. I save it in 2- and 4-cup containers since those are the proportions I use the most. Frozen stock keeps for up to 6 months.

Makes about 3 quarts (2.75 liters)
Serves 4 to 6

1 whole organic chicken, 4 to 4½ pounds, washed and patted dry inside and out
4 wings or extra chicken parts
1 medium white onion
2 carrots
2 celery stalks
1 Roma tomato
1 small head garlic
6 sprigs fresh thyme, or 1 teaspoon dry
2 sprigs fresh oregano, or ½ teaspoon dry
12 sprigs fresh cilantro
4 to 5 sprigs fresh mint (hierbabuena)
⅓ cup white rice
1 tablespoon sea salt
¼ teaspoon black peppercorns
Water to cover the chicken, about 3 to 4 quarts

Optional vegetables to add:
2 zucchinis, cut into 1-inch rounds
1–2 chayote squash (mirliton), cut into quarters
2 medium potatoes, sliced in half
Green beans, about a handful
Fresh cilantro, finely chopped, for garnish
Serrano pepper, finely chopped, for garnish
White onion, diced, for garnish
Limes, cut in wedges for garnish

1. In a large 7- to 8-quart pot, place the whole chicken and add the extra chicken parts, onion, carrots, celery, tomato, garlic, and dried thyme and oregano (do not add fresh herbs yet). Add enough water to cover the chicken, about 3½ quarts. Bring to a boil and then reduce heat to a slow simmer.

2. During the first 15 minutes, pay attention to the stock and remove any foam that forms on top. Once the foam no longer forms, add the fresh herbs and cover with a lid ajar and cook for 30 minutes. Add the rice and cook another 15 minutes.

3. If you want to add the extra vegetables to make it into a meal, add the vegetables according to time of doneness. I like to add baby potatoes and chayote about 15 to 20 minutes before the stock is done. About 10 minutes before the stock is done I add carrots and green beans, and just when I turn off the heat I add the zucchini medallions. Then cover with a lid and let the remaining heat cook them to the right consistency.

4. Serve piping hot, along with an assortment of the vegetables and a scoop of white rice.

5. Garnish with fresh cilantro, white onion, serrano, and a wedge of lime. Serve with a side of warm tortillas.

Corn (Maíz)

Dry cornhusks: The outer corn leaves covering an ear of corn are washed and sun-dried, packed, and ready for sale at supermarkets. When making traditional tamales, cornhusks are a must as they add a great flavor.

Masa harina: Masa harina is nixtamalized corn that has been dried and ground into flour. Masa harina is not interchangeable with cornmeal or corn flour. Masa harina is available in almost every supermarket in the United States, typically in the flour aisle, international food aisle, or Hispanic food aisle. It is a staple in my pantry, because when I crave corn tortillas from Mexico, masa harina tortillas are the closest version easily made at home.

Tortillas: Tortillas are a gift from Mexico to the world. The process of making tortillas dates to about 7,000 to 8,000 years ago. Since then, tortillas have been essential to the soul of Mexican cuisine. They are made from dry corn that has been nixtamalized, then ground to create masa. Fresh masa is shaped into a ball and flattened in a press and cooked on a hot comal (griddle). Each region in Mexico grows a different type of corn and colors can range from blue to yellow to white to reddish and brown.

Fresh: Nothing compares to a freshly made tortilla from freshly ground masa, either *tortearlas* (shaped by hand) or made with a tortilla press, and cooked on a hot comal. The smell while they are cooking is wonderful and the flavor is far beyond store bought.

Masa harina: Tortillas made with masa harina have better taste and quality than store bought, but lack some of the flavor and texture of freshly ground masa. They are a good mid-point.

Store-bought: Convenient for everyday use, but most of them have a lower quality and flavor.

Tostadas: Tostadas are simply deep-fried tortillas. They are usually flat and can be made of white or yellow corn. Some tostadas are just dehydrated tortillas and not fried. You can make tostadas in the oven at a low temperature until toasty or on the comal for a charred flavor.

Nixtamalization

Corn in the Nahuatl language is *tlayolli*. Indigenous people in Mexico domesticated and cultivated corn as far back as about 8,000 years ago. Corn evolved and was crossbred from a sylvan plant belonging to a family of grasses called *teocintle*. This wild grass, endemic in the Mexican territory, has two rows of large kernels, and can still be found growing wild in Mexico. Domesticating this plant led to the corn as we know it today. Cultivating corn has been essential to all of the pre-Hispanic groups in Mexico, the core of their sustenance, and their devoted relationship to nature and their gods. Mexican cuisine relies on corn and a special way to process it. This is what separates Mexican cuisine, its flavors, and its corn culture from the rest of the world.

Nixtamalization has been used for thousands of years by indigenous people in Mexico to precook dry corn, and the process has not changed since ancient times. This process improves and enhances flavor, as well as releases amino acids and niacin in the corn, increasing its nutritional value. Combined with beans, chiles, and vegetables, nixtamal provided a greater balance of amino acids and protein in the ancient Mexican diet.

Nixtamalization is an art in itself, as it requires time and patience. During this process, dry corn kernels are soaked in an alkaline solution of water and food-grade limestone powder (known as "cal," slaked lime powder, or pickling lime). When this powder reacts to the water, it becomes calcium hydroxide. When dry corn kernels are soaked in this alkaline solution, it precooks the kernel and removes the pericarp (exterior hull) of the kernel. The result of nixtamalizing corn is called *nixtamal*. (Other ancient methods used wood ashes mixed with water, creating a potassium hydroxide solution that precooks the kernel. In some areas in Mexico, it is used to make a special type of tamale called tamales de ceniza, or ash tamales.)

Ancient Mexicans also applied different cooking methods to nixtamal, producing diverse flavors and uses. By boiling nixtamal, they made hominy for hearty soups, porridges, and pozoles. By grinding fresh nixtamal, they made fresh masa for tortillas, tamales, atoles, and fermented drinks. Today, modern techniques have been applied to nixtamal. Masa harina, used to conveniently produce tortillas and tamales, is created by drying and grinding nixtamal into flour.

Once you learn the nixtamalization process at home, you will appreciate the flavor and nuances of using fresh nixtamal to make the most delicious hominy for traditional pozoles and soups and freshly ground masa for the fluffiest tamales, soft flavorful tortillas, silky atoles, and all sorts of antojitos Mexicanos.

NIXTAMALIZATION
PROCESS

Choose
Dry Corn Kernels
Use best varieties to make
tortillas and *pozole*:

Make *alkaline solution*
water + limestone powder =
calcium hydroxide

Cook *dry corn kernels*
briefly in this solution.

Soak *corn kernels*
overnight (10–12 hrs.)

Rinse *corn kernels*
draining all the *soaking water*
to remove *alkaline solution* and
disintegrated corn skin.

Rub *corn kernels*
soaked in clean water to
remove the rest of outer skin
and most corn eyelets.

~ Final Rinse ~

Dry corn is now:

Nixtamal

When nixtamal is:

Boiled = *Hominy*
Ground fresh = *Masa*
Ground dried = *Masa harina*

How to Make Nixtamal

It is best to make nixtamal the night before the day you want to use it to make masa or hominy.

Makes about 3.3 pounds of nixtamal

2 pounds dry corn kernels* (about 1 kg)
2 tablespoons pickling lime powder or "cal" limestone powder**
6 to 8 cups filtered water (about 1½ to 2 liters)

The specific kinds of corn kernels most commonly used for nixtamal are: arrocillo, cacahuazintle, mixteco, mushito, tablilla, ocho hileras, and maiz azul. Please check the sourcing ingredients section for the places you can buy the right corn.
**Please check the sourcing ingredients section, page 360.*

1. Sort the dry corn kernels to remove any debris or kernels that are misshapen, off-color, or show obvious defects. Rinse under cold water and drain. Place the washed corn into a nonreactive pot, cover with water about 2 inches above the corn, and bring to a boil. Add the pickling lime/cal powder. When you add the powder to the pot there will be a quick bubbly reaction; don't be startled. Now, stir well with a metal or wooden spoon. The water will immediately turn bright neon-yellow. This means the limestone is active. The nixtamalization has started.

2. Cover the pot with a lid and lower the heat to a gentle simmer. Cook for 25 to 30 minutes, stirring occasionally with a metal or wooden spoon. Carefully check one of the kernels by rubbing it between your fingers. The hull should start to come off. Cut the kernel in half. The outer kernel should look shiny and kind of translucent, and the center should still be opaque. At this point, remove the pot from the stove and uncover. Set it aside to cool down. Once it has cooled down, cover with a clean kitchen towel and leave the corn kernels to soak in this water solution for at least 8 hours. Overnight works best. Do not refrigerate.

3. Next day: Check the corn by rubbing some kernels between your fingers. The outer hull/skin of the kernel should come off easily, and by now the bright yellow-orange water has turned into a yellow-brownish color and part of the kernels' outer hulls are almost disintegrated into the water. Drain the water. Leave kernels in the pot.

4. Using your hands, rub the corn kernels under slow-running water until most of the hull paste (*nejayote*) and some of the dark little eyelets on the kernels fall off. Rinse off the corn kernels 2 to 3 times. Place kernels into a colander and drain. After this process, the corn kernels are now **nixtamal** and are ready to be transformed. At this point the corn kernels are pre-cooked.

5. When **nixtamal** is *boiled and cooked*, it becomes *hominy* to be used in pozole and hearty soups. When nixtamal is *freshly ground* on a stone mill or household mill, it becomes *fresh masa*. When nixtamal is *dried and ground dry*, it becomes what we know as commercial *masa harina*.

Note: Each kind of corn kernel will cook at different ratios, especially depending on the age of the kernels. (This is why it is important to get them from a trustworthy source. See page 361). This is just general guidance. Judge doneness by how it looks. If rubbing the kernels with your fingers releases most of the outer husk completely, you are on the right track. If you want to prepare larger amounts, double or triple the recipe and cook for 35 to 40 minutes until you can rub the outer hull off a kernel. Then leave the kernels soaking overnight 8 to 10 hours for best results. Be patient; nixtamalization takes practice, but the resulting flavor and texture are worth the time invested.

1.

2.

3.

4.

How to Make Hominy

Cacahuazintle is one of the best varieties of corn to make hominy for pozole. It is an heirloom variety of white corn with wide, rounded, flat kernels. When cooked, the kernels bloom into fluffy, tender hominy. The end result is far better in texture and flavor than canned hominy.

Another dry corn that can be used is *maíz rojo*. In the United States, it is known as "purple dry corn for pozole." Look in the bulk section of Hispanic markets for this and other white corn that can be used for pozole. Dry cacahuazintle corn is often difficult to source from regular supermarkets in the United States, but thanks to Steve Sando and his company Rancho Gordo, you can buy heirloom-quality cacahuazintle maize in household quantities when in season, especially around the holidays. For both options check the sourcing list on page 361.

Makes about 3 pounds (1.5 kg) cooked hominy

2 pounds (1 kg) nixtamalized cacahuazintle (see recipe for how to make nixtamal, page 69)
8 cups filtered water, divided
1 head garlic
1 large white onion, halved
1 tablespoon coarse sea salt

1. In a large pot, add the nixtamal, garlic, and onion and cover with water about 6 inches above the kernels. Bring to a boil and cook for 15 minutes, then reduce the heat to a low simmer and cook for about 2½ to 3 hours. Stir occasionally and add boiling water when needed.

2. As in cooking beans, add salt only in the last 15 minutes of cooking, once the hominy has started to bloom. This will prevent toughening of the hominy.

3. You will know when the hominy is done by how it looks and tastes. Hominy is done when it starts blooming. It will look like fluffy white popcorn with the texture of a chewy potato. Both white cacahuazintle and red corn will have the same characteristics when cooked. I recommend cooking hominy al dente, especially when making pozole, since the hominy will continue cooking once it is combined with the meat broth and chile sauce.

Note: It takes about 3 hours to cook the hominy. For pozole, follow the pozole recipe accordingly. You can cook hominy days ahead and it is good refrigerated. Hominy loses its texture when frozen. You can freeze the nixtamalized corn in small batches once rinsed and scrubbed, and then defrost and cook it whenever needed for preparations.

Other hominy options: If you do not want to make your own nixtamal, you can purchase **dry nixtamal** or **fresh nixtamal** that has been vacuum sealed. Good options for buying dry nixtamalized corn can currently be found in the United States: Rancho Gordo, Masienda, Anson Mills, and a Peruvian brand named Inca's Food that sells a pre-nixtamalized mote corn, which is a variety of dried nixtamalized corn. Mote is very similar to cacahuazintle in texture and flavor and only needs to be soaked overnight. I found just one reliable option to buy fresh nixtamal in the United States. Check the sourcing list on page 361. If choosing any of these alternatives, follow the product directions for rinsing and cooking times. You can use the seasoning suggested in this recipe.

Canned hominy: I do not recommend canned hominy; it lacks texture and flavor. If you choose this, make sure to rinse the hominy several times to remove the salty water solution it comes in.

Note: If you are cooking hominy one day ahead, remember to save the broth in which it cooked.

Celeste Leonardo Morales, left, collecting freshly ground masa from the local community electric stone mill (molino) in San Gerónimo, Purenchecuaro, Michoacán. Doña María, right, is the owner of the mill.

How to Make Corn Masa

There are two different ways to prepare masa. One way is to use fresh nixtamal, which yields the most flavorful and delicious fluffy masa. The other option is to rehydrate dry masa harina, which is more convenient, saves time, and results in good flavor. Both processes are acceptable and will make good tamales. In this section I have included both methods for you to choose from.

Fresh Masa

Makes about 3½ to 4 pounds (1.5 to 1.8 kg)

Special equipment:
Grain mill suited for WET nixtamal corn
or
Corn mill/molino (examples on page 42)

2.2 pounds dry corn kernels* (about 1 kg) processed as nixtamal according to instructions on page 69

1. Nixtamal is always ground while its wet. Depending on the mill (read about nixtamal mills on page 42), the nixtamal might have to be ground up to three times to achieve the correct masa consistency. The more finely the corn is ground, the better the masa texture will be, making for softer tortillas. Masa should feel soft and silky when pressed between your fingers.

2. Grind the corn kernels to the specification of your mill. If using a manual mill like the Victoria one, make sure to sprinkle some warm water as you grind the masa. This will help pull the crumbly dough together.

3. Once the corn is ground, if the dough is crumbly, knead briefly, and add warm water as needed to achieve the consistency of moist Play-Doh.

4. Once the masa has the desired consistency, place into a bowl and cover with plastic wrap and then with a damp kitchen towel to keep it from drying. Now your masa is ready to be used according to the many recipes in this book.

Masa from Dry Masa Harina

Dry masa harina is found in most supermarkets either in the ethnic food or the Mexican food aisle. It can also be purchased online.

There are two main dry masa harina brands in Mexico, Maseca and Minsa. I prefer Minsa because it is organic and non-GMO, it makes a softer, fluffier masa, and it has better flavor. It is slightly harder to find in the States but worth looking for.

One of the best ready-to-use masa harinas in the United States is made by Masienda. Their chef-grade masa harina is organic and made with single-origin heirloom corn (white olotillo) from Oaxaca, Mexico. The tortillas made with this masa harina are almost as good in texture and flavor as a fresh masa tortilla.

These are all better options than store bought. Once you taste warm homemade corn tortillas, it's hard to go back.

Makes 2½ pounds (1.1 kg) of rehydrated corn masa

1 pound dry masa harina
1 tablespoon salt
2½ to 3 cups warm water*

If making this masa for tamales, hydrate with 1 cup of water and 1½ cup chicken stock or the broth in which the pork was cooked. And use only one teaspoon of salt.

In a large bowl, mix the dry masa harina and salt. Add warm water a little at a time and knead with your hand until well incorporated and it feels like Play-Doh. Make a round masa ball, place in the same bowl, and cover with plastic wrap or a damp kitchen towel. Let it rest for 15 to 20 minutes and it is ready to use.

Tortillas de Maíz
Corn Tortillas

Makes about 12 to 14 small 4-inch tortillas

Special equipment:
tortilla press
1 plastic bag (see photos for instructions)

From fresh masa*:
Fresh masa (page 75)
¼ teaspoon fine sea salt
Warm water as needed**

To make tortillas from fresh masa, start by following the recipe from Step 2.
**Depending how the masa feels after grinding and kneading.*

From dry masa:
¼ teaspoon fine sea salt
¾ to 1 cup warm water
1 cup dry masa harina

1. Dissolve the salt in the warm water. In a large mixing bowl, place 1 cup of masa harina, mix, and make a "well." Add the water into the center and mix with your hands little by little until you have a soft ball and all the flour is incorporated. Knead for 2 to 3 minutes. Make a ball and cover the masa with a damp towel or plastic wrap. Let it rest at least 20 to 30 minutes to let the masa harina rehydrate as long as possible. Usually after this period you need to make some adjustments:

If too dry: The masa will start to crumble. You need to add more water.

If too wet: The masa will be sticky in your hands. You need to add a bit more masa harina.

The right texture resembles a moister Play-Doh. It is ok for the masa to be a little moist to the touch. Your masa should be room temperature; slightly warm to the touch works best. Making tortillas is a matter of *feeling* the masa. The more you make them, the better you will get at it.

2. While masa is resting, modify a resealable bag by cutting the top sealer lines off the bag and cut open the two sides of the bag. Now you have like a plastic folder. Open the tortilla press and lay down the plastic. Now, start by making a 1½-inch round ball (you can use a small ice cream scooper to help make them evenly sized). Remember to keep your masa covered with a piece of plastic wrap or damp towel at all times to prevent it from drying out. Work with one ball of masa at a time. Place the masa ball in the center of the opened plastic and flatten slightly with your fingers. Fold the plastic over the masa, and fold down the metal tortilla press. Hold the handle and press down gently. Lift the press open and check to see that the dough has spread to about a 4-inch diameter. Rotate the plastic and press again if necessary.

3. Heat up a large cast-iron skillet to medium-high. A griddle, comal, or nonstick pan will work too. With your hand, hold the tortilla in the plastic, and carefully peel the plastic off the tortilla as if you were peeling a sticker. When one side is peeled, flip it onto your writing hand and peel the plastic from the other side of the tortilla. As you peel, allow the tortilla to rest halfway on your hand, and half off. Gently lay down the tortilla on the warm skillet. Once you place it, do not try to reposition.

4. Using a spatula, flip the tortilla when you notice the edges of the tortilla start to release from the skillet. But don't fight it. If the tortilla does not release with ease, increase the heat or give it a few more seconds for a clean flip. When flipped, cook for 20 to 30 seconds, then flip again, and using the spatula lightly press around the tortilla edges to make the tortilla inflate. Cook for another 15 to 20 seconds. As soon as an air pocket forms, the tortilla is done.

5. Place the tortillas as you cook them inside a tortilla warmer or a small basket lined with a clean cotton kitchen towel to keep them warm. Continue making tortillas until you finish the rest of the masa. Once you start getting into a good tortilla rhythm, depending on your skillet size you can make two or three tortillas at a time.

Note: If making tortillas with fresh masa: Fresh masa is already hydrated, but it always needs a little extra warm water and it needs to be kneaded a few times, especially if it has been done earlier in the day. If you bought masa that has been refrigerated, make sure to bring the masa to room temperature, add some warm water to replenish moisture, and knead briefly. The warmth of your hands will help the masa become more pliable and have a better temperature for cooking.

Note: Have some sea salt handy so as soon as you have a chance, you can make yourself a "burrito de sal" when the tortilla is hot off the comal. Sprinkle some sea salt in the middle and—carefully when it is warm enough to handle—squeeze the tortilla into an amorphous shape. Eat while it is warm and enjoy the process!

Antojitos Mexicanos
Mexican Street Food

Mexico is known for its great street food dishes. Popular among them are *antojitos Mexicanos* ("little cravings"). These are the small bites found on the street and in some traditional restaurants. They are the perfect food for an impromptu craving at the fair or the *tianguis* (street market) or as an informal meal at the mercados or in *cenadurías* (little, informal eateries).

A few examples include sopes, gorditas, tostadas, tacos dorados, tlacoyos, tortas, chalupas, huaraches, quesadillas, enchiladas, or flautas. When these small bites are combined, they can become a complete meal for breakfast, lunch, or dinner. These quick bites are often made of fresh corn masa or tortillas. Masa variations include tostadas and gorditas (masa patties) that can be deep-fried, steamed, or cooked on a comal. Antojitos are filled with shredded chicken, beef, cheese, or vegetables, and then served with toppings like shredded lettuce, simple tomato salsa, crema, queso añejo or fresco, radishes, and hot salsas.

These antojitos have rich and mouthwatering flavors that make them some of the most craveable Mexican street foods. With no doubt, they are part of every Mexican folksy or informal celebration.

✻ ✻ ✻

Sopes de Pollo — *Chicken Sopes*   83

Tostadas de Pierna — *Shredded Pork Tostadas*   85

Tacos Dorados — *Deep-fried Tacos*   86

Enchiladas de Plaza en Casa estilo Morelia — *Homestyle Morelia Plaza Enchiladas*   88

Sopes de Pollo
Chicken Sopes

Where I'm from, Guadalajara, these fresh round masa patties are called *sopes de masa*, or *pellizcadas*, which translates into "pinched." Why? Once the patties are cooked on the comal or fried, the edges are pinched all around to create a border to hold the fillings and toppings. Pinching the edges is usually done by an experienced cook, a grandma, or an aunt. These cooks often have developed "Cuauhtémoc fingers," with fingerprints worn away by a generation of hard work in the kitchen. For the rest of us enthusiastic cooks, using two spoons to make the edges will work, saving our fingerprints.

Sopes can be filled with shredded chicken, beef, pork, picadillo, chorizo, requesón (Mexican ricotta), refried beans, potatoes, roasted chile poblano rajas, or mushrooms, to name a few options. Once filled, the sopes are topped with simple tomato salsa, shredded lettuce or cabbage, pickled onions, radishes, crema and queso fresco, or cotija cheese.

The best way I have learned to make these homestyle sopes is to mix a mashed potato into the masa, which gives it a tender bite, crispy exterior, and great flavor. These sopes are festive and a great recipe for any celebration.

Makes 8 (3-inch) round sopes

Masa:
1¼ cup fresh corn masa or masa harina
1 medium waxy white potato, boiled, peeled, and mashed
¼ teaspoon sea salt
¾ cup warm water, add a few more teaspoons if needed
1 tablespoon sunflower or vegetable oil

Fillings:
½ cup refried beans, thick but spreadable
2 cups shredded rotisserie chicken, about 3 pieces of chicken (skin removed)

Toppings:
1 cup shredded iceberg lettuce or green cabbage
¼ cup red onion, diced
4 to 6 radishes, thinly sliced
1 to 2 fresh serrano peppers, thinly sliced
½ cup queso fresco, crumbled
½ cup crema Mexicana
1 cup simple tomato sauce (page 220)

Make the sopes patties:

1. Mix the masa, potato, salt, and water. Knead with your hands until you form a soft dough ball that resembles moist Play-Doh. Cover the ball with a clean damp kitchen towel and let it rest for 15 minutes.

2. Heat up a heavy cast-iron skillet, flat griddle, or comal. Keep it on medium heat.

3. Divide the dough into 8 round balls around 2½ inches in diameter. With your fingers, press one ball down into a round flat shape. Then turn it over and press flat again. Use your fingers to press the rest of the balls until you have flat round patties around 3 to 3½ inches in diameter and a little less than ½-inch thick.

4. Add 1 tablespoon of sunflower or vegetable oil to the comal and place each patty on the comal as you keep shaping the rest of the masa. Check the patties every now and then, and keep rotating them for even cooking. Give each patty about 2 to 3 minutes per side. Start flipping them as they turn golden brown with a few toasty brown spots. Add a bit more oil to the comal if necessary while flipping them.

5. Once both sides are cooked, transfer the sopes to a plate. With the help of two same-sized spoons, make an indentation on the sope about ⅓-inch from the perimeter, then position one of the spoons on the outside sope edge and the other spoon on the indentation you just made. Gently press the masa in between the spoons, "spooning" to create the sope edge all around. If you feel confident enough, you can pinch the edges with your fingers, **but be careful not to burn yourself**. This masa dough is scalding hot. Do this to all eight, placing them on the warm comal at a low heat to keep them warm as you shape the rest of them.

6. When all are ready, the fun begins! I like to spread some refried beans on the bottom as my "glue," then fill them with the shredded chicken. The sticky beans will hold your fillings in place. Garnish with lettuce, onions, radishes, and a spoonful of simple tomato sauce. Then drizzle with crema and sprinkle crumbled queso fresco. Garnish with some thinly sliced serranos and add salt and pepper to taste.

Tostadas de Pierna
Shredded Pork Tostadas

Tostadas are often found in cenadurías, street plazas, and food stands that set up shop during fairs and festive days like Día de Muertos.

Tostadas are flat tortillas that have been sun-dried and deep-fried in oil. These flat, crunchy vessels can hold a tower of toppings and are always prepared in a festive manner. The classic preparation consists of a layer of creamy beans, meat (often shredded), and the classic toppings of finely shredded cabbage or lettuce, onion, tomato, radishes, Mexican crema, and crumbled cotija cheese or fresco. Then we top it off with simple tomato sauce and a few dashes of hot sauce and a squeeze of lime.

These are a textural mouthful of flavors. Tostadas can be served as an appetizer, a complete meal, or as an accompaniment to pozole. You can find corn tostadas readily available at the supermarket. The fun toppings are up to you.

Makes 12 to 14 tostadas

4 to 5 pounds pork shoulder or leg
½ white onion
6 cloves garlic
½ teaspoon oregano
½ teaspoon thyme
1 bay leaf
1 teaspoon sea salt
2 cups pinto or flor de mayo beans*
14 corn tostadas

* See the recipe for refried beans (page 187) and add more bean broth to the recipe and smash on the looser side to make them more spreadable.

Toppings:
½ iceberg lettuce or cabbage, thinly sliced
2 Roma tomatoes, thinly sliced
1 small red onion, thinly sliced
2 avocados, cut into slices
2 cups simple tomato sauce (page 220)
½ pound crema
¼ pound queso cotija, crumbled
4 to 6 limes, cut into wedges
Bottled hot sauce, or salsa pozolera (page 103)

1. In a large pot, place the pork shoulder or leg, add the onion, garlic, oregano, thyme, bay leaf, and salt. Cover with water, bring to a boil, and then decrease heat to a low simmer and cook for about 1 to 1½ hours, until fork tender. Turn off the heat and let the pork rest in its own broth for at least 20 to 30 minutes.

2. Meanwhile, make the simple tomato sauce and smash the beans. Set aside.

3. Pull the pork out of the pot and, using two forks, shred medium fine. *Pork will still be pretty hot, so be careful.* As you shred the pork, add a couple tablespoons of the pork broth to keep it moist.

4. Assemble the tostadas. Take a tostada, smear on about 2 tablespoons of smashed beans, and add an even layer of shredded pork, lettuce, tomato, onion, and avocado. Add 1 to 2 tablespoons of the tomato sauce. Drizzle the crema and sprinkle the cheese on top. Serve with hot sauce and a wedge of lime.

Note: If possible, assemble the tostadas as you go, to keep them from getting soggy. A tostada bar, in which everyone makes their own is a good idea when feeding larger crowds.

Tacos Dorados
Deep-fried Tacos

Tacos dorados are sometimes confused with flautas, or rolled-tacos, in the United States. However these tacos dorados are thin, folded-in-half tortillas, usually filled with refried beans, cheese, requesón (Mexican ricotta), mashed potatoes, chicken, roasted poblanos, or any combination of these fillings. Tacos are secured by toothpicks and deep-fried. They look like half moons, topped with lettuce or cabbage, simple tomato sauce, crema Mexicana, queso, and some dashes of your favorite hot sauce. They are served as an appetizer, a meal, or as part of a platter. In Jalisco and Michoacán, tacos dorados are often served with diced chunks of carnitas on top. They are delicious with a beer, and are often served in informal restaurants, or cenadurías. It's a quick, festive meal to prepare for family and friends.

Makes 24 tacos; serves about 6 to 8 people

Special equipment:
55 round wood toothpicks, soaked in vegetable oil*

24 to 30 thin corn tortillas, just a few more in case one or two break
3 cups grape seed oil or vegetable oil for deep-frying

Fillings:
1 cup roughly mashed potatoes
1 cup refried beans
1 cup requesón or ricotta cheese, drained
1 to 2 poblano peppers, roasted, peeled, and cut into strips
1 cup shredded chicken, roasted or boiled

Toppings:
½ head shredded cabbage or iceberg lettuce
½ cup sliced fresh or pickled white onions (page 221)
8 to 10 radishes, thinly sliced
1 cup Mexican crema
1 cup cotija cheese, crumbled
1 recipe simple tomato sauce (page 220)

*I accounted for extras because some toothpicks will likely break.

1. Warm up the tortillas to make them pliable, and keep them warm under a clean kitchen towel. Place about 2 tablespoons of any of the fillings or a combination of two into a tortilla and fold it in half, being careful not to push the filling to the edges. Insert a toothpick into the tortilla and pass through both sides, as if you were hemming the taco's edge. Place two toothpicks per taco, one on each side of the half-moon taco. Do the same with the rest of the tortillas, covering them as you go with a damp kitchen towel to avoid tortillas drying and cracking. Fill the rest of the tortillas until you have 24 folded tacos.

2. In a 10-inch medium-shallow heavy-bottom pan, add the oil and warm up gradually from low heat to medium-high until it reaches 350 to 375 degrees F (176 to 190 C). Depending on the size of your pan, place 4 to 5 tacos in at a time. Avoid crowding the pan to keep an even temperature. Once the first side of the taco is golden-brown, flip to the other side and cook until evenly golden-brown.

3. Place tacos over a cooling rack lined with a paper towel to allow them to drain, and keep them in a warm oven to keep them warm as you fry the rest.

4. Before serving, carefully remove the toothpicks. Rotate as you pull them so that they come out in one piece. Serve 3 to 4 tacos per person, one of each flavor, and top them with shredded cabbage (or lettuce), 2 to 3 tablespoons of the simple tomato sauce, crema, cotija cheese, and radishes. Finally, add serrano chiles or hot sauce.

Notes: If possible, assemble the tacos as you go to keep them from getting soggy. Make a self-serve taco dorado bar when feeding larger crowds.

Enchiladas de Plaza en Casa estilo Morelia
Homestyle Morelia Plaza Enchiladas

Enchiladas from Morelia are a great example of how antojitos Mexicanos can be a complete meal at a street fair or at home. These are called *enchiladas placeras* or *enchiladas de plaza* because the street vendors place their stands around the plazas downtown under the arched portals that surround the colonial buildings in Mexican towns or small cities.

This style of enchiladas is very different from the traditional saucy, rolled kind. Each corn tortilla is dipped into a guajillo sauce and then fried. The oil seals and caramelizes the tortilla with the garlicky pasilla-guajillo sauce, giving each tortilla an adobo coating. Then they are filled with a little queso fresco and folded like handkerchiefs. Your kitchen might end up with red polka-dotted walls, but it's well worth it!

A piece of parboiled chicken fried in the adobo oil is served on the side, and a generous amount of sautéed potatoes, carrots, and quick-pickled onions and manzano peppers are placed on top of the tortillas, followed by a handful of shredded cabbage or lettuce. Then a generous ladle of simple tomato sauce and crema is added, and cotija cheese or queso fresco is sprinkled over that. If this isn't making your mouth water, I don't know what will.

Since the process is hard work and we are recreating street food, I decided to serve these on a large platter as a homestyle meal. This way you can cook everything at once and take the feast to the table.

Serves 6 to 8 Gueritos or 4 hungry Mexicans

Chicken:
2 chicken breasts and 4 sets of legs and thighs
1½ quarts of water
1 small white onion, cut into quarters
1 head of garlic, cut in half horizontally
½ teaspoon dry thyme
½ teaspoon dry oregano
4 bay leaves
1½ teaspoons sea salt
3 to 4 cranks of freshly ground black pepper
1½ pound waxy potatoes, peeled and cut into medium cubes
4 large carrots, peeled and cut on a bias (diagonally) about ¼-inch thick

Enchilada sauce:
¼ cup apple cider vinegar
2 cups water
3 pasilla chiles about 7 inches long, toasted, stems and seeds removed
4 guajillo chiles about 7 inches long, toasted, stems and seeds removed
6 cloves garlic
½ medium white onion
½ teaspoon dry oregano
¼ teaspoon dry thyme
¼ teaspoon cumin powder
¼ teaspoon fresh ground black pepper
1 teaspoon sea salt

Assemble enchiladas:
1 tablespoon lard
½ cup corn oil, sunflower oil, or vegetable oil
18 to 24 corn tortillas
1 pound queso fresco, crumbled
1 medium white onion, finely diced

Garnish:
Romaine lettuce leaves or shredded iceberg lettuce
1 bunch radishes, cut in halves
2 cups queso fresco
1 cup Mexican crema
Simple tomato sauce (page 220)
Escabeche of manzano (perón) peppers, carrots, and onions (page 224)

1. In a large pot, place the chicken, water, onion, garlic, thyme, oregano, bay leaves, salt, and pepper. Bring to a boil and immediately lower the temperature to a slow simmer. With a slotted spoon, remove all the foam that forms at the beginning of the cooking. Cook the chicken for 25 to 30 minutes, turn off the heat, then cover with a lid and set aside. After cooling off, about 20 minutes, transfer chicken pieces to a cooling rack and let them air dry. Save the chicken stock.

2. Bring the remaining chicken stock to a boil, add the potatoes and carrots, reduce the heat to a simmer and cook for 5 minutes, then turn off the heat and cover the pot with a lid. Set aside and let the potatoes and carrots cook with the remaining heat for about 20 minutes. This will yield al dente potatoes and carrots, perfect for sautéing.

3. Prepare the enchilada sauce: Mix vinegar and water and bring to a boil. Add the toasted pasilla and guajillo chiles and soak for about 25 minutes in the boiling water until rehydrated and plump. Remove chiles and save the liquid. In a blender, place the hydrated chiles, garlic, onion, oregano, thyme, cumin, black pepper, sea salt, and about $\frac{1}{2}$ cup of the water-vinegar mixture in which the chiles soaked. Save the rest of the water-vinegar mixture. Blend until a thick smooth puree. Pour the sauce into a medium-sized bowl, wide enough to dip a tortilla.

4. In a sauté pan, add a drizzle of oil and 2 tablespoons of the enchilada sauce. Briefly sauté for 2 minutes. With a slotted spoon, transfer the carrots and potatoes to the pan, and sauté them for 4 to 5 minutes. Taste and add salt if necessary. Keep carrots and potatoes in the pan near the stove to keep them warm until serving.

5. In a medium frying pan with tall sides, heat up the lard and oil together. When the oil is hot, and using a splatter screen to protect yourself, take one tortilla and quickly dip it into the enchilada sauce, tap to remove the drippings, and carefully, using long metal tongs, place the tortilla into the oil. Place the splatter screen over the pan to contain splattering. Be careful and attentive at all times. Fry each side about 15 to 20 seconds. Do not let them get crispy; they should be fried but soft enough to fold. Promptly remove tortilla from oil, place on a plate, add some crumbled queso fresco and diced onions and fold in half or fourths like a handkerchief. Repeat the same with the rest of the tortillas. Use a platter or a baking sheet in the oven to keep them warm as you go. This process goes quickly, but once you get the rhythm, it's easy.

6. In the remaining adobo oil in the pan, quickly pan-fry the pieces of boiled chicken until the skin has crisped up a bit. Drain the chicken well over a paper towel to absorb the excess oil.

7. Serve as a family-style meal. On a platter, arrange a bed of romaine lettuce on one corner, and place the pieces of chicken on one side and the folded enchiladas on the other side. Add the potatoes and carrots in the middle of the plate. Garnish with radishes, drizzle Mexican crema, sprinkle with queso fresco or cotija, and add a couple of spoonfuls of the simple tomato sauce. Serve with some lime wedges, extra lettuce, crema, queso, and the quick-pickled onions and manzano peppers for everybody to enjoy. *¡Buen provecho!*

Pozole

Pozole comes from the Nahuatl word, *pozolli*, which translates into *hominy*. This soup dates from pre-Hispanic times. It is said that pozole was created in the area of what is today the city of Chilapa, Guerrero. The base of this ancient soup was made by boiling nixtamalized corn kernels (page 69), aromatics, and spices along with chicken or turkey.

The Aztecs prepared pozole only for very special ceremonial rituals. According to the Florentine Codex from Bernardino de Sahagún, in order to commune with their gods, the Mexicas would cook a pozole made with human body parts of the warriors and those who had been sacrificed to their gods. Nothing went to waste, and everything returned to Mother Nature's cycle. When the Spanish friars witnessed these pagan rituals, they prohibited further such practices. Turkey and chicken pozoles endured instead, and with the introduction of pork by the Spaniards, pork has become the traditional choice for this hearty, delicious soup.

Today, pozole is one of the most iconic dishes of traditional Mexican cuisine. It is made all over Mexico, and there are many styles and ways to prepare it, depending on region and seasonality. It is served during many festivities and celebrations that involve large crowds because it's easy to serve and it's a crowd pleaser. It is one of the favorite stews during the fall and winter months, and is always served piping hot and garnished with a large array of toppings.

To prepare a great pozole, nixtamalized corn is a key ingredient. Half of the flavor of the soup comes from hominy. Read more about nixtamalization, how to make nixtamal, and how to cook hominy on page 72.

❋ ❋ ❋

Pozolillo Verde — *Green Pozolillo*   94

Pozole Blanco — *White Pozole*   96

Pozole Rojo, Estilo Jalisco — *Jalisco-Style Red Pozole*   101

Salsa Roja Pozolera — *Red Pozole Hot Sauce*   103

Pozole Verde Guerrerense — *Green Guerrero-Style Pozole*   104

Salsa "Espanta Rabitos," Salsa de Chile Serrano
"Spooky Tail" Sauce, Serrano Salsa   107

Pozolillo Verde
Green Pozolillo

I fell in love the first time I tried this pozolillo. This dish got its diminutive name *pozolillo*, meaning "little pozole," due to its easy, hour-and-a-half preparation. This fresher, lighter pozole is made with fresh white corn kernels sliced off the ear, rather than dry nixtamalized corn cooked into hominy. It is usually made with pork, but I often make it with chicken for a lighter broth. Adding green tomatillos to the broth gives it a bright-green color and a pleasant, fresh, tangy flavor. It is best to prepare this kind of pozole at the beginning of corn season when the corn is tender and fresh. At home, this is one of our favorites.

Serves 4 to 6

Chicken stock:
12 cups water
½ medium white onion
½ head of garlic
½ bunch of cilantro
3 sprigs fresh mint
2 bay leaves
½ teaspoon dry oregano
½ teaspoon dry thyme
2 carrots
1 celery stalk
2 teaspoons sea salt
4 to 4½ pounds whole chicken, skin on, cut in half or pieces

Green sauce:
2 pounds green tomatillos, husks removed and rinsed
3 large poblano peppers, stems and seeds removed, coarsely chopped
½ medium white onion
4 cloves garlic
1 large bunch fresh cilantro
½ teaspoon Mexican dry oregano
2 teaspoons sea salt
2 to 3 serrano peppers
2 tablespoons corn or safflower oil
10 to 12 ears of white corn, dekerneled

Garnish:
1 head iceberg lettuce or green cabbage, finely shredded
1 large red onion, finely diced
1 bunch of red radishes, thinly sliced
1 to 2 avocados, sliced
4 to 6 limes, cut in quarters
½ pound Mexican crema
½ pound queso fresco, crumbled
Corn tostadas

Make the pozole:
1. In a large pot, add 12 cups of water, onion, garlic, cilantro, mint, bay leaves, oregano, thyme, carrots, celery, and sea salt. Add the chicken. Bring to a boil, cook for 5 minutes, then reduce heat to a slow simmer. With a ladle, remove all the white foam that forms as it cooks. Cook for about 40 to 50 minutes, until chicken is tender. Once the chicken is cooked, remove the chicken and aromatics and vegetables and sieve the broth. Let the chicken cool down until it reaches a comfortable temperature. Remove and discard the skin and shred the chicken. Set aside.

2. In a blender, add the tomatillos, poblano peppers, onion, garlic, cilantro, oregano, salt, and one serrano pepper. Add one serrano at a time and taste in between blending so you can measure how spicy it is. The serranos in this recipe are used to add flavor, not heat, as one would season with black pepper. Add a ladle of the chicken stock from the pot to help with the blending. Blend to a smooth puree.

3. In a large, deep pot add 2 tablespoons of cooking oil and warm over medium-high heat until oil is shimmering. Add the blended tomatillo sauce to the oil and cook for 5 minutes. (Note: Introducing the sauce to the hot oil will cause it to splatter; keep your hands and arms away by using a long-handled ladle to avoid burns.) After the sauce is sautéed, add the chicken stock and the corn kernels. Bring to a slow simmer and cook for about 25 to 30 minutes. The broth will change color from emerald green to a bright sage green. At this point taste to adjust for salt. Add the shredded chicken to warm through.

Serve piping hot and garnish with shredded lettuce, chopped onions, slices of radishes and avocado, a squeeze of lime, a dollop of crema, crumbled queso fresco, and tostadas.

Note: If you want a shortcut to recipe preparation, use pre-made chicken stock (in equal amounts to the water), and a prepared rotisserie chicken, shredded.

Pozole Blanco
White Pozole

Pozole blanco is uncommon outside of Mexico, perhaps because its red Jaliscoan cousin, pozole rojo, has stolen all the popularity. Pozole blanco is the original pozole and the hardest to make. Its flavor relies on the magical, cloudy white broth made with pork, chicken, and hominy. Some cooks add some ground hominy to the broth, which gives it more body.

Pozole blanco was one of my Grandma Margarita's to-die-for masterpieces. She is the one who taught me how to prepare it, and by spending time watching her in the kitchen, I learned most of the nuances of flavors and preparations of pozole blanco. Practice, patience, and the memory of the smell of pozole in her kitchen keep me working on my own skills. This recipe is the closest to the way I remember it.

Grandma Margarita's pozole was usually served with a shredded pork tostada on the side, like the recipe on page 85. The pozole itself was always served with shredded lettuce, diced white onions, sliced radishes, lime juice, and the magical chile de árbol salsa roja pozolera (page 103) that my grandma used to prepare to be added "al gusto" (to taste) at the table.

Serves 8 to 10

Special equipment:
20-quart enamel or stainless steel pot

6 to 8 quarts water, plus more to add during cooking
1 large head garlic, cut ¼ off the top to expose the tips of the garlic cloves
1 large white onion, cut into quarters
4 pounds pork leg, cut into 2 or 4 large chunks
2 pounds pork collar joint, or neck, cut into large chunks and washed thoroughly
4 whole pork feet (trotters and knuckles), sliced in quarters and washed thoroughly
1 whole chicken, cut in half
4 medium bay leaves
½ teaspoon dry thyme
1 teaspoon dry oregano
2 to 3 tablespoons sea salt
1 batch hominy (page 72)

Garnish:
1 large white onion, finely diced
1 bunch of red radishes, thinly sliced
1 head of iceberg lettuce or green cabbage, finely shredded (a mandolin works best)
10 to 12 limes, quartered
3 to 4 avocados, optional
Dry Mexican oregano, to taste
Corn tostadas
Salsa roja pozolera (page 103)

Make the pozole:

1. In a large pot add 6 quarts of water and bring to a boil. Add the head of garlic, onion quarters, all pork and chicken. Add water to cover the meat by one inch over. Bring pot to a boil and cook for 5 minutes, then reduce temperature to a low simmer. During the first 20 minutes of simmering, use a metal spoon to remove all the gray foam that forms on top of the stock. After all foam is removed, add bay leaves, thyme, oregano, and sea salt and cover with the lid and cook for about 1 hour, replenishing the water if needed as it cooks down. After this time, remove the chicken. Place it in a tray or bowl and set aside and cover. Transfer all the pork pieces to the pot of cooked hominy along with the water in which the hominy cooked. This will give a better body to the broth. Sieve the pork stock and add to the hominy and pork pot. Stir carefully to combine and increase heat to medium-high. When it starts simmering again, reduce to a low simmer and let the flavors of the stock, pork meat, and hominy marry for at least 30 to 45 more minutes.

2. Check the pork for doneness, tearing a piece with a fork and carefully tasting. At this point, everything should be cooked, the flavors are married, and the pozole is ready. Taste the stock for salt and adjust if necessary. Turn the heat to low to keep the pot warm. Pull out the pig trotters and knuckles, and place them into a bowl and cover. Remove the garlic head and leftover onion pieces. *If you like your broth with more body, place the cooked onion pieces and soft garlic cloves in the blender along with half a cup of hominy and some broth, blend until pureed, and add this to the pozole. The broth will be cloudy and will have more body.*

3. In a separate bowl, place the large pieces of pork leg, add a couple ladles of stock, and cover with a lid to keep it moist. Let it rest for 20 to 30 minutes. When it is warm enough to handle, using two forks shred the pork and add some of the pozole stock to keep it moist. Set aside.

4. Now it's time to serve the pozole! My grandma used to keep the shredded chicken and pork separated, because if added back to the pot it becomes a mess and most likely will overcook. Also because it's easier to portion out to each person and serve the meat option they want. She also kept the pig trotters and knuckles separate to serve them by request. Following her wisdom, I do the same.

5. When it is time to serve the pozole, crank up the heat of the stove; the pozole should be piping hot. Serve a few ladles of the broth and one ladle of hominy. Top with warm shredded pork, and let your diners garnish their own.

6. Garnishes should be set up on a large platter on a side table or at the center of the main table along with all the garnishes with limes and salsas. I like my pozole *con todo*, with everything: onions, radishes, lettuce, a generous squeeze of lime, some drops of the salsa roja pozolera (page 103), a tostada on the side, a large spoon, and a cold beer or agua fresca.

Note: Pozole is one of those hearty soups that taste even better the next day. Invite a few friends the next day for a recalentado, or re-heat. Pozole leftovers freeze well, but last about 2 to 3 months. After that, the hominy texture changes.

Butchers at mercado municipal market in Pátzcuaro. A butcher's knowledge and guidance is an asset when making pozole. Look for a Mexican butcher shop, or carniceria, to get the right cuts and bones for the best broth!

Pozole Rojo, Estilo Jalisco
Jalisco-Style Red Pozole

I'm proud to say that pozole rojo is from the state where I was born, Jalisco. This sassy, porky, red, chile-flavored soup is known worldwide. Pozole rojo gets its color and smoky character from a combination of dry guajillo chiles and anchos. It is served piping hot, garnished with lettuce or cabbage, chopped white onions, radishes, and a good squeeze of lime.

In my family, Aunt Paloma wins the title of "Red Pozole Queen" because she really goes the extra mile. She starts the pozole a week in advance by going to the butcher for the pork head, nixtamalizing the corn, cooking the hominy, and ordering the best sun-dried, fried tostadas from the Mercado de Santa Teresita in Guadalajara, Jalisco. With four boys, a hungry husband, plus daughters-in-law and grandchildren (and the most beautiful niece, wink wink), you can imagine the size of a pot she makes! Enough to fit the whole head of pork, a couple of pork shanks, shoulder, leg, a whole chicken, and other goodies. Eating pozole at my Aunt Paloma's house is a celebration in itself.

The following recipe is fit for a smaller crowd, although leftovers just get better as days go by. It freezes well in airtight containers and keeps for about three months. Do not hesitate to double the recipe.

Serves 8 to 10

Special equipment:
20-quart enamel or stainless steel pot

For the chile puree:
8 to 10 dry guajillo chiles, stems removed and deseeded
4 to 6 dry ancho chiles, stems removed and deseeded
3 to 4 chiles de árbol, stems removed
1 cup water
1 medium white onion
6 cloves garlic
½ teaspoon cumin seeds
½ teaspoon dry Mexican oregano
6 black peppercorns
3 teaspoons sea salt
2 tablespoons cooking oil

For the pork:
½ head of a small pig, about 4 pounds, cleaned thoroughly
4 pounds pork leg or shoulder or combo, cut into 4 large chunks
2 pounds pork collar joint or neck, cut into large medallions and washed thoroughly
4 whole pork feet (trotters and knuckles), sliced in quarters and washed thoroughly
1 large head garlic, cut ¼ of the top to expose the tips of the garlic cloves
1 large white onion, peeled and cut into quarters
6 to 8 quarts water, plus more to add during cooking
4 medium bay leaves
1 teaspoon dry thyme
1 teaspoon dry Mexican oregano
2 tablespoons sea salt
1 batch hominy (page 72)

Garnish:
1 head iceberg lettuce or green cabbage, finely shredded
1 large white onion, finely diced
1 bunch red radishes, thinly sliced
8 to 10 limes, cut in quarters
Corn tostadas
2 to 4 chiles de árbol toasted, for garnish
Salsa roja pozolera (page 103)

Make the pozole:

1. **Make the chile puree:** Slightly toast the guajillo, ancho, and árbol chiles on a comal or cast-iron pan. Then place them in a bowl with enough boiling water to cover them and soak to hydrate for 20 to 30 minutes. In a blender, puree hydrated chiles with 1 cup water, onion, garlic cloves, cumin seeds, dry oregano, black peppercorns, and salt. Sieve if necessary. In a saucepan, heat cooking oil. When oil is shimmering, add the chile puree, being careful not to splatter. Turn the heat to low and cook for 20 minutes, stirring constantly to avoid scorching the sauce. Set aside.

2. **Cook the pork:** In a large pot, place the pork head, leg and shoulder, neck, and feet. Add head of garlic and onion. Add water to the pot until it reaches one inch above the meat. Bring to a boil and cook for 10 minutes, then lower the temperature to a medium-low simmer. During the first 20 to 30 minutes, using a metal spoon remove the gray foam that forms on top of the stock. When all foam is removed, add bay leaves, thyme, oregano, and sea salt.

3. Cover with a lid ajar and cook for about 1 hour and 15 minutes more, until pork shoulder and neck medallions are tender and the meat from the head is falling off the bone. With a fork, remove a piece and taste it. Pork should be tender and juicy. Once pork is cooked, transfer all the pork onto a large tray and separate by cuts. Remove skin of the head, jaws, and other bones and discard. Collect all the meat from the pig head, slice the ears, and set aside. Cover with a lid or use different bowls with lids. Add a couple ladles of the stock to keep the meat moist, and set aside.

4. Once you take out all the pork, using a slotted spoon fish out the garlic head, large pieces of onion, bay leaves, and any pieces of pork gristle or small bones that might have fallen off the pork. Sieve the stock.

5. **Marry the elements:** Add chile puree to the pork broth and simmer for 25 minutes. Then add the chile broth to the cooked hominy along with half of the water in which the hominy cooked, including the onion and garlic head. Add back the large pieces of pork shoulder, neck, and feet, and bring the pot to a rapid simmer, and immediately lower the heat to low simmer and cook for 30 to 45 more minutes. Taste, and adjust salt if necessary. Once the broth-chile puree, pork, and hominy have cooked together, the pozole is ready to serve.

6. **Shred and cut the pork:** While the broth is simmering, take the large pieces of the pork leg and shoulder and shred. Cut the pork neck and meat from the head into small pieces. Leave the trotters and knuckles as they are to serve upon request.

To serve: In a large bowl, serve a ladleful of hominy and piping hot broth. Ask your guests which kind of pork meat they prefer and place it on the top. Arrange all the garnishes on a platter, along with the salsa roja pozolera and tostadas, on a side table or on the middle of the dining table, and let your guests garnish their own bowls. I like my pozole plate *con todo*, with everything, so I top my pozole with lettuce, onions, radishes, and I add a little extra oregano, first rubbing it with my fingers to activate its aroma. Add toasted chiles de árbol and tostadas on the side. I add a squeeze of lime juice and a spoon of salsa roja pozolera to give it a nice kick!

Salsa Roja Pozolera
Red Pozole Hot Sauce

This salsa is a MUST when making pozole blanco. It adds a toasty and bold spicy note to the broth. It should be used with caution because of its intense flavor and heat. Serve it in a small ceramic or glass bowl with a small spoon to encourage small doses.

Makes about 1 cup

25 chiles de árbol, stems removed
2 tablespoons cooking oil
2 large cloves garlic
1 teaspoon sea salt
3 tablespoons white or apple cider vinegar
¾ cup water

Toast the chiles in the oil until dark red and toasty. Let the chiles and oil cool down, then place them in the blender along with garlic and salt, the leftover oil in which the chiles were toasted, vinegar, and water until a smooth paste. If sauce is too thick, add 1 more tablespoon of water or vinegar. Salsa should have a loose paste consistency.

Note: This hot sauce will last for 3 to 4 weeks. Keep it in a glass bottle or jar to best preserve its flavor.

Pozole Verde Guerrerense
Green Guerrero-Style Pozole

Pozole verde is one of the oldest pozoles. It is believed that it was created in the coastal state of Guerrero, thus the name. What makes this pozole so special is the addition of ground pepitas, which gives the broth a nutty flavor, an appealing green hue, and a velvety consistency. Besides its unique flavor, pozole verde is served with an unusual variety of toppings like pork rinds, panela cheese or queso de cincho, Mexican crema, and a fiery serrano salsa, in addition to the regular pozole garnishes such as lettuce, onions, radishes, and lime juice.

The mecca for pozole verde is the city of Chilpancingo, Guerrero, where the best pozolerias can be found and where the Pozole and Mezcal Festival has been held for the last thirteen years. Home-cook pozole makers, *Pozoleras*, gather each year to share their delicious traditional pozole preparations and are hoping that one day in the near future, Chilpancingo will acquire the title of capital of the Pozole Verde. For Día de Muertos, this warm, hearty soup is ideal to serve to family and friends after the long night vigil.

Serves 8 to 10

1 batch hominy (page 72)

Verde sauce:
3 tablespoons cooking oil
½ pound tomatillos, peeled, washed, and cut in halves
2 medium poblano peppers, deseeded and cut into large pieces
1 serrano pepper, stem removed and cut in half
½ white onion, coarsely chopped
4 to 6 cloves garlic, depending on size and pungency
1½ cup of raw pepitas or shelled pumpkin seeds, toasted and finely ground
¼ teaspoon cumin seeds, toasted
4 sprigs epazote
½ teaspoon dry thyme
½ teaspoon dry Mexican oregano

1 teaspoon sea salt
1 cup water

For the pork and chicken:
4 pounds pork leg or shoulder or combo, cut into 4 large chunks
2 pounds pork collar joint or neck, cut into large chunks and washed thoroughly
4 whole pork feet (trotters and knuckles), sliced in quarters and washed thoroughly
1 whole chicken, cut in half
1 large head garlic, cut ¼ of the top to expose the tips of the garlic cloves
1 large white onion, peeled and cut into quarters
6 to 8 quarts water, plus more to add during cooking
4 medium bay leaves
1 teaspoon dry thyme
1 teaspoon dry oregano
2 tablespoons sea salt

Garnish:
3 or 4 avocados, sliced
1 large white onion, diced
1 bunch red radishes, sliced
1 head iceberg lettuce, finely shredded
1 medium bag pork rinds
1 pound panela cheese or queso de cincho
1 pound Mexican crema
6 to 8 limes, cut in quarters
Corn tostadas
Salsa "espanta rabitos" ("spooky tail" salsa, page 107)

Make the verde sauce:

1. In a large sauté pan, heat 2 tablespoons of cooking oil at medium heat until shimmering. Add tomatillos, poblanos, serrano, onion, and garlic and sauté for 3 to 4 minutes until they have some blisters. Carefully transfer pan contents to a blender or food processor. Add toasted, ground pepitas, toasted cumin seeds, fresh epazote, thyme, oregano, salt, and a cup of water. Blend until smooth.

2. In the same sauté pan, add one tablespoon of cooking oil and heat until shimmering and add the blended sauce. Cook over low heat for 10 to 15 minutes, stirring often to avoid scorching the sauce. Once cooked, set aside.

Cook the pork and chicken:

1. In a large pot, place the pork leg, shoulder, neck, trotters and knuckles, and chicken. Add head of garlic and onion. Add water to the pot until it reaches one inch above the meat. Bring to a boil and cook for 5 minutes, then reduce the temperature to a medium-low simmer. During the first 20 minutes, using a metal spoon remove all the gray foam that forms on top of the stock. When all foam is removed, add bay leaves, thyme, oregano, and sea salt.

2. Cover with a lid ajar and cook for about 1 hour and 15 minutes more, until pork shoulder and neck are tender and the chicken is falling off the bone. With a fork, take out a piece of pork and taste it. Pork should be tender and juicy. Once pork is cooked, transfer all the pork into a large tray and separate by cuts. Cover with a second tray or use different bowls with lids. Set aside.

3. After removing all the pork, use a slotted spoon to fish out the garlic head, large pieces of onion, bay leaves, and any pieces of pork gristle or small bones that might be left.

Marry the elements:
Add verde sauce to the broth and simmer for 25 minutes. Then add the green broth to the cooked hominy and the water in which the hominy cooked, including the onion and garlic head. Add the large pieces of pork neck and feet, bring pot to a rapid simmer, immediately reduce the heat to a low simmer, and cook for 15 to 20 minutes. Taste broth, and adjust salt if necessary. Once the verde sauce, broth, pork, and hominy have cooked together, pozole is ready to serve.

Shred and cut the pork and chicken:
While the broth is slowly simmering, shred the chicken, pork leg, and shoulder, and cut the pork neck into cubes. Leave the trotters and knuckles whole to serve upon request.

Serve and garnish:
Arrange on a big serving platter, with all the garnishes in small bowls. Take this platter to the table along with the salsa "espanta rabitos." Serve in large clay bowls one ladle of hominy and 1 or 2 ladles of the beautiful and fragrant green broth. Top with the shredded meat of your choice or a combination of both. Let your guests fix their own bowls with toppings.

Note: Tostadas are an essential complement to a bowl of pozole and easily found at Mexican markets. Make sure to read the list of ingredients and choose ones with no artificial colors or hydrogenated oils. The fewer the ingredients, the better. Or you can make your own by placing corn tortillas in the oven at a very low temperature for about 30 minutes. When they are dehydrated, fry them in corn oil and sprinkle with fine salt.

Salsa "Espanta Rabitos," Salsa de Chile Serrano

"Spooky Tail" Sauce, Serrano Salsa

If you go to Mexico, it's important to know your salsas. One little salsa misstep and you can be on fire. This salsa, for example, can easily be confused for fresh salsa verde. It has almost the same hue, but this salsa has the devil inside. A dear friend, Guillermina Delgado, showed me how to make it, and since then I have been hooked. This salsa is best used to spice up a white pozole, pozole verde, tacos dorados, or flautas. It can also be served with ceviche, aguachiles, shrimp cocktail, and grilled seafood. Beware how much of this salsa you eat today, because (hence the name) you will be remembering it tomorrow.

Makes ½ cup

8 fresh serrano chiles, stems removed
Juice of 3 to 4 limes, about ½ cup
¼ cup water
3 pinches of sea salt

Place chiles in a blender, along with water, lime juice, and salt. Blend until a coarse puree, but well incorporated. Transfer to a bowl and include a **little** spoon, to prevent people from serving themselves copious amounts of this extremely hot salsa. Warn your guests!

Note: This salsa lasts about 3 to 4 days in the refrigerator, and it loses its potency as time goes by. It is best made fresh the day you will use it. You can easily double or quadruple the recipe.

Mole Poblano
Poblano Mole
111

Piernas de Pavo Rostizadas con Mole Poblano
Roasted Turkey Legs with Mole Poblano
117

Mole Verde
Green Mole
119

Mole Amarillo
Yellow Mole
123

Mole Coloradito
Coloradito Mole
126

El Rey de los Moles, Mole Negro Oaxaqueño
Mole Negro, Oaxacan King of the Moles
129

Clemole
136

Cochinita Pibil
Yucatán Pulled Pork
138

Mole

The word mole comes from the Nahuatl word *mulli*, meaning "sauce." The Aztecs ate a diversity of salsas and sauces made with chiles, corn, and seeds, which were prepared for everyday cooking. These sauces were poured over fish, vegetables, and tamales. Some of the sauces were made for ceremonial dishes and they were always present at festive rituals.

This pre-Hispanic recipe, which started as a sauce ground in a volcanic stone vessel called a *molcajete* or a flat mealing stone called a *metate* (page 42), evolved as European cooking techniques and ingredients fused with the traditional methods. Mole as we know it today was created in the convents in Puebla, where nuns combined flavors, ingredients, and techniques to merge the old world with the new world, resulting in a complex mestizo mole.

There are nearly one hundred different moles found in the beautiful state of Puebla, The capital city, Puebla de los Ángeles, is known as *la ciudad de los cien moles*, or "the city of one hundred moles." The most famous is mole poblano, an icon and a national dish (page 111). There are a variety of moles based on ingredients, texture, and flavors: mole almendrado (almond-based), encacahuatado (peanut-based), de fruta (fruit-based), black (charred and chile-based), green (pumpkin seed-based), yellow (chile- and masa-based), and white (pine nut- and almond-based).

Mole has been commonly mistaken as a "chocolate-based sauce," but mole is really all about the chiles. Chiles are the body of mole. They determine the depth of flavor, piquancy, color, and aroma. The right amount and combination of chiles, along with spices, aromatics, fruit, nuts, seeds and chocolate, is what gives each mole its personality and regionality. So when making a mole recipe, it is essential to know how to identify chiles because using the wrong kind can be disastrous. Many chiles are mislabeled in stores, in both bulk sections and packages, so regardless of what they are labeled, you should be able to tell the difference. See pages 52–59 for chile guidance and page 361 for sourcing them.

The following are some of the best-known moles around Mexico. Oaxaca is known for their seven moles: mole negro, mole rojo, mole coloradito, mole verde, mole amarillo, mole chichilo, and mole de novia. Michoacán has their exquisite mole rojo, a simple mole made almost entirely with chiles, corn masa, and fruit. Guerrero's mole rosa is made of pink pine nuts and aromatics. Manchamanteles and Clemole, lighter moles almost like a brothy stew, vary by region in the states of Guerrero, Morelos, Puebla, and Oaxaca. Mole de olla is typically found in Estado de Mexico. Its consistency is more like a brothy soup and includes meat and vegetables. The Mixtecan Huaxmoles of Puebla, Guerrero, and Oaxaca are made with guaje seeds, jalapeños, and goat. Mole Xico from Veracruz is made with fresh apples, pears, pineapple and plantains, and dry fruit and chiles, yielding a unique savory yet fruity mole. Mole Prieto from Tlaxcala is a variation of mole negro made with huitlacoche, which gives it a seasonal flavor.

The recipes I'm sharing are some of the most iconic homemade moles prepared for special celebrations, and are typically prepared for Día de Muertos.

Mole Poblano
Poblano Mole

Mole poblano is one of the greatest icons of Mexican cuisine and represents the fusion of flavors, ingredients, and cultures. In the year 1700, Sister Andrea de la Asunción, intern of the Dominican order of the Santa Rosa de Lima Convent in Puebla, Mexico, created this unique dish to entertain Thomas Antonio, a Spanish viceroy. She magically orchestrated four different chiles and eighteen other ingredients into what we recognize as a Baroque dish because of the array and combination of ingredients and elaborate cooking techniques. It combines ingredients from the Spanish and indigenous cultures and is one of the best examples of *la cocina Criolla Mexicana.*

Because of its elaborate preparation, mole is a celebratory dish, often made for important life events like baptisms, weddings, birthdays, and Día de Muertos, when it is frequently the main food offering on altars. Families gather days in advance and cook together to make this dish.

I must warn you, mole poblano is the antithesis of "quick and easy" cooking; making mole is an arduous process that requires attention, focus, and patience. The road to the best results is long, about 5 to 6 hours of active cooking, but I can assure you every minute is worth it. If you try this recipe, and it is your first time making mole, I recommend you split the steps over three days in the kitchen:

Day One: Buy ingredients and make the chicken stock.

Day Two: Make the first sauce (chile) and the second sauce (tomato and aromatic).

Day Three: Make the third sauce (toasted nuts, seeds, and dried fruit), combine all the sauces, and cook the mole.

On the other hand, if you are like me and enjoy these kitchen endeavors, complete the entire recipe in one adventurous day. Gather all the ingredients a day ahead and get up early. Wear your kitchen-warrior shoes, play some great music, and take your vow of patience because making mole is a rewarding culinary adventure.

This recipe is just to make the mole sauce. You will have to decide what kind of protein to serve with it. Mole is usually served with chicken or turkey, and sometimes pork loin. A neutral protein showcases the flavors of the sauce. I have scaled down this recipe to make at home, yielding enough sauce to serve around 14–16 people. Since you are going through the effort to make it, you might as well have enough mole to save and freeze for other meals. This is actually a small recipe compared to what families in Mexico make. Parties, or *comidas* as we call the festive gatherings, can last from the middle of the day throughout the next day. So people keep feeding their guests and keep on dancing, having fun, celebrating, and eating. Consider that a whole chicken serves about 4 to 6 people and a 16- to 18-pound turkey serves 10 to 12 people. Calculate accordingly and roast or boil the protein of your choice by using the same principles in the recipes for shredded chicken or turkey (page 62).

First things first. When making a good mole poblano you need to have a well-made and flavorful chicken stock. This is the base for building the flavors. The better your chicken stock, the better the mole.

Makes about 4 quarts (3 to 4 liters) of mole sauce, enough sauce to serve about 12 to 14

To make it less overwhelming, the ingredients for this recipe are divided into three main sauces needed to make the mole. Once you have made the three sauces, you just have to combine them to marry the flavors that will become mole.

Chicken stock
1 recipe Mexican homestyle chicken stock (page 65)

1st sauce (chile)
5½ ounces (150 gr) mulato chiles
3½ ounces (100 gr) ancho chiles
2 ounces (60 gr) pasilla chiles
1 (3-inch) chipotle meco chile
⅔ cup pork lard or leaf lard
½ cup extra virgin olive oil
3 cups chicken stock, warm
1 teaspoon sea salt

All chiles should be weighed without stems.

Make the 1st sauce (chile):
Wipe the chiles with a damp towel. Over a medium-size mixing bowl, remove dry chile stems with kitchen scissors. Cut open lengthwise and remove seeds and veins. Do this with all the chiles. Reserve 1 to 2 tablespoons of mixed seeds to use later in the recipe. In a medium-size sauté pan over medium-low heat, melt the lard and olive oil. Fry the chiles about 40 seconds per side. Do this in small batches, paying attention to not scorch the chiles. Carefully shake the chiles to drain the extra oil and place in a separate bowl. Do this with the rest of the chiles. Add boiling water to the bowl of fried chiles just enough to cover them. Place a plate or a lid over the bowl and leave them soaking for about 30 to 45 minutes or until they are rehydrated, soft, and look plumped. Discard water and transfer them to a blender. Puree them in three batches. Small batches work best to obtain the best evenly smooth puree. Add ⅓ of the chiles plus 1 cup chicken stock each time. Set that puree aside, and repeat until all chiles are pureed. Add sea salt, stir, cover, and set aside.

2nd sauce (tomato & aromatics)
8 ounces Roma tomatoes, about 2 large ones
3 ounces tomatillos, about 7
7 ounces white onion, about 1 medium, cut in half
2 white corn tortillas, toasted
1½ ounces day-old crusty sourdough bread
3½ ounces piloncillo, grated
2½ ounces artisanal chocolate tablets, cut into pieces
½ teaspoon anise seeds
5 whole clove buds
4 whole allspice peppercorns
10 black peppercorns
2 teaspoons sea salt
2½ cups chicken stock, warm

Make the 2nd sauce (tomato & aromatics):
Place tomatoes, tomatillos, and onions on a comal over medium heat until they show dark blistered skins and juicy cooked flesh. Cook the onion until charred on both sides. Toast the tortillas directly on the flame or on a separate comal or cast-iron pan. Soak the bread in water. Gather the piloncillo, chocolate, spices, and chicken stock. Place all ingredients of the 2nd sauce into a blender and puree until nice and smooth. Set aside in a bowl.

Sauce 1: Frying chiles.

Sauce 1: Rehydrating fried chiles.

Sauce 2: Charred tomatoes and onions.

Sauce 3: Sautéeing nuts, seeds, garlic, and dried fruit.

Top photo: Large bowl: 1st sauce, chiles; Medium bowl: 2nd sauce, tomato and aromatics; Small bowl: 3rd sauce, toasted nuts and seeds.

3rd sauce (toasted nuts & seeds)
¼ cup pork lard or leaf lard
¼ cup extra virgin olive oil
6 large cloves garlic, cut in half
3 ounces almonds, blanched
3 ounces peanuts, roasted unsalted
2 ounces pepitas, raw
2 ounces sesame seeds, raw
1½ ounces raisins
2½-inch stick canela
1 to 2 tablespoons reserved mixed chile seeds from 1st sauce
2½ cups chicken stock, warm

Make the 3rd sauce (toasted nuts & seeds):
In a shallow frying pan, combine the lard and extra virgin olive oil, and warm up over medium-low heat. Add garlic cloves and sauté until golden brown. Add the nuts, seeds, raisins, and canela and fry until almonds and sesame seeds look golden brown. Remove all the items from the pan and set aside, letting them cool down for a few minutes. Then place the mixture in a blender with 2 cups of chicken stock and puree until a paste. Add ½ cup of chicken stock at the end and blend until a smoother paste. Depending on the power of your blender, you might want to do this in two batches to achieve the smoothest paste possible.

Marrying the sauces:
Marrying the three sauces is the last step. If you are making the mole in one day, take a little break before marrying the sauces. Refresh yourself with a cold agua fresca (or a shot of tequila), take a deep breath, refocus, and start the last and most important step.

If making the sauces ahead of time, remember to bring every sauce to room temperature before combining all the ingredients.

1. Bring to a boil the rest of chicken stock (about 2–3 cups). *Warm chicken stock will make the blending of the three sauces easier and allow you to adjust the thickness of the mole.*

2. In a large clay pot, heavy enamelware, or stainless steel heavy-bottom pot, add ¼ cup extra virgin olive oil or lard, wait until hot, and then add the 1st sauce (chile). Cook for 5 minutes, constantly stirring gently. Then add the 2nd sauce (tomato and aromatics) and stir until well combined. Cook for 5 minutes, constantly stirring gently. Last, add the 3rd sauce (nuts and seeds) and stir gently until well combined. Add 1 to 2 cups of warm chicken stock a little at a time and stir gently, always in the same direction. Lower the heat to medium-low. Cook the mole "low and slow," stirring at all times to avoid scorching the mole.

3. Cook the mole for a minimum of 35 to 45 minutes, up to an hour for best flavor. Add some extra chicken stock along the way if the sauce overthickens. This step is the most demanding of all because you must stir constantly. There is a saying that you should always stir in one direction so the mole won't curdle. Is that true? I'm unsure so I also recommend we stick with using one direction just in case. Nonetheless, the rewards of making this amazing sauce are worth every stroke.

When Is the Mole Ready?
Small craters and bubbles will surface on the top, creating rings of red oil, and small red oil drops will float to the top. The smell and fragrance will be unique, all flavors should be balanced, and the sauce thickness should cover the back of a spoon without separating. Mole should look dark reddish-brown, smooth and velvety. Once the mole is ready, lower the heat and let it rest for 15 to 20 minutes before serving. Mole always tastes better over the next two days when all the flavors have settled together. If you make it ahead of time, the flavor will be even better.

Serve with: Turkey, roasted turkey legs, roasted chicken, pork loin, enchiladas, over tamales, or save some of this mole to make some banana leaf tamales. Include a side of arroz anaranjado, refried beans, pickled onions, and warm handmade corn tortillas, along with a good agua fresca or cold cerveza.

Garnish with: ½ cup toasted sesame seeds, and quick-pickled white onions (page 221).

Notes: Mole freezes beautifully. Save it in airtight containers and make sure to place a piece of parchment paper over the surface of the mole to avoid any freezer burn. You can keep this mole up to 6 months, after which the flavor might be compromised. Imagine, next time you crave this delicious mole sauce you will have it ready to go on hand! When reheating mole, add some chicken stock to the sauce and bring it to a slow simmer. Stir often to avoid scorching the bottom of the pot.

Piernas de Pavo Rostizadas con Mole Poblano
Roasted Turkey Legs with Mole Poblano

What more majestic and decadent way to showcase mole than to serve it over roasted turkey legs. The roasted skin on the turkey adds a layer of flavor and texture that in combination with the velvety rich mole sauce makes turkey legs one of my favorite ways to eat mole. Make a full batch of mole poblano or mole negro and pour the leftover mole over this recipe for turkey legs.

Serves 4 to 6

4 turkey legs
2 tablespoons extra virgin olive oil
Sea salt
Black pepper
½ cup water
6 to 8 cups mole poblano (page 111)

1. Take turkey legs from the refrigerator and bring them to room temperature, about 20 to 25 minutes. Pat the legs dry with a paper towel and place them on a baking pan lined with parchment paper. Rub the legs with olive oil and sprinkle generously with sea salt and fresh cracked pepper. Add ½ cup water to the pan, so the legs cook and steam at first. As the water reduces, the skin will get crispy and golden brown.

2. Roast at 425 degrees F (218 C) for about 30 to 35 minutes until a meat thermometer reads 175 degrees F (78 C) to 180 degrees F (82 C).

3. Remove from the oven and let the legs rest on the pan for 10 minutes.

4. Warm up the mole sauce in a saucepan.

5. Transfer legs to a serving platter. Pour a generous amount of the mole poblano sauce over the legs. Sprinkle some sesame seeds and white pickled onions on the side.

Garnish with quick-pickled white onions for mole poblano (page 221). Serve with a side of arroz a la Mexicana (page 202) or arroz a la mantequilla (page 205), refried beans (page 187), warm corn tortillas or warm bollilos or sweet rolls, and a simple green side salad.

Mole Verde—*Green Mole*

This mole verde tells my story as a cook—the way I've adapted and embraced flavors in a foreign country, and my eagerness to rescue my cooking memories. This recipe is my own translation of the traditional mole verde, not only in flavor but also with a simpler method and an updated way to prepare it at home.

With all the intentions of showcasing the pumpkin seeds' flavor and herbaceous, distinctive smells and colors, I used what is best and available in Texas, where I live. I sought out herbs and ingredients that mimic the traditional flavor in a new way..

The unique flavor of toasted pepitas, chiles, corn masa, and herbs give this beautiful bright-green mole a lighter quality and a velvety texture with a hint of heat that will warm the back of your throat. It is an outstanding combination with any white-flesh fish, shrimp, chicken, or turkey. It also pairs well with many hearty vegetables, like zucchinis, sweet potatoes, mushrooms, chayote squash, carrots, rutabagas, or parsnips. Because of the amount of fresh herbs in the recipe, this mole tastes best the day it is made, and it will hold for the next two to three days in the refrigerator.

Serves 6 to 8

8 to 10 (depending on size) green tomatillos cut into quarters
1 large or 2 small poblano peppers, chopped and deseeded.
3 to 4 serrano peppers, coarsely chopped
¼ medium white onion, roughly chopped
2 cloves garlic
1 to 2 cups slightly packed, fresh epazote leaves*
¼ cup fresh parsley leaves
½ romaine lettuce (use the light-green leaves close to the heart, about 6 to 8 leaves)
2 cups baby power greens, like spinach, kale, arugula, mustard, or chard
½ teaspoon anise seeds, toasted
½ teaspoon cumin seeds, toasted
6 peppercorns
1 teaspoon sea salt
3 to 4 cups of warm chicken stock (page 65)
3 tablespoons extra virgin olive oil
¾ cup raw pepitas, toasted and finely ground**
2 tablespoons white corn masa harina, diluted in 4 tablespoons water or chicken stock

Smell and taste the epazote. If this is the first time you've used it, taste it because it has a minty-licorice flavor. If it is too strong for you, start by adding half the amount and adjust to your taste buds.
I use a coffee grinder dedicated to spices to pulverize the toasted pepitas. Pulsing in a food processor should work too.

1. In a blender, add the chopped tomatillos, poblanos, serranos, onion, garlic, epazote, parsley, romaine, power greens, toasted anise, toasted cumin, peppercorns, salt, 1 to 1½ cups of chicken stock, and a drizzle of extra virgin olive oil, and blend well for about 3 to 4 minutes until pureed.

2. In a 7-quart pot (clay or enamel) drizzle some extra virgin olive oil. Once it starts to ripple, carefully add the green blended concoction. It might splatter, so wear an apron and use a ladle. Stir, and let simmer on low for 10 minutes. Remove any white foam that comes to the surface. Stir now and then.

3. Whisk the pulverized, toasted pepitas into the green sauce little by little to avoid clumps. If the sauce is getting too thick, add one more cup of warm chicken stock a little at a time. Chicken stock has to be warm so the mole does not break and separate.

4. Gently whisk and add the diluted masa harina a little at a time. Add another cup of the chicken stock. Whisk gently. Cook the mole on a gentle slow simmer for another 10 minutes, stirring now and then, making sure you scrape the bottom to avoid hot spots. As it cooks, the mole will thicken. If the consistency is too dense, add more chicken stock a little at a time. You want a creamy consistency that will cover the back of a spoon.

5. At this point I use an immersion blender and blend for 1 minute until smooth and velvety. If you don't have an immersion blender, a regular blender will work. *Please use caution when handling hot sauces in the blender.* Once smooth and velvety, taste for salt level and adjust if necessary. Let it cook at a low simmer for another 15 to 20 minutes.

Serve warm over a piece of chicken, grilled or sautéed white fish, or any vegetables. Be generous with the sauce; cover the entire surface and maybe a little more. Garnish with toasted pepitas, a side of brown rice, or your favorite garlicky rice pilaf.

Variation: This mole makes a delicious adaptation for vegan and vegetarian guests. Use roasted vegetable stock and serve over roasted cauliflower, zucchini, carrots, mushrooms, chayote, and sweet potatoes.

This mole makes a delicious adaptation for vegan and vegetarian guests. Use roasted vegetable stock and serve over roasted cauliflower, zucchini, carrots, mushrooms, chayote, and sweet potatoes.

Mole Amarillo
Yellow Mole

Mole Amarillo is one of the seven moles from Oaxaca. Not all moles are made equal. This one has about one third of the ingredients of other moles. Fewer and more sensible ingredients make this mole shine. Its orange-yellow hue comes from the combination of tomatillos and dry yellow chilhuacle Amarillo, an ancient Oaxacan chile that is hard to acquire even in Mexico due to its small production. Chilhuacle Amarillo is hard to grow, and there are only two growers in Oaxaca. Therefore, mole Amarillo is often prepared with the mild, dry guajillo in combination with the chile costeño, which gives a similar flavor and hue.

This mole has a lighter consistency and is often served with vegetables like green beans, chayote, zucchini, and potatoes. This recipe also includes the delicious and peculiar masa dumplings known as *chochoyote*. The small gnocchi-like chochoyotes are made with corn masa and lard, and then shaped into a small round ball and indented in the middle to create a cavity for the mole to fill. Chochoyotes are added to the mole while it is simmering, and they become tender one-bite pillows of softness to eat along with the mole, chicken, and vegetables.

Mole Amarillo is a complete meal and one of the classic moles made during Día de Muertos in Oaxaca. Its color, aroma, and delicious flavor will embolden you to make it more often.

Serves 6 to 8

1 recipe Mexican homestyle chicken stock, including the chicken* (page 65)
1 tablespoon lard
½ medium white onion, diced
6 cloves garlic
5 whole allspice
5 black peppercorns
3 clove buds
6 guajillo chiles (about 1 ounce), seeds and stems removed, and cut into rings with scissors
4 costeño chiles, seeds and stems removed
3 chiles de árbol, stems removed
½ pound Roma tomatoes (about 2 to 3 medium), roasted
½ pound tomatillos (about 10 to 12), peeled, washed, and cut into quarters
3 sprigs fresh oregano
3 sprigs spearmint (hierbabuena)
1 pinch ground canela
1½ teaspoons sea salt
8 cups chicken stock (from the Mexican homestyle chicken stock previously made)
1 tablespoon vegetable oil
3 tablespoons masa harina diluted in 1 cup water
3 to 4 large leaves of fresh hoja santa, rolled up and sliced into ribbons right before serving

Chochoyotes (corn masa dumplings):
1 cup masa harina or fresh corn masa
1 cup water
2 tablespoons lard, corn oil, or avocado oil
¼ teaspoon fine sea salt

Garnish (chile poblano rajas and onions):
Vegetable oil
5 poblano peppers, sliced into ¼-inch-wide strips
1 medium white onion, sliced into slivers
Juice of 1 to 2 limes
Sea salt to taste

When making the stock for this recipe, use a variety of sizes of chicken pieces, from leg and thigh to half a chicken breast, so it's easy to serve to each guest.

1. In an enamel or heavy-bottom nonreactive large pot, heat up lard until it changes to a golden yellow color. Add onions, garlic, allspice, peppercorns, and cloves, and sauté until the onions and garlic are golden brown and soft. Add guajillos, costeños, and chiles de árbol and fry for another 3 to 5 minutes over medium heat until the guajillos change color to a dark red and the chiles de árbol are toasty.

2. Add roasted tomatoes, tomatillos, oregano, spearmint, canela, salt, and 2 cups of the chicken stock. Cover the pot and slow simmer for 10 to 15 minutes or until tomatillos are soft and guajillos are hydrated.

3. Carefully place everything into a blender and blend until smooth. In the same enamel pot, heat up about 1 tablespoon of oil and then add the blended sauce to cook. Add the rest of the chicken stock and the diluted masa harina, and bring to a low simmer. Using a wooden paddle, stir constantly to avoid scorching the mole as it slowly thickens.

4. While simmering the mole, prepare the chochoyotes. Combine masa harina, water, lard or oil, and salt in a bowl. Knead until well combined and start shaping them. Take about ½ to 1 teaspoon of masa and make a small ball the size of a large marble. Then use your pinkie finger to make an indentation in the center of the masa ball. As you shape them, add them one by one to the simmering mole in different spots to avoid them sticking to each other while they cook. Stir gently to avoid smashing them. As they cook through, they will start to float.

5. Once the chochoyotes are all cooked, add the reserved pieces of chicken that were cooked in the Mexican chicken stock, and add them to the pot of mole Amarillo and simmer for a few minutes until they are warmed through.

6. Add the hoja santa and stir it into the mole, cover the pot, turn off the heat, and let the mole rest for 10 minutes before serving.

7. In the meantime, prepare the poblano pepper and onion garnish. In a cast-iron pan or comal over medium-high heat, warm up a drizzle of oil and add the poblano pepper strips and onions and sauté for a few minutes. You want to quick-char them and leave them al dente. Place them in a small bowl, add lime juice and sea salt, toss, and set on the table.

8. Serve the mole in shallow bowls with a piece of chicken, 2 to 3 ladles of the mole, a spoonful of chochoyotes, and garnish with some of the poblano-onions rajas on the side. Serve with warm corn tortillas, good music, cerveza, and great company!

Notes: Unfortunately in this recipe, hoja santa is not replaceable. The flavor of this herb is unique and exquisite; it tastes like a real root beer plant, a licorice herbal flavor. Other herbs like spearmint or cilantro will make it taste different but can still be delicious. The best way to source hoja santa is to grow it at home! Find a nursery that carries a plant you can grow in a large pot or in a corner of your garden. But check the sourcing ingredients section on page 362 for other suggestions.

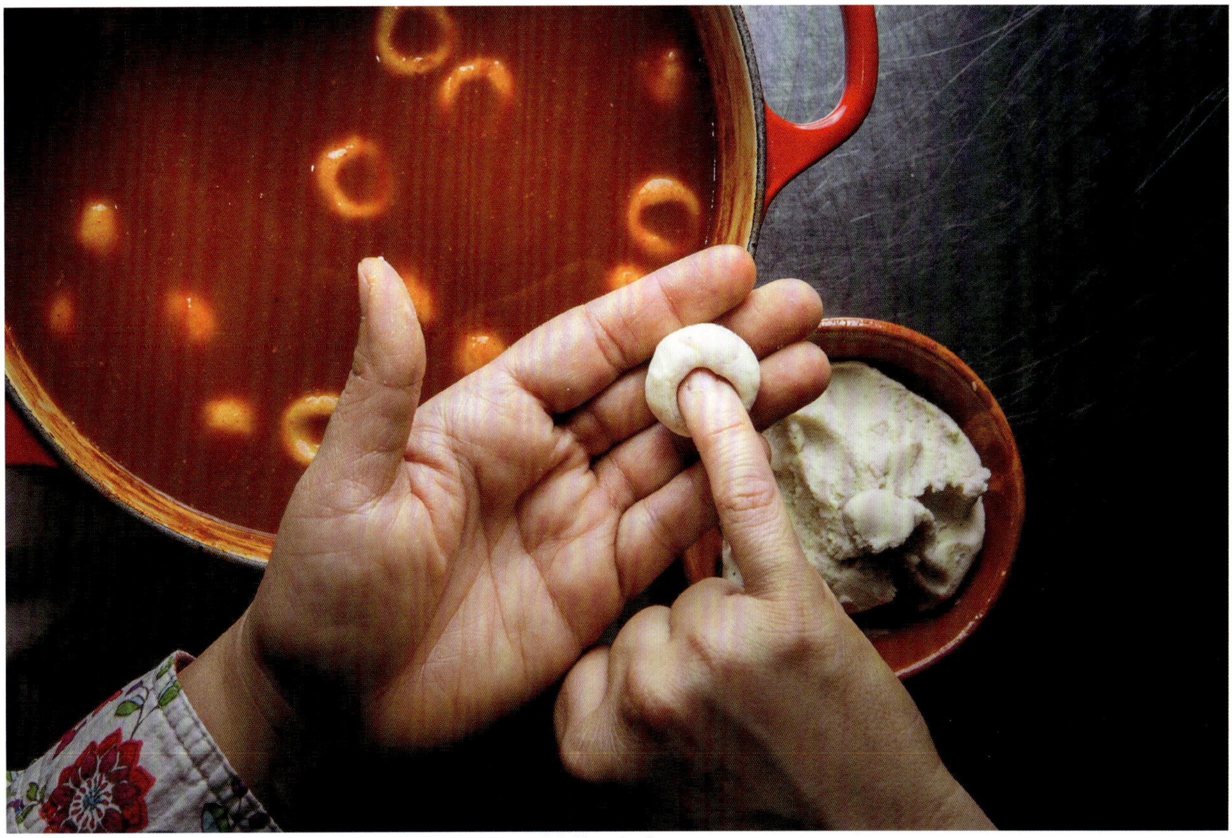

Making chochoyotes.

Hoja santa.

Adding hoja santa to the mole.

Mole Coloradito—*Coloradito Mole*

Oaxaca is the fifth largest state in Mexico, with an impressive culinary diversity throughout its seven regions. Each region has a specialty mole made with ingredients that represent the particular diversity and culture of that region. Thus, Oaxaca is known as *Oaxaca la de los siete moles*—Oaxaca of seven moles. Mole coloradito comes from the central valley region.

Coloradito means "reddish," named for the bright-red hue from the red chilcostle*, guajillo, and ancho chiles. It has a pleasant spiciness and depth of flavor from the anchos and its flavor goes well with pork, chicken, lamb, or beef, or even as a basting sauce for fried fish or shrimp. A mole coloradito taco on a charred corn tortilla, along with grilled nopalito pad strips, and topped with pickled white onions (page 221) is among my favorite ways to enjoy this mole.

Because of its pleasant flavor, this versatile mole is also one of the traditional sauces used for banana leaf tamales, along with pork or chicken. In some Oaxacan towns you can get lucky and have mole coloradito with roasted iguana (not featured in this volume, sorry folks). Talk about versatility! Whether you make this as a meal with a side of garlic rice and corn tortillas to scoop it, or you make it to fill tamales, I assure you it will bring every bite to life!

Serves 8 to 10

- 2 ounces guajillo chiles (around 7 to 8 chiles), seeds removed, lightly toasted
- 2 ounces ancho chiles (around 4 chiles), seeds and veins removed, lightly toasted
- 1 morita chile
- 1 tablespoon lard
- 1 medium white onion, medium diced
- 4 to 6 large cloves garlic, peeled and cut in half lengthwise
- ¼ cup sesame seeds, toasted
- 3-inch stick canela, roughly crushed
- 4 clove buds
- 4 whole allspice
- 8 black peppercorns
- 2 Roma tomatoes, boiled till soft
- 1½ teaspoon Mexican oregano
- 1½ teaspoons cumin seeds, toasted
- ¼ teaspoon thyme
- 2 to 3 one-inch slices day-old baguette, cut into cubes
- 1 teaspoon turbinado sugar
- 1 to 2 teaspoons sea salt
- 3 to 4 cups pork or chicken stock, warm
- 2 tablespoons sunflower oil

1. Place the chiles in a large mixing bowl and cover them with boiling water. Allow them to hydrate for 20 to 30 minutes or until they look plump and soft.

2. Meanwhile, in a large sauté pan over medium heat, warm up the lard until it changes color to a light golden brown. Add the onions and garlic cloves; cook until golden brown. Reduce the temperature and add sesame seeds, canela, cloves, allspice and black peppercorns. Sauté until the canela starts releasing its aromas, then set aside.

3. Drain the chiles and discard the water. In a blender, place the soaked chiles, sautéed onions with aromatics, boiled tomatoes, oregano, cumin seeds, thyme, baguette, sugar, salt, and ½ cup of the chicken stock, and blend. (Start with ½ cup chicken stock, to ensure a smooth paste, and add more stock as needed until you have a smooth thick sauce.)

4. In a large pot over medium-high heat, warm up the sunflower oil. Once the oil is shimmering, carefully add the chile-aromatic blended puree. This might splash, so be careful and use a deep pot and a long-handled ladle to avoid a new pattern on your kitchen walls. Lower the heat to medium-low and cook for 5 to 8 minutes, stirring constantly to avoid scorching the sauce.

5. Bring the rest of the chicken stock to a boil and slowly add into the mole as you stir, until well incorporated. Simmer over low heat for another 15 to 20 minutes, stirring constantly until desired consistency; the consistency is not as thick as other moles, but the sauce should cover the back of a spoon, and when you run your finger over the spoon, the line stays put. Once the consistency is spot on, taste and adjust salt if needed.

Notes: *Mole coloradito is usually made with red chilcostle chiles, a very rare chile from Oaxaca. These chiles are in danger of disappearing. Only a few farmers grow them, and harvest yields are small, so it is even hard to get them in Oaxaca. Because of this, people are using guajillos instead.

El Rey de los Moles, Mole Negro Oaxaqueño
Oaxacan Mole Negro, the King of Moles

Mole Negro is one of Oaxaca's delicacies and has an unmatched, complex flavor. This obsidian black sauce is achieved using a combination of perfectly charred dark chiles. Smoky and mildly spicy with a pleasant, subtle, dried-fruit sweetness, its unique character makes mole negro the King of Moles. Its flavor and consistency is hard to master. With more than thirty ingredients, and because all the chiles and their seeds must be toasted to a charred-but-not-burnt state, it requires an "open-minded" palate. This recipe is a labor of love and concentration and its preparation will challenge any cook, but once achieved, it's the most miraculous sauce. No wonder it is one of the moles almost exclusively made for special celebrations, particularly the Day of the Dead. Ready yourself for this recipe journey.

Chiles:*
3 ounces chilhuacle negro or guajillo chiles
2 ounces mulato chiles
2 ounces pasilla negro chiles
4 to 6 chiles de árbol

Body sauce:
1 large white onion, cut in half
1 medium head garlic, peeled
1 pound Roma tomatoes
1 large plantain, ripe (peel should be black)
½ pound tomatillos
2 corn tortillas
2 to 3 slices day-old baguette, toasted (challah or pan de yema will work too)

Nuts and seeds:
2 tablespoons lard*
2 ounces almonds, blanched
2 ounces pecans
2 ounces sesame seeds
2 ounces roasted peanuts
2 ounces prunes
2 ounces raisins

Aromatics:
4 clove buds
5 whole allspice
14 black peppercorns
1 teaspoon dry Mexican oregano
1 teaspoon dry marjoram
1 teaspoon thyme
3-inch stick canela
3 avocado leaves or 1 teaspoon anise seeds

Rest of ingredients for blending the mole:
1 cone of piloncillo, grated
5 ounces Mexican chocolate, artisanal quality, broken into smaller pieces
3 to 4 quarts (3.5 liters) chicken stock
2 tablespoons lard or extra virgin olive oil
4 to 5 teaspoons sea salt

*Chilhuacle chiles are an endangered species of chiles. Even in Oaxaca, it is hard and expensive to get them, and only two communities in the region still grow them. If you want to go the extra mile, see the online source for them in the Sourcing Ingredients section on page 360. A combination of guajillo and arbol chiles are the closest substitution.

Step 1: Toasted chiles.

Step 2: Charring chile seeds until blackened.

Step 3: Soaking charred seeds and chiles.

Step 7: Frying toasted seeds, nuts, and aromatics.

Preparing ingredients: The first seven steps of the recipe are pre-prep and for processing ingredients. Steps 1 to 7 will take about 2 hours.

1. Char the chiles: Wipe all chiles with a damp towel. Remove the stems from all chiles and seeds from all chiles except the chile de árbols. Seeds should be reserved in a separate bowl. Charring the chiles is hard work but can be simplified by using a grill or toasting them in the oven. Both processes require your attention *at all times*. The difference between charred and burnt takes only a second or two. Mole negro requires a char almost to black to achieve the obsidian color and depth of flavor of the mole and it takes a sensibility and observation to discern when the chiles are at the right point. Here are some tips I have learned when making this mole: How do you tell when your chiles are ready? The shiny outside chile skin should be totally black and the inside of the chile should have a slightly reddish-black hue. Test: If a piece of charred chile crumbles easily like ashes when rubbed between your fingers, your chiles are ready. Char on medium heat to avoid scorching them without toasting them through.

    Oven method: Place all chiles on a baking sheet and preheat the oven to 350 degrees F (180 C). Toast them for 15 to 20 minutes, until blackened. To achieve an even batch, spread the chiles on an even single layer and toss every now and then.

    Grill method: This is the fastest, although the hardest to control, since the chiles can burn fast. Make a low-heat fire using natural charcoal that has burnt down with no direct flames. Char the chiles by tossing them often. Do this in small batches so you can control the heat more accurately. The extra flavor of wood charcoal will impart a delicious layer of flavor to the mole.

    On a comal: Keep in mind this charring process needs to be done in a ventilated area; open the windows and turn on the hood extractor in your kitchen. Charring the chiles on a comal is the best method, because the heat is more even and easier to control. Toast the seeds and the chiles nice and slow to achieve the best results.

2. Char the chile seeds: Place the seeds in a cast-iron pan over medium-low heat. Using a wood spatula, stir the seeds constantly until evenly charred. This process takes about 20 to 30 minutes until they are almost the color of the cast-iron pan.

3. Remove the seeds from the stove, let them cool, and then soak them, and the chiles, in warm water for 15 minutes.

4. Char onion, garlic, and tomatoes: On a cast-iron comal over medium heat, place the halved onion face down, whole garlic cloves, and whole Roma tomatoes until all sides are charred and blistered. You can char onions, garlic head, and tomatoes on the grill if it's easier for you.

5. Roast plantain and tomatillos: Slice the plantain in half lengthwise. Place plantain halves and whole tomatillos on a large pan in a 400°F oven and roast until tomatillos are blistered and the plantains are soft and a golden brown color. This will take about 15 to 20 minutes.

6. Toast tortillas and bread: In the oven, place tortillas and baguette slices at 350 degrees F. Toast bread until golden brown like a crouton and toast the tortillas until they change color to a deep brown and some areas look charred. This will take 15 to 20 minutes; keep an eye on them and rotate and flip them at least twice to ensure even toasting.

7. Toast seeds and nuts: Warm up lard in a large shallow pan until it changes color to a golden brown. Add almonds, pecans, and sesame seeds, and panfry over medium-low heat for 3 to 4 minutes. Stir constantly to achieve an even toasting. Break the canela stick into smaller pieces and add all the aromatics. Toast the aromatics along with the seeds for another 2 to 3 minutes, keeping the temperature on medium-low heat. Toast until almonds change color to golden brown and the canela and spices awaken their aromas. Remember to stir with a wooden spatula at all times to avoid scorching the seeds and nuts. Finally, add the roasted peanuts, prunes, and raisins, toss well, and toast for another 2 to 3 minutes. Set aside and let it cool down a bit.

Traditionally, all this pureeing and grinding is done in a metate, a rectangular stone mortar that has been used since Aztec times. The flavor that the stone gives the ingredients while grinding is very special and hard to achieve with household equipment. The women who use metates learned how to grind ingredients as children. Grinding is a tradition that is passed down though generations. Today, this grinding process is also done in an electric stone mill. In almost every community there is a person who owns an electric mill and charges a small amount to grind nixtamalized corn, chiles, and seeds for moles or other ingredients.

Recipes like this mole are usually made by a group of women who shared the tasks. The grandma or the most proficient cook is the one in charge of orchestrating the final combination of all the purees. It is also said that only one person should be in charge of stirring the mole. After all the prepping, toasting, and blending, you might feel a little overwhelmed but you should also feel very accomplished. The best part is coming up. Take a little break away from the kitchen and drink something refreshing before you continue with the rest of the recipe.

Making the sauces:
When you have all ingredients processed: The next three steps are all about grinding and pureeing in the blender to create three different purees that will be combined and cooked in the same pot to make the magical mole sauce.

To start the process of making the purees, have a pot ready with the chicken stock warmed up, and a measuring cup. Chicken stock is the liquid used for the blending process and must be kept at a slow simmer to help smoothly blend all the ingredients.

Puree #1: Divide the blackened chiles and seeds into three equal amounts. In a blender place one of the batches and ½ to ¾ cup of chicken stock to blend each chile-seed addition. Depending on your blender, you might need to divide the chiles into three or four steps. Be patient. This chile paste needs to be as smoothly pureed as possible—no pieces of skin or grainy texture should be seen. If you have blended as smooth as possible but still see some pieces of skin, use a fine mesh to sieve the sauce. Once all the chiles are processed, pour this smooth puree into a bowl and add 1 teaspoon sea salt, stir, and set aside.

Chiles are the foundation of moles. Learning to identify them and how they taste is a key part of selecting chiles for these delicious sauces. To learn more about chiles and how to identify them, see pages 52–56.

Puree #2: In the blender place the "body sauce" ingredients (charred onion, garlic, tomatoes, roasted plantain and tomatillos, and toasted tortillas and baguette), plus the grated piloncillo, the broken tablets of Mexican chocolate, 1 teaspoon of sea salt, and 2 to 3 cups of warm chicken stock and blend until a smooth puree. Place this puree into a bowl. Set aside.

Puree #3: In a blender add half of the toasted nuts-seeds-aromatics along with 1½ cups of warm chicken stock, and puree until smooth. Add the rest of the nuts-seeds-aromatics, and 1 more cup of chicken stock. Add 1 teaspoon salt and puree until smooth. Set aside.

Marrying the sauces to become mole: These last steps are where the magic happens.

1. In a large 6-quart nonreactive heavy-bottom pot with a lid, heat up two tablespoons of lard until lard changes color to a golden brown. Remove pot from the heat, let it cool for 3 to 5 minutes, and carefully add the **puree #1** chile paste. Stir with a long wood spatula and place back on the heat. It is very important to cook the lard first and to let it cool enough before adding the chile paste to avoid your stove and walls looking like a Jackson Pollock painting. After 2 to 3 minutes, add 2 cups of chicken stock, stir well, and cook for 10 more minutes, stirring every now and then.

2. At this point, add **puree #2** and stir until well incorporated. Add 2 more cups of warm chicken stock and cook for 10 more minutes, stirring slowly at all times to avoid scorching the bottom of the sauce. Last, add **puree #3**, stir until well incorporated, and add the rest of the chicken stock. Stirring slowly and constantly at all times, cook for 30 to 45 minutes on medium-low heat.

3. After 30 minutes, taste to adjust salt or sweetness by adding a bit of sugar or an extra little piece of piloncillo if necessary. Mole is ready when the sauce takes a dark-black hue and a glossy shine. Mole negro is silky and a lighter consistency than mole poblano. The sauce should completely cover the back of a spoon, and when you run your finger through it across the spoon, both sides of the mole should not meet. If mole is too thick, add more chicken stock to desired consistency. Keep mole warm over low heat and stir every now and then to avoid scorching.

Serve mole negro over a juicy piece of chicken, turkey, or pork loin, along with garlicky white rice (page 201), and freshly made corn tortillas.

Notes: This recipe makes about 4 quarts (4.5 liters) of mole. If you are undertaking this long journey, you may as well have mole for seconds or thirds. The good news is that mole freezes beautifully, and it lasts for 6 to 8 months if properly saved in the freezer. Save mole in one-quart containers. To avoid freezer burn, place a piece of plastic wrap over the top of the mole, touching the sauce. This will prevent ice from forming in the gap between the lid and the mole. It keeps best if you can vacuum seal it.

Mole is one of those sauces that get better with time. If you are planning a dinner party, you can make it weeks in advance. It will last about 8 to 10 days in the refrigerator.

Top: Three purees ready to marry—small bowl: nuts, seeds, and aromatics; medium bowl: bread, tortillas, tomatillos, tomatoes, plantains; large bowl: pureed chile and toasted chile seeds.

Bottom: Caution, unattended mole can erupt!

Clemole

Clemole is a slightly spicy, lighter-bodied mole made with chiles and tomatoes or tomatillos, and thickened with corn masa. One of the oldest recipes for clemole, Clemole de Oaxaca, came from the writing of Sister Juana Inés de La Cruz, a 17th-century nun, philosopher, and scholar. Her version calls for pork and a long, Spanish-style pork sausage called *longaniza* with a pasilla chile sauce.

There are a wide variety of clemoles, especially in central and southern Mexico. Some use red chiles or serrano chiles, pork, chicken, beef, or a combination of meats, and it also includes seasonal vegetables. Fish clemole can also be found around Veracruz. My version is slightly spicy, very aromatic, and includes lots of vegetables. It can be made with chicken, pork, or beef-shank medallions. Since it is a lighter but hearty, flavorful, and colorful dish, I think it deserves to be included as an alluring warm stew for enduring the long celebration night.

Serves 4 to 6

4 pasilla chiles, slightly toasted, deseeded, and deveined
2 guajillo chiles, slightly toasted, deseeded, and deveined
3 Roma tomatoes, charred
½ white onion
4 cloves garlic
¼ teaspoon ground clove buds
¼ teaspoon ground cumin
½ teaspoon ground canela
1 bay leaf
10 cilantro sprigs
2 teaspoons sea salt
¼ teaspoon fresh ground black pepper
6 cups chicken stock, divided
2 pounds country-style pork ribs, cut in half
2 pounds pork shoulder, cut into 2-inch cubes
4 tablespoons masa harina diluted in 1 cup of chicken stock
1 tablespoon vegetable cooking oil
1 chayote, cut in quarters lengthwise
5 to 6 baby potatoes cut into halves
2 to 3 handfuls fresh green beans
1 ear of white corn, sliced in ¾-inch wide coins
4 carrots, cut into thick slices or lengthwise
2 zucchinis, cut into thick slices or lengthwise

1. Place the toasted chiles in a mixing bowl and cover them with 3 to 4 cups of warm water to hydrate them for about 20 to 30 minutes, or until they look plump. In a blender, add the chiles, tomatoes, onion, garlic, cloves, cumin, canela, bay leaf, cilantro, plus salt and pepper, along with one cup of the chicken stock. Blend until smooth and set aside.

2. Generously salt and pepper the ribs and the pork shoulder cubes. In a heavy-bottom pan, add a drizzle of vegetable oil and lightly sear each rib and the pork cubes. Do this in batches for best results. Set aside the seared pieces.

3. In the same pot, over medium heat, add a tablespoon of vegetable oil until shimmering. Add chile sauce to deglaze all those bits of pork sediment from the searing, and cook for about 10 minutes, scraping the bottom of the pot to prevent scorching. Add the chicken stock, stir well, bring to a simmer, and then add the seared pork shoulder and ribs. Bring to a slow simmer and cover with a lid. Cook for about 25 to 35 minutes or until pork is tender.

4. Once the pork is done, while constantly stirring, slowly add the masa harina solution and cook covered with a lid ajar for another 8 to 10 minutes. You will notice the sauce will start to thicken and take on a loose soup consistency. Taste and adjust for salt and black pepper.

5. In a separate pot, steam the vegetables. Start with the chayotes and potatoes, cook for 5 to 7 minutes, and then add the green beans and corn coins and cook for another 5 minutes. Add carrots and zucchini at the end. Cook until al dente or to your desired doneness.

To serve: Place meat on a plate and arrange an assortment of vegetables on the side. Ladle the clemole over the meat and add white rice and corn tortillas on the side.

Variation: Adding a few pieces of pork sausage or longaniza will enhance the flavor of clemole and make the flavor richer. Sauté the longaniza links separately and add them at the same time you add the pork pieces back into the stew in step 3. Add about half to one link per person.

Cochinita Pibil—*Yucatán Pibil Pork*

It was in Yucatán that the important culinary fusion of Spanish and Mayan cuisine took place after the Spanish conquest. It is believed that the people of Yucatán were the first Native Americans to eat pork. This culinary fusion was the genesis of a New World mestizo cuisine. Ingredients like pork, spices, and citrus came together with different cooking techniques to create the mestizo fusion.

Cochinita pibil is one of the most renowned dishes in Yucatán. *Cochinita* means "suckling pig" or "small pig," and *pibil* in Mayan means "under the ground," referring to the cooking method that the Mayas developed. It is one of the dishes that I like the most from the Yucatán Peninsula because it is not only flavorful but also fun to prepare. There are two ingredients that give cochinita pibil its character and flavor: annatto seeds and bitter oranges. You might have to go on a retail adventure to find them, although now it is easier than ever with all the specialized spice stores and supermarkets with ethnic foods. Annatto seeds come from a heart-shaped fruit with spiky hairs that grow on little trees in tropical forests. When the fruit is fully mature, it splits open to reveal beautiful red seeds. Annatto seeds are also used for pigments and food coloring.

Cochinita pibil is such a rewarding dish. First, you make a rub for the pork and marinate it overnight or for as long as twenty-four hours. Then you make a pork bundle with banana leaves and bake it in the oven or in an outdoor charcoal pit for 3½ to 4 hours. If you wish, you can go all the way and bury it in the ground, which is the traditional method. You will need to dig a hole in the back of your garden, layer the hole with small leafy tree branches, banana leaves, and a layer of hot coals. Then place the cochinita on a heavy metal tray and cover with a tight lid. Place a wet burlap sack on top, then another layer of banana leaves. Add hot coals and more leafy tree branches, and cover it with dirt to create a sealed underground oven. Cochinita will be done in about 3 to 4 hours, nice and slow. For a less intense cooking method and convenience, I have adapted this recipe for a regular house oven or grill oven.

Cochinita pibil is addictive. The tangy oranges, the floral annatto seeds, and the two types of peppercorns marry the rich pork flavor, creating succulent pork with an extraordinary, complex flavor and tender texture. The pork remains moist in the banana leaf pocket, and the banana leaves perfume the dish giving it even more flavor. It is definitely a dish for special celebrations.

Serves 6 Yucatecos, or 8 to 10 cochinita pibil taco lovers

Special equipment:
Heavy-duty aluminum foil
16 × 13-inch enamel, clay, or stainless steel roasting pan

8 to 10 pounds pork butt or shoulder, cut into large 3 × 4-inch cubes*
2 large white onions sliced into thin wedges

Adobo marinade:
6 tablespoons annatto seeds**
1 tablespoon whole black peppercorns
8 to 10 whole allspice (10 small or 8 medium/large)
6 clove buds
2 teaspoons cumin seeds
2-inch stick canela
½ teaspoon Mexican oregano
12 cloves garlic
1 habanero chile, deseeded
1 tablespoon sea salt
1½ cups bitter orange juice, about 3 oranges depending on how juicy they are***

5 to 6 banana leaves
Quick-pickled charred red onions and habaneros (page 222)

*Pork butt tends to shrink a lot because of its fat content, so always calculate at least 2 or 3 more pounds than you think you will need. In this recipe, 8 pounds yields about 5 to 6 net pounds of pork.
**Using annatto seeds is best because whole seeds preserve their natural oils better than ground spices. Grinding them at home with the rest of the aromatics yields a fresher, more intense flavor for the marinade. Whole seeds are also better because most of the pre-ground annatto powders and annatto paste blocks contain artificial coloring that changes the flavors of the recipe. If you cannot get annatto seeds, read the labels before buying any annatto powder or paste to ensure you will get the best flavor of the ingredients and less artificial coloring. If using achiote paste, three-quarters of the paste bar will be enough, and use only half the amount of salt in the recipe.
***Bitter oranges have a sour, bitter flavor and are highly acidic, which complement and tenderize the meat. They have rough, green and yellow skins (See photo on page 47.) If you can't find this kind of orange, substitute 1 cup orange juice and ½ cup white vinegar.

1. Cut the pork into 3 × 4-inch cubes and set aside.

2. Grind the annatto seeds, black pepper, allspice, cloves, cumin seeds, canela, and oregano until powdered. You can use a stone mortar or a coffee grinder to pulverize the seeds. I prefer to use a mortar; it's more fun and the aroma of the spices while grinding is amazing, but a coffee grinder will work. Just remember: once you use it for spices, only use it for spices!

3. In a blender, combine the garlic cloves, habanero chile, sea salt, and orange juice. Blend.

4. In a glass container, place the pork and the blended marinade, and massage the pork pieces until well coated. Cover with parchment paper and plastic wrap. Refrigerate overnight.

5. **Next day:** Remove pork from the fridge before you prepare the 16 × 13-inch enamel, clay, or stainless steel roasting pan. You don't want the marinated pork to be refrigerator-cold when you place it in the oven. This allows the meat to cook more evenly and it will be more tender. Be sure that it goes into the oven shortly after pork comes to room temperature.

6. Move your oven rack to the lowest position in your oven. Preheat the oven to 325 degrees F (160 C). Place the banana leaves directly on the oven rack for 5 to 7 minutes. Afterward, they should be a little warm, which will make them more pliable. With scissors, cut off the hard middle ribs of the leaves (see step 2 on banana leaves method on page 159).

7. Line the bottom of a large roasting pan with banana leaves in both directions, overlapping the leaves halfway and placing them crossways until you can no longer see the bottom. Place some leaf pieces in each corner to ensure there are no leaks. The overhanging pieces of leaves will be used to help wrap the pork into a bundle.

8. On top of the banana leaves in the roasting pan, add a layer of onions and place the marinated pork meat on top of the onion layer. Add the marinade juices over the pork and cover with the overhanging banana leaves. You are making a pork bundle so make sure it is all fully wrapped. See the photos.

9. Cover the entire bundle with aluminum foil. Tighten the foil all around the edges of the pan to fully seal in heat and moisture. Place the pan into the oven (or the warm charcoal embers in an outside earthen pit or carefully monitored grill) for 2½ to 3 hours. Pull the cochinita out of the oven and let it rest for at least 30 minutes before uncovering it.

10. While the cochinita is resting, prepare the quick-pickled onions. Refresh yourself with a nice cold Mexican beer or agua fresca.

Unveil the cochinita pibil and shred the pork into smaller pieces with tongs or two forks. Let the pork absorb the juices from the pan. The pork should be fork tender, juicy, moist, and fragrant! The smell will fill your kitchen. Cochinita pibil is best served with a side of fluffy white garlic rice, black beans, corn tortillas, and quick-pickled charred red onions and habaneros (page 222). Making tacos is always a great option. And of course save some to make a delicious mukbil pibipollo tamal (page 168.)

Tamales

The tamale, created in Mesoamerica around 8000 to 5000 BCE, is one of Mexico's oldest dishes. From the Nahuatl word *tamalli*, which means "wrapped," tamales were made to feed kings, warriors, and families for both everyday meals and special celebrations. This preparation so important to the Olmecs, Toltecs, Mayas, and Aztecs was made of nixtamalized ground corn masa filled with chile sauces, turkey, hen, fish, frog, iguana, squash, vegetables, beans, or greens and wrapped in corn husks or banana leafs.

There are more than five hundred different kinds of tamales in Mexico, made with an incredible variety of ingredients, and wrapped in various casings such as corn husks, hoja de milpa (corn plant leaves), reed leaves, banana leaves, chard, or chaya (tree spinach), depending on the region and seasonality. Early tamales had no fat in the masa; they were leavened with Tequesquite, a salt from the sedimentary crust that forms on the edges of lakes in Mexico's Central Valley. Since pre-Hispanic times, this alkaline rock has been used to make masa, enhance flavor, soften beans, retain color in vegetables, and tenderize meat. The tamales were steamed in clay pots and cooked over a wood fire, and were eaten mostly during celebrations and as offerings to the gods Mixcoatl and Huitzilopochtli as a thank you for the harvest.

The conquest brought new cooking techniques that blended Mexican ingredients and pre-Hispanic preparations fused with European ingredients that improved flavor and texture. The addition of lard to the masa and the use of pork, fruit purees, sugar, and other spices contributed to the most common flavors of the tamales that we know today.

Tamales are still one of the most traditional preparations in Mexico. They can be made for all kinds of celebrations and usually by groups of people because they can be time-consuming and elaborate to prepare. But the hard work pays off when families and friends gather around these warm, delicious bundles.

❋ ❋ ❋

When Making Tamales   145

Masa para Tamales — *Basic Tamale Dough*   147

Uchepos–Tamales de Elote — *Fresh Corn Tamales–Uchepos*   148

Tamales Tradicionales Rojos o Verdes — *Traditional Red or Green Sauce Tamales*   152

Tamales de Huitlacoche con Quesillo y Epazote
Corn Smut Tamales with Oaxacan Cheese and Epazote   157

Preparing Banana Leaves for Tamale Wraps   159

Tamales en Hoja de Plátano, Rellenos de Mole Negro o Mole Poblano
Banana Leaf Tamales, Filled with Mole Negro or Mole Poblano   161

Tamales de Mole Coloradito en Hoja de Plátano
Coloradito Mole Tamales in Banana Leaves   164

Tamales de Acelgas y Queso Fresco
Swiss Chard and Queso Fresco Tamales   166

Mukbil Pibipollo–Tamal Yucateco — *Yucatecán Ceremonial Tamale*   168

Corundas Tradicionales de Cinco Picos — *Traditional Five Peaks Corundas*   175

Uchepos ready to be cooked. Recipe on page 148.

When Making Tamales

Tamales are great for breakfast, lunch, dinner, or in between.

Breakfast tamales are an easy, substantial, on-the-go meal, and even have their own wrapper. For breakfast at home, people commonly serve them with a sunny-side up egg and refried beans on the side or topped with a simple tomato sauce, crema, and crumbled queso fresco, depending on the kind of tamale.

In Mexico City, tamales are common street food. A bizarre preparation technique from this city are the tortas de tamal served for breakfast and lunch. These tortas are made on a special bread called *telera*, similar to a soft ciabatta, that is cut in half, smeared with smashed beans, and filled with a rojo or verde tamale and a spoonful of salsa, crema, and crumbled queso fresco.

A traditional way to eat them is for merienda or dinner. Usually people eat two savory tamales and one sweet tamalito for dessert. During the fall and winter months, tamales are always served with a cup of atole, champurrado, warm fruit punch, or hot cocoa. Tamales are not an everyday meal, though, and are often saved for special occasions and holidays. For Día de Muertos, tamales go back to the original native celebrations and connect modern Mexican cuisine to its early origins, before European influence. Tamales are a favorite of generations, and these delicious bundles find their way onto many family altars and the centerpiece of fiestas. They are the ultimate Mexican party food.

For corn husk tamales:

- Always rinse the corn husks well and rehydrate them in warm water until soft and pliable. Take them out of the water and place them in a colander to drain out the excess water.

- Use a regular spoon to spread the masa onto the corn husk. It's easy and it slides better when spreading the masa. Some people make a masa ball and then use a tortilla press to make a thick tortilla, then transfer to the corn husk, fill, and close. This technique works great depending on the consistency of the tamale masa.

- Most of the time corn husks come in uneven sizes; save the smaller husks to use on the bottom of the steamer rack and to make strings that will serve to tie the tamales. Also, overlapping two smaller husks works great to make a regular size tamale.

- Tying tamales can be time consuming. To speed up the process, have just one person perform this task.

- When making the sauce for tamales, the flavor should be stronger and saltier than when making a guiso or a stew. Always salt it and season it a little extra to balance the flavor of the masa and the filling. This will make the most flavorful tamales.

- Some people like to marry the sauce with chicken, turkey, or pork to make a guisado. It works well, but I like to cook my sauce separately to avoid overcooking the filling. And add 2 or 3 spoonfuls of the sauce when making the tamales. This ensures that each tamale has enough meat and the same amount of sauce.

- When adding the shredded meat for a tamale filling, spread the shredded meat along the center of the masa in a flat even layer, leaving about a half inch to the bottom. This will ensure that the tamale will have meat from the first bite to the last. Nobody likes a lopsided tamale with all the filling clustered in the center.

For banana leaf tamales:

- Use the freshest banana leaves you can find; they will impart flavor to the masa when cooking.

- Use sharp scissors to cut the banana leaves. For complete instructions, see page 159. And save the scraps to use on the bottom of the steamer rack to avoid wet bottomed tamales.

- Use a trigger ice cream scooper to portion the masa. This will help you make each tamale the same size, and they will cook evenly. I like to use this, especially when making banana leaf tamales, because of the consistency of the masa.

Reheating Tamales

Tamales are easy to reheat. Use a steamer if you want them to taste just like you made them. Another good way to reheat them is on a comal or in a cast-iron pan. For tamales "asados" or "tatemados," place them with the corn husk or banana leaf on the comal over medium heat and cover them with a lid to create a little steam to heat them through. The charred corn husk will add a bit of smoky flavor to the masa. For pan-fried tamales, add a little dab of lard or butter to a cast-iron pan, remove the corn husk or banana leaf, cover a few minutes with a lid to heat them through, and panfry the tamales until slightly golden brown.

Freezing Tamales

Tamales freeze beautifully for 3 to 4 months. Beyond that, the flavors of the masa and filling start to deteriorate. Make sure to wrap the tamales in plastic film and then place them in a resealable bag. Freeze them as airtight as you can to avoid freezer burn. (A vacuum sealer is optimal.) Thaw them for at least 3 to 4 hours before reheating them.

Masa para Tamales—*Basic Tamale Dough*

A light, fluffy, flavorful, and *memorable* tamale depends on good-quality masa and lard and the mixing method you use.

Fresh masa vs. masa harina: Fresh, nixtamalized masa yields a flavorful, fluffy, and tender tamale, which is why it is the best option. Fresh masa can be challenging to find in the United States, but I feel it's my duty to encourage you to search the Mexican markets in your city for a good source of fresh masa. It is certainly worth the effort. For those of you who are eager to try the most traditional method, you can find the recipe for nixtamalized fresh corn masa on page 75. It is a completely different adventure and a bigger investment of time, but without a doubt produces the most delicious results. The alternative to fresh masa is masa harina, which is almost always readily available in large chain supermarkets. Look for a brown package that says "Nixtamal, coarse masa harina for tamales," This kind produces the best texture. Avoid prepared masa for tamales because these products have leavening agents, salt, and other ingredients that you don't want to double up. And keep in mind that *masa harina is not cornmeal.*

The lard: Pork lard is the traditional flavor in tamales. I like to use natural pork leaf lard because of its quality and the flavor it gives to the masa. I buy mine from our local farmer, who raises pork organically and sells at our Sunday farmer's market. You may be fortunate enough to find a similar source where you live. If not, get as good quality as possible. Stay away from hydrogenated lard. Other kinds of fat can be substituted, like canola oil or duck fat. For sweet little tamalitos, try butter or coconut oil.

Whipping lard until light and fluffy is the key to fluffy tamales. Start with room temperature lard, soft but not liquid. Lard takes about 10 to 15 minutes of whipping to fluff up similar to the consistency of whipped butter, which changes its color and texture. I have also used the inverted whip method in which you melt the fat of choice, add it to the masa, and whip it well, and that works great too. To ensure fluffiness, I also get a bit of help from baking powder, which compensates in case the dough is slightly underwhipped. If possible, I use double-acting baking powder, because when mixed into the masa dough, its leavening effect works slower and lasts longer than regular baking powder, giving you more time to assemble your tamales.

The following recipes make a small batch of two dozen tamales, so if you are working alone in the kitchen, it is easy to handle. If you want a larger batch, both recipes double beautifully. If making more than two dozen, I recommend tackling one batch at a time. It's easier to make smaller batches than a huge amount and then not be able to spread the tamales fast enough before the baking powder goes to sleep. If you have a *tamalada* (tamale making gathering), you can make several batches at a time and divide up the tasks with one person prepping the masa; two people spreading the masa, filling, and wrapping; and one person tying the tamales.

Basic tamale masa from FRESH corn masa:
¾ cup lard or leaf lard, room temperature
2½ pounds nixtamalized fresh corn masa, store bought* or recipe (page 75)
2 teaspoons fine sea salt
1 tablespoon baking powder
¾ to 1 cup stock reserved from the meat you cooked for the filling**

You can buy fresh masa at Mexican supermarkets.
**Fresh masa might need more or less stock based on its consistency when purchased.*

In a large bowl, whip up the lard for about 10 to 15 minutes until fluffy. Little by little crumble in the masa, add salt, and start adding some of the stock a little at a time until well incorporated. Mix with your hands or a mixer until all liquid is incorporated and masa is light and fluffy, about 20 to 25 minutes. Sprinkle in the baking powder and mix well for another 3 minutes. Masa should look and feel light and fluffy, with lots of little bubbles and a porous texture that can be seen in the dough.

Basic tamale masa from DRY masa harina:
1 pound dry masa harina
1 tablespoon baking powder
1 teaspoon fine sea salt
¾ cup lard or leaf lard, melted
3 cups stock reserved from the pork/chicken you cooked for the filling

In a large bowl, mix the dry masa harina, baking powder, and salt. Add 2½ cups of warm stock a little at a time and knead with your hand until well incorporated and it feels like moist Play-Doh. Make a round masa ball, place in the same bowl, and cover with plastic wrap or a damp kitchen towel. Let it rest. Meanwhile, in a large bowl, using an electric mixer, whip the lard until fluffy, about 10 to 15 minutes. Crumble in the masa little by little and mix. Slowly add ½ cup of stock until all is well incorporated. Mix for another 10 to 15 minutes until the masa dough looks and feels light and fluffy, with lots of little bubbles and a porous texture that can be seen in the dough.

Note: If using a stand mixer, use the whisk attachment to whip the lard and the paddle attachment when mixing in the rehydrated masa harina.

Uchepos—or Tamales de Elote
Fresh Corn Tamales—Uchepos

These tamales are from the southern region of Jalisco and Michoacán where corn is king. What makes them different from traditional tamales is the use of fresh ground corn instead of nixtamalized corn masa.

The first corn harvest in Mexico starts in August or September, right after the rainy season. The first ears of white corn at the peak of the harvest are reserved to make these tamales because of their tenderness and sweetness. This corn has the ideal amount of starch and sugar for uchepos and makes tamales with a fresh, sweet flavor and a tender, fluffy crumb. They are wrapped in fresh green corn leaves, which add even more flavor and a slight green tint to the tamales. Uchepos have no filling; they are all about the flavor of the corn. They are traditionally served with a thick tomatillo sauce, Mexican crema, or jocoque (fermented milk, similar to yogurt) and a generous amount of crumbled queso fresco or queso cotija or añejo. Leftover uchepos make a great breakfast. Reheat them in a steamer or in a cast-iron pan with a little butter and serve with an egg on the side and a cup of café de olla, page 314.

Makes 28 to 30 small 4½-inch tamales

12 to 14 ears white corn, about 11 cups when dekerneled
12 ounces unsalted butter, melted
1 tablespoon lard
1½ cups sugar
1 teaspoon ground canela
1 teaspoon vanilla extract
¾ teaspoon sea salt
¼ to ½ cup unbleached all-purpose flour
2½ teaspoons baking powder

Salsa Verde de Tomatillo

1 pound milpero tomatillos
½ white onion
1 garlic clove
2 serrano chiles
4 sprigs epazote or a combination of 8 sprigs cilantro and 2 sprigs mint
½ teaspoon sea salt

Place all ingredients in a pot with 2 cups of water, bring to a simmer, and cook for 6 to 8 minutes until the tomatillos and serranos are soft and change color to a bright green. Drain about ⅔ of the cooking liquid. Pour everything into a blender and blend until smooth. Taste and adjust for salt if necessary. This salsa should be served warm on top of the tamales. It should have a nice body—not too thick, not too runny. Consistency is important in order to cover the tamales. If you can't get milpero tomatillos, use the smallest tomatillos you can find; these have the best tangy flavor.

1. Cut about one inch off the tip of each ear of corn and discard the tips. Make a clean cut through the green husks around the bottom of the ear of corn to detach the husks. Peel the corn, saving the tender husks and placing them in a bowl with warm water. Remove and discard all the corn silk. Take some of the longer corn husks and tear with your hands into thin ribbons. Set aside to use later to tie the tamales when assembling.

2. Dekernel each ear of corn. See photo for easy method. Save one of the ears to help prop up the tamales when assembling.

3. In a blender, puree half of the corn kernels along with melted butter, lard, sugar, canela, vanilla, and sea salt, until smooth. If your blender is too small, divide this batch of ingredients in two or three parts to obtain the smoothest masa dough. Then combine all batches into one bowl.

4. In a food processor, pulse the other half of the corn kernels along with the flour, until a coarse paste. This will give a great texture to the tamales.

5. In a large bowl, using a wood spatula, combine the two corn mixtures and add the baking powder, until a uniform paste.

6. Drain the fresh corn husks and organize an "assembly line:" a tray to place the tamales in standing up and a large spoon to fill them. Prepare a steamer pot with water up to the line before the steam rack. Add two pennies to the bottom of the pot. When water is low, the pennies will stop vibrating, letting you know it is time to refill the water. Cover the top of the steamer rack with some of the fresh corn husks, and close the pot with a tight lid.

7. Assemble the tamales: Place a corn husk in your hand and put about two large spoonfuls of the tamale mixture onto the husk. Wrap one side of the husk over the mixture, then the other side. Fold the tail of the corn husk up. Recline the tamalito (little tamale) onto the ear of corn and tie it up with the corn husk ribbons, making sure the fold is contained. Place it in a tray standing up to keep the filling from spilling out. Do the same with the rest of the batter.

8. As you finish with them, carefully place them in the steamer standing up all around the perimeter, and try to leave a hole in the center to allow the steam to roll out so they cook evenly (see photo page 144). Cover the top of the pot with a clean kitchen towel, place the lid on top of the towel, and wrap the four points of the towel over the lid's top. This will keep the vapor in the pot and help absorb some of the extra moisture.

9. Bring the water to a boil, then reduce temperature to medium. Start cooking time for 45 minutes. Keep an eye on the pot; if the coins stop vibrating, carefully refill with hot water. Tamales will be cooked in about 1 to $1\frac{1}{2}$ hours. Tamales are ready when you see the tops have fluffed up like a muffin. Pull one out of the pot, let it cool down for 5 to 10 minutes, and remove the husk. The husk should come off very easily, without sticking. Now your tamalitos are ready! Place them on a tray and cover them with some foil and a clean kitchen towel. Wait for about 20 to 25 minutes to serve.

1.
2.
3.
4.
5.
6.
7.
8.
9.

Tamales Tradicionales Rojos o Verdes
Traditional Red or Green Sauce Tamales

These traditional tamales are essential for any Mexican celebration. Both red and green sauces pair well with any choice of filling: shredded beef, pork, or chicken. If making both kinds at the same time, I prefer to make one sauce spicy and the other mild to please both crowds.

My roasted **green sauce** imparts a spicy kick to complement the succulent shredded pork leg or shoulder. I make my salsa verde roasted on a comal. The tomatillos, serranos, poblanos, and jalapeños make a beautiful, bright-green, flavorful, and spicy sauce for green tamales with lots of character. The sauce is tangy and smoky, complementing the unctuous flavor of the pork, or enhancing the flavor of the chicken. This recipe makes a green sauce that is on the thicker side, so resist the urge to add more liquid. The consistency of the sauce prevents the tamale from absorbing it while cooking.

The garlicky guajillo and ancho **red sauce** is smoky and milder, with a pleasant heat.

I prefer a saucy tamale with a good amount of shredded meat. I pay particular care when assembling to make sure the meat is placed evenly from beginning to end of the masa. And I put 1 to 2 tablespoons of sauce in the middle so you can taste the juicy filling in every bite.

For meatless variations, consider a thick slice of panela cheese and roasted poblano rajas with salsa verde, sautéed mushrooms with red or green sauce, or queso fresco and refried beans with jalapenos.

If this is your first attempt at tamales, please read the tamale tips on page 145 before you start. They will help you feel confident about your choices and techniques. Each of the following sauce recipes makes enough to fill two dozen tamales. To make one dozen red and one dozen green tamales, make a half batch of the red sauce and a half batch of the green.

Important note: When making tamales, always make your sauces a little saltier than you are comfortable with because the masa will absorb more of the salt than you imagine. This is important in order to have flavorful tamales.

Makes 24 medium 2 x 4-inch corn husk tamales

Red ancho-guajillo sauce*:
4 guajillo chiles, stems and seeds removed, toasted
3 ancho chiles, stems and seeds removed, toasted
1 small white onion
6 large cloves garlic
⅛ teaspoon cumin seeds
⅛ teaspoon dry oregano
2 teaspoons sea salt
2 to 3 cups stock in which you cooked the pork or chicken
2 tablespoons lard or cooking oil

*If you want to add a spicy kick add 4-6 boiled chiles de arbol to the sauce and blend along.

Green roasted tomatillo sauce**:
1 pound tomatillos
1 poblano pepper, sliced in half lengthwise, seeds and stem removed
2 jalapeño peppers, stems removed
4 serrano peppers, stems removed
1 medium white onion, quartered
1 to 2 teaspoons sea salt, to taste
4 cloves garlic
2 cups stock in which you cooked the pork or chicken
2 tablespoons lard or cooking oil

**Note: If you want a sauce with a higher fiery kick yielding spicier tamales, don't be shy, double up on the serranos or jalapeños.

Tamale masa:
1 recipe basic tamale dough (page 147)

Assembling:
36 corn husks

Filling:
1 recipe stock and shredded pork (page 63) or chicken (page 62)

1. Prepare the red sauce, the green sauce, or a half batch of each.

   Red sauce: Place the toasted chiles into a bowl and cover with boiling water. Cover the bowl and let them hydrate for 30 minutes until plump. Discard the soaking liquid. In a blender, place the hydrated chiles, onion, garlic, cumin, oregano, sea salt, and 1 cup of the stock. Blend until smooth and add the rest of the stock. In a saucepan over medium-high, heat up the oil until shimmering and add the sauce (be careful; it will splatter) add more stock if necessary. Stir and reduce heat to medium. Cook the sauce for 15 to 20 minutes. Add more stock if necessary. Taste the sauce. It should have full body and taste on the saltier side to correctly balance the seasoning of the masa. Once the sauce is ready, set aside to cool it down.

   Green sauce: On a baking sheet, place the tomatillos, poblano, jalapeños, serranos, onion, and sea salt. Add a little drizzle of oil, toss well, and spread in one single layer. Roast at 450 degrees for 10 to 15 minutes, then broil for 2 minutes until blistered and charred edges and bubbles appear. Remove from oven and let cool down a bit. Place everything roasted and the garlic cloves in a blender or food processor, along with 1 cup of your stock. In a saucepan over medium-high, heat up the oil and add the sauce (be careful; it will splatter) plus the other cup of stock and cook the sauce for 6 to 8 minutes. Taste the sauce. It should be on the saltier side to correctly balance the seasoning of the pork and masa. Once the sauce is ready, set aside to cool it down.

2. Prepare 36 corn husks: In a large bowl rinse corn husks with warm water and place them in a bowl of warm water to soak. Place a can or something heavy on top of them so they stay submerged. *Note: We are making 24 tamales but preparing 36 husks because it's good to have some extras. Sometimes husks are smaller and you might have to overlap two to make a tamale, or they can tear while spreading the masa and you might need to double wrap some. Plus you will need about 2 to 3 husks to make strips to tie the tamales and about 6 to 7 husks to cover the bottom of the steamer pot.*

3. Prepare the steamer pot: Fill with water to the line of the steamer rack and put two pennies on the bottom. When water is low, the pennies will stop vibrating, letting you know it is time to refill the water. Insert the steam rack and place a layer of corn husks on top of the rack, making sure you cover about 1/3 of the side walls of the pot. This will prevent water from getting on the bottom of the tamales. Place steamer on the stove and have it ready to go.

4. Prepare the tamale masa per the instructions on page 147.

5. Assemble the tamales: Arrange the separate sauce, filling, and masa dough elements on a table in an assembly line, with a tray or bowl at the end to put the assembled tamales into. Drain the water from the corn husks and put them in a colander. Squeeze and shake off the excess water. *Now the fun starts.* Place one of the corn husks in your nonwriting hand with the pointy side of the corn husk toward you. Using a large spoon, add 2 or 3 spoonfuls of the prepared masa into the center of the corn husk. Spread it evenly from the center 3 inches to the left and 3 inches to the right. The thickness of the masa should be between 1/8 and 1/4 inch. In the center of the spread-out masa, place a tablespoon of the sauce, then the shredded meat in a flat layer rather than piled up; this will ensure every bite has meat. Then pour another generous tablespoon of sauce on top. Close the tamales by bringing the two sides of the leaf to the center. The masa will stick to itself. Then, fold one side of the husk, then the other, and fold the tail up behind the body of the tamale. At this point you can tie them around with a thin strip of corn husk. This is up to you. I generally don't do this with larger tamales, only with the little ones that tend to unfold more easily when cooking. Do the same with the rest of the masa.

6. Heat up steamer pot: Place the pot on the stove on high. Before it gets hot, place tamales standing up around the inside of the pot in two or three layers, leaving a hole in the center so you can refill with water if needed during the cooking process. Cover the top of the pot with a clean kitchen towel, place the lid on top of the towel, and wrap the four points of the towel over the lid's top. This will keep the vapor in the pot and help absorb some of the extra moisture.

7. Cook the tamales: Bring the water to a boil, and reduce temperature to medium-high. Start cooking time for 45 minutes. Keep an eye on the pot; if the coins stop vibrating, carefully refill with hot water. This size tamale will be cooked in about 1 hour to 1 hour and 15 minutes. After 1 hour, reduce the temperature to low and carefully, using tongs, take one tamale out of the pot and let it sit for about 10 minutes. Check for doneness. The corn husk should come off very easily. If it doesn't, they need more time. Put the tamale back into the pot and cook for another 20 minutes. Turn off the pot and let the tamales rest in the pot for 20 more minutes. Repeat the test. If the corn husk slides off easily, try a bite. The masa should look tender, moist, and fluffy. *Note: It's tricky to tell when tamales are ready. If you judge them from how they look in the pot, you might overcook them. It is very important to do this check-up to avoid overcooking your tamales.*

8. Once they are cooked, using tongs, carefully move all the tamales from the pot into a single layer on a tray. Cover them with aluminum foil and a clean kitchen towel to retain their moisture. Let them rest for 15 minutes before serving. **Serve with:** a side of refried beans (page 187) and Mexican rice (page 202).

Tamales de Huitlacoche con Quesillo y Epazote
Corn Smut Tamales with Oaxacan Cheese and Epazote

Huitlacoche, or corn smut, is technically a fungus that affects corn plants. In Mexico, huitlacoche is a delicacy and is best cooked when it is freshly harvested. It is mushroomy with an intense, earthy flavor, and is known as the "Mexican truffle." Every year, at the end of the rainy season in Mexico, you can find independent farmers selling the most beautiful, fresh huitlacoche at the mercados. For those of us living outside of Mexico, a mellower, yet delicious, huitlacoche is available in jars and preserves.

With all the nostalgia for huitlacoche, I decided to try using a version of huitlacoche preserves bottled in glass jars, which I believe preserves the flavor best. It's not exactly like fresh, but these preserves caught me by surprise because the flavor was quite good. I made some tamalitos with Oaxacan quesillo cheese and fresh epazote, to satisfy my craving for it, and they came out surprisingly delicious! If you are up for discovering a new flavor, this recipe is for you.

Makes about 20 to 24 small 2 x 4-inch tamales

Huitlacoche filling:
2 tablespoons butter
1 medium white onion, small diced
4 cloves garlic, finely chopped
Sea salt, to taste
Black pepper, to taste
1 cup white corn kernels, about 1 to 2 ears of corn
1 (8-ounce) jar huitlacoche
¼ cup chicken stock
6 leaves fresh epazote, finely chopped, plus 20 to 24 whole leaves
1½ pound Oaxaca cheese or string cheese
18 to 22 corn husks, washed and soaked in warm water

Masa:
1 recipe basic tamale dough (page 147)

1. Prepare the filling: In a large skillet, melt the butter and sauté the onion and garlic in it. Season with salt and pepper and cook until translucent. Add corn kernels and sauté for 2 to 3 minutes, then add the huitlacoche and sauté for another 2 minutes. Add chicken stock, cover with a lid, and let it cook for 1 to 2 more minutes. Add the epazote at the end, stir, and taste for salt and pepper. Adjust if necessary. The texture of the filling should be a bit like a paste, but moist and flavorful like a strong earthy mushroom. Add a little more salt than you are comfortable with, since the masa will absorb some of the flavor. The extra salt will balance the flavors to have more delicious tamales. Set filling aside to cool off while you prepare the masa.

2. Prepare the masa per the instructions on page 147.

3. Assemble the tamales: Drain the water and place corn husks in a colander and shake off the excess water. Place one of the corn husks on your nonwriting hand with the pointy side of the corn husk pointing toward you. Using a large spoon, add 2 spoonfuls of the prepared masa. Spread evenly from the center 2 inches to the left and 2 inches to the right. The thickness of the masa should be between ⅛ and ¼ inch. Place two tablespoonfuls of the sautéed huitlacoche, 2 or 3 strips of cheese, and one epazote leaf inside. Close the tamale by bringing the sides of the leaf to the center. The masa will stick to itself. Then fold one side of the corn husk, then the other, and fold the tail up behind the body of the tamale. At this point you can tie them around with a thin strip of husk. This is optional but I generally do this with the smaller tamales, because they tend to unfold more easily when cooking. Do the same with the rest of the masa until you have about 12 to 14 tamales.

4. Prepare the steamer pot: Fill with water to the line of the steamer rack and put two pennies on the bottom. When water is low, the pennies will stop vibrating, letting you know it is time to refill the water. Insert the steamer rack and cover the top of the rack with some of the corn husks. Place the pot on the stove on high. Place tamales standing up around the edges of the pot, leaving a hole in the center so you can refill with water during the cooking process if needed. Cover the top of the pot with a clean kitchen towel, place the lid on top of the towel, and wrap the four points of the towel over the lid's top. This will keep the vapor in the pot and help absorb some of the extra moisture.

5. Bring the water to a boil, then reduce temperature to medium-high. Start cooking time for 45 minute an eye on the pot; if the coins stop vibrating, carefully refill with hot water. These tamales will be cooked in about 1 hour and 15 minutes.

6. After 1 hour and 15 minutes, turn off the pot and carefully, using tongs, take one tamale out of the pot, cover the pot, and let the tamale sit for about 10 minutes. Now check for doneness. The corn husk should come off very easily. If it doesn't, they need more time. In that instance, put the tamale back into the pot and cook for another 15 to 20 minutes or so. Do the same test. If the corn husk slides off easily, try a bite. The masa should look tender, moist, and fluffy. *Note: It's tricky to tell when tamales are ready. If you judge them from how they look in the pot, you might overcook them. It is very important to do this check-up to avoid overcooking your tamales.*

7. When tamales are cooked, using tongs, carefully move all the tamales from the pot into a single layer on a tray, and cover with some aluminum foil and a clean kitchen towel to retain their moisture. Let them rest for about 20 minutes before serving them. These huitlacoche tamales can be served with a salsa martajada en molcajete, and a dollop of Mexican crema.

Fresh corn with huitlacoche/corn smut.

Tamale filling: cooked huitlacoche, epazote, and cheese.

Preparing Banana Leaves for Tamale Wraps

Banana leaves are commonly found in Asian or Hispanic supermarkets and are sold by the pound. To make 12 to 14 tamales, you will need to buy about 4 to 5 leaves. Usually they come cut in half and you will only have to remove the center rib. The 4 to 5 half leaves will weigh about 3 pounds. It is always best to buy them as fresh as you can, about one or two days before making the tamales. (*Remember to save the leftover scraps to cover the bottom of the steamer pot.*)

1. Unfold the banana leaves on a long table, spray them with water, and wipe both sides of the leaves with a clean cotton kitchen towel.

2. Using kitchen shears, cut all along both edges of the center rib of the banana leaf to remove it. Remove the center rib from the rest of the leaves, and discard the ribs.

3. Now you will have about 8 long pieces that can be divided into equal squares of about 12 to 14 inches. Each square will serve as one tamale wrap.

4. Over a warm comal, or electric stove burner, heat up each leaf for about 5 to 7 seconds per side until they become pliable. As you go, pile them up and cover them with a clean damp kitchen towel to keep them moist and pliable.

Tamales en Hoja de Plátano
Rellenos de Mole Negro o Mole Poblano
Banana Leaf Tamales
Filled with Mole Negro or Mole Poblano

Banana leaves are commonly used to wrap tamales in the south-central and southeast regions of Mexico. The leaves keep the tamales very moist and impart a unique herbal flavor to the corn masa. These tamales are wrapped differently than corn husk tamales. To prepare the banana leaves, please follow the instructions on page 159 and allow extra time for preparation.

The resulting tamales are soft and light with a slightly green tint. The decadent mole negro or mole poblano fillings are perfect for a festive meal to share on the ofrenda.

Makes 12 to 14 rectangular 3 x 6-inch tamales

Filling:
2½ cups mole poblano (page 111), mole negro (page 129), or mole coloradito (page 126)
4 to 6 cups shredded cooked turkey, chicken or pork (see basic recipes section, page 61)

Banana leaf wraps:
4 to 5 banana leaves, about 3 pounds*

Tamale masa:
1 recipe basic tamale dough (page 147)

*This amount yields about 14 to 16 (12 x 14-inch) pieces, plus some left over to cover the bottom of the steam rack on the pot.

1. Prepare the mole ahead of time. The mole recipes in this book yield about 2 liters of mole. Making one recipe will be enough for a mole dinner and to make tamales.

2. Prepare the banana leaves: Clean, devein, and cut them into square pieces about 12 to 14 inches wide. Warm them on a comal to make them pliable. See the complete method on page 159. Cover with a damp towel and set aside.

3. Prepare the tamale masa per the instructions on page 147.

4. Assemble the tamales: Using a squeeze-trigger ice cream scooper, scoop a round ball of masa onto the center of the matte side of the banana leaf. Dip your index and middle finger into a cup of cooled chicken stock and gently press the masa ball down until you have a 6-inch round shape about $1/4$-inch thick. (You can use a flat plate or a pan to flatten the masa, as long as it is at least 6 inches in diameter.) Place a generous amount of shredded chicken in the middle, spread evenly in a flat layer, and cover with about 2 or 3 tablespoons of mole sauce.

5. Fold: Take one of the sides of the leaf and fold it over the center of the tamale, then peel back the banana leaf. Do the same with the opposite side, and the same with the other two sides of the tamale until you have a folded square masa envelope. Now take the edge of the banana leaf that is closer to you and fold it over the tamale, pressing gently, then fold over the opposite side. Fold the sides onto the back of the tamale, leaving the smooth side on top. *See steps on opposite page.* They look like envelopes or wallets. Do the same with the rest of the masa until you have 12 to 14 tamales.

6. Prepare the steamer pot: Fill with water to the line of the steamer rack and put two pennies on the bottom of the pot. When water is low, the pennies will stop vibrating, letting you know it is time to refill the water. Use hot water to refill the steamer. Insert the rack and cover top of the rack with some banana leaf scraps. Place pot on the stove on high. Place tamales into the pot by overlapping in a crisscrossed pattern (see photo opposite page). Remember to leave a space in the center for refilling the water if needed. Cover the top of the pot with a clean kitchen towel, place the lid on top of the towel, and wrap the four points of the towel over the lid's top. This will keep the vapor in the pot and help absorb some of the extra moisture.

7. Cook the tamales: Bring the water to boil, then reduce temperature to medium-high. Start cooking time for 45 minutes. Keep an eye on the pot; if the coins stop vibrating, carefully refill with hot water. This kind of tamale will be cooked in about $1 1/2$ hours.

8. After $1 1/2$ hours, turn off the pot and carefully, using tongs, take one tamale out of the pot, cover the pot with the lid, and let the tamale sit for about 5 to 8 minutes. Now check for doneness. The banana leaf should come off very easily. If it doesn't, they need more time. In that instance, put the tamale back into the pot, increase the heat to medium, and cook for another 15 minutes. Do the same test. If the banana leaf slides off easily, try a bite. The masa should look tender, moist, and fluffy. *Note: It's tricky to tell when tamales are ready. If you judge them from how they look in the pot, you might overcook them. It is very important to do this cool-down check-up to avoid overcooking your tamales.*

9. Once they are cooked, turn off the pot and let them rest for 10 minutes. Using tongs, carefully move all the tamales from the pot into a single layer on a tray and cover with some aluminum foil and a clean kitchen towel to retain their moisture. Let them rest for about 20 minutes before eating them. They will remain warm and ready to eat.

Serve with: Tamales can be topped with some extra mole and sprinkled with sesame seeds when served. A side of arroz a la Mexicana (page 202) or refried beans (page 187) can complement the meal.

Tamales de Mole Coloradito en Hoja de Plátano
Coloradito Mole Tamales in Banana Leaves

Anchos and guajillos give mole coloradito its unique flavor, making it one of my favorite moles to fill up a tamale. The banana leaf adds special flavor to the masa, which, in combination with the coloradito, yields a fragrant, and delicious tamale. Make the mole a few days ahead for the best flavor and to save time. These tamales will prove alluring to any guest at Día de Muertos.

Makes about 12 to 14 rectangular 3 x 6-inch tamales

Filling:
2 cups mole coloradito recipe (page 126)
1 basic recipe shredded chicken, turkey, or pork (page 61)

Banana leaf wraps:
4 to 5 banana leaves, about 3 pounds*

Tamale masa:
1 recipe basic tamale dough (page 147)

This amount yields about 14 to 16 (12 x 14-inch) pieces plus some left over to cover the bottom of the steam rack in the pot.

1. Prepare the mole ahead of time. The mole recipes in this book yield about 2 liters of mole. Making one recipe will be enough for a mole dinner and to make tamales.

2. Prepare the banana leaves: Clean, devein, cut, and warm them on a comal to make them pliable. See complete method on page 159. Cover with a damp towel and set aside.

3. Prepare the tamale masa per the instructions on page 147.

4. Assemble the tamales: Using a squeeze-trigger ice cream scooper, scoop a ball of masa into the center of the matte side of a banana leaf. Dip your index and middle fingers into a cup of cooled chicken stock and gently press the masa ball down until you have a 6-inch round shape about ¼-inch thick. (You can use a flat plate or a pan to flatten the masa, as long as it is at least 6 inches in diameter.) Place a generous amount of shredded chicken in the middle, try to make a flat layer, and cover with about 2 tablespoons of the coloradito sauce.

5. Fold: Take one of the sides of the leaf and fold it over the center of the tamale, then peel back the leaf. Do the same with the opposite side and the other two sides of the tamale until you have a folded square. It is okay if the masa is not totally sealed in the center. In fact, this will make a nice red vein in the tamale that I think is very beautiful. Now take the banana leaf that is closer to you and fold it over the tamale, pressing gently, then fold over the opposite side. Fold the sides onto the back of the tamale, leaving the smooth side on top. See steps on opposite page. They look like wallets or envelopes. Do the same process with the rest of the masa until you have 12 to 14 tamales.

6. Prepare the steamer pot: Fill with water to the line on the steamer rack and put two pennies on the bottom. When water is low, the pennies will stop vibrating, letting you know it is time to refill the water. Use hot water to refill the steamer. Insert the rack and cover the top of the rack with some banana leaf scraps. Place pot on the stove on medium-high. Place tamales in the pot by overlapping in a crisscrossed pattern (for step-by-step photos, see page 162). Remember to leave a space in the center to refill water. Cover the top of the pot with a clean kitchen towel, place the lid on top of the towel, and wrap the four points of the towel over the lid's top. This will keep the vapor in the pot and help absorb some of the extra moisture.

7. Bring to a boil, then reduce temperature to medium. Start cooking time for 45 minutes. Keep an eye on the pot; if the coins stop vibrating, carefully refill with hot water. This kind of tamale will be cooked in about 1 hour and 15 minutes. After this time, reduce the temperature to low and carefully, using tongs, take one tamale out of the pot and let it sit for about 5 minutes. Now check for doneness. The banana leaf should come off very easily. If it doesn't, they need more time. Put the tamale back into the pot, increase heat to medium, and cook for another 15 minutes. Do the same test. If the banana leaf slides off easily, try a bite. The masa should look tender, moist, and fluffy. *Note: It's tricky to tell when tamales are ready. If you judge them from how they look in the pot, you might overcook them. It is very important to do this check-up to avoid overcooking your tamales.*

8. Once they are cooked, turn off the stove, and let them rest for 10 minutes. Using tongs, carefully move all the tamales from the pot into a single layer on a tray and cover with some aluminum foil and a clean kitchen towel to retain their moisture. Let them rest for about 20 minutes before serving.

Serve with: Some extra coloradito mole can be spooned when served. A side of garlic rice and refried beans can complement the meal. Add red pickled onions on the side (page 221).

Tamales de Acelgas y Queso Fresco
Swiss Chard and Queso Fresco Tamales

These tamales are originally from Tapalpa, Jalisco. Tapalpa is a beautiful little town located up in the Sierra de Jalisco, where some of the best cheese, crema, jocoque, and milk candies in the state are made. They are one of my favorite tamales because of their unique vegetable flavor. Adding Swiss chard to the masa imparts a delicate herbaceous flavor to the tamale. For the filling, use a fresh cheese, like queso panela or queso fresco. These tamales are light and delicate. I like to serve them with a simple tomato-oregano-cinnamon sauce (page 220), a drizzle of jocoque or plain yogurt, and crumbles of queso fresco.

Makes about 12 to 14 rectangular 3 x 6-inch tamales

Banana leaf wraps:
4 to 5 banana leaves

Tamale masa:
1 recipe basic tamale dough (page 147)
4 cups packed green, yellow, or rainbow chard, chopped or a wide chiffonade

Filling:
1 pound of queso fresco, crumbled, or queso panela cut into ¼-inch slices

1. Prepare the banana leaves: Clean, devein, cut, and warm them on a comal to make them pliable. See complete instructions on page 159. Cover with a damp towel and set aside.
2. Prepare the tamale masa per the instructions on page 147.
3. Add the chard and knead into the masa using your hands or a wood spatula until the chard is evenly distributed.
4. Assemble the tamales: Using a squeeze-trigger ice cream scooper, scoop two balls of masa into the center of the matte side of the banana leaf. Dip your index and middle fingers into a warm cup of chicken stock and gently press the masa balls down until you have a 5 x 6-inch rectangular shape about ¼-inch thick. Place a generous amount (about 2 to 3 tablespoons) of the crumbled queso fresco in the center of the masa rectangle.
5. Fold: Take one side of the banana leaf and fold it over the center of the tamale, then peel back the leaf. Do the same with the opposite side, and then do the same with the other two sides of the tamale until you have a folded square. Now take the banana leaf end that is closer to you and fold over the tamale, pressing gently, and fold over the opposite banana leaf side. Then fold the two sides onto the back of the tamale, leaving the smooth side on top. See steps on opposite page. They look like wallets or envelopes. Do the same process with the rest of the masa until you have 12 to 14 tamales.
6. Prepare the steamer pot: Fill with water to the line of the steamer rack and put two pennies on the bottom. When water is low, the pennies will stop vibrating, letting you know it is time to refill the water. Use hot water to refill the steamer. Insert the rack and cover the top of the rack with some banana leaf scraps. Place the pot on the stove on medium-high. Place tamales in the pot by overlapping in a crisscrossed pattern (see page 162). Remember to leave space in the middle for pouring in water. Cover the top of the pot with a clean kitchen towel, place the lid on top of the towel, and wrap the four points of the towel over the lid's top. This will keep the vapor in the pot and help absorb some of the extra moisture.
7. Bring the water to a boil, then reduce temperature to medium-high. Start cooking time for 45 minutes. Keep an eye on the pot; if the coins stop vibrating, carefully refill with hot water. This kind of tamale will be cooked in about 1 hour and 15 minutes. Keep an eye on the pot and every 30 to 40 minutes refill the water as needed when the coins vibrate. After 1 hour and 15 minutes, reduce the temperature to low and carefully, using tongs, take one tamale out of the pot and let it sit for about 10 minutes. Now check for doneness. The banana leaf should come off very easily. If it doesn't, they need more time. Put the tamale back into the pot and cook for another 15 to 30 minutes. Repeat the test. If the banana leaf slides off easily, try a bite. The masa should look tender, moist, and fluffy. *Note: It's tricky to tell when tamales are ready. If you judge them from how they look in the pot, you might overcook them. It is very important to do this check-up to avoid overcooking your tamales.*
8. Once they are cooked, turn off the stove and let the tamales rest for 10 minutes. Using tongs, carefully transfer all the tamales from the pot into a single layer on a tray and cover with some aluminum foil and a clean kitchen towel to retain their moisture. Let them rest for about 20 minutes before eating them. They will still be warm and ready to eat.

Serve with: A generous spoonful of tomato, oregano, and cinnamon salsa (page 220), drizzle Mexican crema or jocoque, and crumble queso fresco.

Mukbil Pibipollo–Tamal Yucateco
Yucatecán Ceremonial Tamale

This pibipollo is what people from Campeche and Yucatán cook to celebrate Janal Pixán, which is what the Mayan communities celebrate on Día de Muertos. *Janal* (also spelled *Hanal*) means "food" and *Pixán* means "soul." And this tamale is all about satisfying the hunger of both the living and the dead.

What is mukbil? It comes from the Mayan words *muk*, "to bury" and *bil*, "to wrap." Together the word *mukbil* means "to be buried." The second part of the equation is *pib*, which refers to a prepared dish using pork or chicken, lard, spices, and masa. And *pollo* equals "chicken." So if we put it all together, we get "to bury a chicken-masa-wrap." Mukbil pibipollo it is!

These tamales are a delicacy. The traditional cooking process involves burying them in a slow-cooking fire pit in the ground, which develops an exquisite flavor. The unique process is worth celebrating. Do not be alarmed. I have adapted the recipe to mortals like you and me that want to recreate these flavors on the back patio. I scaled down the recipe to make one large tamale, and I cooked it on an ordinary outdoor grill, using natural charcoal and wood. I covered the grill with a lid to mimic a wood oven and to help infuse the tamale with wood smoke flavor. If you have the space and time to create a pit in the ground, it would be ideal and incredible. Nonetheless, this grilling method worked great. Another adjustment to the recipe is the omission of the fresh little beans called either *espelon* or *guaje*. These beans are added to the masa for texture and flavor. It is very hard to find fresh Yucatán ingredients like these beans outside Mexico. I have seen them in my Mexican specialty market. If you are familiar with these beans and can get them, great! If not, the tamale will still taste delicious.

The tamale construction process is a lot like making a pie. I found it extremely easy and fun to make. Because it is just one large tamale, it's not as laborious as making many individual tamales. Besides, I love the fact that all this is cooked outdoors, which makes it more fun and festive.

Makes 1 (9 to 10-inch) round tamale

Special equipment:
4 to 5 large banana leaves
one charcoal grill
natural charcoal*

Adobo sauce:
4 guajillo chiles
3 allspice peppercorns
4 black peppercorns
8 cloves garlic
1 medium white onion, quartered
1 habanero
3 teaspoons achiote powder
2 sprigs fresh epazote or ½ teaspoon dry epazote**
1 to 2 teaspoons sea salt, to taste
2 tablespoons masa harina
2 cups chicken or pork stock (leftover from cooking the meat)

Filling:
½ recipe shredded chicken (page 62)
½ recipe shredded pork (page 63)
2 Roma tomatoes, sliced
½ medium white onion, sliced
1 or 2 habaneros, upon desired heat
2 pinches dry epazote or 4 sprigs fresh mint

Tamale masa:
1 recipe basic tamale dough (page 147)
1 teaspoon achiote powder

*Always use natural charcoal when grilling to avoid chemicals that impart unpleasant flavors to your food. Igniting natural charcoal is easy with a chimney charcoal starter.
**If you can't find fresh epazote, use 3 sprigs mint and ¼ teaspoon Mexican oregano.

1. Using scissors, cut across the top of the dried chiles to remove the stems. Cut along the sides of the chiles to open them up and remove the seeds. Toast the guajillos for 2 to 3 minutes until they show some blistered spots and are pliable and fragrant. Soak them in hot water for 25 to 30 minutes until plump and well hydrated.

2. Heat a comal or cast-iron pan over medium heat, and briefly toast the allspice, black peppercorns, and garlic. Remove from pan and set aside. On the same comal, place the onion quarters and the two habaneros and then char on all sides. Set aside.

3. In a blender, place the rehydrated guajillos, toasted garlic, charred onion, toasted allspice and pepper, achiote powder, epazote, salt, masa harina, and ONE of the charred habaneros. Add 1 cup of chicken stock. Blend well until smooth. Add the other cup of chicken stock and blend for a few more seconds. In a small pot, warm 1 tablespoon of oil and add the sauce. Cook for 8 to 10 minutes until slightly thickened. Set aside.

4. Prepare the banana leaves: Clean, devein, cut, and warm them on a comal to make them pliable. See complete method on page 159. Do not cut into segments; leave them long. Save the long veins to wrap the tamale.

5. Prepare the tamale masa. In ¼ cup of chicken stock, dissolve the achiote powder. Add the masa dough and mix until well incorporated.

6. Assemble the tamale: Overlap 4 veins of the banana leaf to form an asterisk shape. Then place long pieces of banana leaf on top of the veins. Leave a large, wide piece in the center for extra support. Save an extra wide piece of the banana leaf to use later, when wrapping the tamale. Divide dough into ¾ and ¼ portions. Shape the ¾ of the dough into a round flat, and place it in the middle of the banana leaves. Start making a shallow masa container by forming walls of a pie of about 2½ inches tall and a ¼ inch thick. With your fingertips, make sure the bottom of the tamale has an even thickness and no holes or cracks. Once ready, add some of the sauce on the bottom. Add the shredded chicken and/or pork, top with the rest of the sauce, and add some slices of tomatoes and onions on the top. Add slices of the charred habanero chile or—if you want a milder heat—just place the whole chile in the middle to give some flavor. (Remember to take it out when cutting and serving!) Now, place the rest of the dough in the center of that large/wide banana leaf piece you saved, and shaping it with your fingertips, make a large round tortilla about a ¼ inch thick and 11 inches in diameter or large enough to cover the tamale pie. Take the banana leaf and the dough and invert it to top of the tamale. Peel off the banana leaf to make sure your masa lid is covering the whole tamale. Slightly press the edges to close the tamale. Place the banana leaf back on top of the masa lid and start wrapping the tamale as if you were wrapping a round present. Once it is covered in the banana leaves, tie the tamale with the banana leaf veins, being careful not to tighten them too much. You don't want to misshape the tamale.

7. Cook: Start a charcoal fire in an outdoor grill and wait until the charcoal is white with ashes; no high flames needed. Make sure your grill has a lid. If not, use a sturdy inverted metal pot or cake pan to cover the tamale. Put the tamale inside a 12-inch cast-iron pan or a 12-inch cake pan, cover with aluminum foil, and poke some holes in the foil to let steam out. Then place it on the grill close to the charcoal, cover grill with the lid, and cook for about 1 hour and 45 minutes, up to 2 hours. Time may vary depending on how steady you manage to keep the heat of your charcoal grill.

8. Once the tamale is ready, transfer onto a cooling rack and let it rest for 15 minutes before unmolding and opening it. When ready to serve, remove top banana leaves and cut into wedges like a pie. Tamale should be firm and have a juicy filling. Serve with some quick-pickled red onion and habanero salsa, and an *aguacate de agua*.* Have a cold beer or agua fresca and let the celebrations begin! Remember to save a slice for the ofrenda.

*If you can't find this type of avocado, a hass or any other avocado can be a great substitution.

Top left: Five Peaks Corundas with salsa de molcajete. Top right: Rosalba and Mariana.
Bottom: Rosalba's beautiful, traditional Mexican kitchen. Next page: Lake Pátzcuaro, Michoacán, Mexico.

Cooking with Rosalba

The owner of our hotel in the magical town of Pátzcuaro put us in contact with Sra. Rosalba Morales Bartolo, one of the local Cocineras Tradicionales. Knowing the nature of her cooking, I was thrilled. When I talked to her on the phone it felt like I was talking with a long-time friend because of her warmth and friendly disposition. I expressed my desire to learn how to make corundas, the traditional Michoacán tamales, and she sounded eager to teach me. We made an appointment and met at the street market in the nearby city of Quiroga. That morning we shopped for some of the ingredients to prepare the corundas, and then we drove to her home.

Her kitchen was cozy and smelled of fresh corn tortillas. Her daughter, Celeste, was making them on a comal mounted on a traditional wood-fired stove. Rosalba took us back to her kitchen patio, where she cultivated lime, guava, and pear trees, to pick some fruit. In the morning we prepared salsa de molcajete with charred xoconostle (a cactus fruit), tomatoes, chiles, avocado agua fresca, beans, corn tortillas, and her specialty dish, charales dorados (a shortfin silverside fish) with salsa de queso y chile negro, black chili made out of pasilla negro chiles. Then we started on the masa. We took soaked corn kernels to a neighbor's house, where a woman was ready with a huge stone grinding mill, in which she ground an entire bucket of nixtamal (see page 74). In less than five minutes the nixtamal was transformed into the most delicious fresh masa. Celeste and I then carried the ground corn masa back to Rosalba's kitchen.

Rosalba explained that the corundas we were about to make were in the indigenous style in which no oil or animal fat was added to the masa. Instead, she added grated queso fresco, diced carrots, and salt to the freshly ground masa. We kneaded for a few minutes, added salt, warm water, and some wood ashes from the stove to act as a leavening agent. After the masa rested for a few minutes, we wrapped it in fresh corn plant leaves, *hojas de milpa*. A small amount of masa was placed at the end of each leaf and carefully wrapped, giving them a pentagonal shape, then tied with the remaining end of the leaf. The corundas were placed inside a steamer and cooked for about two hours.

While the corundas were cooking, we enjoyed Rosalba's stories while she took us for a walk around San Jerónimo Purenchécuaro. This little town is situated on the east side of the Janitzio Lagoon, with a beautiful view of the smaller islands of Junuen and Pacanda. We visited the church in which the virgin and saints were dressed in traditional embroidered indigenous attire. The church was decorated and prepared for the All Saint's celebrations. A coffin with a skull, surrounded by four tall candelabras, stood ready for mass on November 1. Then we walked to a nearby ice cream parlor to enjoy a *paleta* (ice pop). Rosalba discussed enthusiastically her desire to continue teaching her traditional cooking around the world. Her excitement about the food traditions was contagious.

On the way back to her house, as soon as she opened the door we were confronted by the aroma of cooked masa. A corunda cloud covered the stove, and when she opened the steamer, we knew the corundas were ready. We quickly set the table and I helped her make salsa in the molcajete. She unraveled the beautiful corundas and served them to us topped with some crema, crumbled queso fresco, and spicy salsa.

I felt such gratitude to Rosalba and her daughter for welcoming us to be part of her kitchen, her family, and her story. Thank you so much, Rosalba!

Mariana and Rosalba making corundas de cinco picos.

Corundas Tradicionales de Cinco Picos
Traditional Five Peaks Corundas

As you may have read in the Preface to this book, I was lucky enough to learn how to make these corundas from Rosalba Morales Bartolo, a Cocinera Tradicional and international ambassador of the traditional indigenous Purépecha cooking, in San Jerónimo Purenchécuaro, Michoacán, Mexico.

The green tint and flavor that the corn leaf plant gives to these traditional tamales is indescribable. I had never tasted anything like it. The corundas' texture was less fluffy in comparison to corundas I have tried in the past, certainly because of the omission of fat and leavening, which makes the flavor of the corn shine through. Today, corundas commonly include lard and baking powder to make them fluffy and give them the classic tamale flavor most people are familiar with. The omission of these two ingredients makes them taste closer to a pre-Hispanic tamale. It was a pleasant surprise to find out they were so delicious and easier to digest as well.

I hope you enjoy making this recipe the same way I did when taught by Rosalba. This recipe is an adaptation from notes I took that day. Thank you so much Rosalba for sharing this recipe with us. Your love of cooking is contagious.

Makes about 35 to 40 (3½-inch) corundas

4½ pounds (2 kg) freshly ground nixtamalized corn masa, page 75
2 tablespoons organic wood ashes (any natural charcoal ashes will work)
2 to 4 cups chicken stock, as needed
2 tablespoons sea salt
2 pounds (1 kg) queso fresco
4 cups small-diced carrots
About 25 to 30 fresh corn leaves from the plant,* washed

Ask a farmer in your area when corn is in season. Make sure they have organic, pesticide-free practices, because the leaves will be in direct contact with the masa and will impart flavor. I know this sounds like an impossible ingredient quest. If it's simply impossible to find, use a banana leaf. You might have to shape the corundas differently to adapt to the banana leaf length and how it folds. They will not impart the same flavor but it will suffice. Sometimes we have to adapt and make concessions in the kitchen.

1. In an extra-large bowl, place corn masa, ashes, chicken stock, and salt. Knead well until masa feels soft. Add crumbled queso fresco and knead for about 10 to 15 minutes, until masa is light and fluffy.

2. Add the diced carrots and mix well. Let this masa rest for 1 hour.

3. Once masa is rested, start wrapping it in the corn leaves. Take the end of one milpa leaf and fold it into a cone. Fill up the cone with some masa (about 2 to 3 large tablespoons) and start wrapping the leaf around the masa. To form a pentagon shape, follow the lead of the leaf; it will show you which way to turn the leaf. Keep on wrapping, making sure no dough escapes, until you have wrapped the entire leaf around. Then tuck the end of the leaf in-between layers.

4. Place corundas on a tray and then prepare the steamer pot. Fill with water to the line of the steamer rack and put two pennies on the bottom of the pot. The pennies will vibrate when the steamer is running out of water. Refill water if necessary. Insert the rack and cover the top of the rack with some corn leaves or banana leaves scraps. Place pot on the stove on medium-high. Place tamales in the pot by overlapping them all around the perimeter of the pot. Remember to leave a space in the center for refilling the water. Cover the top of the pot with a clean kitchen towel, place the lid on top of the towel, and wrap the four points of the towel over the lid's top. This will keep the vapor in the pot and help absorb some of the extra moisture. Once water is boiling, lower the heat to a rapid simmer and cook for about 1 hour and 45 minutes, up to 2 hours and 15 minutes. Using tongs, take one corunda out of the pot and let it cool off for 10 to 15 minutes. The leaves should come right off when unwrapping and the masa should be nice and fluffy. Once cooked, turn off the heat, and let them rest for 20 to 30 minutes inside the pot.

To serve: Unwrap them and top with Mexican crema, crumbled cheese, and a spicy red charred salsa de molcajete (page 210) or chunky manzano (perón chile) salsa (page 212).

Accompaniments

In Mexican cooking, a side of rice and beans are considered as important as the main dish. I can't imagine a plate of mole poblano without a heaping serving of fluffy arroz a la Mexicana, a mole coloradito without a side of garlicky rice, or any traditional guiso without a side of buttery rice and refried beans. On the other hand, beans are more than a side and can be the main dish or merienda along with the proper accoutrements, like handmade corn tortillas, queso fresco, and a spicy molcajete salsa. In fact, if I had to choose my last meal, my frijoles de la olla (page 184) would be my choice to leave this world with a happy stomach. And of course the same meal would lure me back for Día de Muertos!

❋ ❋ ❋

Frijoles de la Olla — *Pot Beans*   184

Frijoles Refritos — *Refried Beans*   187

Frijoles Negros Refritos — *Refried Black Beans*   191

Frijoles Con Chorizo y Chile de Árbol — *Spicy Chorizo Beans*   193

Sopa Tarasca — *Tarascan Bean Soup*   194

Enfrijoladas — *Pinto Bean Sauce Enchiladas*   197

Arroz al Ajo — *Garlic Rice*   201

Arroz a la Mexicana — *Mexican-Style Rice*   202

Arroz a la Mantequilla con Rajas, Elote y Queso Adobera
Buttered Rice with Roasted Poblanos, Corn, and Queso Adobera   205

Arroz Verde estilo Puebla— *Puebla-Style Green Rice*   206

What I Know About Beans That You Need to Know Too

Cooked, de la olla, or refried, I want to share with you my love for beans. When my brother and I were babies, my mom used to give us a couple ounces of bean broth in a bottle; she said all the vitamins were in the broth. So the love affair started early on!

In Mexico, this simple ingredient is a staple in our national diet. There are many great foods from my homeland, but the earthiness, texture, and flavor of well-prepared homemade beans are my definition of comfort food and are special to me.

There are so many versions of "how to cook beans" out there, using many ingredients, cooking methods, pots, herbs, you name it. Yet most miss the mark when it comes to traditional Mexican-style beans. I can't understand how something so simple has been so misunderstood and feel a responsibility to clear up the confusion.

Keep it simple. Respect the ingredient. Slowly and patiently cooking a pot of beans will yield the best you ever had. Why cook them from scratch? Because the right method and seasoning are in your control, and done correctly, the results are exceptional compared to the salty, mushy, and lifeless canned versions.

How to Choose Beans

There are near-infinite possibilities when it comes to beans, from the dark black beans with intense delicious flavor, to the medium-brown creamy pinto beans, to the light, creamy, and potatoey peruano, mayocoba, or flor de mayo beans. Each of these varieties has different purposes, and they pair with different Mexican meals, cooking styles, and regions.

For example, black beans are found in East-Central and Southeast Mexico, Mexico City, Oaxaca, Chiapas, Veracruz, Campeche, Yucatán, and Quintana Roo. Peruano and flor de mayo are more common in South-Central Mexico areas like Jalisco, Michoacán, Zacatecas, and San Luis Potosí. Pinto beans are the beans of choice for almost all of northern Mexico, all the way from Tijuana to Monterrey.

The traditional store-bought varieties are naturally the most common: Pinto, peruano (also called canary or mayocoba), flor de mayo, and black. These four kinds are available in most supermarkets in the United States.

Heirloom beans are the caviar of beans. If you truly want to experiment and try new flavors and textures, these varieties are going to make you crave beans more often. At this time, my favorite source for heirloom beans in the States is Rancho Gordo New World Specialty Food. Steve Sando has made it a mission to rescue the almost-lost varieties of heirloom beans in Mexico and Latin America. My favorite beans from Rancho Gordo are rebosero, rosa de castilla, acoyote negro, rio zape, pintos, and of course, being from Guadalajara Jalisco, flor de mayo or peruano for refried beans.

Where to Buy Beans

I shop for beans online from Rancho Gordo or at Mexican or ethnic supermarkets where they have newer beans because of quicker turnaround. When buying pre-bagged, I like to make sure that the bag looks shiny; plastic bags can get a little opaque the older they are. Look for well-sealed bags with no holes or insect webs on the inside corners.

When buying them from bulk sections, shiny beans are a good sign. The smell of the bean will indicate freshness. Old dry beans start to smell a bit nutty and rancid.

I always buy dry beans one or two days before I cook them and I don't usually have lots of bean bags in my pantry. I would rather cook them all at the same time and keep them in the freezer ready to thaw and reheat.

What to Cook Beans In

The pot you choose makes the difference when cooking beans. From flavor to cooking time, always choose whatever is best or most convenient for you.

Clay pot: This is the traditional bean-cooking vessel. There are no greater beans than the ones cooked in clay pots. The clay imparts great flavor to the beans and cooks them quickly. Make sure your clay pot is from a reliable source and that it is made for cooking. Cooking time: 1½ to 2 hours.

Dutch enamel: This creates a great heat source. Your pot might get stained or darken a little bit. Cooking time: 2 to 2½ hours.

Cast-iron: The beans will get an extra dose of iron. A slightly metallic flavor might be added. It's a great choice for cooking on the stove or outdoors over a wood or charcoal fire. Make sure to use a well-seasoned pot. Cooking time 2½ hours.

Stainless steel: This might take longer to cook because stainless steel pots don't retain as much heat as clay or cast-iron, but it will get the job done. Cooking time: 3 hours.

Slow cooker: This is the safest bet for people with busy schedules. I love the slow cooker's results. When using a slow cooker, I cook them in my enclosed patio to avoid the bean smells inside my house during the cooking time. It works like a charm! Cooking time: On high about 4 pounds of beans need 5 to 6 hours. Set a timer

Rebosero beans.

Pinto beans.

Mayocoba beans.

Black beans.

and check beans for doneness so next time you know exactly how long they need. Also, *never salt slow cooker beans until they are fully cooked*. Add the salt when the beans are done cooking, then let them cool down in the pot and they will absorb the salt.

Pressure cooker: The reverse of the slow cooker, this is the fastest method. Less romantic, but your beans will be ready in approximately 35 to 45 minutes.

To Soak or Not to Soak?

I never soak my beans and I always have great results. I don't like to soak them because the beans split and the skins separate from the bean. As I mentioned, buy beans from a reliable source, and always cook them on a slow simmer. How slow? Well, you barely see one or two bubbles coming up. Beans prefer low and slow.

Bean Seasoning

Very few seasonings are needed. When cooking a basic pot of beans, I just add ½ of a medium-size white onion, one whole chile (fresh or dry), and water. Sea salt is always added at the end.

Experiment. I usually prefer to use a fresh serrano or jalapeño with mild-flavored beans like pinto and peruano. For reboseros and black beans I go for a cascabel, morita, or chipotle. Fresh chiles complement milder beans, whereas the deeper-flavored beans (like negros, acoyotes, and reboseros) because of their color and flavor benefit from a dry or smoky chile. There is no rule, of course.

When it comes to herbs and spices, you can add some fresh epazote or garlic, especially when cooking black beans, which will complement the flavor and turn the broth into an herbaceous licorice flavor. Epazote is known to aid in the digestion of the beans.

Salt Matters

Use good quality sea salt. The recipe is simple, so the quality of the salt you are using is going to shine through. I use sea salt from Cuyutlán, Colima, Mexico, because I love the flavor. Always salt your beans about 30 minutes or so before you think they are done. If the beans are ready and you have not salted them, no worries, you still have a chance to add the salt. Stir carefully, cook for 5 more minutes and turn the heat off. The beans will keep absorbing some of the salty broth. The biggest mistake would be salting the beans at an early stage of cooking. This will make the skins tough, and they will not cook evenly. So remember to *always* salt your beans at the end!

When Cooking Frijoles de la Olla

Sort thoroughly to remove little stones or dry sticks. Rinse the beans thoroughly in cold water, rubbing them well one or two times until the water comes out clear. Place the rinsed beans in a pot and cover them with about 3 to 4 inches of water above them.

Bring them to a boil, and then lower the heat to a slow simmer. Cover with a lid slightly ajar. If the beans look a bit dry while cooking, add *boiling* water. It will keep the beans from splitting and will keep them at an even temperature. Beans like to be stirred now and then while cooking, but not too often. Gently stir the beans by inserting the spoon around the edges of the pot all the way to the bottom and gently bring the spoon up, like you are folding them. Always salt your beans about 20 to 30 minutes before they are fully cooked (except when cooked in the slow cooker, in which case add salt at the end; with the remaining heat they will keep absorbing salt from the broth), and when ready let them sit on the stove to slowly cool down. If you live in a warm, humid climate, you might want to cool your beans faster and transfer them sooner to the refrigerator, since they can turn sour in a blink of an eye.

Fat

Lard, safflower oil, corn oil, coconut oil, bacon. No matter what kind of fat you choose, one of the most important steps when preparing refried beans is to heat your fat properly. Place the oil or lard or a combination of both in the pan and let it warm up slowly until it is rippling hot. The fat must change to a deep golden color before adding your onions.

Traditional refried beans are made with lard, and the flavor is incomparable. But for everyday beans, safflower or corn oil is what most home cooks use, saving the pork lard for holidays or special celebrations.

To avoid animal fat, use safflower oil or coconut oil.

Freezing

Beans freeze beautifully. Freeze them whole in their broth or refried. They stay good for six to eight months! This is why I encourage you to cook a *big* batch of beans every time you make them. I portion out for 2 to 4 dinners and I freeze them in small plastic containers that will fit my sauté pan or soup pot, so I can defrost directly in the pot on the stove if I forget to thaw them (which seems to happen to me all the time). I am not fond of reheating in plastic containers and always reheat or defrost on a stovetop; we don't even own a microwave! These portions last me 1 to 2 months and they are lifesavers of convenience. On weekends I reheat some frijolitos and serve with tortillas and a good salsa and a couple of eggs for a royal breakfast.

Now that you have a better grasp on the bean matter, the following are four basic bean recipes for you to try.

Frijoles de la Olla
Pot Beans

Beans are at every table of Mexican families, at least once or twice a day for breakfast, with lunch or dinner, all week long. This is the dish that I often long for. When I come to visit from the other realm, I want a bowl of frijoles de la olla, with pico de gallo, salsa macha, crema, queso fresco, and handmade corn tortillas on my altar. I will find my way back just to inhale the essence of this dish.

The preparation is pretty simple once you read and apply the rules in "What I Know About Beans That You Need to Know Too" on page 179.

Finish this recipe with these indispensible toppings: salsa fresca, chopped tomatoes, onions, serrano chiles, cilantro, sea salt, and a little squeeze of lime. Handmade corn tortillas are the perfect match with queso fresco or frijolero, as well as a dollop of crema Mexicana, which is similar to crème fraîche as it has a little sweetness and mellow richness.

Makes 2 pounds of beans

2 pounds (1 kg) dry beans, any kind, sorted, and rinsed
2½ quarts (3 liters) water
½ large white onion
1 chile (I prefer serrano or cascabel)
4 to 5 sprigs fresh epazote (or a couple pinches dry)

1. Sort the beans and remove any debris. Rinse well.

2. Place all ingredients in a clay pot for best flavor. Otherwise, cook in a cast-iron or enamelware pot. Bring the pot to a boil and immediately lower the temperature to low simmer. Cook for about 1 to 1½ hours until soft and creamy. Once they are cooked, add about 1 to 2 teaspoons sea salt.

3. Stir gently, turn off the heat, and let them rest for 25 to 30 minutes. Minutes before serving, warm them up over medium-low heat and stir as little as possible. Serve piping hot!

Serve 1 to 2 ladles of beans with broth in a deep bowl. For a hearty meal, top with pico de gallo; avocado slices; Mexican crema; queso fresco, añejo, or frijolero; warm freshly made corn tortillas, and a spicy salsa.

Note: Beans taste great the day they are made, and even better the next day. I always make 4 to 6 pounds so I can freeze them in little containers. Beans thaw out in a flash and taste like fresh made. They last in the freezer for up to 6 to 8 months.

Frijoles Refritos
Refried Beans

Traditional refried beans are made with lard. The flavor is incomparable. Vegetable, safflower, corn, and even coconut oil are popular choices for everyday cooking, saving the lard for the holidays or special celebrations. Cooking the fat of choice at the proper temperature before introducing the beans is critical and often overlooked when making refried beans, yet it is the specific act from which the recipe gets its name. Refrying changes the flavor and consistency of the beans. You can make refried beans with almost any kind of bean. My favorite versions are flor de mayo, pinto, rebosero, peruano, and black beans.

Makes about 10 to 12 cups

½ cup safflower oil, corn oil, or lard
½ cup finely chopped white onion
Pinch sea salt
8 cups cooked rebosero, pinto, or rosa morada beans
4 cups bean broth

1. In a sauté pan, place the oil or lard (or a combination of both) in the pan and let it warm up slowly until the color on the oil or lard changes to a deeper golden color. Then crank up the heat to medium-high until the oil is rippling hot. Add diced onions and a pinch of salt and sauté them until they have golden-brown edges and are translucent.

2. Carefully add the beans and bean broth, pouring away from you to protect your hands from splatters. Bring beans and broth to a boil, then decrease heat to low simmer and start mashing up the beans until creamy. Some visible skins are ok; they add a better texture.

3. Once beans are well smashed, start stirring constantly until they look pasty and start separating from the edges of the pan. If you can shake your pan and all the beans stay together like a blanket that slides on the pan, your refried beans are ready!

To serve: Slide beans onto a platter and fold, making a big oval shape. Top with crumbled queso fresco or cotija añejo. Add *totopos* (corn chips), and serve warm.

Variations:

Chiles: Add one or two whole dry or fresh chiles, like árbol, cascabel, or serrano to the oil and sauté along with the onions to give some extra spice to the beans. Remove the chile before smashing the beans, or smash along if you want a spicy kick.

Lard: If using lard, it is a must to cook the lard on low-medium heat until it changes color to a light golden brown. This is a key step that will give the best flavor to the beans.

Herbs: Any addition like avocado leaf, hoja santa, epazote, or poblanos can be added when sautéing the onions for extra flavor. Removing the herbs before smashing the beans will add aromatic flavor to the beans, great as a side or accompaniment. Smashing or blending the herbs with the beans will result in intensely flavored beans, best used when making bean tamales.

1.

2.

3.

4.

5.

6.

7.

8.

Frijoles Negros Refritos
Refried Black Beans

Black beans are one of my favorites. They are full of flavor, decadent, rich, and versatile. Serve them "Veracruz-style" with some sautéed plantains on the side, chiles toreados, or charred habaneros and you will have the best side dish for cochinita pibil, pork banana leaf tamales, chile con carne, chilaquiles, or a simple breakfast with two sunny-side up eggs. They also make a delicious filling for vegan/vegetarian tamales and tacos.

Yields 10 to 12 cups

½ cup safflower oil, corn oil, lard, coconut oil, or a combination
½ cup finely chopped white onion
pinch sea salt
4 large cloves garlic, smashed
8 cups cooked black beans
4 cups bean broth (the liquid in which you cooked the beans)

1. In a cast-iron or stainless steel sauté pan (avoid nonstick for this recipe) heat up the oil on a medium-high heat until rippling hot. Add onions and a pinch of salt and sauté until golden brown. Add smashed garlic and sauté for 1 minute. Be careful not to scorch the garlic; that would add a bitter aftertaste.

2. Carefully add the beans and bean broth. Use a long-handled ladle to protect your hands from any splatter. Bring to a boil, decrease heat to slow simmer, and start mashing up the beans until creamy. Some visible skins are ok.

3. Once they are smashed, stir constantly until they look pasty and start separating from the edges of the pan. Usually if you can shake your pan and all the beans stay together like a blanket that slides on the pan, your refried beans are ready!

To serve: Slide them onto a platter. Garnish with some sautéed serrano peppers or charred habaneros, plantains, a crumble of queso fresco or cotija añejo, and *totopos* (corn chips).

Note: Traditionally these black beans are made with lard. Get the best pure lard you can, leaf lard if you can find it. A combination of two oils will work too. A great alternative to animal fat is coconut oil. It adds great flavor, and is a perfect combination with plantains.

Frijoles Con Chorizo y Chile de Árbol
Spicy Chorizo Beans

My grandma Margarita was famous for her Chorizo beans. Family and friends would ask her to make them for special events. The paprika, ancho chiles, and spices in the chorizo, along with the pork fat, add a pleasant, unctuous spicy flavor to the beans. I add two or three whole chiles de árbol to the oil while it is warming up for a hint of extra spice, just like she used to do. I save the toasted chiles for whoever wants to crush them and sprinkle some over their beans to add an extra kick.

These beans are simply scrumptious, especially if you use a good-quality chorizo. Look for a chorizo that is made with finely ground pork and is not too fatty. Try a few kinds until you find the one you like best. Usually, commercial brands tend to have a higher fat content, leaving the beans too greasy and with unpleasant little pieces of gristle instead of delicious ground pork morsels. I have found great options and better quality chorizos from butcher shops and farmer's markets.

Yields 8 cups

4 tablespoons safflower oil or corn oil
6 dry chiles de árbol
12 ounces fresh chorizo
½ cup chopped white onion
8 cups cooked beans (rebosero, pinto, or flor de mayo)
4 cups bean broth (from cooking the beans)
1 teaspoon apple cider vinegar

1. In a large sauté pan, heat up the oil and toast the chiles de árbol in the oil until dark mahogany red. Remove the chiles and set them aside. Remove the chorizo from its casing and add the chorizo to the chile-flavored oil. Using a wooden spatula, crumble the chorizo to help cook into small morsels.

2. Halfway before the chorizo is done cooking, add onions and sauté until they are soft. Add cooked beans, bean broth, vinegar, and one of the toasted dry chiles. Bring to a boil and decrease to a slow simmer.

3. Remove the softened chile and using a machacadora or bean smasher (page 43), smash the beans until creamy. Its okay if some pieces of bean skin and little chorizo crumbs are visible.

4. Once smashed, cook for about 5 to 7 more minutes until desired consistency. I like these beans on the loose side; if you like them pastier, keep on cooking and stirring for another 5 to 10 minutes.

To serve: Transfer onto a platter, sprinkle on some queso fresco, cotija añejo or frijolero, and garnish with the reserved chiles de árbol. Serve warm along with totopos, corn tostadas, or warm corn or flour tortillas for some delicious bean tacos.

Sopa Tarasca
Tarascan Bean Soup

This Tarascan soup is primarily made with home-cooked beans with the addition of some chiles and tomatoes for flavor. I have included this easy-to-make recipe because it is a crowd-pleaser, loved by both the living and the dead. Although very simple, it is one of the most delicious soups from the region of Michoacán. In Pátzcuaro you can find several versions of this soup, and every cook seems to believe they have the "original" version. After investigating, I'm not certain who made the authoritative version, but I can assure you that the indigenous Purépecha people have had some sort of bean soup as a staple in their cooking repertoire for ages. What I do know for sure is that this soup will warm up your supper table on any given night.

Serves 4

3 tablespoons safflower oil
1 guajillo chile, deseeded, leave in one piece
2 pasilla chiles, deveined and deseeded, cut into rings
½ white onion, diced (about ½ cup)
2 cloves garlic
3 roasted tomatoes
1 cup cooked beans*
1 cup bean broth from your cooked beans
5 cups chicken stock
¼ teaspoon marjoram
2 to 4 fresh epazote sprigs

Garnish:
Crema Mexicana
Queso fresco or quesillo
Fried tortilla strips
Fried pasilla chiles

*Bayo or Rosamorada beans work best; use pinto if you can't find those better options. For best results, always use home-cooked beans. To cook beans, see page 179.

1. In a large pot, heat up the oil, add the guajillo chile and pasilla chile rings, and fry until the chiles darken. Pull them out and set aside. Set aside half of the fried pasilla rings for garnish.

2. In the same pot, with the remaining oil, sauté the onion and garlic until golden brown.

3. Add the tomatoes. Sauté the mixture for 2 to 3 minutes, smashing the tomatoes as you cook them. Then add the fried guajillo, half of the fried pasilla, beans, bean broth, chicken stock, marjoram, and epazote. Bring to a simmer for 15 minutes.

4. Next, puree the soup with an immersion blender, food processor, or blender. Add the soup back to the pot and cook for about 10 minutes over low heat, until it reaches a creamy consistency. Adjust salt to your taste.

5. Serve warm and garnish with crema Mexicana, fried tortillas, and fried pasilla. Avocado makes a great garnish as well.

Notes: This soup should be creamy and light. If it is too thick, add more chicken stock or a bit of water. It is best made with home-cooked beans. If you want to use canned beans instead, rinse them well and discard the broth they came with as it will make the soup too salty. Substitute 1 cup of water for this discarded broth. Results may vary.

Enfrijoladas
Pinto Bean Sauce Enchiladas

Imagine fresh corn tortillas smothered in smooth velvety bean sauce that has been seasoned and tinted with dried chiles. There are many versions of enfrijoladas. This sauce is made with smoky anchos, guajillo chiles, sweet sautéed onions, and a couple of garlic cloves blended to create a light, smooth, mildly spicy bean sauce. Enfrijoladas are the lighter cousins of enchiladas and are often vegetarian when made with crumbled queso fresco and onions. Shredded chicken or cooked chorizo also make great fillings for these handkerchief-folded tortillas. When you make these enfrijoladas, the heavenly smell from the kitchen will welcome every wandering soul near or far.

Serves 4 to 6

Sauce:
3 tablespoons safflower oil or other mild cooking oil
1 medium ancho chile, deseeded and stem removed
2 long guajillo chile, deseeded and stem removed
½ cup diced white onion
2 large cloves garlic
½ teaspoon sea salt
2 cups cooked pinto beans
2 cups bean broth
1 cup chicken stock or water
½ cup extra water or milk
16 corn tortillas, 5-inch
4 tablespoons safflower or corn oil, to lightly panfry the tortillas

Filling:
1 pound requesón cheese, ricotta cheese, queso fresco, or crumbled goat cheese
½ medium red onion, diced small
Sea salt

Garnish:
Cotija añejo or queso fresco cheese
Crema Mexicana
2 or 3 avocados, sliced
Salsa mucha muchacha (page 216)
Quick-pickled red onions (page 221)

1. In a large saucepan, warm up the oil over medium heat. Add the dry chiles, onion, garlic, and a pinch of salt. Sauté until onions are softened and dry chiles have a bright color and are slightly blistered. Add the cooked beans, bean broth, and chicken stock. Bring to a boil and let it simmer for about 10 to 15 minutes until the dry chiles look rehydrated and plump.

2. Set beans aside, covered, for 5 minutes. Then place the sautéed bean mixture into a blender. Remember to be careful when pouring hot liquids into a blender. You can also use an immersion blender, or a food processor to make this sauce, although I've found that the blender works best to make a smooth, velvety sauce.

3. Transfer the sauce back to the saucepan and keep it warm at the lowest temperature, stirring now and then. Taste and adjust for salt, or liquid if too thick. Sauce should be loose enough to pour and thick enough to cover a tortilla. To test thickness, submerge a wooden spoon into the sauce to coat the spoon, and run your finger over the back of the spoon through the sauce. If the sauce remains separated, it is the right consistency.

4. Prepare the cheese filling by crumbling the cheese in a small bowl. Add the onions and combine. Set aside to have it ready when folding the tortillas.

5. Warm up each tortilla by quick frying it in a little oil. You want them soft and pliable, but with a little color. Gently, using tongs or a flat spatula, submerge each tortilla into the warm bean sauce until fully coated. Place them onto a platter and fill them with the requesón-onion mixture and fold them in half or into fourths like you would do with a crepe. When you have them all folded, keep them warm in the oven. Reheat the remainder of the bean sauce and add a little more milk or water to adjust consistency.

To serve: Serve 3 to 4 enfrijoladas per plate and ladle one or two spoonfuls of the bean sauce on top. Add a dollop of crema, sprinkle the cotija cheese, garnish with avocado and red onions, and add a little drizzle of salsa mucha muchacha.

Note: Enfrijoladas are usually filled with cheese, but to make a more complete meal, fill them with shredded chicken or chorizo.

When making rice

Some people think rice is one of the hardest things to cook, but it is quite the opposite. If you follow the instructions below, I assure you of rice success every time. Let go of your rice fears!

- When making rice pilaf, always take the time to toast the rice in butter or oil until the rice changes color from translucent to white to off-white to slightly golden beige. This step along with the right amount of water will result in fluffy, separate, cooked grains.

- Always use two cups of water for every one cup of rice as a good measure for long-grain rice. Use the same container or cup to measure the rice and water.

- After adding the cooking liquid to the rice, always bring rice to a boil, then immediately turn down the heat to slow simmer, and cover with a lid.

- Once the lid is on, do not poke, stir, lift the lid or disturb the rice; let it cook in peace. Every time you lift the lid to check on it, you lose heat and steam. So the rice loses moisture, and the temperature change makes for uneven cooking. Stirring the rice just makes for mushy, soggy rice.

- Once the rice is cooked, remove it from the burner, keep the lid on, and set aside.

- Let the rice rest for 5 to 10 minutes before serving for best flavor and texture.

- Fluff the rice with a fork before serving and enjoy!

- If doubling, tripling or quadrupling the following recipes, follow the water ratio of two cups of water to one cup of rice and adjust the salt to your taste.

- Rice freezes well for about 2 to 3 months. And it reheats beautifully; just add a sprinkle of water to revive it first.

Arroz al Ajo
Garlic Rice

This rice is a great accompaniment to mole negro, coloradito, or Amarillo, and a faithful companion to cochinita pibil. The way the garlic infuses the oil and cooks along with the rice gives the rice an incredible aromatic and savory flavor. Always remember to remove the garlic halves before serving. If you are doubling or tripling the recipe, add a whole head of garlic cut in half horizontally to expose all the garlic cloves, allowing it to infuse the oil. This makes it easy to remove the whole head at the end rather than fishing out individual garlic cloves.

Serves 4

2 tablespoons butter
1 tablespoon safflower oil
1 cup long-grain white rice
4 medium-large cloves garlic, cut in halves
2 cups chicken stock
1 bay leaf
½ teaspoon sea salt

1. In a medium-size pot over medium heat, add the butter and oil. When butter is melted, add the rice and garlic cloves, tossing constantly, and cook until the grains of rice become off-white. Keep tossing and soon they will turn into a light golden-tan color. At this point the garlic should have the same color as well. This is the perfect time to add the stock.

2. Add two cups of chicken stock or water, the bay leaf, and salt. Cover the pot with a lid until the water reaches a rolling boil. Immediately turn down the temperature to a low simmer and keep the lid on the pot.

3. My advice for good rice is to not look at it and not stir it. Do not keep poking it or removing the lid. Rice cooks best if left alone. Let it cook for 20 minutes.

4. Check the rice for doneness, turn off the heat, move to the side and sprinkle about a tablespoon of water over the rice. Cover with a lid and leave it resting for 5 to 10 more minutes. Right before serving, fluff up the rice with a fork.

Note: If you like your rice to have a bold garlic flavor, remove the garlic cloves when golden brown and quickly puree them along with some of the chicken stock. Add this loose puree to the rest of the chicken stock and add to the rice.

Arroz a la Mexicana
Mexican-Style Rice

In the United States, arroz a la Mexicana is known as orange rice, Spanish rice, or Mexican rice. In Mexico, this tomatoey pilaf is the classic side for many home-cooked dishes, and it is mole poblano's best friend.

My Grandma Margarita used to add little diced carrots and peas, and some boiled eggs to garnish. So I decided to go with her version, since shelling peas was one of my first tasks in the kitchen when I was a little girl. I always felt so happy when the rice was ready and I saw my shelling efforts of the little green confetti peas in the rice. Over the years I observed how my Grandma prepared her dish, and one thing I learned is that in order for the rice to be consistently orange, the chicken stock has to be warm or boiling when added to the rice. This prevents the tomato puree from separating. This little trick will help you make the most scrumptious arroz a la Mexicana.

Makes about 4½ cups of rice

½ medium white onion, cut into quarters
2 cloves garlic
2 large Roma tomatoes, boiled and navel removed
Sea salt
2 tablespoons safflower or vegetable oil
1 cup long-grain rice
2 cups chicken stock, simmering hot
1 to 2 carrots, small diced, about ½ cup
1 bay leaf
¼ cup peas, freshly shelled or frozen
2 boiled eggs, cut into quarters for garnish (optional)

1. In a blender, place ¼ onion, garlic, tomatoes, a pinch of salt, and ¼ cup water. Blend until pureed. Set aside.

2. In a 3-quart pot over medium heat, heat the oil and add the rice along with the other ¼ onion wedge. Stir constantly until rice grains turn to a cream or golden-brown color.

3. Add the tomato puree and ½ teaspoon of sea salt. Cook for 1 to 2 minutes. Add the simmering 2 cups of chicken stock, diced carrots, and bay leaf and stir until well combined. Bring rice to a boil, then lower the heat to low, and cover with a lid. The secret to good rice is to **let it be** once you place the lid on. Do not stir! Keep the pot covered for at least 20 to 25 minutes.

4. Check for doneness. If still al dente, put the lid back on and cook 5 more minutes on low heat. When rice is almost done, turn off the heat, add the peas, and leave it covered for 5 to 8 minutes. The remaining heat will cook the peas to a bright green. When ready to serve, fluff up the rice with a fork, transfer to a serving dish or clay cazuela, and arrange the boiled egg on the edge for garnish.

Serve alongside any mole or other main dish, or with some tamalitos and a side of refried beans.

Note: If the tomatoes are not in season, use organic whole roasted canned tomatoes and add a small pinch of paprika to improve color and flavor.

Arroz a la Mantequilla
con Rajas, Elote y Queso Adobera
Buttered Rice
with Roasted Poblanos, Corn, and Queso Adobera

My mom used to make this rice for us when my brother and I were little. She made it with such care, tenderness, and delicious flavor that we would always have seconds and sometimes if we tried hard enough we would get thirds. We loved it. When the rice was ready, my mom would turn off the stove and add slices of adobera cheese over the top, cover the pot, and allow the cheese to melt before serving. Talk about gilding the lily. Thank you, Mamá, for making the most delicious rice for us. Feel free to double up the recipe, because you will want seconds . . . or thirds.

Makes about 4½ cups

3 tablespoons butter
1 teaspoon cooking oil
1 cup long-grain rice
¼ medium white onion, sliced into 3 wedges
1 clove garlic, sliced in half
¾ cup white corn kernels, about 2 ears worth of corn
2 cups chicken stock,* simmering hot
½ teaspoon sea salt
1 large poblano pepper, charred, skin removed, sliced into long strips
4 to 6 ounces adobera cheese, queso fresco, or Monterey Jack cheese, sliced**

My mom would use powdered chicken bouillon, about a heaping teaspoon. If you use this option, omit the sea salt.
*** If a good quality adobera cheese is not available, I suggest Monterey Jack cheese or just a good crumbly queso fresco.*

1. Add oil and butter in a 3-quart pot over medium heat until butter is melted. Add the rice along with onion and garlic. Stir constantly until rice grains become opaque white and slightly toasted. Add corn and sauté for 2 more minutes.

2. Add the chicken stock and ½ teaspoon of sea salt. Stir until well combined. Bring pot to a boil, lower temperature to low heat, and cover pot with a lid. Once you place the lid on, don't poke or stir. Keep pot covered for at least 20 minutes.

3. Check on rice doneness and cook for 5 more minutes if needed. Once rice is done, turn off the heat and quickly top the rice with the poblano pepper strips and the sliced cheese, alternating them to make a pattern if you like. Cover with a lid and let it rest for 5 to 10 minutes until the cheese has melted. When ready to serve, fluff up the rice with a fork and transfer to a serving dish or serve individual portions. Add some dollops of Mexican crema for garnish.

Serve with any mole or main dish as a side. This rice goes great with pork enchiladas or chicken. I love leftovers with a sunny-side up egg on top for lunch or a light supper.

Arroz Verde estilo Puebla
Puebla-Style Green Rice

This is a traditional, easy-to-make recipe from the central state of Puebla, Mexico. It is a family-style recipe so there are many variations. This is my version and the flavors I like. This fluffy rice gets its emerald-green color and herbaceous buttery flavor from the combination of fresh poblanos, serranos, and cilantro. This rice pairs especially well with homemade guiso, pork, chicken, or seafood. It is a great new recipe to add to your ofrenda.

Makes about 4 cups of cooked rice

½ medium white onion, cut into quarters
2 cloves garlic
1 large poblano pepper, tail and seeds removed, coarsely chopped
1 small serrano pepper
1 medium-size bunch cilantro, about 2 cups, including stems
½ teaspoon sea salt
¼ cup water
1 tablespoon safflower oil or a good extra virgin olive oil
1 tablespoon butter
1 cup long-grain rice
2 cups chicken stock, simmering hot

1. In a blender, place ¼ onion, garlic, poblano, serrano, cilantro, a pinch of sea salt, and ¼ cup water. Blend until pureed. (If the blender needs more liquid, add some of the 2 cups of chicken stock.) Set aside.

2. Combine oil and butter in a 2-quart pot and warm up over medium heat. Add the rice along with the other ¼ onion wedge. Stir constantly until rice grains are opaque and slightly toasted. They should have a creamy white almond color.

3. Add the green puree, stir for 2 minutes, then add the chicken stock and ½ teaspoon of sea salt. Stir until well combined. Bring pot to a boil, then lower heat to low simmer, and cover pot with a lid. Once you place the lid on, do not poke or stir. Keep pot covered for at least 20 minutes.

4. Check if rice is done. If al dente, cook 5 more minutes on low heat. When rice is almost done, turn off the heat and leave it covered for 5 to 7 minutes. When ready to serve, fluff up the rice with a fork, then transfer to a serving dish or serve individual portions.

Salsa Roja Asada con Chile de Árbol y Chile Cascabel
Roasted Red Salsa with Árbol and Cascabel Chiles
210

Salsa Martajada de Chile Manzano en Molcajete
Chunky, Mortar-style Manzano Chile Salsa
212

Salsa Verde de Tomatillo Asada
Roasted Tomatillo Salsa Verde
215

Salsa Mucha Muchacha (Salsa Macha)
Ground Chile de Árbol Salsa
216

Chiles Toreados
Bullfighting Chiles
218

Salsa de Jitomate Sencilla para Antojitos Mexicanos
Simple Tomato Sauce for Mexican Antojitos
220

Salsa de Jitomate, Oregano y Canela
Tomato, Oregano, and Cinnamon Salsa
220

Cebollitas Desflemadas para Mole Poblano
Pickled White Onions for Mole Poblano
221

Curtido de Cebolla Morada
Quick-Pickled Red Onions
221

Encurtido de Cebolla Morada y Habaneros Tatemados
Quick-Pickled Red Onions and Charred Habaneros
222

Chiles Manzanos (Perones), Zanahorias y Cebollas en Escabeche
Escabeche of Manzano (Perón) Peppers, Carrots, and Onions
224

Verduras en Escabeche
Escabeche-Pickled Vegetables
226

Salsas, Quick Pickling, and Escabeches

I still remember the first time Grandma Margarita allowed me as a young girl to use the molcajete. I had watched her make salsa many times, and I always asked questions and observed her hand and wrist movements, the way she mashed chiles, and how and when she would add each ingredient. She always made the salsa after cooking the meal so it was slightly warm when she took it to the table. A warm corn tortilla with a spoonful of her salsa; I lived for that. So the day she thought I was ready and finally asked me to start making the salsa was a privilege. As my little hand held the mortar stone, called a *tejolote*, I had not anticipated how heavy it was, so I didn't do very well that first time. But I remember my grandma wrapping her hand around mine and explaining to me how it needed to be done. She taught me step-by-step until we finished making the salsa. I felt very happy and accomplished, and since then making salsa in a molcajete has been one of my biggest pleasures in the kitchen.

The sound of the sea salt rubbing against the stone while mashing the garlic cloves. The smell of charred tomatoes and crackling chiles toasting on the comal. These are my motives to start a cooking storm in the kitchen. Each family has their own style of making salsas, and each salsa has a purpose and pairs differently with specific dishes. For example, a salsa martajada (roughly smashed) is carne asada or quesadilla's best companion. Roasted tomatillo and chile de árbol salsa makes the best salsa for tacos. Fresh salsa verde is a must for chicken flautas. The list is endless. We Mexicans are very particular about how salsas are made, seasoned, and paired with food. The salsa recipes in this book are among my personal favorites. Making salsa is an art in itself, and I hope you embrace them in your kitchen. You can read more about molcajetes and how to cure one on page 42.

This section is also about the Mexican pickles we call escabeche or encurtido. They are macerated fruit, vegetables, and legumes in a savory solution of vinegar, salt, and spices—or a sweet solution of sugar and aromatic spices like canela and allspice.

The most popular escabeches used every day in Mexican homes and as street food are verdura en escabeche, a vegetable medley, and japapeños en escabeche. Store-bought canned jalapeños are convenient, but the homemade version is far better in flavor and texture.

Each of the chiles and vegetables keep their crisp and crunchy bite. They are easy to make and a great addition to your pantry. Whether preparing a salsa or an escabeche, I have always found the process and results very rewarding. Each family has their own salsa and escabeche recipes. I would definitely return every year to look for these in my ofrenda.

Salsa Roja Asada con Chile de Árbol y Chile Cascabel

Roasted Red Salsa with Árbol and Cascabel Chiles

This salsa roja is the first salsa I learned to make in the molcajete. In my house, it is a must on the table. I use it on huevos rancheros or with carne asada, beans, quesadillas, tacos, or even to make carne guisada. Adding finely chopped fresh cilantro and red onion makes it a great hot salsa snack with tortilla chips and a couple of beers. The special chile in this salsa is the cascabel. It has a round cherry shape and it rattles when shaken like a bell. *Cascabel* means "bell." These sassy chiles have a spicy side, with a pleasant smoky, fruity flavor. Cascabel chiles are now easy to find at Hispanic markets or spice shops.

Makes 4 cups

3 medium-large steak tomatoes, about 4 inches wide, or 5 Romas*
6 to 8 dried chiles de árbol
2 dried cascabel chiles
2 medium cloves garlic, peeled
½ to 1 teaspoon sea salt
1 to 2 tablespoons water
½ medium red onion, finely diced, for garnish
Small bunch cilantro, finely chopped, for garnish

Any juicy, meaty tomato with high acidity content will work best, like better boy, early girl, or big boy tomatoes.

1. In a cast-iron pan or comal, toast the chiles at medium heat, turning them constantly with a wooden paddle or spoon. When they look evenly toasted and show an intense dark red color, remove pan from the fire and let them cool a bit until easy to handle. Remove the stems.

2. Using the same cast-iron pan, place tomatoes upside down, and set the heat to medium. Cover them with a lid smaller than the pan's rim to apply some pressure on them so the heat will cook them more evenly. Turn them right-side up and keep rotating them until they have well-blistered, charred skins and they are cooked through, about 8 to 10 minutes. Once the tomatoes are charred and cooked, set them aside until easy enough to handle. Remove the skin and with a paring knife remove the cores of the tomatoes.

3. If making salsa in a food processor or blender: Place tomatoes, garlic, sea salt, and toasted chiles in blender or food processor and pulse until coarsely blended. Add a little water if needed. Taste and adjust for salt if needed.

4. If making salsa in a molcajete or mortar: Place garlic cloves and half of the sea salt in the mortar and smash until garlic and salt form a smooth paste. Add toasted chiles two at a time and smash until a coarse paste, making sure you smash almost all the chile seeds. If you need more traction, add a pinch of sea salt. Once you have a course paste, add one tomato at a time into the mortar and smash until well combined. Repeat until you smash all three tomatoes. Taste and adjust for salt and consistency. If you feel the salsa is too thick, add a bit of water until you feel it's the right consistency for you.

5. Top with finely diced onion and cilantro. Serve at room temperature with chips and a nice cold beverage or along with your favorite meal.

Salsa Martajada de Chile Manzano en Molcajete
Chunky, Mortar-style Manzano Chile Salsa

Making salsa in the molcajete or a stone mortar is an art. The action of mashing the ingredients in a volcanic lava-stone molcajete leaves a rough texture and imparts the minerality from the stone to the salsa. It is the rubbing of the ingredients that makes them share their flavors in a unique way. Salsa martajada takes its name from its consistency. This salsa is not pureed until smooth. Instead, large pieces of tomatoes, onions, and smashed chiles make this salsa juicy and toothsome, like a chunky relish.

Salsa martajada is the kind of salsa you will make on a family grilling day, since you can char all your tomatoes, onions, and chiles right before the grilling starts and have an amazing complement to all those grilled steaks, fish, chicken, or vegetables. Or quickly make it in the kitchen, charring the chiles and tomatoes over a comal to serve with a bowl of frijoles de la olla (page 184), tamales, eggs, enfrijoladas (page 197), corundas (page 175), or quesadillas. Try a tablespoon of this salsa over a warm homemade corn tortilla and you'll consider making a double batch.

Makes about 4 to 5 cups

- 3 large Roma tomatoes, charred
- 3 medium green onion bulbs, charred
- 2 manzano (perón) chiles, charred
- 1 to 2 jalapeños, charred
- 2 cloves garlic
- ½ teaspoon sea salt
- 2 to 3 tablespoons water

1. Grill or char on a comal the tomatoes, onions, manzanos, and jalapeños.

2. Before starting a salsa, rinse and pat dry your stone mortar or molcajete. (Wetting the stone will prevent it from absorbing the delicious juices, while patting dry allows enough traction when smashing ingredients.) Smash garlic and a generous pinch of sea salt until pureed. Add chiles and smash unevenly. The secret of martajada is to leave it chunky.

3. Cut onions into quarters, add salt, and smash briefly in the molcajete containing your garlic and chiles. Do the same with the tomatoes and add one tomato at the time and smash briefly, leaving medium-sized chunks.

4. Add a couple tablespoons of water if the tomatoes didn't provide enough liquid or you want a more loose consistency. Taste for salt and adjust if needed. Serve salsa directly in the molcajete or stone mortar at the table with a wooden spoon. Watch it disappear in seconds!

Salsa Verde de Tomatillo Asada
Roasted Tomatillo Salsa Verde

Tomatillos are a beloved ingredient in Mexico because of their tangy and mild characteristic flavor. Whether raw, boiled, charred, or roasted, tomatillos are very versatile and used in a variety of simple and complex dishes, including chilaquiles, flautas, tacos, eggs, moles, and guisos. One of the best ways to enhance the flavor in tomatillos is by roasting them. Roast them at a high temperature for enough time, until they show some charred blisters. This develops a slightly smoky flavor that gives a depth of character to the salsa. This roasted tomatillo salsa is especially good when used along with pork or chicken for tamale filling.

Makes 2 to 3 cups

1 to 2 drizzles vegetable or corn oil
1 pound tomatillos (about 14 to 16 average size), peeled and washed
1 poblano pepper, sliced in half lengthwise
1 medium white onion, cut into thick slices
2 jalapeño peppers, cut in half lengthwise
2 to 3 serrano peppers, cut in half lengthwise
1 teaspoon sea salt
2 cloves garlic
½ cup water

1. In a large baking pan, toss with a little vegetable or corn oil the tomatillos, poblano, onion, jalapeños, and serranos. Distribute into an even layer and sprinkle on some sea salt.

2. Roast in the oven for 20 minutes at 425°F (218°C) until tomatillos have charred spots and chiles are blistered.

3. Place all the roasted vegetables into a blender along with garlic and ½ cup water. Blend until a smooth puree. Taste for salt and adjust if necessary. If sauce is too thick, add more water.

Notes: If you are making this sauce for tamales, keep it on the thicker side. If you are making this sauce for tacos, chilaquiles, or huevos rancheros, adjust the water up to ¾ to 1 cup. If making a double batch remember to adjust the salt if needed.

Salsa Mucha Muchacha (Salsa Macha)
Ground Chile de Árbol Salsa

This is one of my salsa obsessions. Mucha muchacha rules the salsa realm with spice, color, and flavor. It is smoky and nutty with an intense chile aroma. The notes from the chile de árbol bring depth and spiciness, then just when you think your mouth is going to be on fire, the moritas hit you with their sweet spicy cherry-like flavor, followed by sharp garlic and nutty notes from the peanuts and oil, and everything starts to mellow down. It is a rollercoaster! Afterward, a pleasant spice lingers on your tongue and warms up your taste buds leaving you wanting more. Salsa macha is best portioned sparingly in **drops not spoonfuls**. It is both exhilarating and potent.

Please do not be alarmed when you read the ingredients for the recipe. I know 64 to 68 chiles seems excessive, but this is exactly the type of salsa preparation that shows the versatility of chiles and the spectrum of flavor versus a scorching heat of chiles.

Salsa macha is a good salsa for white or red pozole, antojitos Mexicanos, beans from the pot, a simple sunny-side up egg, greens, quesadillas, or you name it!

Makes an 8 to 10-ounce jar

64 to 68 dried chiles de árbol, between 3½ inches and 4 inches long*
3 to 4 morita chiles, about 2 to 3 inches in size
1 cup safflower or avocado oil
2 tablespoons roasted salted peanuts
2 tablespoons toasted sesame seeds
2 large cloves garlic
1 to 1½ teaspoon sea salt

Make sure they are chiles de árbol, not Japonés chiles, since they are often mislabeled. For the specifics of chile de árbol, see page 55.

1. Remove the chile stems. In a medium-size pot place oil and warm up over medium heat. Add the árbol chiles and carefully toss constantly until all chiles look dark mahogany red but not burnt. If some of the chiles get darker than others, remove them promptly and keep frying the rest. Remove the pot from heat, carefully take out all the fried chiles, and place them in a bowl to cool down a bit.

2. Return the oil pot to the stove and add the 3 morita chiles. Watch carefully, because these moritas tend to inflate like balloons. Once they are dark red, almost black, remove chiles from the oil and let them cool off.

3. Place the pot with the oil in a safe place to cool off for about 3 minutes. Then add the peanuts and sesame seeds into the oil and toss. Wait for another 3 to 5 minutes until the oil is a lukewarm temperature.

4. Place the fried árbol chiles, moritas, garlic cloves, salt, and all the oil with the sesame seeds and peanuts into a blender or a small food processor or for best results use an immersion blender, and puree everything until it becomes a loose paste. The salsa should look smooth but still have some texture left from the seeds.

Note: The day this salsa is made it has a fiery kick. Watch out! The next couple of days it will mellow down. Keep the salsa in an airtight glass jar in the refrigerator or in a cool, dry place. The chiles and oil tend to separate. Just shake or mix well with a spoon before using. This salsa will last about 4 to 6 weeks. It gets better and better every day.

217

Chiles Toreados
Bullfighting Chiles

If I had to translate *chiles toreados* into English, I would call them bullfighting chiles. When the matador teases the bull, the bull gets flaming mad. When making chiles toreados, its almost the same action. You make these chiles in a scorching-hot pan drizzled with a bit of oil and sea salt. Over high heat you shake the pan to get the chiles blistered. As they rub against the hot pan, they get spicier. These actions get the chiles spicy level to a top notch. After coming out of the pan they are tamed with a good squeeze of lime juice and sea salt. They are the best companion to a queso fundido, quesadillas, refried beans, tacos; you name it! You can "torear" any kind of fresh chile, from jalapeños, serranos, güeros, habaneros, verdes de árbol, or manzano (perones).

Makes . . . you cry. So spicy, so good!

1 teaspoon any mild cooking oil
6 to 8 fresh jalapeños or serranos, whole or cut in half lengthwise
½ to 1 teaspoon sea salt
Juice of one lime, plus a couple lime wedges

Heat the oil in a shallow cast-iron pan on medium-high. When the oil is rippling hot, add the chiles and 2 good pinches of sea salt. Shake the pan back and forth at all times until the chiles show large blisters and charred spots. The chiles will look shiny and like they are about to burst. Transfer them to a shallow bowl, squeeze some lime on top, and sprinkle 1 or 2 generous pinches of sea salt. Serve while they are hot.

Chiles Toreados.

Salsa de Jitomate Sencilla para Antojitos Mexicanos

Simple Tomato Sauce for Mexican Antojitos

This light sauce is bright and herbal. It is usually used to top the many kinds of antojitos Mexicanos, from tacos dorados, to flautas, tostadas, sopes, enchiladas de plaza; you name it. The acidity of the tomatoes, the oregano, and the sharp garlic and onions juice up and balance the crunchy fried concoctions.

Makes about 2 to 3 cups

3 to 4 large Roma tomatoes
2 cloves garlic
¼ medium white onion
3 pinches dry oregano
1 pinch dry thyme
1 pinch ground clove buds
½ teaspoon sea salt

1. In a small pot, place tomatoes, garlic, and onion. Cover with water and bring to a simmer. Cook until a pairing knife is easily inserted into a tomato. Set pot aside, reserve the water, and let the tomatoes cool.

2. When cool enough to handle, use a pairing knife to remove the little navels of the tomatoes, but leave the skins on. Transfer tomatoes to a blender along with the onion, garlic, oregano, thyme, cloves, and salt. Add ¼ cup of the water in which you cooked the tomatoes and blend until pureed. Consistency should be of a loose, light sauce. If the sauce is too thick, add 1 or 2 more tablespoons of the reserved water until you get your desired consistency.

Serve slightly warm over antojitos Mexicanos (page 81), like sopes, tacos dorados, shredded chicken or pork tostadas.

Salsa de Jitomate, Oregano y Canela

Tomato, Oregano, and Cinnamon Salsa

This salsa is a variation of Salsa de Jitomate Sencilla. Adding a serrano chile and a hint of canela gives the salsa a pleasant warmth. Tomatoey, herbaceous, and fragrant, this salsa is a perfect companion to serve over swiss chard and queso fresco tamales (page 166), enchiladas de plaza en casa (page 88), eggs, vegetables, or any antojito. This mild and delicious salsa should have a loose consistency. When adjusting the body of the salsa, use the water in which the tomatoes were cooked, for best flavor.

Makes about 2 to 3 cups

3 to 4 large Roma tomatoes
½ white onion
1 clove garlic
1 serrano chile
1 generous pinch dry Mexican oregano
2 generous pinches canela
¼ to ½ cup water in which the tomatoes boiled
Sea salt to taste

1. In a small pot, place the tomatoes, onion, garlic, and serrano. Cover with water and boil until tomatoes are tender when a knife is inserted. Set aside and allow them to cool a little. Reserve the water.

2. Place everything in a blender, except the water, and blend until smooth. If the consistency is too thick add ¼ or ½ cup of the water in which the tomatoes were cooked.

3. In a small pot cook the sauce for 3 to 5 more minutes.

Cebollitas Desflemadas para Mole Poblano
Pickled White Onions for Mole Poblano

Desflemar (dephlegmate) is a process in Mexican cooking used to remove strong flavors or slimy matter from foods like onions, nopalitos, and chiles. The process consists of soaking the vegetable in a solution of either water and lime juice or vinegar and sea salt. By soaking thin, raw slices of white onions in this solution, they lose their pungency, making them more pleasant and friendly to eat. Cebollitas desflemadas are the best garnish and a must when serving a plate of mole poblano.

Makes about 1 to 1½ cups

2 medium white onions
Juice of two limes
3 tablespoons water
¼ teaspoon dry oregano
1 teaspoon sea salt

Peel onions and cut into round thin slices. Rinse the slices in cold water and drain well. In a small bowl combine lime juice, water, oregano, and sea salt. Add the onion slices and toss well, cover, and let them marinate for 20 minutes before serving as a garnish.

Curtido de Cebolla Morada
Quick-Pickled Red Onions

Sweet and salty, sharp and tangy, these briny magenta-hued pickled onions are delicious and addictive. The brine tames their sharp piquancy, making them the perfect quick-pickled garnish to brighten up any mole, taco, or antojito Mexicano.

Makes a 2-quart jar

1¼ cups water
1¼ cups white vinegar
¼ cup sugar
¼ cup sea salt
2 bay leaves
4 whole allspice
1 tablespoon coriander seeds, optional
6 to 8 small to medium red onions

Make the brine: In a small pot place water, vinegar, sugar, and salt and warm up over medium heat until sugar and salt are completely dissolved. Remove from heat. Add bay leaves and allspice, and let it steep. Cut onions in half lengthwise and remove ends and outer skins. Place onion halves flat-side-down and from pole-to-pole radially slice to create slivers. Cutting the onions this way will keep their shape, staying crunchy for longer. With your fingers separate the onion segments. Layer onion slivers in the glass jar halfway and add half of the warm brine. Add rest of the onions and brine until you fill the jar and brine completely covers the onions. Close the jar with a tight lid and shake the jar to distribute the solution and spices. Refrigerate overnight or at least 4 to 6 hours before serving.

Note: These pickled onions last about 6-8 weeks in the refrigerator if you resist eating them all in the first couple of weeks!

Encurtido de Cebolla Morada y Habaneros Tatemados
Quick-Pickled Red Onions and Charred Habaneros

The Yucatán Peninsula produces some of the best habanero chiles in Mexico. These quick-pickled onions and charred habaneros are an essential complement to cochinita pibil (page 138) or the traditional Yucatecán tamales, mukbil pibipollos (page 168). I included my favorite variation of this spicy hot pickling. Be aware this quick-pickled concoction gets hotter as it marinates. It pairs well with any of the eastern peninsula's flavors.

Makes about 3 cups

¼ cup apple cider vinegar
1 teaspoon turbinado sugar
1 to 2 teaspoons sea salt
8 to 10 habaneros, a mix of green, orange, and yellow
3 medium red onions, cut in half lengthwise
Juice of 2 limes
2 to 3 pinches dry oregano

1. In a small pot slightly warm up the vinegar and add sugar and salt and mix until dissolved. Set aside to cool down.

2. On a griddle, place the habaneros and halved onions. Quick-cook until habaneros are charred and blistered on all sides but still hold their shape and have some bright colorful spots. Halved onions should be quick-charred only on the flat side, and removed from the griddle promptly to avoid cooking them. (You just want a slight onion char to impart flavor to the pickled concoction.)

3. Remove onions and habaneros from griddle. Cut onions radially from the center into crescent moon slivers* and habaneros into slices. Use a fork to hold the habaneros while slicing them to avoid burning your fingers. Place sliced onions and habaneros into a bowl and add the lemon juice and solution of vinegar, sugar, and sea salt. Sprinkle on dry oregano by rubbing it between your fingers to release its fragrant oils. Toss until well combined. Set aside, and let marinate for 15 to 20 minutes before serving. Serve as a garnish over cochinita pibil tacos (page 138), or on the side with a slice of Yucatecán mukbil pibipollo tamale (page 168).

*Notes: This salsa is best made the same day, but it will last in the refrigerator for 3 to 4 days. *It is important to cut the onions into slivers, since they will keep their shape and crispness. If you cut them into rounds or other directions, they tend to become mushy with time.*

Chiles Manzanos (Perones), Zanahorias y Cebollas en Escabeche
Escabeche of Manzano (Perón) Peppers, Carrots, and Onions

The first time I tried these delicious peppers was in Patzcuaro, Michoacán, and I fell in love with them. Known as manzano or chile perón, these fragrant, fruity, spicy peppers, with black seeds, a slightly sweet end note, and a bright egg-yolk yellow color, stole my heart.

Quick-pickled onions, crunchy carrots, and strips of manzano peppers are all you need in a quick-pickled concoction. Briny, salty, crunchy, spicy, sweet, this is the perfect complement to any antojitos Mexicanos, or to brighten up any rich meal, like the enchiladas de plaza en casa (page 88).

The recipe makes two quarts. I split it into two 1-quart mason jars. Once you try them you'll be so happy to have an extra jar in your refrigerator.

Special equipment:
2 (1 quart) mason jars

Brine:
1½ cups of water
1 cup white vinegar
1 cup apple cider vinegar
2 tablespoons sea salt
4 tablespoons sugar

Pepper mix:
1 pound large carrots, cut into round slices a little less than ¼-inch
1½ pounds white onions, about 4 medium-size onions, sliced into wedges
12 ounces (about 6 to 8) manzano peppers, tail and seeds removed, sliced into wedges
¼ cup extra-virgin olive oil or vegetable oil
1½ teaspoons dry Mexican oregano
6 bay leaves
2 sprigs fresh oregano or marjoram

1. In a medium-size pot, combine all the ingredients for the brine. Bring to a simmer and stir until sugar and salt are dissolved. Add sliced carrots to the simmering brine and cook until al dente, about 2 to 3 minutes. Turn off the heat and set aside to cool off for about 20 minutes.

2. Meanwhile, in a large bowl mix onions, manzano peppers, and extra virgin olive oil. Toss well and set aside.

3. Once brine is lukewarm, add the carrots and brine to the onions and peppers. Crush the dry oregano by rubbing between your fingers, add to the brine and pepper mix, and toss well.

4. Pack a large glass jar with the onion-carrot-pepper mixture. As you fill them, add 3 bay leaves to each jar, along with 1 oregano sprig for each jar. Pack down well, then add brine to each jar. It should be enough to fill up the two jars. Clean the sides of the rim and attach and tighten the lids. Shake them well and place them in the refrigerator. They will be ready to eat in 3 hours, but it's best to leave them overnight. They will get better with time, and they will keep for about 3 to 4 weeks . . . if you can resist!

Verduras en Escabeche
Escabeche-Pickled Vegetables

Escabeche is one of many pickled recipes the Spaniards introduced to Mexico after having borrowed them from the Arabs and Persians. It has many variations. In Mexico it is more commonly served with seafood, fish, or pork. And the well-known street food, "the torta" (the equivalent of the American sandwich), is almost always accompanied by pickled jalapeños, carrots, and onions. Escabeche can be a simple informal appetizer with a beer on the side.

This escabeche vegetable medley is the "supporting cast" I crave when I'm eating a taco, enchiladas, or antojitos Mexicanos. It's a bright, tangy, sweet, crunchy, spicy mix. Please don't limit yourself to this cast of ingredients; cauliflower, green beans, beets, or other vegetables can be included. The proportion of chiles and vegetables is up to you; just consider that the more chiles you include, the spicier the vegetables will be.

This is a refrigerator pickling method and it's best to let it marinate overnight. It will last in the refrigerator for about 4 to 6 weeks (if you let it).

Makes about 6 (8-ounce) jars or one large (48-ounce) jar

½ cup sunflower oil, grapeseed oil, or any mild oil
1 pound white pearl onions, peeled, and halved if larger
1 to 2 heads garlic, depending on size, halved
6 to 8 fresh jalapeños, cut into ¼-inch round slices or cut in half lengthwise
4 to 6 carrots, cut in ¼-inch thick round slices, blanched and drained
1 pound little red new potatoes, cut in halves and cooked al dente
1 pound white button or cremini mushrooms, cut in halves

Brine:
1 cup apple cider vinegar or rice vinegar
1 cup white vinegar
2 cups water
1 tablespoon sea salt
¼ to ½ cup of white sugar
8 bay leaves
8 sprigs fresh thyme or 1 teaspoon dry thyme
8 sprigs fresh oregano or 1 teaspoon dry oregano
6 sprigs fresh marjoram or ½ teaspoon dry marjoram
1 tablespoon black peppercorns

1. In a large pot, add the oil and sauté the pearl onions and garlic for about 2 to 3 minutes. Add the jalapeños and sauté for 1 minute until bright green. Add the carrots, potatoes, and mushrooms, and toss well. (If you are adding any other vegetables, like cauliflower or green beans, this is the time to add them.) Cook for 2 to 3 more minutes, remove from heat, and set aside.

2. In a separate medium-size pot, add vinegar, water, salt, and sugar. Bring to a simmer until sugar dissolves. Once the sugar dissolves, turn off the heat, wait 3 minutes, and add all the fresh and dry herbs and black peppercorns. Then cover the pot and let the herbs steep for 5 more minutes.

3. Add the still warm vinegar solution to the vegetable pot, turn off the heat, remove from stove, and let it rest until it cools down. Once cooled, fill up sterilized glass jars, place them into refrigerator, and give them a little shake every now and then to keep the juices and vegetables well distributed.

Note: These escabeche-pickled vegetables get better with time. It takes at least 2 to 3 days before they are ready to eat. Keep jars in the refrigerator, or use a canning or pickling technique to seal them, and keep them in the pantry in small batches to use later.

Street Snacks

Mexicans are true snack aficionados at heart. From early in the morning to late at night you can find some sort of delicious impromptu treats along the streets and roads in little towns or large cities. From the outside of the churches and in the mercados to street markets, plazas, and office buildings, the snacks are part of our food culture. Mouthwatering street snacks sneak up on you when you least expect them. Street vendors sell churros, paletas, ice cream, toasted pepitas and nuts, roasted sweet potatoes, and calabaza en tacha (page 248). Every city, town, and province has its own style. Offerings include fresh cucumber, jícama, watermelon, huge mangoes on a stick, pineapple, oranges, and other seasonal fruits, either combined or sold individually with lots of lime juice, chile powder, and sea salt. Hungry pedestrians can often be found snacking on kettle-cooked potato chips, guasanas, boiled peanuts, toasted peanuts, elotes (corn on the cob), and esquites. In Mexico, there is always a seasonal street snack waiting for you.

✣ ✣ ✣

Papas Fritas en Cazo de Cobre — *Copper Pot Potato Chips*   232

Chile Para Papas — *Chile Sauce for Potato Chips*   234

Chile Pasilla en Polvo — *Pasilla Chili Powder*   234

Elotes Asados — *Charred Street Corn*   235

Esquites — *Mexican Street Corn Kernels*   236

Cacahuates Chile-Ajo — *Chile-Garlic Peanuts*   238

Guasanas al Vapor — *Steamed Fresh Young Chickpeas*   239

Papas Fritas en Cazo de Cobre
Copper Pot Potato Chips

Santa Clara del Cobre in the state of Michoacán is a little town known worldwide for their copper craftsmanship. The people there have dedicated their lives to making beautiful jewelry, kitchen tools, cups, pots, pans, cutlery, and platters. They have passed down their knowledge through generations. The cooks and street vendors of Michoacán use these famous copper pots to make carnitas and street snacks like potato chips. The way that copper transfers the heat, and the flavor and color that cooking in these pots give foods, is unique.

These potato chips are a labor of love. The oil has to be at the right temperature and the pot large enough to have space to cook evenly. Done right, you have the most delicate, paper-thin, crunchy potato chips. I know you can buy "kettle" chips at the store, but it doesn't compare to making them fresh at home for a special celebration.

Serves 4 to 6

Special equipment:
Copper pot that holds 2 to 3 quarts (if you don't have copper pot, use a deep cast-iron or heavy enamelware pot)
Mandolin
Frying thermometer
Stainless steel spider strainer
Cooling rack
Brown paper bags or newspaper

32 to 48 ounces (1 liter) peanut oil*
Sea salt
4 to 5 yellow wax potatoes, washed, well scrubbed, and peeled
Lime juice, for garnish
Hot chile sauce, for garnish (recipe below)

1. Place copper pot on a large burner of a gas stove or portable gas burner if cooking in open air. Place the thermometer in the copper pot, making sure it is well attached. Add the oil and sea salt and warm up slowly and gradually.*

2. While the oil heats, peel the potatoes, wash them, and then pat them dry with a kitchen towel. Using a mandolin (and a protective mesh glove), set the blade to about $1/16$-inch (about 1 mm). Slice the potatoes thin enough to almost see through but thick enough not to tear apart. Slice one potato at a time to fry in small batches. If you slice all potatoes at once, they will oxidize and turn brown.

3. When the thermometer in the pot reads 360°F, you are ready to start frying. Being really careful, add the potato slices one at a time, trying not to clump them. Move around so the potatoes do not fall in one spot and overlap.

4. Using a stainless steel spider strainer, gently move potatoes around until they have ruffled edges, look and sound crispy, and turn to a light golden color. Use the strainer to remove them from the oil, gently tap the strainer on the edge of the pot to allow extra oil to drip off into the pot, and transfer the potatoes to a cooling rack set up with brown bags or newspaper underneath to absorb the extra oil. Sprinkle on some extra fine sea salt immediately.

5. Once the oil heats back up to 360°F, repeat the same process until you are done with all the potatoes. Turn the heat off and allow the oil to cool in the pot until safe to remove from the burner.

6. Drizzle potato chips with a squeeze of lime juice, sea salt, and some hot sauce. If possible, serve and eat them while they are slightly warm. When they are this freshly made, the only other thing you need is an ice-cold beer.

*WARNING: Hot, frying oil should never be left unattended or accessible to children (or most adults) in any way, ever. Before frying these potatoes, have all your tools and ingredients prepared and handy. The best way to avoid burns and fires is to stay with the hot oil and concentrate on your cooking procedures. Afterward, monitor the hot oil until safely cooled before leaving it unattended.

Chile Pasilla en Polvo
Pasilla Chile Powder

This chile powder is addictive. When sprinkled onto juicy fruit, corn on the cob, or esquites, along with a generous squeeze of lime juice, it's smoky, spicy, and salty. Just thinking about it makes my mouth water. Feel free to double or triple the recipe and keep it in a small airtight jar for future spicy sparks.

Makes about ¼ cup

2 pasilla chiles
1 teaspoon cooking oil
1 tablespoon whole dry pequin chiles
1 teaspoon fine sea salt

Using scissors, cut the pasilla chiles open, discard the stems, and save the seeds. In a small pan pour the oil and add the sliced pasillas, seeds, and the piquins. Toast the chiles over medium-low heat until the seeds are brown and the pasilla takes a deep burgundy color. A fragrant aroma will permeate the kitchen. Remove from pan and place them on a plate to cool. Once they are completely cooled, put the toasted chiles and sea salt in a small mortar or spice grinder and grind to a medium-fine powder. Put in a little dish and it is ready to use. Keep leftovers in an airtight container.

Chile Para Papas
Chile Sauce for Potato Chips

2 tablespoons chile powder, something mild like Anaheim or guajillo, or usually sold as chile para fruta (chile powder for fruit); just make sure it does not contain salt
¼ teaspoon fine sea salt
2 tablespoons vinegar-based Mexican hot sauce, like Valentina or Cholula
2 to 3 tablespoons water

In a small glass jar, combine all the ingredients, close with the jar lid on tight, and shake until all ingredients are mixed. Use a spoon to drizzle this sauce over the potato chips.

Elotes Asados
Charred Street Corn

Another great way to prepare Mexican street corn is to slowly char the ears of corn over wood or natural charcoal. In Mexico they are also known as elotes tatemados. This charring gives the kernels a different texture and a depth of flavor. I love the flavor of charred corn, but sometimes the corn can get a little dry. My trick to prevent the corn from drying out is to baste it with a solution of sea salt and water as it chars over the fire. As you baste the ears of corn, the kernels stay moist and as the water evaporates it leaves a salty crust that seasons the corn and complements the flavor of the char.

Once they are charred and ready to eat, the only thing you need to add to this corn is a squeeze of a juicy lime and some chile powder or hot sauce.

Special equipment:
1 hot grill with natural charcoal or a wood fire and a rack

4 to 6 ears of white corn
2 cups water
3 teaspoons sea salt
Limes
Pasilla chile powder (page 234)

1. Pull back all the corn leaves on each ear of corn, and tie them up. Remove all the corn silk and wash the ears gently. Place all the ears in a bucket of water and soak the corn for 30 minutes. This will help keep them hydrated.

2. Prepare the salty solution by diluting the sea salt into 2 cups of warm water. Keep it in a glass jar and set aside.

3. Meanwhile, prepare your grill, light the fire, and allow it to burn down until you have gentle medium-warm coals, no large flames. Place the corn over the grill and leave the leafy parts hanging off the edge of the grill so these parts can be handled as you rotate the corn. Regularly baste each ear of corn with the salty solution and rotate every 30 seconds or so to provide the corn with an even char. Cook for 5 to 7 minutes.

4. When they are ready, transfer to a platter and serve with lime wedges, chile paste, crema, queso, or straight up, enjoying the flavor of salty corn.

Esquites
Mexican Street Corn Kernels

Suddenly the whole world is falling for Mexican street corn. Why? Because it is so scrumptious and appetizing. For us Mexicans, this is usually not a snack we make at home; it's the perfect excuse to go out in the evening to find a street vendor (elotero). I remember as a child hearing the little bell and the loud voice of the elotero man around 7 p.m. each night: "Haaaay Eloooteeees y tamales de elooteee!" And I would run out to get a warm elote snack.

Esquites is corn that has been sliced off the fresh ears and cooked in a pot of water and sea salt. They are served in a disposable cup topped with crema or mayonnaise, queso fresco, or cotija enchilado, chile powder, chile paste or hot sauce, sea salt, and fresh lime juice, and they are eaten with a spoon. It is almost half a meal on its own. In Mexico City, esquites are often seasoned with fresh epazote and chiles de árbol. In Texcoco, esquites are served with bone marrow, a delicious gourmet variation offered by an old man named Josué who has owned a street stand for more than 40 years. You can stand in line for an hour and a half for his esquite delicacy.

In Guadalajara, Jalisco, the city I'm from, esquites are known as *elote de vaso*, corn in a cup. Fresh ears of corn are boiled in their tender green husks with some sea salt. They are sliced and served with some of the liquid in which they were cooked to enhance the corn flavor, then served with the classic toppings. And since Jalisco has a great milk industry, crema Mexicana is often used (instead of the more common mayonnaise), along with queso fresco or cotija fresco enchilado. I crave these esquites during corn season August through November.

We usually use white corn in Mexico. It is less sweet and a little more starchy than the yellow sweet corn in the USA, making the snack more savory. So try to find white corn if possible. Esquites are easier to eat and less messy than whole ears of corn. Serve in glass jars or cups, and set up all the ingredients on the table so people can prepare as they like.

Serves 4 to 6

10 to 12 large ears of white corn in green husks
8 to 10 cups water, enough to cover the corn
2 teaspoons sea salt
1 cup crema
1 to 2 cups queso fresco, crumbled, or queso cotija enchilado, finely grated
4 to 6 limes, cut in halves
Sea salt
Pasilla chile powder (page 234) or your favorite hot sauce

1. Remove the first couple husk layers of each ear of corn, leaving only the lightest green husk. These husks will add a touch of flavor when cooked. In a large pot, place the ears, sea salt, and enough water to cover. Bring to a boil, reduce the temperature, and simmer for about 1 hour. Turn off the heat and set them aside until they are cool enough to handle. Save about half the water in which the corn cooked. Peel the husks from the corn and remove the corn silk.

2. In a large bowl, place a small upside-down bowl securely in the middle. Place an ear of corn vertically on top of the upside-down bowl and slice off the corn kernels. This setup will contain all the kernels without making a confetti mess. When all corn kernels are sliced, place them in a pot with the reserved water, reheat, and keep them warm until serving.

3. To serve, place all the toppings on the table, and then carefully place the warm pot on the table. Using a ladle, serve corn kernels with a bit of the water in which they were cooked. Encourage your guests to customize their own esquites. I like mine with lots of crema, queso, a good squeeze of lime, and two or three pinches of my chile pasilla powder.

Cacahuates Chile-Ajo
Chile-Garlic Peanuts

These delicious, toasted, spicy peanuts are the perfect *botana*, a little afternoon snack. We make them on a weekend afternoon to serve with a cold beer or refreshing agua fresca. The peanuts can be toasted on a comal and slightly charred or panfried in a little oil. The combination of chile de árbol, garlic, and sea salt give the peanuts the right amount of seasoning to make them irresistible. Make a double batch and once they are cool, save them in an airtight jar for impromptu snacking.

Makes 4 cups

1 tablespoon safflower or avocado oil
4 to 6 large cloves garlic
6 dry chiles de árbol
4 cups large premium raw peanuts, shelled
1 teaspoon fine sea salt

On a comal or in a cast-iron pan, warm up the oil over medium-low heat. Add garlic cloves, and chiles de árbol. Toast until the chiles are dark red and the garlic cloves are golden brown. Remove chiles and garlic cloves and add the peanuts. Shake the pan and toss peanuts constantly with a wood spatula until they change color and get toasty and fragrant. Lower the heat. Meanwhile, in a small mortar, crush one of the toasted chiles. Mix in 1 teaspoon of fine sea salt and continue crushing until finely ground. Sprinkle this spicy sea salt mixture over the peanuts while they are warm. Toss well and transfer to a flat ceramic platter to cool off. Once cool, serve them in a ceramic bowl with some of the toasted chiles de árbol and garlic. Add a few wedges of lime and a cold beer or agua fresca.

Note: If you want them more garlicky, slice a whole garlic head equator-wise and experience the marvelous aroma!

Guasanas al Vapor
Steamed Fresh Young Chickpeas

Another delicacy of street botanas is guasanas, the Mexican edamame. Guasanas are green baby garbanzo beans that are cut early while still fresh. Big steamer pots of this snack can be found around the streets or plazas of Mexico on the weekends. The steamed beans are sold in newspaper cones or plastic bags, seasoned with a squeeze of lime juice, sea salt, and hot chile sauce. Guasanas are eaten with bare hands like edamame: Squeeze the outer pod and suck out the tender chickpea inside. The salty juice inside makes this little botana sing. You can find these little, green chickpea pods at Hispanic markets in the produce section.

Serves 4

½ to 1 pound fresh chickpeas (guasanas)
½ teaspoon fine sea salt
2 limes, cut in wedges
Hot sauce

Thoroughly rinse the guasanas and remove any debris or squashed beans. In a large steamer pot, place the guasanas and sprinkle about ½ teaspoon sea salt over them. Cover with a lid, bring pot to a boil, and steam for about 15 to 18 minutes. Turn off heat and taste one. They should be al dente and taste sweet and juicy, somewhere between a pea and an edamame. Transfer to a large bowl and serve with wedges of lime and hot sauce. They taste better while slightly warm.

Aguas Frescas

Aguas frescas are a daily part of Mexican life. *Frescas* means "fresh." These drinks should be sweetened judiciously, emphasizing the sweetness and quality of the ingredients. Aguas frescas are always good drinks to prepare for celebrations and gatherings. Two or three flavors will please all kinds of crowds, from little niños to uncles and grandmas.

The following recipes are simple aguas frescas that use fruits in season for the months of October through December in Mexico. Some of them are variations of classics that you can prepare all year, like the "Oat-chata" in which oats replace rice for a heartier flavor. In my hibiscus agua fresca, I use a stick of cinnamon to balance the acidity. I always use dry whole hibiscus flowers because they yield the best flavor and can be purchased in the bulk section or prepackaged around the produce area in Mexican markets here in the States. You can find mandarin oranges everywhere during those months in Mexico and in the United States you can find this kind of citrus in the fall. Mandarin agua fresca is aromatic, light, fresh, and full of citrus flavor. It's one of my favorites. Among my favorites, a bizarre flavor: banana, one of my brother's and my favorite agua fresca flavors when we were little. Here are a few recommendations when making agua fresca:

- The secret of good agua fresca is ripe fruit in season for the best fruity aromatic flavor. Also, when fruit is ripe, it is naturally sweeter so you don't need to add a lot of sugar.
- Always taste the fruit before sweetening the water. Fruits vary in sweetness and flavor, and this will help you calculate how much sugar is needed.
- Add a pinch of salt to brighten up the flavor of the fruit.
- If you want to use other sweeteners in your agua fresca, like coconut sugar, agave nectar, honey, or raw sugar cane like piloncillo, consider that some of these are stronger or weaker than white granulated sugar, so adjust the amount of sweetener accordingly.
- When making agua fresca on hot days, leave the fruit concentration a notch stronger and sweeter that you would normally drink, since ice will tend to water down the flavors. Chill the agua fresca at least 1 to 2 hours before serving, to further prevent dilution.
- Make a larger batch than you think you will need. And drink with reckless abandon!

❈ ❈ ❈

Agua Fresca de Jamaica con Canela — *Hibiscus and Canela Agua Fresca*   244

Agua Fresca de Sandía con Hierbabuena — *Watermelon and Mint Agua Fresca*   244

Agua Fresca de Melón Chino — *Cantaloupe Melon Agua Fresca*   244

Agua Fresca de Mandarina — *Mandarin Orange Agua Fresca*   244

Agua Fresca de Guayaba — *Guava Agua Fresca*   245

Agua Fresca de Plátano — *Banana Agua Fresca*   245

Agua Fresca de Avena — *Oat-chata Agua Fresca*   245

Agua Fresca de Chia con Limón y Hierbabuena — *Chia, Mint, and Lime Agua Fresca*   245

Agua Fresca de Jamaica con Canela
Hibiscus and Canela Agua Fresca

Canela and hibiscus have a special synergy. It is not a very common combination to find but is my personal favorite. The fragrant and floral hibiscus flavor is incredible and reinvigorating. I like my hibiscus agua fresca lightly sweetened. I often keep a concentrated hibiscus syrup in the refrigerator to add to sparkling water or to make a small batch of agua fresca for lunch or dinner. Always buy dried hibiscus flowers in bulk at the produce section of Hispanic supermarkets. They are more flavorful and make the best ruby-red concentrated hibiscus agua fresca.

**Serves about 6 to 8,
depending how thirsty your guests are!**

½ cup dry hibiscus flowers
4-inch stick canela
¾ cups turbinado sugar, piloncillo, or ½ cup agave syrup
10 cups cold water

In a small colander, rinse the dry hibiscus flowers. In a small pot, bring 4 cups of water to a boil, add hibiscus flowers and crushed cinnamon stick, and slow simmer for 20 minutes. Remove from stove, cover with a lid, and let it steep for 30 minutes. In a large glass pitcher, sieve the hibiscus flowers while the solution is still warm, and stir in sugar until it dissolves. Place the flowers back in the pot and add 1 to 2 cups of water to give a second rinse and extract the remaining flavor from them. Discard flowers. Add the rest of the cold water and stir well. Taste and adjust sugar. Serve over ice in a large glass.

Agua Fresca de Sandía con Hierbabuena
Watermelon and Mint Agua Fresca

6 to 8 cups cubed ripe watermelon, seeds removed
1 to 2 sprigs mint
½ cup turbinado sugar or ¼ cup agave syrup
8 cups cold water

In a blender, place watermelon, mint leaves, 2 cups of water and ½ cup of sugar. Blend until smooth. Add this to a glass pitcher. Then add the remaining 6 cups of water. Taste to adjust sugar. Refrigerate. Serve with lots of ice in a tall glass and garnish with a sprig of mint or a piece of watermelon.

Agua Fresca de Melón Chino
Cantaloupe Melon Agua Fresca

If you are tossing the fleshy innards and seeds of a cantaloupe when making agua fresca, you are wasting the best part. Part of the flavorful essence of the melon is here. I like to blend all the seeds and innards along with some of the melon, then sieve this cantaloupe puree and add to the agua fresca for the best concentrated floral and fruity melon flavor. This method only works with cantaloupe and honeydew. I like to use honey or agave in cantaloupe agua fresca to enhance its floral flavor qualities. You could also use regular turbinado sugar.

½ medium ripe cantaloupe melon, including the seeds and fleshy innards
¼ cup of honey or agave syrup
8 cups cold water

Cut melon in half and scoop the seeds and innards of one half into a blender. Peel the melon skin off, cut melon into large chunks, and place half of the chunks into the blender along with 1 cup of water and honey. Then blend. Sieve this melon puree into a glass pitcher, scraping with a spoon to help the juices come through. Add the rest of the water and stir well. Taste and adjust sweetness if necessary, and refrigerate. Serve over ice in a tall glass.

Agua Fresca de Mandarina
Mandarin Orange Agua Fresca

Juice of 2 pounds of mandarin oranges, about 16 ounces of juice
Zest and segments of 2 small mandarin oranges
½ cup of turbinado sugar or ¼ cup agave syrup
6 cups water

In a large glass pitcher, add 6 cups of lukewarm water and dissolve the sugar or agave. Add mandarin juice and zest, and stir well. Taste and adjust sweetness if necessary. Refrigerate. Serve over ice in a tall glass, and add some mandarin segments as garnish.

Agua Fresca de Guayaba
Guava Agua Fresca

½ pound fresh guavas, cut in halves, end knobs removed
⅓ cup turbinado sugar or ¼ cup plus 1 tablespoon agave syrup
8 cups cold water

Place guavas, sugar, and 1 cup of water into a blender, and blend until a smooth puree. If the seeds did not blend, sieve the puree. In a large glass pitcher, dissolve sugar into 7 cups of water, add guava puree, and stir well. Taste and adjust sweetness if necessary and refrigerate. Serve in a tall glass over ice. Sprinkle some cinnamon for garnish.

Note: Guavas tend to be very sour because of a high level of vitamin C, so guava agua fresca might need a little more sugar than the rest of the aguas frescas.

Agua Fresca de Plátano
Banana Agua Fresca

This agua fresca is not very common, but it is surprisingly delicious and refreshing. Bananas are available year-round, making it a convenient and delicious fruit to showcase. It was one of my brother Manuel's and my favorite childhood agua fresca flavors. We ordered it every time grandma Ana would take us for lunch at a restaurant in Guadalajara called Las Vías. It brings me lots of good memories, and agua fresca de plátano will definitely be something to look forward to in my ofrenda.

2 medium bananas, ripe with 70 to 80% brown stains on skin
2 medium bananas, soft ripe with yellow skins with no brown spots
1 cup whole milk (or soy milk)
7 cups cold water
½ teaspoon vanilla extract
¼ cup turbinado sugar or 2 tablespoons agave syrup

Place peeled bananas, milk, 1 cup water, vanilla, and sugar into a blender and puree until smooth. In a large glass pitcher, combine banana puree and the remaining 6 cups of water, and stir well. Taste and adjust sweetness if necessary and refrigerate. Serve in a tall glass over ice.

Agua Fresca de Avena
Oat-chata Agua Fresca

¾ cup oats (old fashioned or quick oats)
2 cups almond milk, whole milk, or soy milk
2-inch stick canela, crushed
½ teaspoon vanilla extract
Pinch salt
½ cup turbinado sugar or ¼ cup agave syrup
6 cups cold water

Place oats, milk, canela, vanilla, salt, and sugar into a blender and puree until smooth. Add 2 cups of water and blend until smooth. In a large glass pitcher, combine oats puree and the remaining 4 cups of water and stir well. Taste and adjust sweetness if necessary and refrigerate. Serve in a tall glass over ice.

Agua Fresca de Chia con Limón y Hierbabuena
Chia, Mint, and Lime Agua Fresca

8 cups water
½ to ¾ cup turbinado sugar or ¼ to ½ cup agave syrup
½ cup chia seeds
1 cup lime juice
10 to 12 limes, plus more to garnish
6 sprigs mint, plus more to garnish

In a large glass pitcher, add 8 cups of lukewarm water and dissolve the sugar. Add chia seeds and lime juice and stir well. Taste and adjust sweetness if necessary and refrigerate for at least 3 to 4 hours to let the chia seeds bloom. Stir vigorously before serving. Serve over ice in a tall glass with some lime slices and a mint sprig for garnish.

The best piloncillo cones come from Tlaltetela, Veracruz.

Sweets, Preserves, and Desserts

In Mexico, the wide variety of desserts reflects the diversity of fruit used to prepare them. These confections and desserts bear Spanish, Arab, and French influence. The Spanish contributed the combination of piloncillo with spices and aromatics. Spanish nuns used old-world kitchen methods to adapt recipes using seasonal Mexican produce. These adaptations resulted in confections like braised sweet pumpkin, a variety of candied fruits, fruit rolls, and preserves, all part of the traditional Mexican confections and desserts we know today.

Due to their concentrated flavor, these fruit desserts are often served in small portions after the main meal of the day, or as a merienda or light dinner. A piece of cheese like manchego or asadero is often served with fruit *ates* (pastes) and preserves. Fruit rolls are also made of the ates, and are filled with condensed milk, shredded toasted coconut and nuts. A cup of unsweetened cinnamon tea, coffee, or a glass of milk is always the best way to enjoy a delicious, slightly warm piece of calabaza en tacha (sweet braised pumpkin) or camotes enmielados (braised sweet potato).

❈ ❈ ❈

Calabaza En Tacha — *Syrup and Cinnamon Braised Pumpkin* 248

Guayabate — *Guava Preserves* 252

Camotes Envinados — *Rum and Orange Glazed Sweet Potatoes* 253

Palanquetas de Nuez y Pepitas — *Mexican Pecan and Pumpkin Seed Pralines* 254

Obleas con Miel, Sal de Mar y Pepitas
Mexican Wafers with Honey, Sea Salt, and Toasted Pumpkin Seeds 255

Alegrías de Amaranto y Miel — *Amaranth and Honey Treats* 257

Calaveras de Amaranto y Miel — *Amaranth and Honey Skulls* 259

Buñuelos 260

Flan de Cempasúchil — *Marigold and Caramel Flan* 267

Calabaza En Tacha
Syrup and Cinnamon Braised Pumpkin

There are few Mexican desserts more iconic than fruit that has been cooked or crystallized in piloncillo. Calabaza en tacha is one of them—pumpkin braised in piloncillo, cinnamon, and aromatics. The dark syrup coats the pumpkin flesh, which is soft and buttery with a delicious concentration of caramel and cinnamon flavor. From street vendors to convenience stores, fairs, and plazas, this pumpkin is everywhere in Mexico during the fall.

Calabaza de Castilla is the pumpkin variety commonly used for this preparation. It has fleshy, floral insides, and almost every part of the pumpkin can be used. The seeds are toasted, the leaves of the plant and flowers are cooked and used in stews, and the flowers are used in quesadillas. The varietal I used for this recipe is kabocha squash, which has a flavor and texture that closely resembles Calabaza de Castilla. It's easy to find and the modest sizes of these pumpkins are also more reasonable to make at home, especially when preparing just a few servings.

My favorite way to eat calabaza en tacha is the way my Grandpa Guillermo used to eat it, first dunking a couple of spoonfuls of the pumpkin into milk. He called this his "burrito canelo." I don't know why he called it that, but I know it's delicious! You end up with caramel-colored milk with the most delicious sweet cinnamon pumpkin flavor. Guillermo never had the chance to meet any of his grandchildren, so my grandma Margarita often shared these kinds of stories with us. It was her way of keeping his memories alive. So every time I make calabaza en tacha, I eat it "burrito-canelo-style" at least once.

Make a large batch and share with friends, family, and neighbors, or freeze in small quantities to add to cold blended drinks, like smoothies. Calabaza en tacha is also great to use as filling for empanadas, pies, and bread.

Makes about 12 to 14 pumpkin pieces

2 kabocha squash (around 6 pounds total)

Syrup:
1½ cups water
3 (3-inch) sticks canela
6 clove buds
½ teaspoon sea salt
3 piloncillo cones, about 8 ounces total
½ teaspoon baking soda
Salted, toasted pepitas, for garnish
Flake salt, for garnish (optional)

1. Cut the pumpkins along the equator to separate the top half from the bottom. Scrape out innards until smooth and remove seeds. Carefully, using a sharp knife, cut each pumpkin half into triangular wedges and remove the hard stem. Lightly sprinkle baking soda over the pumpkin flesh.

2. In a small pot, add water, canela, cloves, salt, and piloncillo, and slow simmer until piloncillo is dissolved. Remove from heat and set aside.

3. In a large, wide pot, place the triangular pieces of pumpkin skin-side down in a single layer. Pour some of the syrup over the top and add one of the canela sticks, broken into pieces. Place a second layer of squash and pour extra syrup. In the third and final layer, face the pumpkin skin-side up and pour on the rest of the syrup. Cover with a lid and slow simmer for about 35 to 40 minutes.

4. When done, the pumpkin should be soft but not mushy, and syrup should have a thicker consistency. Remove pot from stove and let it sit uncovered for 30 minutes to cool. When the pumpkin is cool enough to handle, transfer into a baking pan or tray and arrange in a single layer. Pour the rest of the syrup on top of the pumpkin so it keeps absorbing the flavors while still warm.

To serve: sprinkle with toasted pepitas and sea salt flakes, and serve with a cold glass of milk.

Notes: This recipe is good for 2 small to medium pumpkins, and it can be easily divided in half. Leftover pumpkin can be saved in containers in the freezer to be used in breads, as filling for pies and empanadas, in flavored atoles, and as other fall preparations.

For atole de calabaza (pumpkin atole): *Prepare one recipe of atole blanco (page 317) and add about 1 cup of calabaza en tacha flesh or puree. Stir well into the atole and let it warm up for 10 minutes, stirring often. Taste, and adjust sugar if necessary. This is one of the most delicious ways to use the calabaza en tache leftovers.*

Guayabate
Guava Preserves

Guava season is October to February in Mexico. This fragrant, floral, and citrusy fruit is often made into atoles, added to syrups, or used for buñuelos to brighten up the flavors. Guava is a little fruit, often misunderstood because of its hard seeds and strong flavor. The most common guavas in Mexico are pink and yellow. Both are high in vitamin C and in the fall are often made into confections called *ates*, which are firm, sweet, fruit blocks made of sugar and fresh fruit pulp high in pectin, like from guavas, quince, and arrayan (a fruit from a Mexican myrtle tree). Ates are also made into jelly rolls and sweet preserves.

This version of guava preserve or dulce de guayaba is on the loose side, and can be eaten with a spoon in small amounts. Despite the consistency, my grandma Margarita used to call it guayabate and place it in glass jars in the refrigerator and serve it cold in small amounts for all the family.

Makes about 1 (16-ounce) jar of preserves

1 pound (½ kg) guavas, pink or yellow, washed
1 cup water, divided
Pinch sea salt
½ to 1 piloncillo cone (about 8 ounces)*
3 whole allspice
2 clove buds
1 (3-inch) stick canela

* When making fruit preserves, always taste your fruit first. If guavas are too sweet, add just ½ cone of piloncillo. If they are too acidic, use the whole cone.

1. Slice guavas in half lengthwise. Using a melon baller, remove the seeds. Place seeds into a pot with ½ cup of water and a pinch of salt and bring to a simmer until all the seeds are loose. Sieve this fleshy water, discard seeds, and set aside.

2. In a medium heavy-bottom pot, add ½ cup water, piloncillo, allspice, cloves, and cinnamon stick. Bring to a simmer until piloncillo has dissolved. Add the sliced guavas and the fleshy guava water you sieved. Toss all this until well combined. Bring to a low simmer, cover, and cook for 8 to 10 minutes. Then uncover and let simmer for another 2 to 3 more minutes until the syrup starts to reduce. Stir very gently just a few times to avoid breaking up the fruit. Remove from the stove and let the preserves cool down.

Serve warm or cold. Garnish with some toasted pecans or almonds, or over ice cream.

Camotes Envinados
Rum and Orange Glazed Sweet Potatoes

Inspired by fall flavors and a special rum-like drink made in Michoacán called Charanda, I offer a variation on sweet potatoes. We tried Charanda while visiting for the celebration of Día de Muertos, and I decided to add a good kick to a delicious root vegetable.

Charanda is a spirit distilled from sugarcane and aged in oak barrels made from the wood found on a hill called *Cerro de la Charanda*. To the Purepechas (the indigenous people from the Michoacán area), Charanda means *Tierra roja*, or red soil. The trees that grow on this hill give this rum its characteristic reddish color and its delicious buttery vanilla flavor.

I think braising with rum to flavor and infuse these sweet potatoes creates a delicious result. Use the most tender, organic (if possible) sweet potatoes you can find. Charanda can be ordered online, or use a good spiced rum.

Serves 4 to 6

1 cup of water
1 (3-inch) stick canela, crushed
1 piloncillo cone
2 pounds tender sweet potatoes, scrubbed, washed, and pricked with a fork
6 clove buds
Peel of one Valencia orange
½ cup Charanda rum añejo
2 tablespoons butter
Sea salt

1. In a small pot, add water, canela, and piloncillo, and bring to a slow simmer. Cook until the piloncillo has dissolved.

2. In a baking pan lined with parchment paper, place the sweet potatoes and insert cloves into them. Add pieces of orange peel, pour in the piloncillo syrup over the sweet potatoes, dot them with butter, and add the rum.

3. Braise at 375°F for 30 minutes or until a knife is inserted easily and skin looks wrinkly and crisp. Right before taking them out of the oven, broil for 5 minutes as you baste them using the bottom of the pan syrup to glaze the tops. Serve warm, and sprinkle on some sea salt and a spoonful of the rum glaze.

Note: If you buy organic sweet potatoes, leave the skin on; if not, peeling them is recommended.

Palanquetas de Nuez y Pepitas
Mexican Pecan and Pumpkin Seed Pralines

The word *palanqueta* comes from the Nahuatl word *papaquili*, which means happy or joyful, a perfect name since those are the emotions inspired by the flavor of these Mexican pralines. These cloudy clusters of pecans, pepitas (pumpkin seeds), peanuts, or almonds are a classic candy you can get at fairs and from street vendors in the plazas around any holiday and, of course, at the celebrations for Día de Muertos. This version of pecan palanquetas is from the small city Ciudad Guzmán in the state of Jalisco. What makes them special is how sugar is mixed with milk and brought to a slow rolling boil to achieve a buttery, soft, crumbly cluster. The combination of roasted nuts, milk, and sugar melt in your mouth as you eat them and leave you craving more. I added a little cinnamon and vanilla for extra flavor. Make them any size you want, from bite-size to four-inch pieces for sharing.

Makes 8 to 12 round 4-inch palanquetas

Special equipment:
Candy thermometer

½ cup whole milk
2 cups sugar
Pinch sea salt
2 tablespoons butter
¼ teaspoon cinnamon powder
¼ teaspoon vanilla extract
1½ cups toasted pecans or roasted pepitas

1. Line two half-sheet baking trays with parchment paper or a nonstick silicone pad. In a medium heavy-bottom pot, place the milk, sugar, and salt. Bring to a rolling simmer, stirring at all times until temperature reaches 228 to 230°F. Using a candy thermometer, it should read below "soft ball" stage. Add butter, cinnamon, vanilla extract, and toasted pecans and stir well for 1 to 2 minutes.

2. Remove from heat and promptly spoon onto the lined baking trays, making 4 to 6 palanquetas in each. Let clusters cool for 20 to 30 minutes. Enjoy!

Note: Store them in an airtight container in a dry place.

Obleas con Miel, Sal de Mar y Pepitas
Mexican Wafers with Honey, Sea Salt, and Toasted Pumpkin Seeds

In Mexican street markets, there is a version of these wafer sandwiches known as *pepitorias*. They are made of two wafers, either whole or folded in half, filled with a thin layer of thick piloncillo syrup or honey, and laboriously decorated with lined-up pepitas, peanuts, toasted amaranth, or nuts all around the perimeter of the wafer. They are colorful and scrumptious. The thin wafers are easy to find in Hispanic supermarkets or Mexican candy shops in the States. My favorite combination of filling is orange-blossom honey with toasted pepitas, and I like to add some flaky sea salt to balance the sweetness and brighten up the flavor. This fun snack is quick and delicious. Don't worry about lining up each pepita; sprinkling them will suffice. These wafers make for a tasty colorful ofrenda on the altar.

1 package thin Mexican wafers (obleas)
2 to 3 tablespoons honey
½ cup toasted or roasted pepitas or sunflower seeds
Sea salt

Drizzle some honey over one wafer. Sprinkle on some pepitas and sea salt. Drizzle a little more honey and add another wafer on top, like if you were making a sandwich. So simple and so delicious.

Alegrías de Amaranto y Miel
Amaranth and Honey Treats

Alegrías translates to "joys." These sweet Mexican snacks date from pre-Hispanic times, when amaranth seeds were used as currency and were found in a wide variety of dishes. One of the most important uses of amaranth seeds were in rituals. The seeds were toasted, puffed, and mixed with honey and sometimes blood to form a dough that was shaped into skulls and god figurines for worship. One important ceremony consisted of creating a large figure resembling their deity, Huitzilopochtli, which was then offered to him and eaten by the people as a symbol of communion with him. To avoid these religious practices, Hernán Cortés prohibited the cultivation and consumption of amaranth on penalty of death. The plants decayed and the people stopped growing them, losing some of the traditional dishes in which these nutritious seeds were used. Amaranth was an essential ingredient in tamales, atoles, and even tortillas. Eventually, the plant was found growing in the wild and reestablished.

Today, amaranth is used as a dietary supplement and in confections like alegrías. Every February since 1971, the town of Santiago Tulyehualco, Xochimilco, Mexico City, has held "La feria de la alegría y el Olivo," the Amaranth Fair. All sorts of food, drinks, and confections made with amaranth are sold and celebrated. During the rest of the year, it is very common to find puffed amaranth in bulk in grocery stores and mercados, and alegrías squares are sold at street markets for a quick snack. During fall, alegrías are made into skull shapes and form part of the sweet array of candies offered on the altars for Day of the Dead.

Alegrías are the Mexican equivalent of marshmallow rice cereal treats and are just as easy to make. They can be shaped with skull molds, into bars, or into rounds using a muffin tin. Dried seed and fruit combinations can be used to decorate and make them taste delicious. These bars are mildly sweet, crunchy, and make for a healthy snack that can be enjoyed all year round.

Makes a 9 x 13-inch pan

Special equipment:
9 x 13-inch rectangular baking mold
2 pieces of parchment paper

¼ cup toasted peanuts
¼ cup toasted and salted pepitas
2 tablespoons chia seeds
½ cup water
1 (8 oz, 123 gr) piloncillo, chopped
½ cup honey
Pinch fine sea salt
1 teaspoon lime juice
½ teaspoon baking soda
4 cups (6 oz) puffed amaranth

*You also can add any of the following: almonds, pecans, pine nuts, raisins, cranberries, or any other diced dry fruit or toasted nuts of your preference.

1. Prepare the mold: Line the inside of the mold with a large piece of parchment paper. Place an even layer of the peanuts, pepitas, and chia seeds on top of the parchment paper.

2. In a heavy-bottom pot, place water and piloncillo. Bring to a simmer and stir until piloncillo is completely dissolved and has no lumps. Add honey and sea salt, stir well, and bring to a simmer again. Once the mixture starts bubbling up, turn off the heat, add lime juice, and stir well. Sprinkle in baking soda and stir well. The consistency of this syrup should be foamy, caramel colored, and create ribbons when stirred with a spatula.

3. Promptly add the puffed amaranth to the piloncillo syrup and stir quickly until well incorporated. While still warm, pour this mixture over the top of the nuts and seeds in the prepared mold. Place a piece of parchment paper on top of the mixture then with a flat cup, or using your fingers, lightly press to make the layer flat and even. I used a flat-bottom measuring cup to flatten the layer, just like when you make marshmallow treats.

4. Let this cool off for about 30 minutes. Unmold and remove the parchment paper. Lightly oil the blade of a sharp knife to prevent stickiness and cut into rectangles or squares.

Note: Alegrías keep best in an airtight container. If made into bars or squares, wrap them individually in waxed paper to keep them crunchy.

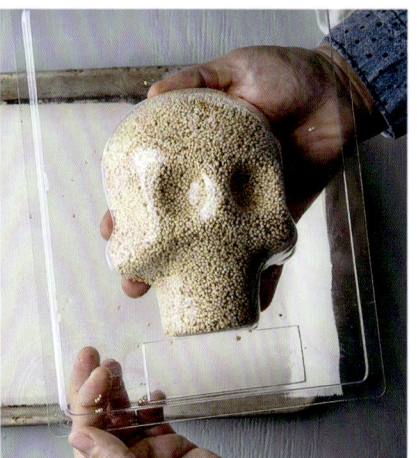

Calaveras de Amaranto y Miel
Amaranth and Honey Skulls

Today, these amaranth skulls are rarely found because they have been replaced by sugar, alfeñique paste, and processed chocolate. I'm not opposed to the new as long as we also remember the traditional. Amaranth puffed seeds are delicious and nutritious. So for the sake of tradition, I want to maintain the practice of using a honey and amaranth concoction. I decorate these skulls with toasted seeds and dried fruits such as pepitas, roasted peanuts, almonds, pecans, raisins, prunes, and dried cranberries. These skulls look and taste more like what the Aztecs would have made, and, in my opinion, are much tastier than the sugar skulls. The amaranth-honey mixture has the texture of marshmallow rice cereal treats. This recipe is also used to make alegrías treats (page 257) that are commonly sold as snacks at fairs on Día de Muertos.

Makes 2 large amaranth skulls

Special equipment:
1 or 2 large skull molds
1 folded paper towel with a few drops of cooking oil

¼ cup water
150 grams piloncillo, grated
½ cup honey
1 teaspoon lime juice
16 ounces puffed amaranth
2 pinches ground canela

1. In a small pot, heat up water and piloncillo and stir until piloncillo dissolves. Add honey and lime juice and bring to a low simmer. Stir constantly until half the liquid has evaporated and it has the consistency of honey. Remove from heat and let the syrup cool down for 2 to 3 minutes.

2. Add the puffed amaranth and gently stir using a wood spatula. Once the amaranth is cool enough to handle, rub your hands with some cooking oil and gently knead the mixture until the syrup is evenly distributed.

3. Promptly fill the molds and press down to get a solid skull. If the dough is too sticky, add more oil to your hands. Level and even out the back of each skull. Place a piece of cardboard behind the mold and flip it over. To help release the mold, tap on the skull forehead and chin. Let the skull dry for about 24 hours. The next day, carefully glue the two skull halves together using some royal icing (page 346).

4. At this point your skull is still fragile but dry enough on the outside to decorate. Use royal icing to glue the seeds onto the face. I used pepitas around the eyes, prunes for the eye cavity, roasted peanuts for the forehead and teeth, two almond halves for the nose, and pecans for the top of the skull.

These skulls are edible within 2 to 3 days, and good to display for more than a month.

Buñuelos

"When Tita felt Pedro's burning gaze on her bare shoulders she understood exactly how the raw dough of a buñuelo must feel when it comes in contact with the oil. The heat that invaded her was so real, that she feared that just like dough, bubbles would break out all over her body. . ."

—From *Like Water for Chocolate*, by Laura Esquivel

Buñuelos are one of the most beloved autumn confections in Mexico. It's hard to resist the thin flaky fried dough covered in warm fruity syrup with a hint of cinnamon and cloves. Spanish nuns would make buñuelos and other confections to sell at Christmastime around churches and posadas. Today buñuelos can be found almost year-round at fairs, street markets, and plazas all over Mexico.

When I was young, my father would take my brother and me to Plaza Santuario in Guadalajara. Outside the church, street stands served all kinds of buñuelos. We would go on a rainy or cold day and sit on wooden benches at narrow tables and watch the "buñuelera" lady breaking huge buñuelos onto a plate and ladling warm syrup over them. When we were served, we had a variety of atoles to choose from. Atole blanco was my favorite because it was unsweetened and a great contrast to the sweetness of the syrup. Warm, sweet and crunchy spoonfuls of buñuelos warmed us. What a delicious indulgence! I highly recommend you pair buñuelos with atole blanco (page 317).

Thin and crisp, buñuelos can range in size from 20 to 40 inches or larger. Expert "buñueleras" have mastered the art of making larger sizes over generations. I have adjusted the recipe to make a more manageable size for the home cook, and I also recommend you try a mini version (buñuelito) that is equally delicious.

Buñuelos can be glazed in syrup or sprinkled with sugar and cinnamon. The very thinnest buñuelos are broken in pieces in a bowl and covered with a light, sweet syrup, to be eaten with a spoon. All three variations are included in this recipe, and you can easily play with the sizes and syrup flavors for variety.

Buñuelos can be served after a meal like a dessert, or as a merienda or a late-afternoon snack, and are best served freshly made. They do not keep too well, maybe one day at the most; they will start getting soggy and a bit stale after two days.

Makes about 14 (7-inch) average size or about 22 (4-inch) minis

1 cup water
6 tomatillo husks
1 pinch sea salt
2 cups plus 1 tablespoon all-purpose flour, sifted
1 tablespoon sugar
½ teaspoon baking powder
1 tablespoon butter, room temperature
1 whole egg, room temperature
½ teaspoon anise seeds, ground (optional)
2 cups (16 oz) grapeseed oil or other frying oil

1. In a small pot, boil water, tomatillo husks, and salt until water is reduced by half. Remove husks, and let water cool until tepid. You should end up with about ½ cup of liquid.

2. In a small bowl, mix flour, sugar, and baking powder until well combined. Add butter, egg, ground anise seeds, and ½ of the tomatillo husk water. Combine all ingredients with your hand, add the rest of the water, and incorporate until a dough ball is formed. Lightly dust a clean surface with flour and knead dough ball for 10–12 minutes until soft and elastic. If dough feels too sticky, sprinkle on some flour until you have moist but not sticky dough. After kneading, do the dough windowpane test* to ensure your dough is kneaded well. Shape dough into a ball, cover with an upside down bowl, and let it rest for 20–30 minutes.

3. Once dough is rested, divide into small balls about the size of a walnut. This size makes about 6 to 7-inch buñuelos. For 4-inch mini buñuelos, make balls the size of half a walnut. Shape each ball and cover with a towel or plastic wrap as you roll the rest of the dough. Let the balls rest for 10–15 more minutes.

4. Using both hands, flatten each ball with your fingers into a flat disk. Gently start stretching the dough into a circle using the tips of your fingers, forming a round disk shape. Rotate the disk as you stretch the dough. Continue until you have a 4-inch round or a 6-inch round depending on the size of the ball. You can also use a rolling pin in the same way you might when making flour tortillas.

5. Place a clean cotton towel on a table. Place the thin round doughs on the towel and cover them with a damp cotton towel to avoid over-drying. Shape the rest of the dough.

6. Once all the dough is shaped, heat the oil to 350°F and fry one buñuelo at a time. It will take about 30–40 seconds per side. When they have blistered and are a golden-brown color on both sides, use tongs to take the buñuelo out of the oil and gently tap it on the side of the pan to remove excess oil. Place on a cooling rack. Fry the rest of them. Watch the oil temperature at all times to avoid burning; this part of the process goes really fast. USE CAUTION when cooking with hot oil; be attentive at all times, use the right equipment like long metal tongs, and use the back burner to avoid oil spattering onto the floor. Keep children out of the kitchen!

Once all the buñuelos are fried, choose any of the following buñuelo styles: thick syrup glaze, light syrup broth, or sugar-canela coating.

Dough windowpane test: If well kneaded, the gluten in the dough will create a stretchy membrane. Stretch a piece of dough as much as you can until it creates a thin membrane that doesn't break. If it breaks easily, the dough needs to be kneaded longer.

Traditionally these buñuelos are called Buñuelos de rodilla, *or knee buñuelos, because once each dough ball was flattened, a damp towel was placed on top of the cook's knee, and the flattened dough was placed over the towel and the roundness of the knee helped shape the buñuelo while stretching it as thin as possible.*

Another technique includes using an inverted bowl to form the dough, but I prefer to stretch the dough with my hands instead. It's easier to feel the dough and to detect the thicker areas I need to stretch more. This produces the thinnest dough and will not flatten the little bubbles you work so hard to create when kneading. This yields a more bubbly and flaky buñuelo.

Variations:

Thick syrup glaze:
¾ cup water
2 cones piloncillo
1 (4-inch) stick canela
4 clove buds
2 guavas, cut in halves
1 pinch of salt

Place everything in a small pot and bring to a low simmer until piloncillo is completely dissolved, cinnamon is fragrant, and fruit is soft. Consistency should look like honey. Set syrup aside to come up to room temperature.

Once buñuelos are fried and cool enough to handle, use a pastry brush to glaze both sides and edges of each buñuelo. Place glazed buñuelos on a rack so they can drip off extra glaze. Once dry, stack them with a piece of parchment paper in between to avoid them sticking to each other.

Light syrup broth:
4 cups water
1 piloncillo cone
1 (6-inch) stick canela
4 clove buds
4 guavas, cut in halves
1 pinch salt
Extra ground canela, for garnish

Place everything in a small pot and bring to a low simmer until piloncillo is completely dissolved, canela is fragrant, and fruit is soft. Consistency should look like a thin sticky broth. Keep warm and set aside.

In a small bowl, break 2 to 3 buñuelos into bite-size pieces, and pour 1 or 2 ladles of syrup over them. Sprinkle some ground canela on top and serve with a spoon. Eat them while they are warm.

Syrup flavor variations: Instead of the guavas, add 1 quince cut in fourths, or 5 dry figs cut in halves, or the zest of ½ orange, or 2 star anise, or 3 inches of sliced fresh ginger, or substitute pomegranate juice for 2 cups of water.

Sugar and canela coated:
½ cup sugar
1 tablespoon ground canela

In a small bowl combine sugar and canela. Sprinkle over both sides of the buñuelos while still warm. Place on a rack to keep them crunchy.

Previous page: Buñuelos in light broth with atole blanco. Top photo: Sugar and canela buñuelos. Recipes are on page 260.

Flan de Cempasúchil
Marigold and Caramel Flan

Flan is a creamy custard dessert that Mexico inherited from the Spaniards and adopted as our own. There are many variations out there. Besides the classic vanilla and caramel flavor, there is orange, dulce de leche, and flan de queso (also known as *flan napolitano*), all equally delicious to me. I wanted to create a flan using one of the symbolic elements of Día de Muertos: the Mexican marigold flower, or cempasúchil. I used the dry petals of one of the edible types of this family of flowers, the calendula, to infuse the milk. The result is a delicate orange-colored flan with the scent of honey and flowers. I made a light golden caramel mild enough not to overwhelm the delicate flavor of the flowers.

The bain-marie technique I use to cook the flan produces the smoothest flan. Placing a cotton kitchen towel between the two pans avoids the contact of metal to metal, which would otherwise bring the milk and egg mixture to a boil too fast, creating unwanted little pearls of egg protein called *segnoritas*. Using this little trick creates a creamy, smooth, and silky flan.

Makes a 10-inch round, 1½-inch-tall flan or an 8-inch round, 2-inch-tall flan

Special equipment:
2 (3 to 4-inch-tall) aluminum cake pans to be nested (*either a 10-inch and a 12-inch or an 8-inch and a 12-inch, depending on the size of flan you want to make*)

½ cup (120 ml) water
¾ cup (150 gr) sugar
1½ cup (354 ml) organic whole milk
1 (12 oz/354 ml) can evaporated milk
½ cup (8 gr) calendula marigold dry tea, preferably just the petals
2 (14-ounce) cans condensed milk
½ teaspoon (2.5 gr) vanilla paste or 1 teaspoon (4 ml) vanilla extract
4 eggs
4 egg yolks

1. Prepare your two nested pans by placing a cotton kitchen towel on the bottom of the larger pan and adding enough boiling water to wet the kitchen towel. Place the smaller pan on top of the towel inside the larger pan.

2. Make the caramel: In a small heavy-bottom pot, add the ½ cup water and ¾ cup sugar. Heat over medium-high, stirring just a little to help dissolve the sugar. Once the sugar is dissolved, remove the spoon and reduce temperature until the sugar starts turning a bright golden yellow. Remove from heat and immediately pour into the smaller of your two pans. Spread the caramel all around the bottom. Do not worry if the caramel starts to crack; it will not affect the look of the flan.

3. In a 3-quart, heavy-bottom pot, combine the whole milk and evaporated milk. Warm up until small bubbles form around the edge. Remove from heat and add the dry calendula petals. Cover with a lid and let infuse for 20 to 25 minutes.

4. Preheat the oven to 325°F.

5. Sieve the milk into the container of a blender to remove the petals. Add condensed milk and vanilla and blend. Then add the eggs and egg yolks and blend until frothy. Pour this mixture into the pan with the caramel, and cover tightly with aluminum foil. Carefully transport the nested pans with the flan mixture into the middle rack in the oven. Once in the oven, pull rack a third of the way out and carefully pour boiling water into the larger pan, being careful it does not reach the edge of the aluminum foil. This prevents water from filtering into the flan.

6. Bake flan for about 45 to 60 minutes. Turn off the oven and with the door ajar let the flan cool slowly. After 20 minutes, remove flan pan from the oven and remove aluminum foil carefully because it might have trapped hot steam. Let it cool for 30 to 40 minutes. If the bottom of the pan feels slightly warm, the flan is ready to flip. Run a flat knife around the edges of the flan to release the sides and create an air bubble. Place a large flat plate on top of the pan and flip it over with conviction! Remove the pan and your flan should look as sleek as a mirror. Do not attempt to move or rearrange the flan on the plate. At this stage it is too fragile. Cover with the same pan used for cooking and refrigerate for at least 4 to 6 hours before serving.

When flan is cool and ready to serve, garnish the edge of the flan with some dried marigold petals.

Sweet Tamales

Tamales in Mexico are also made with sweet ingredients. The concept of sweet tamales might sound a little strange to you, but if you have never tried them, it is a must! The origins of sweet tamales are largely unknown. We can deduce that they appeared during Colonial times. Sugar, butter, aromatics, and in some cases fruit purees, nuts, and dried fruit were inherited from Spanish and Moorish cuisine. I imagine these tamales being created by a nun with a sweet tooth.

Regardless of the origin, they are a fun variation and make a pleasant end to a meal. They can also be a good little afternoon snack, or, as in Mexico, we have them as part of a breakfast or a *merienda* (light, early dinner) because they are usually smaller than the savory tamales. They are best eaten with a cup of warm atole, champurrado, or café de olla. These tamalitos will warm you up while waiting for the souls during the night vigil.

✳ ✳ ✳

Tamales de Piña, Coco y Pasas al Ron
Pineapple, Coconut, and Rum Raisin Tamales   271

Tamales de Chocolate Obscuro con Trocitos de Cacao
Dark Chocolate and Cacao Nib Tamales   275

Tamales Dulces de Betabel — *Sweet Red Beet Tamales*   277

Tamales de Zarzamora — *Blackberry Tamales*   279

Tamales de Piña, Coco y Pasas al Ron
Pineapple, Coconut, and Rum Raisin Tamales

One of the classic sweet flavor combinations for tamales is pineapple and raisins. I decided to add more flavor by soaking the raisins in spiced rum and adding toasted coconut. For the dough, I used half butter and half extra virgin coconut oil to give more flavor and a fluffier texture. You can also use the traditional lard instead. I think these tamalitos are delicious with a cup of cinnamon tea or coffee while you wait for the visiting souls to arrive and celebrate.

Makes 12 to 14 small 2 x 4-inch tamales

Filling:
4 cups (16 oz/450 gr) dry masa harina
½ teaspoon fine sea salt
2 cups (500 ml) whole milk
1 stick (4 oz/113 gr) butter, softened
½ cup (4 oz) extra virgin coconut oil
¾ cup (5.3 oz/150 gr) sugar
1½ teaspoons ground canela
½ teaspoon vanilla extract
1 can (20 oz/570 gr) pineapple, ⅔ of the slices small diced, the rest ⅓ of the slices crushed along with ½ cup (125 ml) of the pineapple can juices
1 tablespoon baking powder
½ cup (4 oz/80 gr) raisins, soaked in ¼ cup of spiced rum until raisins look plump
¼ cup toasted, shredded coconut

Wraps:
18 to 20 corn husks washed, soaked in warm water, and drained before using

1. In a large mixing bowl, mix masa harina with salt, rehydrate with milk, and knead until well combined.

2. In a separate bowl, whip butter, coconut oil, and sugar until lightly colored and fluffy.

3. Add ground canela and vanilla and mix until well combined.

4. Add the rehydrated masa in small chunks and mix in between additions until well incorporated. Add the crushed pineapple and mix.

5. Mix the masa for about 8 to 10 minutes. Once fluffy, sprinkle the baking powder over the masa, add soaked raisins, toasted coconut, and diced pineapple, and mix for 2 more minutes until well incorporated.

6. Assemble the tamales: Using a large soup spoon, add 2 spoonfuls of the masa dough into the top center of a corn husk. Fold each side of the husk and form a slightly flat little flat cylinder. Fold the tail of the corn husk behind the seam of the tamale, tie with a corn husk strip, and proceed with the rest.

7. Prepare the steamer pot: Fill with water up to the line of the steamer rack and put two pennies on the bottom. When water is low, the pennies will stop vibrating, letting you know it is time to refill the water. Insert the rack in the steamer and cover the top of the rack with some corn husks. Place tamales standing up all around the pot, cover the top of pot with a clean kitchen towel, and then place the lid over the towel and wrap the four points of the towel over the lid's top. This will keep the vapor in the pot and help absorb some of the extra moisture.

8. Bring the water to a boil, then reduce temperature down to medium-high. Start cooking time for 45 minutes. Keep an eye on the pot; if the coins stop vibrating, carefully refill with hot water. After 45 minutes, reduce the temperature to medium-low and carefully, using tongs, take one tamale out of the pot and let it sit for about 5 minutes. Now check for doneness. The corn husk should come off very easily. If it doesn't, they need more time. Put the tamale back into the pot and increase the heat to medium and cook for another 15 minutes or so. After 15 minutes, do the same test and try a bite. The tamales should look tender, moist, and fluffy.

Note: It's tricky to tell when tamales are ready. If you judge them from how they look in the pot, you might overcook them. It is very important to do this check-up to avoid overcooking your tamales.

9. Once they are cooked, using tongs, carefully move all the tamales from the pot into a single layer on a tray and cover with some aluminum foil and a clean kitchen towel to retain their moisture. Let them rest for about 10 minutes before eating them.

Tamales de Chocolate Obscuro con Trocitos de Cacao
Dark Chocolate and Cacao Nib Tamales

Chocolate tamales are not a traditional flavor. After experimenting with cocoa powder and cacao nibs, I was pleased and surprised by the delicious combination. The dark chocolate, cacao nibs, and corn masa yield a nutty, rich, and intense flavor. I used butter instead of lard and milk instead of stock or water and Dutch cocoa powder. However, if you have a good, unsweetened *chocolate de metate* (stone-ground chocolate), dissolve 1 or 2 tablets in warm water to form a paste and substitute for the cocoa powder. These tamalitos will bring any chocoholic soul to the ofrenda.

Makes 12 to 14 small 2 x 4-inch tamales

Filling:
4 cups (16 oz/450 gr) dry masa harina
½ teaspoon fine sea salt
2 ½ cups (625 ml) whole milk
2 sticks (8 oz/226 gr) butter, softened
¾ cup (5.3 oz/150 gr) sugar
1 ½ teaspoon ground canela
1 teaspoon vanilla extract
1 tablespoon baking powder
4 tablespoons Dutch cocoa powder, sifted and dissolved into an **extra ½ cup (125 ml) whole milk**
3 tablespoons (45 gr) cacao nibs

Wraps:
18 to 20 corn husks washed, soaked in warm water, and drained

1. In a large bowl, mix masa harina with salt, rehydrate with 2½ cups of whole milk, and knead until well combined. Set aside.

2. In a separate bowl, whip butter and sugar until light and fluffy.

3. Add ground canela, vanilla, and baking powder and mix until well combined.

4. Add the rehydrated masa in small chunks and whip in between additions until well incorporated.

5. Dissolve the cocoa powder into ½ cup milk. Add to masa and mix for about 8 to 10 minutes. You can add about ¼ cup to ½ cup more water or milk if masa feels too stiff. Once masa is fluffy and airy, add the cacao nibs and mix for one more minute.

6. Assemble the tamales: Using a large soup spoon, add two spoonfuls of the masa dough into the top center of a corn husk. Fold each side of the husk and form a little slightly flat cylinder. Fold the tail of the corn husk behind the seam of the tamale, tie with a corn husk strip, and proceed with the rest.

7. Prepare the steamer pot: Fill with water up to the line of the steamer rack and put two pennies on the bottom. When water is low, the pennies will stop vibrating, letting you know it is time to refill the water. Insert the rack and cover the top of the rack with some corn husks. Place tamales standing up all around the pot, leaving a hole in the center so you can refill with water during the cooking process. Cover the top of pot with a clean kitchen towel, place the lid on top of the towel, and wrap the four points of the towel over the lid's top. This will keep the vapor in the pot and help absorb some of the extra moisture.

8. Bring the water to a boil, then reduce temperature to medium. Start cooking time for 45 minutes. Keep an eye on the pot; if the coins stop vibrating, carefully refill with hot water. After 45 minutes, reduce the temperature to medium-low and carefully, using tongs, take one tamale out of the pot and let it sit for about 5 minutes. Check for doneness. The corn husk should come off very easily. If it doesn't, they need more time. Put the tamale back into the pot and increase the heat to medium and cook for another 15 minutes or so. After 15 minutes, do the same test and try a bite. The tamales should look tender, moist, and fluffy. *Note: It's tricky to tell when tamales are ready. If you judge them from how they look in the pot, you might overcook them. It is very important to do this check-up to avoid overcooking your tamales.*

9. Once the tamalitos are cooked, using tongs, carefully move all the tamales from the pot into a single layer on a tray and cover with some aluminum foil and a clean kitchen towel to retain their moisture. Let them rest for about 10 minutes before eating them.

Tamales Dulces de Betabel
Sweet Red Beet Tamales

Very few Mexican recipes use beets. Mostly they are prepared in very simple ways—made into juice as a morning elixir, shredded, steamed, or boiled, and in salads. As children, my brother and I would snack on thick slices of steamed beets with lime and sea salt prepared by my mother. I loved their sweet, earthy flavor. With that flavor in my memory, I played with some recipes, and incorporated beet puree into masa to make beet tortillas. The combination of corn and beets yielded a delicious earthy flavor and beautiful bright-colored tortillas. Based on how good these beet tortillas tasted, I used the masa to make a sweet tamale. I added shredded beets for texture, ground canela to enhance the sweetness of the beets, and butter to give the masa the right moisture. The result is a festive, bright-magenta tamalito with a delicious sweet beet flavor.

Makes 12 to 14 little 2 by 4-inch tamales

4 cups (16 oz/450 gr) dry masa harina
½ teaspoon fine sea salt
1½ cups (375 ml) beet juice
1 cup (250 ml) whole milk
1 cup (8 oz/226 gr) butter, softened
¾ cup (5.3 oz/150 gr) sugar
1½ teaspoons (6 gr) ground canela
½ teaspoon (2 ml) vanilla extract
1 tablespoon baking powder
1 to 2 cups shredded raw beets*

Wraps:
18 to 20 corn husks, washed and soaked in warm water, drained

*To shred beats, I use a mandolin for best results. Food processors work great too.

1. Mix masa harina with salt. Add beet juice and milk to rehydrate. And knead until well combined.

2. In a separate bowl, whip butter and sugar until light colored and fluffy.

3. Add ground canela and vanilla extract and mix until well combined.

4. Add the rehydrated masa in small chunks to the whipped butter one at a time and mix in between additions until well combined.

5. Using a handheld or a stand-up mixer, mix the masa for about 8 to 10 minutes. Once masa looks airy and fluffy, sprinkle the baking powder over the masa, and mix for 2 more minutes until well incorporated. With a spatula, fold the shredded beets into the masa until evenly combined.

6. Assemble the tamales: Using a large soup spoon, scoop 2 spoonfuls of the masa dough into the center of a corn husk. Fold over each side of the husk and form a little flat cylindrical tamale. Fold the tail of the corn husk behind the seam of the tamale, tie with a corn husk strip, and proceed with the rest.

7. Prepare the steamer pot: Fill with water up to the line of the steamer rack and put two pennies on the bottom. When water is low, the pennies will stop vibrating, letting you know it is time to refill the water. Insert the rack and cover the top of the rack with some corn husks. Place the pot on the stove on medium-high. Place tamales standing up around the inside of the pot in two or three layers, leaving a hole in the center so you can refill with water during the cooking process. Cover the top of pot with a clean kitchen towel, place the lid on top of the towel, and wrap the four points of the towel over the lid's top. This will keep the vapor in the pot and help absorb some of the extra moisture.

8. Bring the water to a boil, then reduce temperature to medium-high. Start cooking time for 45 minutes. Keep an eye on the pot; if the coins stop vibrating, carefully refill with hot water. After 45 minutes, reduce the temperature to medium-low and carefully, using tongs, take one tamale out of the pot and let it sit for about 5 minutes. Now check for doneness. The corn husk should come off very easily. If it doesn't, they need more time. Put the tamale back into the pot, increase heat to medium-high, and cook for another 15 minutes or so. After 15 minutes, do the same test and try a bite. The tamales should look tender and moist. *Note: It's tricky to tell when tamales are ready. If you judge them from how they look in the pot, you might overcook them. It is very important to do this check-up to avoid overcooking your tamales.*

9. Once they are cooked, using tongs, carefully move all the tamales from the pot into a single layer on a tray and cover with some aluminum foil and a clean kitchen towel to retain their moisture. Let them rest for about 10 minutes before eating. Serve with atole, milk, or cinnamon tea as a merienda or dessert.

Notes: Use fresh beet juice for best results. And when hydrating the masa, use a fork to avoid staining your hands.

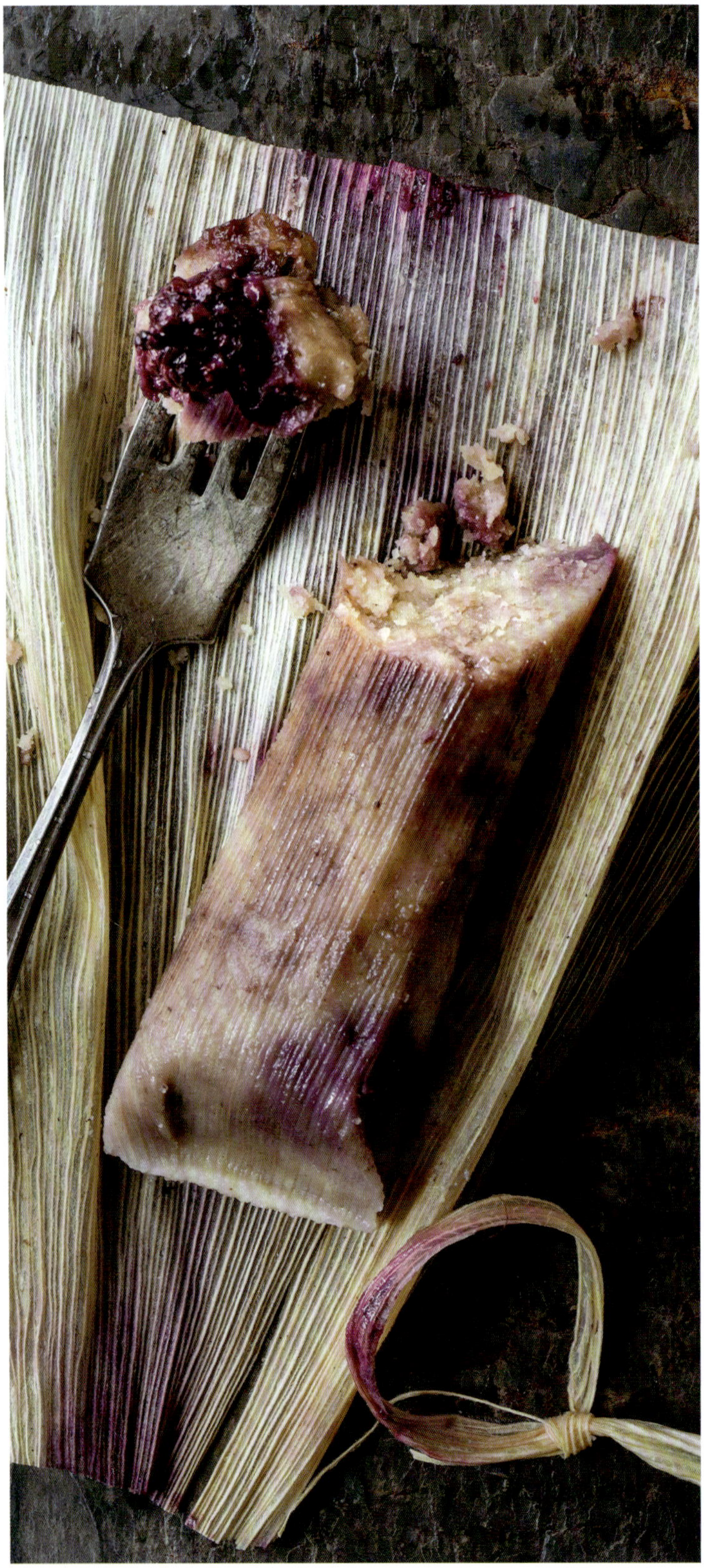

Tamales de Zarzamora—*Blackberry Tamales*

Blackberries grow abundantly in the south of Mexico. When in season, blackberries are used in several Mexican dishes and preparations, including atoles, marmalades, salsas, and, of course, sweet tamales. I used a combination of fresh berries, which give a tangy tart note, and marmalade to add sweetness and a swirl of flavor to the masa. These tamales are best made with fresh whole milk and butter instead of lard. The result is a tender, fruity, not overly sweet, little tamale that is the perfect ending to a big celebratory meal. Make a café de olla or a cinnamon atole to accompany these delicious tamalitos.

Makes 12 to 14 small 2 x 4-inch tamales

4 cups (16 oz/450 gr) dry masa harina
½ teaspoon fine sea salt
2½ cups (625 ml) whole milk
2½ sticks (10 oz/280 gr) butter, softened
¾ cup (5.3 oz/150 gr) sugar
1½ teaspoons ground canela
½ teaspoon vanilla extract
1 teaspoon lemon juice
1 tablespoon baking powder

Swirl:
⅓ cup blackberry jam

Filling:
24 to 36 fresh blackberries, about 2 or 3 per tamale

Wraps:
18 to 20 corn husks, washed, soaked in warm water, and drained

1. In a large bowl, mix masa harina with salt, rehydrate with 2½ cups whole milk, and knead until well combined. Set aside. Using a paddle attachment on a stand mixer, whip butter and sugar until light and fluffy.

2. Add ground canela, vanilla, and lemon juice and mix until well combined.

3. Add the rehydrated masa in small chunks and mix in between additions until well incorporated.

4. Using a stand mixer, mix the masa on medium speed for about 8 to 10 minutes. Once masa looks airy and fluffy, sprinkle the baking powder over the masa, and mix for 2 more minutes until well incorporated. With a spatula, fold blackberry jam into the masa until dough has purple stripes.

5. Assemble the tamales: Using a large soup spoon, add 2 spoonfuls of the masa dough into the top center of a corn husk. Add 2 to 3 fresh blackberries in the center. Fold each side of the corn husk and form a little slightly flat cylinder. Fold the tail of the corn husk behind the seam of the tamale, tie with a corn husk strip, and proceed with the rest.

6. Prepare the steamer pot: Fill with water up to the line of the steamer rack and put two pennies on the bottom. When water is low, the pennies will stop vibrating, letting you know it is time to refill the water. Then insert the rack and cover the top of the rack with some corn husks. Place tamales standing up all around the inside of the pot. Cover the top of the pot with a clean kitchen towel, then place the lid on top of the towel and wrap the four points of the towel over the lid's top. This will keep the vapor in the pot and help absorb some of the extra moisture.

7. Bring the water to a boil, then reduce temperature to medium-high. Start cooking time for 45 minutes. Keep an eye on the pot; if the coins stop vibrating, carefully refill with hot water. After 45 minutes, reduce the temperature to medium-low and carefully, using tongs, take one tamale out of the pot and let it sit for about 5 minutes. Now check for doneness. The corn husk should come off very easily. If it doesn't, they need more time. Put the tamale back into the pot, increase the heat to medium, and cook for another 15 minutes or so. After 15 minutes, do the same test and try a bite. The tamales should look tender and moist. *Note: It's tricky to tell when tamales are ready. If you judge them from how they look in the pot, you might overcook them. It is very important to do this check-up to avoid overcooking your tamales.*

8. Once they are cooked, using tongs, carefully move all the tamales from the pot into a single layer on a tray and cover with some aluminum foil and a clean kitchen towel to retain their moisture. Let them rest for about 10 minutes before eating them.

Notes: For the most flavorful blackberry tamales, use the best-quality jam you can find. I use a 100% fruit version that contains no additives other than cane sugar and lemon juice. Its best to make your own berry preserves when in season.

Variation: Add ½ cup of Mexican ricotta (*requesón*) or goat cheese along with the fresh berries to make a more decadent filling.

Pan Dulce

Pan dulce translates to "sweet bread." These baked goods are a big part of Mexican gastronomy and an important inheritance from Spanish and French family bakers who adapted their techniques and combined flavors using Mexican ingredients. Each state has their own varieties and every family has their favorites, which include the beloved conchas, semitas, orejas, pan de chochitos, puerquitos, cocoles, chilindrinas, cuernitos, pan de yema, hojaldras, ojos de buey, rebanadas, corbatas, and garibaldis, to name a few. It is traditional that early in the morning or at night around 6 or 7 p.m., people go to bakeries or street vendors and choose an assortment of pan dulce to be arranged on the table for breakfast and merienda. Families gather and enjoy pan dulce with a cup of hot cocoa, milk, coffee, or tea.

During the week around Día de Muertos, the most popular pan dulce, and significant to the celebration, is pan de muerto. This bread is thought to have been prepared to resemble a skull and bones soon after the Spanish friars came to Mexico. The friars found this bread with its distinctive shape to be a good substitution for real skulls that were part of native rituals. It was also part of Spanish Catholic tradition to share *Huesos de Santo*, candies and breads shaped like holy relics of the Saints, as part of the Catholic rituals on All Saints' Day and All Souls' Day.

Today, eating pan de muerto as part of the offerings on the altars represents the communion with the souls of our departed. While the rounded bone-shaped loaf with a sugary top is the primary design, there are several variations in certain Mexican states. In Michoacán, Estado de Mexico, Morelos, Guerrero, and Guanajuato, pan de muerto is shaped like birds, rabbits, dogs, sheep, fish, jaguars, butterflies, and horses. These animal shapes represent psychopomp creatures from the Purépecha and Otomi indigenous cultures. They believed that these animals, also found on altars during the holiday, will protect and help the souls through their journey.

In Oaxaca, pan de muerto is made of a traditional bread dough called *pan de yema*, which is richer in butter or lard and egg yolks. Its buttery soft crumb with a dark shiny crust resembles challah bread. Pan de yema is often topped with sesame seeds or colored sugar, or is decorated with intricate royal icing designs. Pan de yema is also shaped into anthropomorphic figures of various sizes to represent the bodies of those who have passed. These human-like bread shapes are decorated with clay or plastic faces of saints, cherubs, and small baby faces to represent the small souls on the altars.

Another ofrenda bread variation is rosquillas de muerto (or golletes), found primarily in Estado de Mexico and Oaxaca. This bread has a flat round shape with a hole in the middle, like a large stretched bagel covered with bright-pink granulated sugar. Rosquillas de muerto were also made by the friars to substitute for skulls. In this case, the skulls of warriors and people honorably sacrificed were displayed in rows on a wooden structure called a *tzompantli* along the pyramids on the Calzada de los Muertos (Dead Avenue). To mirror the rows of skulls, rosquillas were baked with a hole in the center to hang horizontally on a sugarcane on top of the altars.

The following recipes include a traditional version of pan de muerto and pan de yema, beloved conchitas with their sugary topping, and classic puerquitos (piglets) with their dark caramel and spice flavor. There is also a favorite recipe from my childhood—a soft vanilla-lemon cookie topped with nonpareils called grageitas or *pan de chochitos*.

Pan dulce and pan de muerto are essential offerings for the Día de Muertos altar. I hope you make time to bake and enjoy any of these recipes as part of your celebration.

❋ ❋ ❋

Pan de Muerto — *Bread of the Dead*   282

Pan de Yema Oaxaqueño — *Oaxacan Egg Yolk Bread*   289

Querubines Oaxaqueños de Pan de Yema — *Oaxacan Egg Yolk Bread Cherubs*   292

Conchas de Pan Dulce — *Sweet Bread Shells*   295

Puerquitos — *Lil' Piglets*   300

Galleta de Grageitas–Pan de Chochitos — *Rainbow Nonpareil Sprinkle Cookies*   302

Calaveritas de Galleta de Amaranto — *Amaranth Skull Cookies*   304

Pan de Muerto
Bread of the Dead

Pan de muerto is the most iconic food ofrenda of Día de Muertos, and no altar is complete without this delicious and unusual bread. It is the ultimate offering to the visiting souls.

The enticing smell of pan de muerto announces Día de Muertos during the fall harvest season. Bakeries start baking this bread one or two weeks before the celebrations and some continue for the rest of November. The soft, luscious dough is prepared with orange peel, anise, cinnamon, and orange blossom water. Once baked, it is brushed with melted butter and covered in granulated sugar that gives it a golden brown exterior and sugary top. The bread's crumb is soft and sturdy, and a slice of it can withstand a dunk into café de olla or hot chocolate. This dunking is called *sopeadito*, the best way to enjoy pan de muerto.

This recipe takes two days to make. The first day will be to make the dough and let it rest for 8 to 10 hours (overnight) in the refrigerator to develop the best flavor and crumb. So read the recipe once or twice before making it, and plan accordingly for best results. *This recipe also works well as half a batch.*

Makes 6 medium (6 to 7-inch) breads or 12 to 14 small (4-inch) breads

Sponge:
1 cup (4 ounces/125 ml) whole milk
2 tablespoons (25 gr) sugar
2 tablespoons (16 gr) unbleached all-purpose flour
4½ teaspoons (½ ounce/14 gr) active dry yeast

Dough:
7 cups (850 gr) unbleached all-purpose flour
1 cup (150 gr) whole wheat or rye flour
1 cup (200 gr) white sugar
2 teaspoons (10 gr) fine sea salt
4 teaspoons (4 gr) ground canela
1 cup (8 oz/227 gr) European-style butter, room temperature
4 large whole eggs
2 large egg yolks
1 tablespoon (15 ml) orange blossom water*
1 teaspoon (2 gr) orange zest**

Sugar topping:
1 stick (4 oz /115 gr) butter, melted
1 cup granulated white sugar
1 to 2 pinches ground canela

Orange blossom water is easy to find in Middle Eastern specialty markets and is absolutely delicious in this bread!
**Valencia oranges have the best zest flavor for baking.*

First day:
1. Make the sponge. Warm the milk to lukewarm. In a small bowl, combine warm milk, sugar, and flour, and whisk well to avoid any lumps. Sprinkle the yeast over milk mixture and gently mix in. Cover bowl with plastic wrap and let this mixture bloom in a warm place for 15 to 20 minutes, until the mixture looks foamy and creamy and the top resembles a sponge.

2. Make the dough. In the bowl of your stand mixer, add all the dry dough ingredients—flours, sugar, salt, and canela. Set on slow speed and mix well. Add butter to the flour bowl in small chunks and mix in for a few seconds. Add eggs, egg yolks, orange blossom water, orange zest, and the yeast sponge. Using the hook attachment of your stand mixer, mix dough on medium-low speed for 2 to 3 minutes until it forms a ball in the center. Then mix for 5 minutes on medium and at last crank your mixer to medium-high speed and mix dough for 2 to 3 more minutes. If making dough by hand, knead for 25 to 30 minutes, until dough is smooth, soft, elastic, and does not stick to the surface. Dough should have a shine and should not be sticky to the touch.

3. Gently remove the dough from hook and place it on a lightly floured table. Knead dough briefly to shape into a ball. Place dough in a large lightly buttered bowl, cover with plastic wrap and then with a clean kitchen towel, and place it in the refrigerator overnight. I've tried different methods, but 8 to 10 hours overnight is the right amount of time for the dough to develop. This method allows you to develop flavor in the dough without having to keep an eye on it all day.

Second day:

1. Pull the dough out of refrigerator, gently punch and reshape the dough, kneading gently, and briefly transfer to a baking tray and cover with plastic wrap and then a kitchen towel. Place in a warm place for about 2 to 2½ hours to come to room temperature. At that point, your dough should be soft, malleable, and ready to be shaped.

2. Over a lightly floured surface, divide the dough in half. Shape one half into a ball, cover with plastic wrap, and set aside. Then divide the other half into 4 equal parts. Reserve one part for the skulls and bone shapes, cover with plastic wrap, and set aside. Shape the other 3 pieces each into a ball by taking the piece of dough and wrapping the edges underneath itself to form a round ball. Place rounded dough on the table, and using your hand, create a concave shape and gently cup your hand over the dough ball. Gently, create a circular motion with the dough under your hand by rubbing against the table until you have formed a smooth, round, tighter ball. Refer to the photos for help.

3. Place each of the 3 large formed balls onto either a buttered pan or a baking sheet lined with parchment paper. Using your fingers, press the center of each ball to flatten to about ½-inch thick, and flatten the edges of the round ball against the baking sheet.

4. Using the fourth small reserved piece of dough, divide and make 3 balls the size of a key lime, about 1-inch across, then equally divide the rest of the dough into 3 balls about the size of a small plum, about 2½ inches around. See page 286.

5. *To make the skull:* Take one small key-lime-sized dough ball and make one round ball and set aside. *To make the crossbones for each top:* Take one small plum-sized dough ball and divide dough into two equal portions. Roll one portion into a small cylinder. Roll the other portion into another cylinder. Using your fingers, roll the cylinders against the table. As you roll, spread your fingers to create four bumps. These bumpy strips will represent the bones. Place the two bone strips one across the other over the top of each large dough ball, forming a cross shape. Please see the photos on page 286 for help.

6. Now we are ready to place the round center ball that represents the skull on the main bread portion. Use your fingers to make a deep indentation in the center of the shaped dough about halfway to the bottom of the tray, being careful not to tear the dough, and place the small skull ball in the center. Do not worry about pushing the center down a bit; this will prevent the ball from falling off when baking.

There is no need to add water or eggwash to glue the dough decorations over the dough; just make sure you flatten them against the body of the main dough ball so they stick together.

7. Now, do the same to decorate the other two dough balls in the tray. Then cover the three with plastic wrap and then a kitchen towel. Place the tray in a warm place in your kitchen and proof them for 25 to 30 minutes or until they double in size. *Time of proofing will depend on how warm your kitchen is. Check on them after 15 minutes to avoid overproofing, and decide if they need more or less time.*

8. Adjust oven rack in the middle and preheat oven to 350°F.

9. In the meantime, shape the second large half of the dough in the same way. By the time you finish shaping the second batch of dough, the first batch should be doubled in sized and ready to bake. Place tray in the oven and bake for 20 to 22 minutes, until bread is golden brown and produces a hollow sound when tapped gently. *Take into consideration that you can make smaller size breads, two large, or one extra large. I love to make little breads for kids or individual sizes for adults to give as gifts during the celebration. If making smaller sizes, make sure to place same sizes of shaped dough in baking trays for even baking. Also adjust baking times. Bake small breads for 15 minutes and medium breads for 18 minutes.*

10. Once baked, let them cool on the tray for about 10 minutes. In a small bowl, mix granulated sugar and canela. While the bread is still slightly warm, brush them generously with melted butter and coat heartily with the sugar and canela mixture, then hold the bread upside down and tap the bottom to remove the excess sugar. See the photo on page 287. Place bread on a rack to keep cooling. Prepare a pot of hot chocolate (page 322) or a café de olla (page 314) and call everybody to the table because it's time to celebrate!

Notes: Plan ahead and make this bread over the weekend. For example, make the dough on Saturday night, and then wake up Sunday and shape and bake your bread. You will have it warm and ready for breakfast. This bread can be made about 1 to 2 days before the celebration and will last soft and fresh for about 4 to 5 days when kept in an airtight container.

Pan de Yema Oaxaqueño
Oaxacan Egg Yolk Bread

Pan de yema is one of the iconic Día de Muertos breads in the region of Oaxaca, from the town of Santo Domingo Tomaltepec. The rest of the year, pan de yema can be found in round loaves sized from 5 to 12 inches and made for other special occasions. This beautiful, mahogany crusted bread has a soft crumb, rich flavor, mild sweetness, and a unique anise flavor. Bakers in Oaxaca make it into different shapes and sizes, and the ladies are in charge of the decorations on top, which include flowers made of sugar icing, stenciled flowers made with colored caster sugar, or just a sprinkling of anise seeds or sesame seeds. Pan de yema is commonly baked in wood-fired brick ovens, which also adds flavor to the dough. If you are lucky enough to have a brick oven, I encourage you to use it to bake this bread. For the rest of us mortals, a good oven will suffice.

Pan de yema's spongy crumb makes it ideal to be *sopeadito*, dunked in a warm cup of hot cocoa. So whether you follow tradition to the letter or just make this bread to the delight of your family and friends, you will enjoy this delicious celebration with pan de yema.

Makes 4 to 6 medium (7-inch) loaves or 8 small (4-inch) loaves

Sponge:
1 tablespoon (15 gr) sugar
½ cup (4 oz/120 ml) whole milk, room temperature
2¼ teaspoons (7 gr) dry active yeast
1 cup (140 gr) unbleached all-purpose flour

Dough:
3⅓ cups (460 gr) unbleached all-purpose flour
½ cup (100 gr) granulated sugar
1 teaspoon (3 gr) fine sea salt
1 tablespoon (4 gr) anise seeds, coarsely ground
3 large whole eggs
3 large egg yolks
½ cup (4 oz/113 gr) European-style butter, room temperature
Extra butter to grease the baking sheets
¼ cup (30 gr) sesame seeds, for topping the bread

Egg wash:
2 egg whites
1 egg yolk
1 tablespoon water
pinch fine sea salt

1. Make the sponge: In a small bowl, dissolve the sugar in the milk and sprinkle the yeast on top until it dissolves. Add flour and mix until you get a smooth, sticky paste. Cover the bowl with plastic and let it bloom for about 1 hour. In baking this is called a sponge; it will develop and feed the yeast. After an hour of sitting you should have a foamy, textured sponge, doubled or tripled in size and resembling a sponge with big and small bubble holes.

2. Make the bread: In a mixing bowl, add flour, sugar, salt, anise seeds, eggs, egg yolks, butter, and the yeast-sponge and mix on low speed for 3 to 4 minutes until well incorporated, then mix on medium-high for 7 to 8 minutes, or once ingredients are combined, knead the dough by hand for 15 to 20 minutes. Turn off the mixer and let dough stand 1 minute. The dough should look smooth and show some elasticity. Sprinkle some flour onto the top of the hook and run your fingers through the dough hook to remove dough from hook. Using a scraper, pull the dough out of the bowl onto a clean, floured surface.

3. Slightly sprinkle some flour onto the dough, and briefly knead and shape into a ball. Place dough ball seam side down in a large bowl lightly sprinkled with flour. Cover with plastic wrap and a clean kitchen towel. Let dough rest in a warm place in your kitchen to rise until it doubles in size, which takes about 1 to 2 hours, depending on the temperature of your kitchen.

4. Once dough has doubled in size, gently punch down the dough, transfer onto a lightly floured surface, and briefly knead gently to deflate as you shape it into a round ball. Divide dough into fourths and remove and reserve about 15 grams (½ ounce) of each ball. Shape large pieces of dough into rounds. Place the shaped round dough onto two separate greased baking trays, two round pieces per tray. Give them enough room to grow. As you situate the ball, press down the center to flatten the ball, and with the outside of your hand, make a little indentation on the dough. This will make the shape of your bread grow more evenly. With the rest of the dough, using about 30 to 50 grams (1 to 1½ ounces) per bread, shape into logs, then divide into thirds. Take one piece and roll into a log using your fingers, and as you roll, spread your fingers to create little bumps in the log. This will represent the bones. Place one strip across the middle of the bread, then roll the other strip and place it across perpendicular to the first strip to form a cross. With the last third, make a round ball and place it on the center. Brush the shaped dough generously with egg wash. Do the same with the rest of the shaped dough. *Note: See page 286 for how to shape pan de muerto. This amount of dough makes four 6-inch round breads.*

5. To make just round shapes of pan de yema, punch and knead the dough, and then weigh it and divide the total weight by the number of breads you wish to bake. You can make two mediums and four smalls or one large and two medium breads, or just small breads or any combination. Make sure you place the same size of shaped dough on each tray for even baking.

6. Once dough is all shaped: take a large piece of plastic wrap, dust some flour on it, and crinkle it up into a ball. Then, over the sink, pull the plastic apart again and shake off the excess flour. Loosely cover the shaped dough trays with the floured plastic. Finally, cover the trays with a light clean kitchen towel. Let the dough rise until doubled in size, about 30 to 60 minutes in a warm place. Check the rising at 30 minutes to avoid overproofing. You will be surprised how fast it proofs once the dough is shaped, so watch carefully.

7. Once dough has doubled in size, gently brush the dough with egg wash and sprinkle the tops with sesame seeds. Preheat the oven to 375°F, place bread in oven, and lower the temp to 350°F. Bake for 18 to 20 minutes until it has an even dark mahogany brown color. This bread must achieve this color, due to the egg yolk content. Watch closely and make sure your oven is at the right temperature for an even bake. Adjust baking time to 12 to 15 minutes for smaller sized bread.

8. Once they are baked, cool them on a rack for 15 minutes before serving. Serve with a good cup of hot cocoa (page 322), café de olla, or a calientito (page 314).

Notes: Bake with the best eggs you can; the flavor of this bread relies on the egg yolks. Have all the ingredients at room temperature. If you do not want to make the bread into the skull shape, round shapes work well too. See the next page for small little cherub shapes.

Querubines Oaxaqueños de Pan de Yema
Oaxacan Egg Yolk Bread Cherubs

One of the characteristics of Oaxacan pan de yema, besides its delicious flavor, is that in certain regions of Mexico this bread is made into anthropomorphic shapes. *Querubines* translates as "cherubs." This doll-shaped bread represents what in Mexico we call *angelitos*, the innocent babies, children, saints, or young adults. The bread dough is shaped into body silhouettes, and after it's baked, a small clay or plastic figurine head of a child, cherub, or saint is inserted into the bread to represent the body of the soul in transit.

These breads indicate that an altar is made for a small soul, like a baby or a child. It is believed that any food or bread placed on the altars as offerings should be thrown away the next day, since the souls will eat the "essence of the food," leaving the bread and food flavorless and odorless. This is why people don't eat any of the food placed on the altars.

Eager to carry on the traditions, I included some drawings on the next page, which you can photocopy onto card stock. Then cut and tape a toothpick onto the back of each face and insert into the bread.*

Makes 4 large and 4 small querubines de pan de yema

1 pan de yema recipe (page 289)
¼ cup (50 gr) sesame seeds or colored sugar
Card stock
6 to 8 wood toothpicks*
Clear tape

1. Follow the instructions on the Pan de Yema recipe. Once you have punched down the dough in step 4, divide it into 6 to 8 pieces, depending on the size of the querubines-muñequitos you want.

2. Shape each piece into an oval. Then with a metal scraper or a sharp knife, cut some slivers into the sides to make the arms, and then make a partial cut down the center to make the legs. Pull arms and legs carefully to separate from body. You can cross the arms up in the top of the body or you can even make them hold hands. Place them on a baking tray with plenty of space in between them so they do not stick to each other when they rise and bake.

3. Proceed to proof the body shapes for about 15 to 20 minutes or until almost doubled in size.

4. Once proofed, brush them with egg wash and sprinkle on some sesame seeds or colored sugar crystals.

5. Bake at 350°F for about 12 to 15 minutes until dark mahogany color. Remove from the oven and let them cool. Then insert the little faces, and you are ready to decorate your altar!

Remind your guests to remove the toothpick before eating the bread.

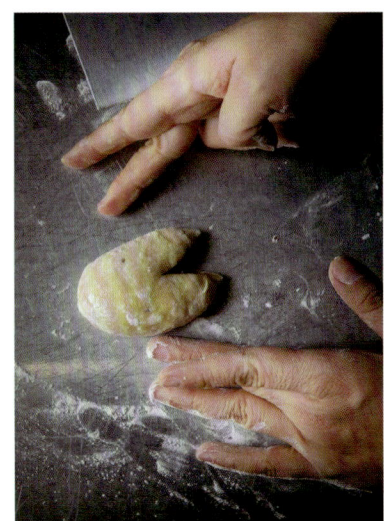
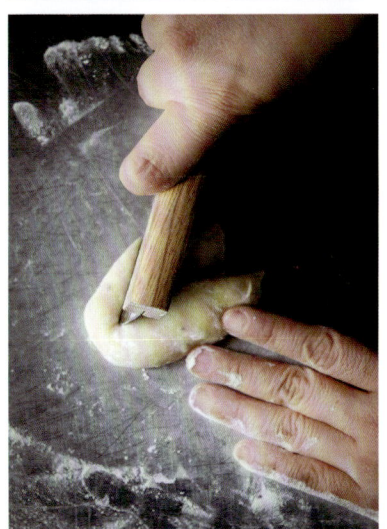

photo copy and cut - - - ✂

Conchas de Pan Dulce
Sweet Bread Shells

The beloved conchas, buttery and fluffy baked pastries with a sugary top, are an irresistible, iconic pan dulce in Mexico. They get their name from the imprinted sugary design on top that, when baked, makes this round soft bun look like a seashell. The classic flavors are vanilla and chocolate. I love to crank up the flavor volume with a touch of canela in the dough and on the sugary crust paste. And for the chocolate conchas I use the best Dutch process cocoa powder, which gives them a truly dark chocolate flavor. When coming out of the oven, these conchas warm up your home with a heavenly smell. You must eat one or two while they are warm! Make a pot of hot chocolate (page 322) or café de olla (page 314) to accompany them.

Makes 12 to 14 conchas

Special equipment:
1 concha cutter, to imprint the shell motif into the sugar paste (see sourcing list page 361)

Starter dough:
3 tablespoons (45 ml) whole milk, lukewarm
1 tablespoon (15 gr) sugar
1 heaping teaspoon (5 gr) dry active yeast
1¼ cups (150 gr) all-purpose flour
1 large egg

Vanilla sugar paste topping:
¾ cup plus one tablespoon (110 gr) all-purpose flour
1 cup (100 gr) confectioners' sugar
7 tablespoons (100 gr) butter, softened
¼ teaspoon (1 ml) pure vanilla extract
¼ teaspoon (1 gr) ground canela

Chocolate sugar paste topping:
¾ cup plus one tablespoon (110 gr) all-purpose flour
1 cup plus one tablespoon (110 gr) confectioners' sugar
½ cup (110 gr) butter, room temperature
1 tablespoon (15 gr) Dutch process cocoa powder
¼ teaspoon (1 gr) ground canela

Dough:
2½ cups (350 gr) all-purpose flour
½ cup (100 gr) sugar
¼ teaspoon (1½ gr) fine sea salt
4 eggs
½ cup (113 gr) butter
¼ cup (60 ml) whole milk
½ teaspoon (2½ ml) vanilla paste

1. Make the starter dough: Pour lukewarm milk into a small bowl and dissolve the sugar in it. Sprinkle dry yeast over the milk and let it bloom. In a mixer bowl, add the flour and egg and the bloomed milk-sugar-yeast mixture, and mix for 3 to 4 minutes until a soft ball forms. Place this ball in a clean bowl. Cover the bowl with plastic wrap and a clean kitchen towel and let it develop for 2 hours.

2. Make the sugar paste topping: Choose either the vanilla or chocolate option. Place all the ingredients in a mixing bowl and mix until it forms a soft dough ball. Do not overmix. Shape into a ball, cover with plastic wrap, and chill for 20 minutes before using.

3. Make the dough: In a mixer bowl, add flour, sugar, salt, eggs, butter, milk, and vanilla. Add the dough starter in small pieces. Using the dough hook of your mixer, mix for 3 to 4 minutes on medium-slow speed. Then 5 to 6 minutes on medium-high. Add a tablespoon of flour around the edge of the bowl to help the dough come off the bowl and form a ball in the center. Dump the dough onto a floured surface and gently knead and shape into a ball. Place dough ball in a clean bowl dusted with flour. Cover bowl with plastic wrap and a clean kitchen towel. Let the dough rest and proof in a warm place for about 1 hour.

4. After 1 hour, punch the dough and gently reshape it into a ball. Place ball in the same bowl, cover, and let rest and proof for 1 more hour. Repeat this process for a total of 3 hours.

After the last proofing hour, punch down the dough, gently shape into a ball, and start cutting and weighing out small balls of 60 grams (2½ ounces). Once you have all the dough divided into approximately 12 to 14 60-gram (2½ ounce) pieces, shape each piece into a ball: Place your hand around the dough in a concave shape, and apply light pressure while making circular movements until you have a round little ball.

5. Line a baking sheet with parchment paper, or grease the surface of the baking sheet with some butter, and place each shaped ball onto the baking sheet about 3 inches from each other so they don't stick to one another when risen. As you place each ball onto the sheet, apply some butter in your hand and press gently to flatten the ball as you grease the surface of the balls. This will give your conchas a good, domed shape when baked.

6. Chill the sugar paste topping for 20 minutes. When it's cold but pliable, cut pieces that weigh about 15 to 20 grams. Use your hands to shape the pieces into small balls, but handle briefly to avoid melting the paste. With scissors, cut a resealable plastic bag along the seams and cut off the resealable part. Place the sugar paste ball in between the plastic flaps. Using a tortilla press or a flat heavy pan, gently press to make a 3 to 4-inch round flat sugar paste patty. Peel one side of the plastic to expose the sugar paste patty, dunk your concha cutter into flour, and then gently press it into the sugary patty to emboss the shell segments. See steps on page 297.

7. Take the plastic with the pressed shell, place the exposed sugar patty in your hand, and peel the back plastic layer, as if you were peeling off a sticker. Carefully place the embossed patty on top of the dough ball. Press down gently so the sugary top takes the shape of the round ball. Now transfer the beautiful and delicious sugar topping onto the rest of the dough balls.

8. Cover the shaped conchas on the baking sheet with a large piece of plastic wrap dusted with flour to avoid sticking, and put a clean cotton kitchen towel over the plastic.
   Let the conchas rise in a warm cozy place until doubled in size. This can take 30 to 60 minutes, depending on the warmth of your kitchen.

9. Preheat oven to 375°F. Reduce the oven temperature to 350°F and bake the conchas for 15 to 18 minutes or until the sides and bottom of the bread golden brown. Remove from oven and leave on the sheet pan for 3 more minutes. Then transfer to a cooling rack.

Variation: Mini Conchitas
These are about half the regular size, and best of all you can eat two or three different flavors. Mini conchitas are ideal for little kids and for altars. If the previous recipe dough is divided as follows, this recipe makes about 20 to 24 mini 3-inch conchitas: Divide the dough into small balls of 1½ ounces (30 to 40 gr) each. Make topping balls of ½-ounce (10 to 15 gr) pieces. Proof them for half the time and bake them at 350°F for 10 to 12 minutes.

Variation: Conchitas de Naranja y Limon Real (Orange and Lemon Citrus Conchitas)
I wanted to experiment using citrus flavors with the conchas. I think the soft and delicate buttery notes of the dough complements the fragrant flavors of the orange and lemon really well. The result is so scrumptious that these citrus conchitas are my new favorite variation. Make them regular size or minis.

Add 2 teaspoons of lemon or orange zest to the dough in step 3.

Orange sugar topping paste:
¾ cup (110 gr) flour
¾ cup (100 gr) powdered sugar
7 tablespoons (100 gr) butter, softened
½ teaspoon (2 gr) orange zest

Lemon sugar topping paste:
¾ cup (110 gr) flour
¾ cup (100 gr) powdered sugar
8 tablespoons (110 gr) butter
½ teaspoon (2 gr) lemon zest

Notes: The sugary top might make a little more than you will need, just in case you need more or want to make it thicker. Conchitas keep well in an airtight container for about 2 to 3 days.

Puerquitos—*Lil' Piglets*

Puerquitos are one of the beloved pan dulce classics in Mexican bakeries. This soft-crumb, cakey, piglet-shaped cookie has a strong spiced-caramel flavor from the piloncillo, canela, ginger, and anise seeds freshly ground into the dough, making them a delicious fall treat. I felt compelled to include the recipe because these are my mom and brother's favorite pan dulce. Thinking of them, I created a recipe that is improved by making them at home. I used organic butter, coconut oil, and freshly ground spices to enhance the flavor and quality. I would love to see these ultimate puerquitos in my ofrenda.

Makes about 10 to 12 puerquitos, depending on cookie cutter

Special equipment:
1 piglet cookie cutter* (see Sourcing Ingredients, page 362)
Large rolling pin

Dough:
2½ cups (350 gr) all-purpose flour
½ teaspoon (1½ gr) baking soda
½ teaspoon (1½ gr) baking powder
¼ teaspoon (¾ gr) sea salt
½ teaspoon (1½ gr) ground canela
½ teaspoon (1½ gr) ground ginger
4 tablespoons (2 oz/60 gr) butter, softened
3 tablespoons (1½ oz/40 gr) extra virgin coconut oil, melted
1 egg
¼ cup (60 ml) molasses
1 cup piloncillo syrup (recipe below)

Piloncillo syrup:
1½ cups (355 ml) water
2 (8 ounce, 225gr) piloncillo cones, shaved or cut into smaller pieces
3-inch canela stick
½ teaspoon (1½ gr) anise seeds, crushed
4 whole allspice
4 clove buds
Pinch fine sea salt

To roll and shape the cookies:
1 cup (140 gr) all-purpose flour
¼ cup chocolate chips or raisins, for the pig eyes

Eggwash:
1 egg
1 teaspoon water

Notes: These piglets will get better the next day once all the flavors have settled. And they keep really well in a plastic bag or a plastic container for about 5 to 8 days.

1. Make the piloncillo syrup: Bring the water to a boil and add piloncillo, canela stick, anise seeds, allspice, cloves, and salt. Cover with a lid and stir every now and then until piloncillo is dissolved and the syrup is fragrant. Reduce the syrup by about a third, so you will end up with about 1 cup of piloncillo syrup. Remove cloves, allspice, and canela stick. Leave the crushed anise seeds; they will continue to give flavor to the batter as the piglets bake. Let the syrup cool down completely.
2. Make the dough: In the bowl of a mixer, combine flour, baking soda, baking powder, salt, ground canela, and ginger. Mix until well combined. Add butter, coconut oil, egg, molasses, and piloncillo syrup, and mix on medium-low until well combined, about 3 to 4 minutes. Form a ball with this dough, cover it with plastic wrap, making sure the plastic is touching the dough to avoid forming a skin, and refrigerate for at least 30 to 45 minutes.
3. Use ½ cup of flour to generously dust a clean surface where the dough will be rolled. Dust the top of the dough generously with flour and roll the dough slightly thicker than ¼ inch. Once rolled, dust more flour on top of the rolled dough and rub it in before cutting out the shapes (to obtain a clean cut). Using the pig cookie cutter, cut out the piglets. Line a baking sheet with parchment paper, and place the piglets on it, about 5 or 6 per tray. Give plenty of space in between each piglet so they can bake well. Place the trays with piglets in the refrigerator for about 15 to 20 minutes before baking.
4. Preheat oven to 375°F.
5. Remove trays from refrigerator and give each pig cookie an eye by pressing one chocolate chip tip upside down into the area between the ear and the forehead of the piglet profile. Make the egg wash by whisking one egg and one teaspoon of water. Then with a pastry brush, generously apply egg wash on top of each piglet. Give two coats of egg wash to each piglet.
6. Bake them for 10 to 12 minutes or until reddish brown on top with toasty bottoms. Cool them on a rack. Serve them with a glass of milk or a coffee for a late afternoon snack or merienda!

Galleta de Grageitas–Pan de Chochitos
Rainbow Nonpareil Sprinkle Cookies

Making this cookie recipe with children can be a fun way for them to help you in the kitchen while you prepare for Día de Muertos. *Galleta de grageitas* (or *pan de chochitos*) is another classic of Mexican bakeries and was my favorite childhood pan dulce. I used to remove all the *chochitos* from the cookie and eat them first. Then I would eat the cookie. Now as an adult I just love the fun crumbly, buttery texture contrasting with the playful crunchy sprinkles. And if you dunk the cookie in milk, you end up with rainbow milk.

These delicious cookies have a soft and cakey crumb. I pumped up the flavor of the dough by adding vanilla paste and lemon zest to the batter. It works really well to balance the sweet layer of sprinkles. I included the recipe for the Día de Muertos celebration because its colorful, fun to make, and great as a display on the altars. Making them with a skull cookie cutter is fun too.

Makes 8 to 10 (4-inch) cookies

Special equipment:
1 (3- or 4-inch) fluted round cookie cutter

1¾ cup (250 gr) unbleached all-purpose flour
½ cup (100 gr) sugar
1 teaspoon (4 gr) baking powder
¼ (1 gr) teaspoon sea salt
1 stick (4 ounces/115 gr) butter, softened
1 egg
½ teaspoon (2 gr) vanilla paste
Zest of 1 small yellow lemon
¼ cup whole milk

Egg wash:
1 egg
1 teaspoon water

½ cup *grageitas* (rainbow nonpareil sprinkles)

1. Place into a mixing bowl, the flour, sugar, baking powder, and salt, and mix well using a mixer paddle attachment. Add butter and mix on medium-low for about 3 minutes. Then add 1 egg, vanilla paste, and lemon zest and mix for 1 minute until egg is well incorporated. Add milk and keep mixing on medium speed for another 2 minutes.

2. Cover the dough mixture with plastic wrap and refrigerate for 20 to 30 minutes.

3. On a well-floured surface, roll the dough to about ⅓-inch thick. Flour the top of the dough lightly. Dip the round cutter into flour and cut about 8 to 10 cookies. Reroll the rest of the cutout dough and make 1 or 2 more cookies. (Reroll only once to obtain the same quality crumb.)

4. Apply a generous layer of egg wash with a pastry brush, and then flip each round over and press lightly into the bowl with the sprinkles to ensure all the egg surface is covered with sprinkles. Place the cookies onto a baking sheet lined with parchment paper, allowing about 2 inches of separation between each cookie, and proceed with the rest.

5. Place cookie trays in the refrigerator and preheat oven to 350°F. Bake cookies for 20 to 25 minutes until bottoms are slightly golden. Transfer to cool on a rack. These cookies are best served with a glass of milk. Remember to dunk them to get the rainbow milk!

Note: Keep cookies in a plastic bag or airtight container up to 8 days.

Calaveritas de Galleta de Amaranto
Amaranth Skull Cookies

Amaranth was cultivated in Mexico by the Aztecs for eight thousand years. It was a great source of nutrition for them. The real value of amaranth lies in its seeds. These tiny seeds are loaded with 12 to 17% protein, and are high in lysine and essential amino acids. Amaranth seeds are also plentiful in calcium, iron, magnesium, and many more minerals and vitamins.

Puffed amaranth seeds taste like nutty popcorn. They are soft, tender, and hold a great natural flavor. My intention was to make a delicious natural cookie without too much sugar or added colors. I like to leave the bright colors to the decorations on the altar, and leave the food more natural.

These cookies are a great modern treat for Day of the Dead. They are only mildly sweet, the amaranth gives the cookie a great texture, and the nuts and seeds add flavor and character to the buttery dough. It is fun to decorate with seeds. This can be a great project to involve your children, family, and friends.

Makes 12 to 14 (4-inch) cookies

Special Equipment:
Skull-shaped cookie cutter

Piloncillo syrup:
1 8-ounce (225 gr) piloncillo cone, chopped or grated
3-inch stick canela
½ cup (125 ml) water

Dough:
1 cup (2 sticks/8 oz/226 gr) butter, room temperature
Zest of 1 large lime
Juice of ½ lime (about 2 teaspoons)
1 teaspoon (4 ml) vanilla extract
½ cup melted piloncillo syrup*
1 cup (140 gr) unbleached all-purpose flour
1 cup (140 gr) unbleached whole wheat flour
½ teaspoon (2 gr) fine sea salt
1 cup (30 gr) puffed amaranth

Decorating the cookies:
1 egg whisked with 1 teaspoon of water
¼ cup raw pumpkin seeds, *for around the eyes or to make the lady's nostrils*
2 tablespoons raw almonds, *for the gentleman's nostrils*
2 tablespoons pine nuts, *for the teeth*
2 tablespoons cashew halves, *for mustaches*
2 tablespoons golden raisins, *for eyeballs*
1 tablespoon cranberries, *for eyeballs, lips, and cheeks*
1 tablespoon dark chocolate chips, *for eyeballs*
1 tablespoon white chocolate chips, *for eyeballs*

1. Make the syrup: In a small pot, place the piloncillo cone, cinnamon stick, and water. Heat up and bring to slow simmer until the piloncillo cone has dissolved and is the consistency of a thick syrup or honey. Let it cool off while you prepare the rest of the ingredients.

2. Make the dough: In a medium-size bowl using a stand or hand mixer, whip the butter until fluffy and pale. Add the lime zest, lime juice, vanilla extract, and the cooled piloncillo syrup. Whip for 2 more minutes.

3. Sift both flours and salt over the butter mixture. Using the hand blender on low, mix until flour is incorporated, for about 15 seconds. Add the puffed amaranth and whip for 5 seconds until it's incorporated. Do not overmix.

4. Dump the cookie mixture onto a baking sheet lined with parchment paper. With a flat spatula, spread the cookie dough into an even rectangle. Place another piece of parchment on top of the spread-out cookie dough. With a rolling pin, evenly flatten the dough until it's about ¾ of an inch thick. Refrigerate the baking sheet with the dough for 30 minutes.

5. When the cookie dough is chilled, prepare a baking sheet lined with a silicone pad or parchment paper. Place the cookie dough onto a flattened clean surface, peel off the top parchment paper, and cut out the cookies with a skull-shaped cookie cutter. Place the shaped dough onto the tray with about ½-inch separation between each cookie. By now you should have about 14 to 15 uncooked cookies. Gather the rest of the dough and gently press it together, place the parchment paper on top, roll it up, and refrigerate for the next batch.

6. Now the fun begins! Brush each cookie with some egg wash and start decorating the cookies. Make sure when placing seeds to GENTLY press them into the cookie. I used half of dried cranberries and chocolate chips for eyeballs, then pumpkin seeds around them. Two pumpkin seeds make the perfect skull nostrils. For the skull ladies, I used cranberries to make the lips, cut with scissors, and the gentleman skulls have mustaches made with cashew halves. For the teeth, halved peanuts look great; place them all aligned on the lower third of the skull cookie. See photos for instructions on page 307.

7. After decorating, lightly brush the cookies for a second time with egg wash, being careful not to remove any decorations. The egg wash will protect the seeds from burning when baking, and it will give the cookies a beautiful glossy finish. Place the cookie tray in the coolest part of your refrigerator for about 15 minutes before baking.

8. Preheat the oven to 375°F. Remove the cookie tray from the refrigerator, put it in the oven, and bake for 15 to 18 minutes. Check cookies at 10 minutes and rotate the pan so they brown evenly, and give them another 5 to 8 minutes to finish cooking. Keep a close eye on them and pull them out right when they look golden brown. Check the bottom of one cookie; it should be a deep golden brown, and the seeds should look toasty. By now, your home will smell fragrant, buttery, and citrusy.

9. Remove the tray from the oven and allow the cookies to rest for 2 to 3 minutes until they firm up and are ready to handle. With a spatula, gently transfer them to a cooling rack. Please eat a cookie while they are slightly warm.

Notes: Once they are completely cool, keep them in an airtight container. These cookies last for 4 to 5 days (if you don't eat them before that). They are great for breakfast with a cup of tea or coffee, or ideal for an afternoon snack.

Chocolate skulls, for Día de Muertos, Patzcuaro, Michoacán.

Café de olla and pan de muerto. Warm up!

All of the drinks in this section can be spiked with alcohol. A popular option in Mexico is a strong alcohol called Aguardiente (30 to 59 percent alcohol) often distilled from sugarcane and flavored with anise. There are many styles of aguardiente made in Mexico. A couple made from sugarcane are Charanda from Michoacán and Zacualpan from Morelos. Jobito from Veracruz and Mosquito or Moscos from Toluca are made from a combination of fruit and aguardiente. The Spanish version of aguardiente is known as Orujo.

Hot Drinks

Ready to warm up? The cemetery vigil can be hard to endure, but it can be more livable when holding a cup of something warm. On these cold nights, a café de olla, atole, ponche de frutas, or the beloved calientitos is what you need to keep spirits high and the celebration going. So make a large pot of any of these drinks, share with family and friends, and gather in a circle to tell stories.

❋ ❋ ❋

Ponche de Frutas — *Warm Fruit Punch*   312

Calientitos — *Hot Spiced Punch*   314

Café de Olla — *Clay Pot Coffee*   314

Atole Blanco — *White Atole*   317

Atole de Calabaza — *Caramel Pumpkin Atole*   317

Atole de Nuez — *Pecan Atole*   317

Atole de Guayaba — *Guava Atole*   319

Atole de Canela — *Cinnamon Atole*   319

Champurrado   320

Chocolate Mexicano — *Mexican Hot Cocoa*   322

Ponche de Frutas
Warm Fruit Punch

Imagine fall fruits slowly simmering to magically deliver aromas and flavors with only one mission: warm you up! *Ponche de frutas* is a traditional punch made during the rainy and cold days of autumn and winter in Mexico. Making it is simple as long you use at least two kinds of stone fruits, one type of citrus, and either hibiscus flowers or tamarind, which add acidity to balance the sweetness. The sweetness from the fruits and a small amount of piloncillo with its caramel flavor gives a pleasant sweetness to the punch. Turbinado sugar and dark agave nectar are also good alternatives for sweetening.

Serve ponche de frutas in clay or peltre (enamel) mugs, along with a little spoon or a long skewer so you can eat the fruit chunks as you drink. Young ones love it, but for the grown-ups I highly recommend a little splash-a-roo of your favorite rum, charanda, or whiskey.

Serves 6 adult cups or 2 Sasquatch cups

12 cups water
½ to 1 piloncillo cone*
3 (4-inch) sticks canela
3 clove buds
2 star anise
¼ cup (35 gr) dried hibiscus flowers, flor de Jamaica (see Sourcing Ingredients)
Pinch fine sea salt
2 apples (Jazz apples and Pink Ladies work well)
2 pears (Bosc or Seckel hold their shape)
4 guavas
6 to 8 small crabapples
14 to 15 tejocotes (Mexican hawthorn), optional
1 to 2 quinces
10 prunes
12 to 15 (2-inch) pieces of sugarcane
Rind of one large orange
Spiced rum, optional**

Add more piloncillo depending on how sweet you like your punch. I recommend starting with a small amount, taste, and add more if needed. If you are using any other sweetener, start with a ¼ cup and work your way up.
**For an extra joyous party, add liberal amounts of spiced rum or bourbon to your adult guests' cups, if they like. Customizing each cup allows the little ones to enjoy some child-appropriate fruit punch too.*

1. In a 4- to 6-quart large pot, add water, piloncillo, cinnamon sticks, cloves, star anise, hibiscus flowers, and salt and bring to a boil.

2. Meanwhile, core the apples and pears and cut them into medium-size pieces. Cut the ends and deseed the guavas with a small spoon or melon baller, and then cut into quarters. Slice the crabapples in round slices and tap the slices to remove the seeds. Remove the end core of the tejocotes with a paring knife, leaving them otherwise whole. I like to cut each fruit a little differently, so people can recognize what fruit they are eating. For the orange rind, you can use an orange peel curler to make a long strip, or add smaller pieces using a vegetable peeler. Just make sure not to add the white part of the orange, since this will add some unpleasant bitterness to the punch.

3. Add all the chopped fruit, prunes, sugarcane, and orange rind to the pot and cover ¾ of the way with a lid. Bring to a slow simmer and simmer for about 15 to 20 minutes. Carefully taste the punch and adjust sweetness if necessary. When the fruit is fork tender, your punch is ready to serve.

Prepping the guavas, quince, hawthorns, and sugarcane.

Calientitos—*Hot Spiced Punch*

This hot brewed tea is a favorite of those who await the spirits on cold nights. It has no rules for flavoring; people use whatever fruit and spices are available. Made on an *anafres* outdoors or over a wood fire, the wood smoke adds a wisp of smoked flavor to the tea. The distinguishing ingredient is the *piquetito*, meaning a little splash of a strong liquor or traditional spirits like rum, mezcal, or aguardiente added when served to the guest.

Makes 1 pot, serves 6 to 8 adults

5 (3-inch) sticks canela
3 clove buds
4 guavas, 6 to 8 *tejocotes* (hawthorns) or 1 quince, quartered
1 cone (8 ounce, 226 gr) piloncillo, or ½ cup (100 gr) turbinado sugar
6 cups (48 ounces, ½ L) water
Pinch fine sea salt

Place all the ingredients into an enamel or clay pot. Make a wood or natural charcoal fire on your grill. Place the pot on top of the grill and let it slow simmer for 25 to 30 minutes. Add 1 cup of cold water to the pot and stir. Cover with a lid for 15 to 20 minutes. Uncover and suddenly you will see the color of the brew has changed to a bright-reddish hue. Serve piping hot in terra cotta, ceramic, or enamelware mugs, along with a little splash of charanda, mezcal, or aguardiente.

Café de Olla—*Clay Pot Coffee*

Café de olla is best made in a clay pot. The coffee we Mexicans crave on a cold November night derives flavor from the vessel, the spices, and the caramel-like sweetness from the piloncillo. Café de olla is warm and comforting while waiting and celebrating with family and friends. It can be prepared with any medium-roast coffee you like, and can be made as strong as you like. To lift their spirits, many people during the night of the Day of the Dead celebration add a little *piquete*, which means to spike the drink with a little *aguardiente* or rum. Café de olla is also a breakfast staple served with a side of sweet bread, like a conchita, and during the last weeks of October and the month of November a slice of pan de muerto with café de olla is a must.

Makes about 4 cups

4 to 5 cups (32 to 40 ounces) water
½ cone piloncillo, or turbinado sugar
3-inch stick canela
6 clove buds
Pinch fine sea salt
6 to 8 tablespoons coffee, medium ground

Bring the water to a slow simmer in a small pot. Add piloncillo, cinnamon, clove buds, and a pinch of sea salt and simmer until sugar is dissolved. Add ground coffee, stir, and bring to a slow simmer. Then turn off the heat. Cover with a lid and let it steep for 8 to 10 minutes. Sieve coffee and return back to pot. Leave the cinnamon stick in and keep the coffee warm. Serve in clay cups for best flavor and aroma.

Atoles

The word *atole* comes from the Nahuatl *atolli*, which translates as "stirred corn water." As far as we know, this drink originated long before the conquest. Corn was the main source of sustenance for the ancient Mexicans and this drink was made every day as a mainstay of their nutrition. Recipes have been found as far back as 1545 in Friar Bernardino de Sahagún's chronicles in the *Florentine Codex*.

Women prepared the atole. They used nixtamalized corn masa, toasted corn, or old ground tortillas mixed with a variety of seeds, beans, fermented corn water, fruits, chile, and/or honey. Cold atole was prepared with chia seeds, fruit juice, bee honey, "nectar" from honeypot ants, spices, and chiles. It was served in gourds decorated with flowers.

Chile atole is one of the pre-Hispanic savory atoles that is still prepared today in some areas like Veracruz, Guerrero, and Michoacán. It is made from anise, herbs, chile, and a combination of corn masa and fresh corn kernels. It is often served with lime juice and sea salt in clay cups in the morning or late at night.

One method of preparing atole is by dissolving corn masa in water or milk. Its consistency resembles a velvety, loose porridge. It is often flavored using seasonal fruits like guavas, berries, pumpkin, sweet potato, tamarind, plantains, pineapple, and quince; spices and aromatics like cinnamon, vanilla, and cacao; and nuts like pecans, pine nuts, and almonds.

Atoles are usually sweetened with piloncillo. There is also an unsweetened atole variation called atole blanco, which is usually made out of masa and water or milk, along with vanilla and canela. This unsweetened atole is often paired with buñuelos (page 318) as a foil to the sweet buñuelos syrup.

Atole is the drink of choice during Día de Muertos, and must be served warm. It is the faithful companion to tamales and buñuelos, or to accompany antojitos Mexicanos. Drinking atole during these cold nights is part of the tradition and will warm you from the inside out.

The following recipes are my favorite atole flavors. You can easily double or triple the recipes for bigger crowds; just remember to adjust sugar to your taste. I hope you enjoy them as much as I do.

Atole Blanco—*White Atole*

This atole is the best choice to have with buñuelos. Since it is unsweetened or only lightly sweet, it allows you to balance the sweet flavor of the deserts like calabaza en tacha, guayabate, and sweet tamales. Atole blanco is the loyal companion of buñuelos and can be flavored with aromatic spices like vanilla, canela, or anise. It can be made with water or milk. It can also be the base for any fruit puree you want to add, and if you have some calabaza en tacha (p. 248) leftovers, adding some to this will make for the best caramel pumpkin atole.

Makes 4 mugs

5 cups water or whole milk (or half water, half milk)
½ teaspoon vanilla extract
1 pinch salt
¾ cup dry masa harina or fresh masa
1 (4-inch) stick canela

In a small, heavy-bottomed pot, add cold milk, vanilla, and salt and then add in the masa harina with a whisk until smooth and well incorporated. Add cinnamon stick and warm up over medium-low heat. Stirring at all times, cook atole for 15–20 minutes until it starts to thicken and the cinnamon has released its flavor and scent. Serve hot in generous mugs.

Atole de Calabaza
Caramel Pumpkin Atole

Makes 4 to 5 mugs

1 recipe atole blanco
1 cup hot water
½ cup piloncillo
1 cup calabaza en tacha or pumpkin puree

Prepare one recipe of atole blanco. Dissolve piloncillo in hot water. Add calabaza en tacha or pumpkin puree, mix well, and add to the atole blanco. Bring to a slow simmer. Simmer for 6 to 8 minutes just to marry the flavors.

Atole de Nuez—*Pecan Atole*

Living in Texas makes it easy to love pecans. Atole de Nuez is one of the most traditional atole flavors and a favorite of mine. The toasted ground pecans along with the piloncillo and cinnamon give this atole a nutty caramel flavor. I added extra chopped pieces of toasted pecans at the end of the preparation because I really enjoy biting into these little pecan morsels when sipping it.

When making atole de nuez on a cold night, to warm up I add a splash of spiced rum or Charanda rum from Michoacán, along with a sweet tamalito on the side.

Makes 6 cups

3 cups water, divided
3-inch stick canela
½ cup piloncillo, grated
¼ cup sugar
⅛ teaspoon salt
6 tablespoons masa harina or fresh masa
½ cup pecan halves, toasted and ground
¼ teaspoon vanilla
3 cups whole milk
3 tablespoons pecan halves, toasted and roughly chopped, for garnish

Instead of milk, you can use almond milk, soy milk, or flax milk. Instead of piloncillo, you can use raw agave or honey. And instead of sugar, you can use another sweetener of your choice.

1. In a 3-quart, heavy-bottomed pot, bring to a simmer 1½ cups of water, along with the cinnamon stick, piloncillo, sugar, and salt. Cover with a lid and simmer for about 8 minutes until the sugar and piloncillo dissolves, stir occasionally.

2. Meanwhile, in a small bowl, dissolve the masa harina into 1½ cups of water, and whisk until there are no lumps.

3. Remove the cinnamon stick, and slowly add the masa harina mixture, whisking to avoid lumps. Cook for 2 to 3 minutes. Add the toasted, ground pecans and vanilla and slowly incorporate milk. Keep stirring until well combined.

4. Cook on low heat, stirring continuously for 20 to 25 minutes until small bubbles start erupting on the surface as the consistency of the atole thickens. Do not let the atole boil; cook it nice and slow. The consistency should be thick enough to cover the back of a spoon but thin enough to drink, like a very light and velvety porridge. Taste for sweetness before serving and adjust if needed.

Serve in clay mugs and sprinkle some roughly chopped, toasted pecans on the top.

Atole de Guayaba—*Guava Atole*

From August to February, guavas (*guayabas*) are in season in Mexico. This delicious, aromatic, and tangy fruit makes for one of the best fruit-flavored atoles. The pulp adds great texture and citrus flavor along with its particular and distinctive floral aroma. Can you imagine the smell? If you want to try some of the most iconic flavored atoles, guava is the one to start with. This light-yellow, fruity drink is perfect for an instant warm up when the night temperature drops.

Makes 6 cups

1½ cups water
12 fresh guavas*, pink or yellow, cut in halves
3-inch stick canela, cut in half
½ cup piloncillo, grated
¼ cup sugar
⅛ teaspoon salt
4 tablespoons masa harina or ½ cup fresh masa
1½ cups water
3 cups whole milk**
¼ teaspoon vanilla

There are two kinds of commonly used guavas in Mexico. Yellow guavas have light-yellow creamy flesh. Pink guavas with yellow-lime-green skin and rosy pink flesh are the most floral and sweet.
**Instead of whole milk, you can use almond milk, soy milk, or flax milk. Instead of piloncillo, you can use raw agave or honey. And instead of sugar, you can use any other sweetener of your choice.*

1. In a 3-quart, heavy-bottomed pot, bring to a simmer 1½ cups of water, the guavas, the halves of cinnamon stick, piloncillo, sugar, and salt. Cover with a lid and simmer for about 10 minutes until the sugar and piloncillo dissolves and guavas are soft, stir occasionally.
2. Meanwhile, in a small bowl, dissolve the masa harina into 1½ cups of water and whisk until there are no lumps.
3. Remove half the cinnamon stick from the guava-sugar mixture. Place guavas, the rest of the cinnamon stick, and the syrup in a blender and puree until smooth. Sieve the puree. Set aside.
4. In the original pot, add milk and the masa harina mixture, whisking at all times to avoid lumps. Add the sweet guava puree and vanilla and stir well. Cook on low heat, stirring constantly for 20 to 25 minutes, until small bubbles start erupting on the surface and the consistency thickens, resembling a loose porridge. **Do not let it boil** or you will burn the atole and the delicate fruit flavor; cook it nice and slow. Before serving, taste for sweetness. Adjust sweetness if needed. I always take into consideration what the atole is going to be served with. If it is served with savory tamales, I will make the atole a little sweeter. If I plan on serving with pan dulce or buñuelos, I like my atole a little less sweet to balance out the sweetness.

Atole de Canela—*Cinnamon Atole*

The most fragrant of all atoles is made with cancla, Mexican cinnamon. The masa and milk in this atole make the perfect vehicle to showcase the flavor and aromatic virtues of canela. I like to sweeten this atole using half sugar and half piloncillo because it enhances the woodsy spice flavors of the canela and gives it a hint of caramel. When ready to serve, finely grate some extra canela on top of each cup of atole for an extra burst of flavor and aroma. You can read more about canela on page 48.

Makes 6 cups

3¼ cups water, divided
4 sticks (3 inches long) canela
½ stick canela, ground, to sprinkle over atole cup when serving
½ cup piloncillo, grated
¼ cup sugar
⅛ teaspoon salt
6 tablespoons masa harina or ⅔ cup fresh masa
3 cups whole milk
¼ teaspoon vanilla extract

Instead of milk, you can use almond milk, soy milk, or flax milk. Instead of piloncillo, you can use raw agave or honey. And instead of sugar, you can use any other sweetener of your choice.

1. In a 3-quart heavy-bottomed pot, bring to a simmer 1½ cups of water. Using your fingers, break the canela sticks apart lengthwise to separate the multiple layers into various sticks. This will make a better infusion. Add the broken canela sticks to the simmering water along with piloncillo, sugar, and salt. Cover with a lid and simmer for about 12 to 15 minutes until the sugar and piloncillo dissolves. Stir occasionally. Turn off the heat, add ¼ cup cold water, cover pot with a lid, and let it sit and infuse for 10 more minutes.
2. Meanwhile, in a small bowl, dissolve the masa harina into 1½ cups of water and whisk until there are no lumps. Sieve the infusion in step 1 to remove all woody canela pieces, discard canela, and set infusion aside.
3. In the same pot you boiled the canela, add milk and the masa harina mixture. Whisk constantly to avoid lumps. Add vanilla extract and the canela-sugar infusion and stir until well combined. Cook this mixture over low heat, stirring constantly for 20 to 25 minutes, until small bubbles start erupting on the surface and the consistency thickens to a loose porridge. Do not let it boil; cook it nice and slow. Before serving, taste for sweetness. Adjust sugar if needed. I take into consideration what the atole is to be served with.

Serve atole in clay mugs, and sprinkle some freshly ground canela on top.

Champurrado

We can't talk about atoles without discussing the delicious, cacao-based king of atoles, champurrado. This atole, descended from the Aztecs, is one of the oldest versions. It was originally made of water, corn masa, honey, dry chiles, spices, and cacao that had been ground into a fine powder. Why is it the king? Because for many cultures, such as the Olmecs, Mayas, and Aztecs, cacao was a symbol of abundance and used as currency. Cacao drinks were intended only for gods, emperors, nobility, and warriors. They had many uses in rituals, and also had medicinal, commercial, and gastronomic uses. Cacao became one of the most precious offerings for the souls on the indigenous altars.

Today, champurrado in Mexico is served for breakfast alongside tamales, or with a late dinner of antojitos Mexicanos, or with sweet treats like churros, tamales, or pan dulce, often in the fall and winter months. Champurrado is a welcome indulgence during Día de Muertos, along with some good tamales. This Champurrado recipe is the mestizo version, made with whole milk to make it extra creamy and velvety. Using piloncillo to sweeten is a must. I recommend toasted cacao nibs as a garnish.

Makes 6 cups

3 cups water, divided
1½ chocolate tablets, like Taza, Casa Crespo, or any stone-ground Mexican chocolate
3-inch stick canela
½ to ¾ cup piloncillo, grated, about ½ large cone*
⅛ teaspoon salt
6 tablespoons masa harina
3 cups whole milk**
½ teaspoon vanilla
2 tablespoons toasted cacao nibs, for garnish

Instead of piloncillo, you can use raw agave, honey, or a combination of them.
**Instead of milk, you can use almond milk, or soy milk.*

1. In a 3-quart, heavy-bottomed pot, bring to a slow simmer 1½ cups of water, along with chocolate tablets, cinnamon sticks, piloncillo, and salt. Cover with a lid and simmer for about 10 minutes until the piloncillo and chocolate tablets dissolve. Add ¼ cup of cold water so the cinnamon releases its color. The water will turn slightly reddish.

2. Meanwhile, in a small bowl, dissolve the masa harina into 1½ cups of water and whisk until there are no lumps. In the same pot, add milk and masa harina mixture whisking at all times to avoid lumps. Add vanilla and stir well until the chocolate-canela syrup is well incorporated into the milk-masa mixture. Cook on low heat, stirring continuously for 20 to 25 minutes, until small bubbles start erupting on the surface and the consistency thickens. Do not let it boil; cook it nice and slow. Before serving, taste for sweetness and adjust to your taste if needed. Serve in clay mugs and sprinkle some cacao nibs for garnish.

Note: It is important to use good-quality Mexican chocolate tablets, if possible; stone-ground chocolate tablets make the best champurrado and hot cocoa. A few options are listed at the end of the book on page 361.

Chocolate Mexicano—*Mexican Hot Cocoa*

Chocolate is one of the best gifts from Mexico to the world. Mayan and Aztec gods' "seed of love and generosity," manifested in a cacao bean, which they transformed into a beverage known as *xocolatl*, meaning "bitter water." Xocolatl was a bitter, complex, and invigorating drink often served after a meal to kings and warriors. It was prepared with equal parts of cacao and corn or cacao and vanilla beans in cold water. It was frothy, and was mixed with honey, chile, spices, and/or herbs. Xocolatl was served to the king of the Aztecs in gold cups, and to the warriors in beautifully carved stone vessels or gourd cups that were painted and embossed, with lids to shake the mixture.

Modern drinking chocolate is the result of seventeenth-century European changes. A monk sent cacao seeds and the xocolatl recipe to the Monastery of Aragon in Spain where they added the milk, sugar, and cinnamon that ultimately created the hot chocolate drink we know today.

One of my favorite fall and winter pleasures is a cup of Mexican hot chocolate. I have fond memories of my Grandma preparing a cup of frothy hot cocoa for dinner. I loved the sound of her molinillo frothing the milk and the aroma of chocolate, cinnamon, and vanilla coming out of the kitchen. A molinillo is a wood tool that is used to mix chocolate into warm milk. By spinning the long handle between two hands, air is churned into the liquid, creating a fine froth. My Grandma definitely knew how to use her molinillo; her hot chocolate was like sipping a cloud.

This delicious Mexican hot chocolate is an exciting experience much different from mixing water with a little packet of powder. In this recipe, I added ancho chile powder and a hint of pasilla, which tickle and warm the throat, enhancing the chocolate flavor. The difference between a good cup of cocoa and a GREAT cup of cocoa is the quality of the cacao, so consider that when buying chocolate tablets. I recommend chocolate de metate, which is cacao seeds that have been toasted and hand-ground on a stone mortar called a metate. My favorite chocolate de metate tablets come from Casa Crespo in Oaxaca, Rancho Gordo Stoneground chocolate from Guerrero, and La Lucha in Uruapan, Michoacán. See the sourcing list on page 361.

Makes 4 generous mugs

Special Equipment:
1 wood molinillo or blender
1 tall clay or enamel pot

4 cups whole organic milk
2 cups almond milk
2 Mexican chocolate tablets, preferably chocolate de metate*
1 teaspoon Mexican vanilla extract or 1 vanilla bean pod
1 teaspoon ancho powder
2 generous pinches dried chile pasilla powder (optional)
1 (3-inch) stick canela
2 tablespoons piloncillo, agave nectar, or turbinado sugar, to taste*

* *The sweetness of the chocolate is up to you. I like mine barely sweet, but some people like it extra sweet. I would say start with 2 tablespoons of the sugar you choose.*

1. Add all the ingredients to a tall pot, over medium-low heat. Stir with a wood spoon until the chocolate tablet becomes a soft paste and the heat starts dissolving the chocolate.

2. Increase the heat to medium and **watch the pot at all times.** Believe me, the worst spills on the stove are from milk, and it can happen in a fraction of a second, so watch out!

3. As soon as you see bubbles on the edge of the milk, and the color of the milk has changed, start frothing the chocolate with the molinillo. Place the handle between your palms and rub your hands back and forth as though you're warming them, thus spinning the molinillo back and forth. Make sure the molinillo is half in the milk and half out to incorporate as much air as possible into the milk. Once you see a thick layer of chocolate foam, it's time to serve the chocolate. I usually pour it from up high to achieve even more foam. At this point, anything goes; sprinkle some cinnamon and extra cayenne powder or spike it up with some mezcal, rum, hazelnut liquor, or coffee liquor.

Notes: Why Mexican vanilla and canela? Mexican vanilla comes from an orchid endemic to Veracruz, Mexico, and canela is a distinctive, traditional flavor; both are delicate and extremely fragrant. These two ingredients and a good quality chocolate tablet from Mexico make a cup of cocoa that is a chocolate revelation. Always use quality organic milk for best flavor and consistency.

For vegan or lactose intolerance substitutions, use a combination of soy milk and almond milk or rice milk and almond milk. For nut allergies, use a combination of two of the following: soy, coconut, or rice milk.

The perfect match for a cup of hot chocolate is a concha (page 295).

Alipuses y Chamucos
Booze and Little Devils

✼ ✼ ✼

Mezcal con Sal de Gusano — *Mezcal Shots with Worm Salt* 327

Banderitas — *Mexican Flags* 329

Jarritos de Tequila estilo Jalisco — *Citrus Tequila Jarritos, Jalisco Style* 330

Ponche de Membrillo — *Quince Punch* 331

Ponche de Granada — *Pomegranate Punch* 333

Ponche de Zarzamora — *Blackberry Punch* 334

Ponche de Mandarina y Anís — *Mandarin and Anise Punch* 335

During Día de Muertos, people toast the memories of their deceased family and friends. These drinks make them remember or forget, or simply set the festive mood of the party. A bottle of mezcal or tequila, or a special drink or cocktail, is always part of the traditional ofrendas.

One drink not included here because of the nature of its ingredients and preparation is the ancient Aztec fermented drink called pulque. Dating from pre-Hispanic times, pulque was a ceremonial drink made for the harvest and ancestor's festivities, and its importance was recorded in the mural, "Los bebedores de Pulque" inside a chamber of the Great Pyramid of Cholula in San Andrés Cholula, Puebla, Mexico. This painting depicts 110 men drinking pulque as part of a ritual for the festivities celebrating Mayahuel, the deity of pulque.

Today Pulque is making a comeback in Mexico, and because it is one of the oldest traditional drinks, it is a significant presence during Día de Muertos. Ian and I had the chance to try a delicious homemade pulque in the town of Tarimbaro, Michoacán, where the national pulque fair takes place every year around the beginning of December. It was served in a tall, iced glass with wedges of oranges and limes. We drank it straight with no flavor or juices added, and it was refreshing and absolutely delicious.

Pulque is a type of aguamiel, or "honey water," and has a milk-like color, slightly viscous consistency, and a sweet, starchy, yeasty flavor and aroma. It is made from the nectar that collects in the hollowed-out center of the maguey plant. This nectar used to be fermented in leather sacks but is now fermented in wood or fiberglass vessels for about three to four days to produce the final beverage. Pulque has a short shelf life and is best drunk fresh. Specialty shops called *pulquerias* around central and southern Mexico are the best places to enjoy it, sometimes in new flavor combinations and with different fermentation levels.

As younger generations are taking an interest in the craftsmanship of pulque, various attempts have been made to bottle and commercialize it. But none of them have been successful because bottling drastically changes the flavor. So if you ever visit Mexico, be sure to stop by a pulqueria and try a jicara de pulque or a mixed drink combining pulque with other fruit juices.

In the meantime, any of the following traditional drinks like fruit punches and shots are made with the mission to lift the spirits of the celebration.

Left: Tinajero extracting the aguamiel from the maguey. Right: Freshly made pulque in Tarimbaro, Michoacán.

Mezcal con Sal de Gusano
Mezcal Shots with Worm Salt

It is thought that mezcal was created when the Spanish invaders distilled a variation of the Natives' agave mash. My favorite way to drink this smoky spirit is with wedges of tangy fruit like oranges, grapefruits, limes, mandarins, guavas, or even quince.

The secret to pairing juicy fruits with mezcal is using the right salt. Sal de gusano, or worm-flavored sea salt, is made mainly in the city of Mitla in Oaxaca, Mexico. To make the salt, worms called chinicuiles, which are found on the maguey agave plants, are toasted over a wood-fired comal. They are meaty and have a salty, smoky, umami flavor. When the worms are crushed and combined with sea salt, the salt becomes brown and acquires its unique flavor. The worms themselves are also a delicacy since they are only available in the rainy season when they can be harvested from the maguey roots. They are eaten in tacos, salsas, guacamoles, and many other dishes.

Since the worms grow on the same plant from which we get mezcal, it's like they say, "What grows together, goes together."

Serves 2 to 4

**8 ounces smoked mezcal
1 wedge orange
1 wedge grapefruit
1 wedge lime
1 teaspoon Gran Mitla sal de gusano***

*I have added a few sources of one of the best worm salts in Sourcing Ingredients. Gran Mitla is by far the best sal de gusano I have tasted.

Serve mezcal in 2-ounce shot glasses, with the citrus wedges on a plate or wood board. Serve the worm sea salt on the side in a little ramekin. To drink, take a wedge of any of the citrus and dip the tip of it in the worm sea salt. Take a sip of the mezcal, then squeeze the citrus wedge juice into your mouth and eat the citrus flesh. Repeat the same, choosing a different citrus wedge every time you sip.

*"Para todo MAL un mezcal . . .
y para todo BIEN . . . tambien!"*

*"For every malady, drink one mezcal . . .
and for every goodness, one mezcal as well."*

Banderitas
Mexican Flags

Mexicans have a robust love and respect for *La Patria*, the homeland, and this iconic, national favorite tequila trio is a fine way to receive our beloved ones from the far dimensions in celebration.

The drink is served in three shot glasses, one filled with lime juice, one filled with tequila, and one filled with *sangrita* of your preference.

Sangrita translates to "bloodlike"; the color combination of the juices yields a red-orange beverage. The traditional sangrita was created in the 1920s in Chapala, Jalisco, Mexico, to complement the flavor of a lesser-quality tequila. Legend has it that it was inspired by the leftover juices of a commonly served botana at restaurants and cantinas called pico de gallo, which was made of orange wedges, jicamas, and cucumbers dressed with lime juice, sea salt, and chile de árbol powder. The leftover juices on the plate were poured into a shot glass and drunk with a tequila shot. There are many stories about who created the sangrita and most natives from Chapala attribute the creation to LaViuda de Sánchez, the wife of one of the oldest restaurateurs in Chapala. Her recipe consisted of orange juice, lime juice, chile piquin powder, chile de árbol powder, and sea salt. If the oranges were too sour, she added some pomegranate juice or grenadine to sweeten the reddish drink.

Today, traditional sangrita recipes use the same original ingredients. Outside of Jalisco, sangrita is commonly made with tomato juice and resembles a savory clamato or bloody mary mix. You will find both sweet and savory versions in this recipe. Both options work great as long as they are served in the color sequence of the Mexican flag (green, white, red). A banderita must be sipped in the same order so that the tangy lime prepares you for the warm smooth burn of 100% blue agave tequila, followed by the sweet-savory sangrita to tame and balance the fiery sequence. For a great beginning to your celebration, serve them alongside a good appetizer, street botanas (page 81), or a platter of pico de gallo Jalisco-style, combining chopped cucumbers, orange slices, and jicama, dressed with lime juice, sea salt, and chile powder.

Makes 1 banderita

Special equipment:
3 (2-ounce) shot glasses

For the green shot:
Juice of 3 lemons
Pinch sea salt

For the white shot:
2 ounces 100% agave tequila, blanco, silver, or reposado

For the red shot:
Traditional sangrita, mix the following:
1 ounce seville orange juice
1 ounce grenadine or pomegranate juice
½ ounce lime juice
2 to 3 dashes hot sauce, like Tapatío or Cholula
1 or 2 pinches of chile de árbol powder or any prepared chile powder for fruit

OR

Tomato sangrita, mix the following:
1 once tomato juice
1 once orange juice
⅓ ounce lime juice
Pinch celery salt
Pinch freshly ground black pepper
2 dashes Worcestershire sauce
2 to 3 dashes hot sauce, like Tapatío or Cholula
Extra lime wedges, for rim garnish
Chile powder, for rim garnish

To form the flag:
1. **Green shot:** Fill the first shot glass with the lemon juice and a pinch of sea salt and stir well.
2. **White shot:** Fill the second shot glass with tequila.
3. **Red shot:** Combine either the traditional or tomato sangrita of your choice. Pour into the third shot glass.

Serve the three shot glasses aligned together sequenced like the colors of the Mexican flag: Green, White, and Red. And sip away in that order. Salud!

Jarritos de Tequila estilo Jalisco
Citrus Tequila Jarritos, Jalisco Style

This refreshment is served at fairs, on the street, and in restaurants in almost all states in Mexico. In Jalisco, where I'm from, they are known there as *jarritos* or *cazuelas*. They are served in Tlaquepaque in a well-known traditional restaurant, accompanied by the music of mariachis and warm plates of birria de cabrito (goat stew).

Jarritos are festive, easy-to-prepare, and a crowd-pleasing drink. You can serve them with or without alcohol or set up a bar station with instructions so guests can prepare their own. Or serve in a big cazuela (clay pot) with a ladle, as a refreshing punch, and each guest can refill their jarrito. These are a good family-friendly drink for a Día de Muertos party.

Makes 4 (12-ounce) jarrito drinks

Special equipment:
4 clay clay jarrito pots
4 straws

4 cans grapefruit soda
Juice of 4 to 6 limes, plus 2 limes cut in
    ⅛-inch slices
Juice of 5 oranges, plus 1 orange cut in
    ¼-inch slices
Juice of 3 pink grapefruits, plus 1 grapefruit
    cut in ¼-inch slices
4 to 8 ounces white tequila (to your taste)
Fine or coarse sea salt

1. Soak the clay jarrito pots in water for 10 minutes to hydrate them.
2. Use a lime wedge to wet the rim of each jarrito, and dip the rim into fine sea salt.
3. Combine all the citric juices in a jar.
4. Add into each jarrito about ½ cup of ice cubes, 1 to 2 ounces tequila, and an equal portion of the juice concoction, and fill the rest of the jarrito with grapefruit soda. Stir vigorously until well combined.
5. Add some halves of each citrus into each jarritos, and/or use some to decorate the rim. Insert a straw and make a toast.

Note: If making a big self-serve cazuela punch, combine all ingredients in the cazuela except the ice. Add the slices of orange, grapefruit, and limes. You can freeze the citrus slices ahead of time and add them to cool the drink without watering down the flavor. Provide an ice bucket for your guests to fill each jarrito with ice and a ladle of the refreshing drink.

Ponche de Membrillo
Quince Punch

Quince season in Mexico usually starts in mid October, just in time for the celebration. A quince looks like a yellow apple, and the flavor resembles a citrus fruit married with a green apple—tart and highly acidic. It's the perfect base for a fruit punch that is tart, citrusy, and refreshing.

This punch is best served in short glasses with plenty of crushed ice, and makes a great late afternoon pick-me-up drink while you prepare decorations and build your altar. Play some festive music and you will have a great afternoon.

Makes 1½ liters

Special equipment:
1-liter glass bottle with a seal or a 64-ounce mason jar with lid

2 cups small-diced quince, about 2 or 3 medium, divided
¼ cup lemon juice
2 cups water
½ cup turbinado sugar
2-inch stick canela
1 star anise
Peel of one lemon
1 liter white tequila, white mezcal, or aguardiente
Lemon wedges, for garnish

1. Marinate 1 cup of the diced quince in the lemon juice and set aside.
2. In a medium pot, simmer water, sugar, cinnamon, star anise, lemon peel, and 1 cup of the small-diced quince. Cover and cook until sugar dissolves and the quince is soft enough to puree, about 8 to 10 minutes. Reserve cinnamon stick, and place the rest in a blender. Blend until it's a smooth puree, strain, and discard the pulp.
3. Place this juicy syrup back into the pot. Add the cup of quince soaked in lemon, the cinnamon stick, and the liter of tequila. Stir well. Transfer the concoction into a bottle or a jar. Place in refrigerator and let it brew for 2 to 3 days for best flavor.

Serve over generous amount of crushed ice.

Ponche de Granada
Pomegranate Punch

This pomegranate punch is best known and made in the state of Jalisco. Made with tequila, mezcal, or aguardiente, this delicious punch is infused with pomegranate juice and pomegranate seeds. The punch is extremely easy to prepare, and after a few days it develops a fruity and luscious flavor. It is a magical concoction that yields effortless awesomeness.

Due to its strong flavor and alcohol concentration, it is best served over a generous amount of crushed ice, as a refreshing aperitif or digestif. On any given afternoon, rain or shine, this punch will sparkle up your welcoming spirit. Ponche de granada might be the best way to receive your special guests from near or far.

Makes 1½ liters

Special equipment:
1-liter glass bottle with a seal or a 64-ounce mason jar with lid

1 cup water
¼ cup turbinado sugar
4-inch stick canela
¼ cup dried hibiscus flowers (flor de Jamaica)
2 cups pomegranate juice
2 cups pomegranate kernels (about 1 extra-large or 2 medium pomegranates)
1 quart (1 liter) white tequila, white mezcal, or aguardiente
Lime wedges, for garnish

1. In a 3-quart pot, heat up water, sugar, cinnamon stick, and hibiscus tea until sugar dissolves and the water is red from the hibiscus flowers, about 5 minutes. Add pomegranate juice, bring to a simmer, and cook for 5 minutes. Remove from heat and let it cool.

2. Once liquid is lukewarm, add the pomegranate kernels and tequila. Stir until well incorporated and transfer this concoction into a bottle or a jar. Place in refrigerator and let it brew for 2 to 3 days for best flavor.

3. Strain. Add back some of the pomegranate seeds and serve over crushed ice with a thin wedge of lime.

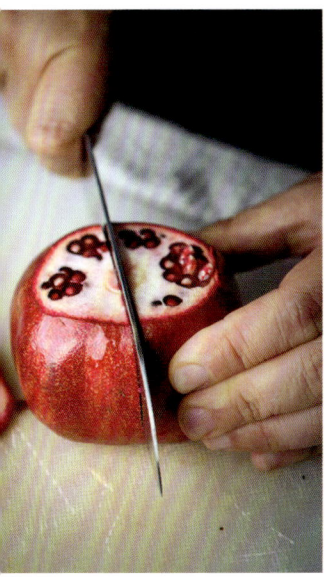

Ponche de Zarzamora
Blackberry Punch

November is the last month you can find blackberries in the markets in the south of Mexico. While we were in Michoacán during Día de Muertos, we bought plenty of fresh wild berries at the mercado every morning, and we gobbled them like kids eating candies. Those berries inspired me to make this fruity dark-purple punch.

When preparing, please get the ripest blackberries and taste them for sweetness so that you can adjust the amount of sugar to your taste. Usually a half cup is just right if the blackberries are in season. The punch should be middling sweet, letting the bright berry flavor come through. Make it three or four days in advance for the best developed flavor. Serve with lots of crushed ice in small glasses.

Makes 1½ to 2 liters

Special equipment:
One liter glass bottle with a seal or a 64-ounce mason jar with a lid

1 cup water
½ cup turbinado sugar
2-inch stick canela
2 allspice buds
Pinch salt
2 cups fresh blackberries
1 liter white tequila, white mezcal, or aguardiente
1 yellow lemon
Blackberries or lemon wedges, for garnish

1. In a medium-size pot, simmer water, sugar, canela stick, allspice, and salt. Cook until sugar dissolves, about 4 to 7 minutes. Remove from heat, cover with a lid, and let it cool off completely.
2. Wash blackberries and crush them manually or in a food processor (pulse 4 to 6 times until crushed but not pureed). Then sieve them to remove the small seeds.
3. Combine the crushed and sieved blackberry puree with the cooled sugar syrup and add mezcal. Stir until well combined. Transfer this concoction into a glass bottle or mason jar. Don't forget to include the cinnamon stick so it keeps on flavoring while macerating. Place in refrigerator and let it brew for 2 to 3 days for best flavor.
4. Serve over generous amount of crushed ice with a squeeze of lemon wedge and fresh blackberries added for garnish.

Ponche de Mandarina y Anís
Mandarin and Anise Punch

Everybody looks forward to enjoying juicy Mandarin oranges in the autumn in Mexico. The beautiful deep orange skins of the fruit announce their sweet and tangy juice.

The floral, sweet, bright Mandarin orange juice combined with star anise pods make this punch a one-of-a-kind beverage. Make it a week (or at least two or three days) in advance for the most developed flavor. Serve in small glasses with plenty of ice and sip slowly while waiting for the souls. Enjoy!

Makes 1½ liters

Special equipment:
1-liter glass bottle with a seal or a 64-ounce mason jar with lid

1 cup water
⅓ cup turbinado sugar
4 whole star anise pods
Zest of 1 mandarin orange
2-inch stick canela
2 cups fresh-squeezed mandarin orange juice, plus the zest of two mandarin oranges
1 liter white tequila, white mezcal, or aguardiente
Sprigs fresh mint, for garnish

1. In a medium pot, simmer water, sugar, star anise pods, mandarin zest, and cinnamon stick. Cook until sugar dissolves, about 5 to 8 minutes. Remove from heat, cover with a lid, and let it cool off completely.

2. To the pot, add mandarin juice and mezcal. Stir well. Transfer this concoction into a glass bottle or a mason jar. Place in the refrigerator and let it brew for 2 to 3 days for best flavor.

Serve over a generous amount of crushed ice, and add a sprig of fresh mint for garnish.

Altars and Ofrendas at Home

✳ ✳ ✳

How to Make an Altar   339

Calaveras de Azucar — *Sugar Skulls*   343

Decorating Sugar Skulls   345

Royal Icing   346

Papel Picado Mexicano — *Mexican Cutout Paper*   348

Large Multilayer Tissue Paper Flowers   351

Paper Flower Making Party   353

Marigold Paper Flowers, Pom-Poms, and Garlands   354

Long-Stem Marigolds   356

How to Make an Altar

In Mexico, we gather all the family members to help set up the altar. It's especially important to have the younger ones help, under supervision, as a means to pass down the tradition. These gatherings enrich family ties and make memories.

Altars and ofrendas are usually set up in the closest room to the entrance of the house, whether that's the dining room, a patio or terrace, a corridor, or the living room. An entryway made of flower petals is often placed at the bottom of the altar and sometimes leads all the way to the entrance of the house to serve as a path for the soul in transit. This path is a guide to go back to their realm as well, which avoids any souls staying too long or getting lost.

Setting up the altar is like setting the table for a beautiful dinner party. It should be thoughtfully arranged. Once the location is decided, a combination of tables, wood or cardboard boxes, chairs, or anything else can be used to create levels of the altar. Each box can be covered with colorful tissue paper, tablecloths, or table runners to make it festive.

An altar can be as big as an entire room or as small as a shoebox. Large families often create a multifamily altar with many photos of relatives. Smaller families dedicate intimate altars for one or two people. Three-level altars are the most common because they represent Heaven, Earth, and Purgatory. Levels can also be dedicated to specific members of the deceased.

Some people have made parallels between the number of altar levels with the nine levels of the Aztec afterworld known as Mictlan. This place in Aztec mythology was where most of the souls live in peace in the afterlife after a difficult four-year journey fraught with challenges through nine different worlds. Today, the levels of the altars don't mean quite as much and it's your choice how many to include.

Table Altar

I started with two boxes that gave a nice height that served as a platform to place the decorations all around. I painted the boxes in bright colors and then added a woven runner for texture. On the top level, I placed the picture of the departed, a sugar skull with his name, fresh and paper marigolds, a glass of water, and a little chair so the soul can take a seat, rest, and quench his thirst after the long journey.

On the second level, I placed the sanctification elements: sea salt, holy water, and incense. On the third level, over the table, I placed fruit, pan de muerto, candies, special prepared foods, drinks, personal objects, and memorabilia. Along the three levels, I taped paper flowers to the wall. Then on each level, I added some glass candles to create a staggered light to guide the soul. And his favorite tunes are playing. (See page 340.)

Small Altar

Setting up an altar is easy. I used a shoebox, painted the box with acrylic paint, and used some craft paper to cover the inside. You can use fabric, cardboard or any kind of decorative paper. I kept the basic elements: photo, candles, pan de muerto, flowers, a cross made with sea salt, water, small food offerings, some memorabilia, and papel picado. When the holiday is over, I use the same box to keep all the elements neatly in storage for next year. (See opposite page.)

Multi-family Altar

There are no specific rules about how many levels there should be or how many people the altars are dedicated to. This is an example of a large family altar. Ian and I decided to combine our relatives into one big family tree. We made papier-mâché skulls for each of our relatives and included a little chair for each soul, water, cross of salt, copal, flowers, fruit, tequila, pan de muerto, memorabilia, and votive candles. On November 2 at 12 a.m. we included the food ofrendas. (See page 341.)

Three-level table family altar.

Left: Altar on November 1 guiding the souls to find their way home. Right: Altar with food ofrendas right before 12:00 a.m. on November 2.

Calaveras de Azucar
Sugar Skulls

Making sugar skulls for Day of the Dead is a lot of fun. Mexicans often decorate them alongside family and friends. It's an opportunity to remember loved ones with lighthearted stories from the past and plenty of laughing and joking. You can pipe the name of the lost loved one right on the skull.

Sugar skulls are both decorative and delicious, though extremely sweet. I have made some sugar skulls in the past to be reused the next year. To prevent moisture from degrading them, seal them in a plastic bag inside an airtight container with a couple silica gel envelopes. Next year you will find them intact and ready to use! Spruce them up by re-piping some colors or applying some glitter. They will last for many years.

This recipe is very simple once you have the necessary ingredients and molds. After that, it's all about preparing the sugar mixture, paying close attention to the consistency. This will ensure an easy time when unmolding. I recommend making these skulls at least three days before you intend to decorate them to be sure the sugar skulls are as dry as possible. I add orange blossom water to the recipe for a delicious floral scent that will help lure our faraway guests.

Makes 3 extra-large skulls or 6 to 8 small skulls or 12 to 18 half-faces*

Special equipment:
1 extra-large skull mold
1 small skull mold
1 or 2 small face Posada Sugar Molds* (optional)
4 to 6 pieces corrugated cardboard the size of the mold

6 pounds (2.7 to 3 kg) sugar
⅓ cup meringue powder
¼ cup water
1 to 2 tablespoons orange blossom water

1. In a large metal bowl, mix sugar and meringue powder until well combined. Add water and orange blossom extract, and mix thoroughly with your hands until it resembles moist sand. To start molding the sugar mixture, it has to have the correct consistency. Grab a handful of the sugar mixture and press tightly, and then open your hand. If the sugar holds the shape of your fingers and does not crumble easily, then it is ready to mold. If it's too crumbly, cracks easily, and does not hold the shape, it needs more water. In that case, add half a teaspoon at a time, mix thoroughly, and do the hand test again until you achieve the right moisture and consistency.

2. Using a paper towel dabbed with a bit of cooking oil, rub oil onto the insides of the molds. Pack the mold with the sugar mixture, pressing tight as you fill them. To level the back of the skull, use a piece of cardboard and scrape evenly so the back is smooth and level.

3. Cover the back of the mold with the cardboard and flip it over. With your fingers, gently tap the eyes, forehead, and chin of the mold to help it release. If the consistency of the sugar mixture is spot on, you will have no trouble. Remove the mold and set the cardboard with the sugar skull aside in a dry safe place. Placing them on a baking sheet allows you to move them all easily. Let them air dry for 48 to 72 hours for best results.

Note: The proportions of this recipe are a base start. Weather tends to affect the sugar consistency, so if you live in a humid climate, you might need less water, and if you live in a hot dry city, you might need slightly more water.

1.

2.

3.

4.

5.

6.

7.

8.

9.

Decorating Sugar Skulls

This is a basic list of what you need to decorate the sugar skulls. Small sugar skulls can be eaten, so it is best to decorate with edible soft candy and royal icing. If you intend to store the skulls instead, and no one is going to mistake them as edible, you can add anything from your imagination. For storage, place each large sugar skull in a single airtight bag to avoid damage. Then place inside a sealed plastic tub, and store in a dry place. The following materials can be found online, in bakery supply stores, and in craft stores.

- 1 royal icing recipe. You will need at least one batch of royal icing to make all the colors, and ½ recipe to make white royal icing to glue the large skulls, with some leftover for decorating.
- Gel colors: magenta, red, orange yellow, green, turquoise, purple, black
- 8- to 10-inch size piping bags, one per color, plus a few extras in case one bursts
- Decorating coupler sets, one set for each bag/color you plan to make
- Metal piping tips, read next page for advice
- Rubber bands or pins, to close the back of the bags
- Cotton kitchen towel, damp
- 2 black food-safe markers
- 4mm silver dragées and 6mm white dragées. Dragées are small round sugarcoated candies, used to decorate cakes, cookies, and confections.
- Edible glitter—pixie dust, any color you like. I used red for the lips on the woman skull page 342 and ice-blue for general sprinkling.

Royal Icing

makes 4 cups

1- to 2-pound bag confectioners sugar, sifted
½ cup meringue powder
½ cup water
3 tablespoons lemon juice

In a metal bowl, sift the powdered sugar along with the meringue powder. Add water and lemon juice and whip with a hand mixer until there are stiff peaks. The icing should feel drier than toothpaste. With a spatula, gather the royal icing from the sides of the bowl to the center, and cover the bowl with a damp cotton towel. Keep the icing covered at all times to avoid it drying out.

✳ ✳ ✳

Decorating with royal icing: Before making the colored icing, select which colors you will be using for decorating and consider which metal tips you will need. In the photo at right there is a guide with the metal tip numbers and examples of icing lines. There are plenty more styles and piping shapes, but two or three tip sizes should be enough. I recommend a fine tip no. 1, 2, or 3 for thin lines, dots, swirls, details, and writing; a petal tip no. 101 or 102 for teardrop shapes, petals, and small flowers; a star-shape tip no. 16 for drop flowers, borders, and stars; and finally a nontoxic food-safe marker for shades, lines, and details. Once you have a plan, start making the colored icing.

Making the colored icing: In a small bowl, place about ½ cup of icing and add a few gel color drops. Mix well. Using a small plastic spatula, transfer to a piping bag fitted with a plastic coupler and metal tip. Make one color at a time and fill the bags as you go. After filling the bag, make sure all the icing is pushed neatly down inside the bag. Twist the top of the bag and tie a rubber band around the end of the bag. Place bags on a tray lined with damp paper towels, and cover the tips of the piping bags with a damp towel to keep icing from drying on the metal tips. To unclog a metal tip, use a needle or toothpick.

For the large sugar skulls: I used 3 to 4 different colors, two solid lines, one petal, and one star. Once sugar skulls are completely dry, you can use a light-color edible marker or a pencil to lightly draw thin lines of the pattern you want on the skull to serve as guides for icing. Then, pipe the icing directly onto the dry sugar skull.

For the small black and white sugar skulls: Use tip no.1 and pipe icing around the main perimeters of the skulls. Let it dry completely. Then, using the edible marker, gently trace lines to make the shadows and smaller details. For sourcing José Posada sugar molds, see page 362.

How to hold a piping bag: Hold out your hand, palm up. Place the twisted part of the bag in the curve of your thumb and index finger. Grab the body of the bag with your fingers and gently squeeze. For better control, use your other hand to help guide the hand that is piping. But most important, have fun!

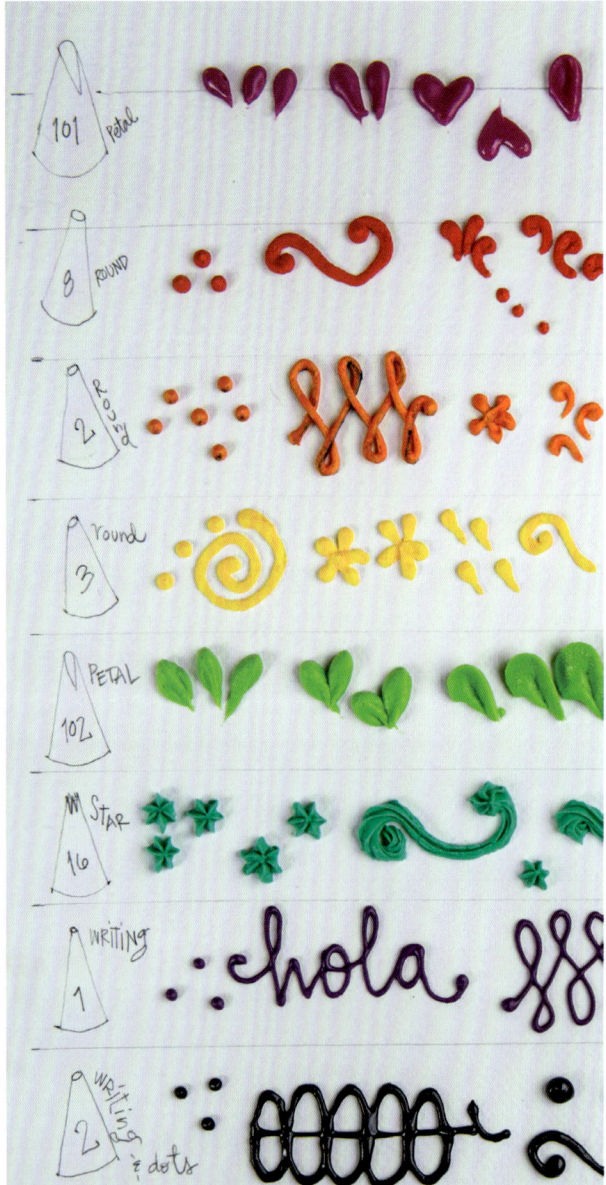

Papel Picado Mexicano
Mexican Cutout Paper

Papel picado is a must for Day of the Dead. This colorful, festive paper is part of almost every celebration in Mexico from weddings to baptisms to birthdays. During the Day of the Dead celebration, papel picado decorated with skulls, skeletons, fruit, ofrendas, crosses, and Catrinas fill the streets and decorate the altars inside of churches, atriums, plazas, and mercados.

Making Papel Picado is an art unto itself. Entire families in Mexico make papel picado in elaborate, beautiful designs as a business. Making papel picado at home is fun and easier than you might think. All you need are scissors, hole punches, glue, tape, light thread, and colorful tissue paper.

You can make designs intricate or simple. You might not be depicting skeletons or the face of Catrina with this technique, but fun geometrical shapes and flower cutouts are a good start. These instructions will help you create great designs and personalize your altar. Cutting papel picado is a craft that kids, friends, and family will enjoy making together.

Makes 8 to 12 rectangular sheets of papel picado

Special equipment:
8 to 12 sheets 20 x 20-inch multicolored tissue paper
Ruler
Scissors
Hole punch
Lightweight cotton or nylon thread

1. Fold paper in half, and then in half again.

2. From the fold crease, measure two 2½-inch segments and draw a little mark on both sides to help keep the line straight when folding. (See side photo of green paper.)

3. Now take the opposite end of paper and fold toward the crease. With your thumb, make a nice crease on the new fold. Take the same paper end and fold back like an accordion to the second 2½-inch mark. Then fold toward the crease one more time. Do the same on the other side of the paper fold. (See side photo of yellow paper.)

4. Notice that the two side ends of the accordion have the open ends of paper. Flip them up so they can be together, and cut out a little rectangle from the open edge. (See side photo of yellow paper.)

5. Now, these two long ends are the sides of the paper. Make a nice trim. I made little scallops using the scissors. Do it by hand or you can use special scissors that cut trimmed designs. You can be as elaborate or as simple as you want. (See side photo of pink paper.)

6. Fold these edges back and fold the 2½-inch strip of paper accordion in half lengthwise. Using the hole punch, make sets of three holes, like if you were punching a hole on each vertex of a triangle. Do this four times along the outside edge of the paper strip. Do the same on the opposite folded edges; punch in-between gaps to have a patterned design. (See side photo of pink paper.) Using the scissors, cut a small triangle in the center of each set of circles. (See side photo of pink paper.)

7. Open accordion into the center and there is another fold. Cut bigger triangles in the center gaps between the groups of triangles.

8. Now it's time to unveil. Unfold the accordion and try to flatten it as much as you can to remove the hard creases. Since the paper was doubled in half, you have two sheets that can be used as singles or as one double. I like to use them doubled up because they are less likely to tear and easier to hang. Using a light cotton thread, pass it in-between the sheets and you are ready to hang the papel picado. To hold it in place, you can staple the ends or use a piece of tape on the top corners to secure the paper to the thread and avoid sliding. Now you are ready to decorate.

Large Multilayer Tissue Paper Flowers

Hands down, these are my favorite paper flowers to make. The first time I made them was with my friend Paige and her mother, Felipa, for a Mexican fiesta birthday party. It took the three of us two Saturdays to make sixty flowers. That sounds like a lot but we had so much fun, listening to music, talking, and joking around. We stapled all the flowers to the arch entryway of her house and it looked amazing! The effort was worth it; she even kept the flowers for future decorations after the party because they looked so beautiful!

In the past I have held craft nights at my home, making projects that can be completed in one afternoon. I had such a great time with these two ladies that for this book I decided to gather up six of my friends,* make some aguas frescas and botanas, and have a paper flowers party. The flowers are fun to make and in some of the simpler steps you can encourage your children to help out. Involving the entire family can be entertaining, and in a couple hours you can have a good number of flowers to decorate your altars. At the end of the party you can exchange different types, sizes, and color flowers so everyone goes home with a good assortment.

Makes 12 to 24 flowers of different sizes, colors, and shapes

3 packages of multicolored tissue paper in 20 x 20-inch sheets
Scissors
Zigzag scissors
Stapler
Clear tape
30 gauge floral wire or nylon thread

1. Using a minimum of three sheets of tissue paper per flower, start by deciding your colors. As you can see in the photo, I used pink, orange, and lime green. Layer the three sheets, and measure about 1½ to 2 inches from the bottom up. Fold up and make a sharp cross. Fold backward and start making an accordion strip, and keep folding until you have a long strip 20 inches long and 1½ to 2 inches wide.

2. At this point decide how many flowers you want to make from that strip. You can divide the strip into:

    Half, for 2 medium to large flowers
    ⅔ and ⅓ for one large and one small flower
    ⅓ for three small flowers

The flower I made for this photo was cut into ⅔ and ⅓.

3. Once cut, staple the middle and attach a wire around each accordion strip for future attachment. Make a loop and twist around the center of the strip. Decide which color will be your center so the wire comes straight down the opposite side. (See photo. I chose green to be my flower center so the wire is placed down the pink side.)

4. Now trim the two ends of the paper strip. The shape of this cut will determine the shape of each of the petals of the flower. There are many ways to trim it to resemble different flowers. Pointy petals can look like a zinnia, round can look like a daisy, and thin strips can look like a marigold. See page 352 for different petal trims and decide which you want to make.

5. Once the ends are trimmed, the fun begins. Open up the accordion strip and tape two of the side ends. This will allow you to start unfolding all the tissue layers in the same direction to complete the circle. Now start lifting up toward the center each layer of tissue paper one at a time. Go all the way around with the green, then with the orange, then with the pink until you have the full circle. As you lift, reshape the creases of each petal to keep it perky and fluffy. Do not worry about perfect petals or shape. Do this process with the large ⅔-strips and do the same with the ⅓-strip.

6. Once you have both flowers shaped, turn the flower upside down and gather the two final ends and tape to close the full circle. Now attach the small flower to the center of the large flower, passing the wires in between the center fold. Twist the wires and refluff petals if necessary. Your flower is ready to hang.

Tips:
- Flowers can be made as simple as three layers or as elaborate as five to six layers for a fuller look.
- Make different sizes and shaped petals of each type and combine them.
- Combine different colors in harmony, monochromatic, or gradient tones.
- Use this same folding principle to make other types of flowers with different colors and sizes.
- You can attach smaller flowers for the center of large flowers, or just leave the large flower as is with a simple center.

Special thanks to my friends Viviana, Victoria, Sharlene, Jess, and Andrea for helping out with this fun project!

Paper Flower Making Party

Gather your family and friends and make an afternoon of crafting a few days prior to the Day of the Dead. This can be a great excuse to get together during the summer, and to get ahead with the preparations for your altar. Make copies of the instructions to have them at the table; people can work in teams of two to learn how to make one type of flower per team. At the end of the party, everyone can exchange flowers and go home with an assortment. Prepare some refreshments like the citrus jarritos (page 330) and any of the mexican street botanas (page 81) for a great complement to the party. Have fun!

Marigold Paper Flowers, Pom-Poms, and Garlands

Marigolds (*Cempasúchil*) are the flower of choice for this celebration, not only for their bright colors but also for their scent, which is believed to attract and direct the souls to the altars. In south and central Mexico at the end of October, the marigold season is at its peak, just in time for November festivities. These flowers are endemic in Estado de México and its surroundings. They have been used in many rituals and ceremonial festivities since the Aztec times.

Today there are large cultivars of marigolds, along with the white baby's breath and red velvet flowers, that supply Día de Muertos in Mexico. But for people and expatriates who would love to celebrate but have no way to get fresh flowers, paper flowers are a good alternative. They are fun to make and the perfect excuse to gather friends and family around a table. If you decide to celebrate next year, keep them in a box in a dark place to avoid paper discoloration. They will last for many years.

These little yellow and orange marigold pom-poms are a very basic way to represent the marigolds on an altar, using simple and inexpensive materials. Each sheet of tissue paper makes two little flowers. The scale of these flowers is perfect for decorating a home altar. The pom-poms can be displayed individually arranged in small bowls or scattered around the altar. You can cover a small arch like you would with real flowers. My favorite way to use these flowers is by threading them into a garland. One only needs about eight flowers (four of each color), a single ribbon, and a needle, and your garland is ready to hang. And if you store them in a dark airtight box, they will keep for many years. The yield is more than enough for a 5-foot garland and a few extras to decorate a small altar.

Makes 16 (3-inch) pom-poms

2 orange tissue paper sheets sized 20 x 20 inches
2 yellow tissue paper sheets sized 20 x 20 inches
Scissors
Stapler
Tape
5 feet of $1/8$-inch wide lime green ribbon
One large-eye hand needle

1. Layer all the tissue sheets and cut them into thirds lengthwise. This will yield 20-inch long × 6.6-inch wide strips.

2. Layer and line up three strips, and cut in half. Now you have two 10-inch long × 6.6-inch wide strips.

3. Take one of those three-layer strips and measure $3/4$ inch from the short side up. Now, fold paper into an accordion like a paper fan. (See opposite photo.)

4. Gather this entire accordion into a small strip and staple right in the middle. Using zigzag scissors, trim the short edges. Using regular scissors, cut about $1/2$-inch strips on each vertex of the zigzag.

5. Fan the paper out and use a small piece of tape to gather the two ends of paper to one side of the accordion.

6. Carefully, starting from the open end, begin pulling up one layer of the tissue paper toward the center. Go all the way around, and do the same for the other two layers, until it starts looking like a fluffy pom-pom. Flip the flower upside down and use a little piece of tape to gather the two ends.

Fluff up the petals and your pom-pom is ready. Continue with the rest of the paper.

To Make a Garland

Cut 5 to 6 feet of ribbon and tie a bow on one end. Thread the ribbon through the large-eye needle on the other end. Take a pom-pom and thread the needle right in the middle, in-between the layers. Thread one orange, then one yellow, and so on, until you have 8 to 10 pom-poms. Remove the needle and tie a double bow. Your garland is ready to hang!

Note: You can make longer garland as needed, but keep in mind that the longer they are, the more likely they are to tangle. So make them shorter and then connect to cover a longer distance. Mix and match the colors of the tissue paper, like using two yellows and one orange or using ombré sets of colors. For storage: These flowers will last a long time if you keep them in a closed box so light won't fade the colors.

Long-Stem Marigolds

These long-stem paper flowers are ideal for the altar. They are made of crepe paper, which is sturdy and has a great texture and flexibility, giving these flowers a funky look. These flowers can be made in different colors or gradient shades of oranges and yellows, from light yellows to dark orange, or in a single tone. I mixed and matched using three colors, dark orange, medium orange, and yellow, and I covered the stem using floral tape. I really liked the way they came out: funky, festive, and fun.

Makes 8 (3-inch) flowers

1 sheet of dark orange crepe paper
1 sheet of medium orange crepe paper
1 sheet of medium yellow crepe paper
8 paper straws
Ruler
Paper scissors
Zigzag scissors
Floral tape
Clear tape

1. Cut eight 2-inch-wide by 15-inch-long strips of the dark-orange crepe paper. Using the zigzag scissors, trim one of the long edges of each strip.

2. Cut eight 2-inch-wide by 12-inch-long strips of the medium orange and yellow crepe paper. Using the zigzag scissors, trim one of the long side edges on each strip.

3. Align one strip of crepe paper of each color, starting with the dark orange, medium orange, and then yellow. Fold them in thirds and make long cuts in between each zigzag about $1/2$ to $2/3$ of the width of the strips. Once you cut them all, unfold and attach them with a little piece of tape at the end.

4. Cut a $2 1/2$-inch piece of tape and attach one end to the back of the three crepe paper strip at the end of a straw, and wrap. Make sure to align the tip end of the straw halfway to the width of the crepe paper strip.

5. Keep rolling into the straw all the strips of crepe paper. Keep it as tight and aligned as you can. When you're finished rolling, the entire perimeter of the roll should be orange. Use a piece of tape to close.

6. Wrap floral tape twice around the bottom of the rolled flower base. Then slightly change the angle of the tape as you go around, wrapping the base of the flower onto the straw. This can be a little tricky because of the difference in thickness, but be patient and keep on rolling all the way down the straw until it is completely covered.

7. Now, using your hand, push down all the paper petals until fluffy, round, and perky. If there is a wider set of petals, just trim them into strips. Place them on a flower base and keep on rolling.

Acknowledgments

We are enormously grateful to all the people of Mexico, especially to the residents in and around Patzcuaro. Our fruitful adventure was possible because of the humble and friendly people we met everywhere in the mercados and plazas; farms, flower fields, and taco stands; at the churches and the cemeteries; and all the places you allowed us to witness and record your lives and bountiful celebration.

Special thanks to Victoria Ryan for introducing us to one of the best *cocineras tradicionales* in Mexico, Rosalba Morales Bartolo, and her daughter Celeste Leonardo Morales, and thanks to them for sharing their love and knowledge in the kitchen with us.

A big thank you goes to the personnel at LLILAS Benson Latin American Studies and Collections at the University of Texas, and to the folks at the Austin Public Library for making our research possible and easy to manage. Professor Manuel Aguilar-Moreno, thank you for your valuable academic support. We would also like to thank the late Professor Elsa Malvido, investigator at INHA, Mexico, for her valuable scholarly contributions.

All our gratitude to all those who helped us test recipes and for their feedback. To our generous prop loaners: Barbara Fregoyle for her beautiful handmade ceramic creations and Elizabeth Winslow. For photographic equipment: Jack Salamanchuk and Panasonic, Dan Heldmann and Nikon, Jimmy Ton and Sony, Ruben Cruz, and Chris Paine and Hoodman USA for memory card generosity!

For digital resources and technical support: Rick Garanflo (Rick you rock!); for technical support, Fernando Naranjo, Joseph Simms, Thomas Bacon, and Austin Macworks. We will always be grateful for your advice, knowledge, and expertise. Thank you to all the good people at Precision Camera and Video for your friendly support.

Special thanks to Mariana's grandmas: my *traditional* Grandma Margarita Sánchez for her whispering in the kitchen, and my *modern* Grandma Ana Fernanda Lund aka "abuelita voy al baile," for always encouraging me to look up. "Se diferente; hay que ver para arriba."—"Be different; look up!"

To our parents, Yolanda Ruiz Pickard and Manuel Nuño Sánchez, and Betsy Cleghorn McEnroe and Gregg McEnroe; we love you. Thank you for giving us the strength and courage to pursue our dreams. To all our close relatives who supported us during this journey, thank you!

Thank you our friends for their perpetual positivity and support: Paul Bardagjy, Viviana Canepa and family, Jessica Lantz, Sharlene & Douglas Eaton-Landis, Andrea Gomez-Gregoriades, Jerry and Rosemary Sullivan, Kirk Tuck, and Liliana Valenzuela. *And to all our friends who stayed close and helped us during the creation of this book, thank you so much!*

Muchas Gracias to everyone who contributed to our crowdfunding campaign, which made the printing of our first edition possible.

A special thanks goes to our dear editor, Aaron Downey, for all his encouragement and support in creating this book. Thanks to Caroline Cook for her editorial help, Tony Sedgwick for his editorial review, and Preston Thomas for his patience and allowing us to collaborate on the book layout and design. We would also like to express our immense gratitude to the team at Rio Nuevo Publishers and owners Ross and Susan Humphreys, who believed in the project and gave us the opportunity to publish our first book with their publishing house. Thank you so much!

Sourcing Ingredients

This is a list of some reliable online companies where you can source almost all of the ingredients for this cookbook, in case you cannot find them in specialty stores where you live. Today, you are likely to find many of the ingredients at international or Hispanic markets, and often in regular grocery stores. Look around and you might be surprised how easy it is to find these ingredients.

I have also included a few websites where you can find Mexican kitchen utensils, clay pots, comals, and great quality stoneware, like molcajetes and metates. And there are sources for making the decorations and molds for sugar skulls and altars, as well as a website where you can find crepe paper in all the colors of the rainbow.

Your best bet for locating a Mexican or Latin American grocery in your area is an online search. These are currently growing in number in Texas where we reside and may be opening in your area as well. If you patronize a local supplier, you are supporting a system that helps availability and your local economy as well. Here is a good guide to Mexican grocery stores in the United States by *Saveur* magazine: www.saveur.com/article/Travels/Guide-Mexican-Grocery-Stores.

Mexican and Latin Foods Markets in the United States

Fiesta Mart—www.fiestamart.com
Texas: Houston, Austin, Dallas–Fort Worth
One of the largest international and Latino food stores in Texas. Visit their website to find a location near you. Fresh fruits and vegetables, pantry items, and kitchen equipment.

GourmetSleuth, Inc.—www.gourmetsleuth.com
Mexican spices and herbs, chiles, dry corn, clay cookware, mortars, pestles, grinders, novelties. One of the only online stores that carry chilhuacle negro chiles!

MexGrocer.com—www.mexgrocer.com
A traditional ingredient online store for one-stop shopping. Pantry items, dry chiles, dry corn, beans, salsas, spices and herbs, drinks, snacks, candy, piñatas, votives, and traditional kitchen equipment. Eighteen years of experience in the market back up this great company.

Spices, Inc.—www.spicesinc.com
Dry chiles, organic spices, herbs, and condiments.

World Spice Merchants—www.worldspice.com

Specific Ingredient Sources

AMARANTH:
Angelina's Gourmet Puffed Amaranth—
www.amazon.com
Amaranto is direct from Mexico—
www.amaranto.com.mx

Arrowhead Mills organic amaranth is available at Whole Foods and healthy food shops.

BANANA LEAVES:
Hispanic and Asian supermarkets commonly carry fresh banana leaves. Or try Walmart supermarkets, www.mexgrocer.com, and www.amazon.com.

BEANS:
Rancho Gordo—www.ranchogordo.com
Currently the ultimate online source for beans and grains. Their impeccable products from Mexico are sold in small amounts, perfect for household cooking. Their great service is a plus. My favorite products there are acoyotes, reboseros, rosa morada, hominy, and pineapple vinegar. You might want to get a *machacadora,* a wooden bean masher, from them as well. Also look for other heirloom beans, chocolate a mano, vinegars, corn, xoconostle, dried chiles, and kitchen gadgets.

CALCIUM HYDROXIDE FOR NIXTAMALIZATION:
Pure calcium hydroxide by Modernist Pantry—
www.amazon.com

Mexican cal by Mi Costeña—www.amazon.com
Also known on the web as Mexican cal, limestone powder, slaked lime powder, or pickled lime powder, this is the essential component in the nixtamalization process. It is found at Hispanic markets in the spices and dried herbs section.

CANELA:
All of the previously mentioned online supermarkets carry canela sticks.

CHOCOLATE TABLETS:
Taza Chocolate—www.tazachocolate.com
Casa Crespo Chocolate—www.casacrespo.com

Chocolate Joaquinitas
Tablets, whole toasted cacao, and cacao nibs from Pátzuaro, Michoacán, if you are visiting Mexico.

La lucha—www.cafelalucha.com.mx
Chocolate de metate; sweet, semi-sweet, and bitter.

Rancho Gordo—www.ranchogordo.com
Stone-ground chocolate from Guerrero.

Moctezuma and **Mayordomo**
Commercial brands of great quality chocolate tablets, both available at www.amazon.com.

CHIA SEEDS: Whole Foods or www.amazon.com.

CONCHA CUTTERS: www.amazon.com.

CORN:
Dry organic corn to prepare nixtamal for fresh masa:
Masienda is a good source for heirloom white, blue, and yellow corn; heirloom black beans; heirloom Jamaica (hibiscus) flowers; masa harina; and equipment—www.masienda.com.

Dry pre-nixtamalized corn to make hominy for pozole:
Rancho Gordo—www.ranchogordo.com
White corn and, in season, cacahuazintle.

Los Chileros—www.amazon.com
White and Blue corn pre-nixtamalized.

Inca's Food Mote Pelado—www.amazon.com

Fresh nixtamal mailed to your door:
Three Sisters—www.threesisterspdx.com

Masa harina:
Maseca and Minsa brands are the most popular masa harina brands in Mexico. Both can be purchased at www.amazon.com or at regular supermarket stores. Look in the international or Latin food sections. For more information, visit their sites at **Maseca**—www.mimaseca.com and **Minsa**—www.minsa.com.mx.

CORN HUSKS:
Almost all Hispanic supermarkets carry them. If you want to but them online, www.amazon.com or www.mexgrocer.com are good options.

DAIRY PRODUCTS:
Los Altos—www.losaltosfoods.com
Don Francisco—www.donfranciscocheese.com
These brands have the best flavor and product selections for things like queso fresco, queso cotija, requesón, jocoque, panela, queso Oaxaca, and Mexican crema. Shop directly from their websites or at www.amazon.com.

DRIED CHILES:
El Guapo is one of the brands I trust most. They label their chiles correctly, and they have great quality, from chiles de árbol and guajillos to spices and dried herbs. They also sell achiote seeds, canela, and corn husks. Purchase at www.amazon.com or www.mexgrocer.com.

Casa Ruiz is another great brand of quality dried chiles—www.amazon.com

GourmetSleuth is one of the few online stores that carry black chilhuacle negro chiles!—www.gourmetsleuth.com

Spices, Inc. is one of the greatest selections of dried chiles, chile powders, and chile flakes—www.spicesinc.com

FRESH FLOWERS IN TEXAS *(Cempasúchil, Marigolds and Cresta de Gallo, Cockscombs):*
Arnosky Family Farms Texas Specialty Cut Flowers—www.texascolor.com, @arnoskyfamilyfarms
13977 FM 2325, Blanco, TX 78606
Arnosky Family Farms grows the largest, most beautiful crop of marigolds and cockscombs in the US. People travel from all over to attend the Marigold Festival. Every year in October and November you can find buckets of freshly cut orange and yellow marigolds, cockscomb, floral perfumed fresh air, and friendly smiles. We spent hours walking through the flower fields and felt transported to the Tarímbaro, Michoacán, flower fields. Then it took only one minute to fall in love with Pamela and Frank.

GARDENING, GROWING CHILES, AND MEXICAN HERBS:
Annie's Heirloom Seeds—
www.anniesheirloomseeds.com/mexican-pepper-collection/
This website carries a Mexican pepper seed collection that includes poblano, jalapeño, serrano, habanero, and chile de árbol. Ideal for beginners!

Baker Creek Heirloom Seeds—www.rareseeds.com
If you want to grow your own Mexican heirloom herbs, chiles, tomatoes, sweet potatoes, pumpkin, flowers, and corn. You will find seeds for red cockscomb flowers, more than ten kinds of marigold flowers, calendula, Aztec sweet nicotiana flowers, covent garden baby's breath, etc.

Dwarf Tomato Project—www.dwarftomatoproject.net
Created by Craig LeHoullier, one of the best authors on heirloom tomatoes, the Dwarf Tomato Project has been working for more than ten years with growers around the world to create delicious tomatoes of all flavors and sizes on small, easy-to-maintain dwarf tomato plants. If you are invested in creating an heirloom garden to make delicious salsas, this is the place to start.

Reimer Seeds—www.reimerseeds.com
An amazing source for seeds from their country of origin, including Mexican seeds for cactus, peppers, greens, tomatillos, herbs (like epazote), tomatoes, and jicamas. Shop by world map.

Seed Savers Exchange—www.seedsavers.org
Since 1975, Seed Savers has been growing, saving, and sharing heirloom seeds, to keep heirloom varieties in our gardens and on our tables for generations to come.

Dried Hibiscus Flowers / Jamaica
Always buy them loose in bulk. Avoid versions that come in tea bags. Available at www.amazon.com and www.mexgrocers.com.

HOJA SANTA:
Fresh: **Marx Foods**—www.marxfoods.com/Fresh-Pepperleaf-Hoja-Santa
Dried: **El Guapo**—www.amazon.com

HUITLACOCHE:
When buying huitlacoche, fresh is best, but it's nearly impossible to get in the United States. The best varieties I have tried come in preserved jars. They have the closest flavor. Avoid canned huitlacoche because it has a metallic flavor.

MARIGOLD FLOWERS (DRIED):
Whole Foods Market in the bulk tea section.

Herbs of Mexico—www.herbsofmexico.com
Many different brands for dry marigold flowers are also available at www.amazon.com.

OVERSEAS MEXICAN INGREDIENTS:
For cooks living abroad, here are some online stores for sourcing chiles, masa harina, and other Mexican goods.

Cool Chile—www.coolchile.co.uk
Monterey—www.montereyfoods.com.au
All About Cuisines—www.allaboutcuisines.com
World of Chillies—www.worldofchillies.com
Holamexico—www.holamexico.de

PAPEL PICADO, DECORATIONS, AND DAY OF THE DEAD FOLK DECOR:
Mexican Sugar Skull for pre-made papel picado in different sizes, styles, and colors—www.mexicansugarskull.com

Paper Mart has the most complete assortment of premium colored tissue paper, crepe paper, floral tape, and pre-made tissue pom-pons—www.papermart.com

Viva Oaxaca—www.vivaoaxacafolkart.com

PIGLET COOKIE CUTTER:
search for: piglet cookie cutter 5-inch cutter www.amazon.com

SPICES:
Organic Spices, Inc.—www.organicspices.com
Spicely Organics—www.spicely.com
Penzey's—www.penzeys.com
Savory Spice—www.savoryspiceshop.com

STONEWARE & KITCHENWARE:
If you are interested in buying a molcajete or metate, make sure the description says lava stone or volcanic natural stone. Also these online shops sell great quality tortilla presses, comals, clay cazuaelas, and pots and pans:

Ancient Cookware—www.ancientcookware.com
Direct From Mexico—www.directfrommexico.com
MexGrocer—www.mexgrocer.com

SUGAR SKULL MOLDS:
Mexican Sugar Skull—www.mexicansugarskull.com
This is one of the best websites to get the traditional-shaped sugar molds. These molds can also be used to make chocolate skulls. They come in a variety of sizes and styles. And the website also carries a large array of decorating supplies, papel picado, and oilcloth tablecloths.

The molds I used to make the sugar skulls in this book are:

For the large skulls: Oaxaca X-Large Sugar Skull Mold W3480

For the small skulls: Mini Sugar Skull Mold W3502

For the half-skull faces with Catrinas: Catrina Skull Mold C4405

For the Frida and revolutionary sombrero skulls: Posada Mold C4400

Wilton offers different styles of skull molds, skull baking pans, and chocolate molds. www.wilton.com

VANILLA MEXICANA:
Villa Vainilla—www.villavainilla.mx

Blue Cattle Truck—www.vanillaimports.com
Villa Vainilla and Blue Cattle Truck are two of the best Mexican vanilla sources in the United States. Both companies are family-owned and source the vanilla directly from Papantla, Veracruz, Mexico. They carry some of the best responsibly sourced, authentic Mexican vanilla extracts and beans available. Both brands are also available at www.amazon.com.

Glossary

acitronar: Sauté until translucent.

aguacate de agua (water avocado): A type of avocado, also known as *pagua*. It has green skin even when ripe, its flesh is bright yellow, and it has a higher water content than other avocados, making it lighter and less oily. This avocado grows in the states of Veracruz, Tabasco, and Oaxaca, and is mostly found as part of traditional dishes in Campeche, Yucatán, and Quintana Roo. Pan de cazon and pibipollos are a couple dishes that use this as garnish. It's known for quelling the fiery habanero's heat.

aguardiente: Hard liquor distilled from sugarcane.

aguas frescas: "Fresh waters." These non-alcoholic beverages are made with fresh seasonal fruit to flavor water, sweetened with sugar or agave nectar, and served cold. People drink them during summer in the middle of the day. In Mexico, aguas frescas are an essential part of *comida*, when we have our strong meal of the day. Aguas frescas are sold at stands in plazas, mercados and sometimes by street vendors. Popular flavors all year round are hibiscus/Jamaica, horchata, tamarind, and lime and chia. Season favorites include pineapple, mango, papaya, melon, watermelon, yellow plums, alfalfa, guava, and mandarin.

ajonjoli: Sesame seeds.

alipús: General name for popular alcoholic beverages or distilled hard liquors.

anafre: A small portable oven, made of laminated metal or clay. It has a bottom chamber that is fed with wood or natural charcoal. On the top it has a grid where clay pots and comals are placed to prepare food.

antojitos Mexicanos ("little cravings"): The generic name for a series of informal foods, typically corn-based, such as quesadillas, gorditas, tlacoyos, tacos, tacos dorados, sopes, tostadas, enchiladas, tamales, empanadas, or tortas. Each state in Mexico has its own varieties. They can be eaten at restaurants, street stands, state fairs, plazas, or in mercados as an appetizer, a small informal meal, or as a complete meal. Antojitos Mexicanos are often served on large platters, and can be served during special celebrations.

ate: Fruit paste.

atole: A traditional warm beverage made with water or milk, masa sweetened with piloncillo, and sometimes combined with a seasonal fruit, dried fruit, or nuts.

botana: An informal snack, usually served with drinks, as appetizers or as an afternoon snack.

cal: Calcium hydroxide or limestone powder. Also known as Mexican cal, slaked lime powder, or pickled lime powder. This powder is what makes nixtamalization possible. To learn about the full process, see page 67, and to buy, see Sourcing Ingredients, page 360.

canela (Mexican cinnamon): The bark of the *Cinnamomum verum* tree. Mexican cinnamon is a type of cinnamon from Sri Lanka called Ceylon, and is known as *canela* in Mexico. It is often considered "true" cinnamon. Its unique flavor is essential in Mexican recipes like hot chocolate, breads, moles, and sauces. See page 48.

cazuela: Clay pot used for cooking.

cempasúchil: The iconic flower of Día de Muertos, also known as the Mexican marigold.

chipotle meco: A dry, twice-smoked jalapeño. Its appearance and color resembles dry tobacco leaves.

Chochoyotes: Corn masa dumplings.

comal: Flat griddle made of metal or ceramic. See cooking equipment, page 41.

encurtido: Pickled.

epazote: Fresh herb used often in Mexican cooking. See fresh herbs, page 51.

escabeche (verdura en vinagre): Light-pickled vegetables and/or chiles.

flor de calabaza: Squash blossom.

guiso/guisado: General name for a protein or vegetable dish, usually cooked in a sauce, gravy, or salsa along with chiles, herbs, and vegetables. Guisos can be sautéed with strips of pork or chicken, or use a tougher cut of meat and simmered to a stew-like consistency.

hoja santa: An herb known in English as eared pepper, anise piper, piper auritum, or root beer plant. Known in Spanish as anisillo, sabalero, hoja de la estrella, hoja de anis, allacuyo, or yerba santa. For description and how to use, see page 51.

hominy: Cooked, nixtamalized corn, used for pozole.

huitlacoche (or cuitlacoche): Corn smut. It is considered a delicacy in Mexico and is sometimes referred to as the Mexican truffle. It is usually sautéed with onions, garlic, and epazote to be incorporated into many dishes, like tamales, quesadillas, gorditas, and in meat sauces. It can be found at Mexican markets only once a year, during corn season.

jocoque: "Soured milk," similar to yoghurt, this was a Lebanese influence. It is used similarly to Mexican crema or in savory preparations like uchepos.

leaf lard: The highest grade of lard, usually extracted from around the kidneys of the pig. The flavor is mild and clean, giving dishes a more subtle pork flavor. It has a higher smoking point suitable for frying.

machacadora: Bean masher.

maiz cacahuazintle: One of fifty-nine types of native corn in Mexico, this is the most commonly used dry corn for making pozole and corn masa because of its size, consistency, and flavor.

masa: Raw dough made from nixtamalized corn.

masa harina: Nixtamalized corn flour.

merienda: Late afternoon small meal, often consisting of milk, coffee, tea, or hot cocoa with pan dulce or a small pastry.

metate: A flat rectangular three-legged stone used to grind chiles, corn, and seeds. See cooking equipment, page 42.

molcajete: Mexican mortar. See cooking equipment, page 42.

molinillo: Hand-carved wooden utensil used to froth milk and hot cocoa. See cooking equipment, page 43.

nejayote: The lime-water solution, including the disintegrated corn hull, that is leftover from the nixtamalization process. Aztecs used this water to make papel amate.

nixtamal: From the Nahuatl words *nextli* (ashes) and *tamalli* (amorphous dough made of corn, tamale). The end product of the nixtamalization process.

nixtamalization: The process in which dry corn is cooked in an alkaline solution made with limestone to precook the corn kernels to remove the hulls and pericarps. This process is used to make hominy and masa. See page 67.

nopales: Often referred to as nopalitos, these are tender and succulent cactus paddles. Part of a regional Mexican gastronomy, they are grilled, used in salads and light sauces, and used in smoothies and juices. Nopalitos have many nutrients and health benefits.

ofrenda: Offering. In Día de Muertos, the ofrendas are the components on the altar, such as food, drinks, and memorabilia. In some regions in Mexico, "La ofrenda" refers to the altar itself. See page 31.

papel picado: Colorful tissue paper that is used for decorating Mexican festivities, especially on Día de Muertos. Learn how to make it on page 348.

pepitas: Pumpkin seeds.

piloncillo (panela or panocha): Unrefined whole sugarcane that is boiled until dark and shaped into cones or blocks. There are two varieties of piloncillo, light brown and dark brown. The best quality piloncillo comes from the state of Veracruz, Mexico. It is commonly used in Mexican cooking to sweeten atoles, aguas frescas, desserts, and fruit.

pimienta gorda: Whole allspice.

queso fresco: A kind of cheese with a soft crumb made with fresh milk. Also known as queso de rancho.

refritos: Refried beans.

Seville oranges: Bitter oranges.

tacha: Term used to describe fruits, like pumpkin and sweet potatoes, that are braised in a dark syrup made with piloncillo, cinnamon, and spices until crystalized in a thick glaze.

tatemar, tatemadas: To char on a comal. Tortillas are often left on a low-heat comal to the point that they are toasty and charred. This term also applies to corn on the cob, cactus, tomatoes, chiles, vegetables, fruits, or seeds that are toasted and charred on a comal.

tejocote (Mexican hawthorn): Native of Mexico, this small, round fruit with bright orange-yellow skin resembles a crabapple. Its flavor is tangy and acidic, and it is mostly used in warm punches, preserves, and fruit jelly rolls.

tequesquite: A natural mineral salt, an alkaline rock that was used since the Aztec times to flavor food, as a food tenderizer as a leavening for tamales, and to help improve the flavor and texture in corn masa, tortillas, beans.

uchepo: Tamale made with fresh corn that is slightly sweet and served with a savory green sauce, typically from the state of Michoacán and the south of Jalisco. See page 148.

Bibliography

Adapon, Joy. *Culinary Art and Anthropology*. New York: Berg, 2008.

Andrews, Jean. *Peppers: The Domesticated Capsicums*. Austin: University of Texas Press, 1995.

Anonymous. *El Cocinero Mexicano 1831*. Mexico: Imprenta de Galván, 1831.

Arau, Alfonso, dir. *Like Water for Chocolate*. 1993; USA: Miramax, 2000. DVD.

Beezley, William. "José Vasconcelos, National Education, and Revolutionary Culture in Mexico." *Oxford Research Encyclopedia of Latin American History*. September, 2016. http://latinamericanhistory.oxfordre.com/view/10.1093/acrefore/9780199366439.001.0001/acrefore-9780199366439-e-268.

de Benítez, Ana M. *Cocina Prehispánica/Pre-Hispanic Cooking*. México, D.F.: Ediciones Euroamericanas Klaus Thiele, Biblioteca Interamericana Bilingue 5, 1980.

Biblioteca Digital de la Medicina Tradicional Mexicana. "Sauco-Sambucus Mexicana," www.medicinatradicionalmexicana.unam.mx/index.php.

Brodman, Barbara. *The Mexican Cult of Death in Myth, Art and Literature*. iUniverse, 2011.

Carmichael, Elizabeth, and Chloe Sayer. *The Skeleton and the Feast*. Austin: University of Texas Press and British Museum Press, 1997.

Carrasco, David. *Daily Life of the Aztecs*. Westport, CT: Greenwood Press, 1998.

Carrasco, David, and Eduardo Matos Moctezuma. *Moctezuma's Mexico Vision of the Aztec World*. Niwot: University of Colorado Press, 1992.

Clendinnen, Inga. *Aztecs: An Interpretation*. New York: Cambridge University Press, 1991.

"Codex Borbonicus." Assemblée Nationale. http://www.assemblee-nationale.fr/histoire/7gf-borbonicus.asp.

"Codice Borbonico, un legado ancestral prehispanico, conocelo." Taringa! http://www.taringa.net/posts/imagenes/17033637/Codice-Borbonico-un-legado-ancestral-prehispanico-conocelo.html

Coe, Sophie D. *America's First Cuisines*. Austin: University of Texas Press, 1994.

Couch, N. C. Christopher. "Images of the Common Man in the Codex Borbonicus." Institutuo de Investigaciones Históricas. http://www.historicas.unam.mx/publicaciones/revistas/nahuatl/pdf/ecn17/267.pdf.

Dahl-Bredine, Phil, Jésus León Santos, Judith Cooper Haden, and Susana Trilling. *Milpa! de semilla a salsa/Milpa: From Seed to Salsa*. Santa Fe: Judith Haden Photography, 2015.

"Dia de Muertos." Visit Mexico. Accessed April 10, 2018. www.visitmexico.com/es.

Díaz del Castillo, Bernal. *Historia Verdadera de la Conquista de la Nueva España*. 19th edition, México: Editorial Porrúa, 2000.

Diego Rivera Retrospective. Madrid: Ministerio de Cultura, Reproducciones Visual, 1992.

"El maíz fue creado por antiguos mexicanos a partir del teocintle." Más de MX. Accessed April 10, 2018. http://masdemx.com/2016/03/el-maiz-fue-creado-por-antiguos-mexicanos-a-partir-del-teocintle-video/.

Fernández-Armesto, Felipe. *Near a Thousand Tables: A History of Food*. New York: The Free Press, 2002.

Godoy, Juanita Garcia. *Digging the Days of the Dead: A Reading of Mexico's Días de Muertos*. Boulder: University Press of Colorado, 1998.

Iglesias y Cabrera, Sonia C. *Cuando lod Abuelos Regresan: Origen y simbologia de Día de Muertos en Mexico*. Distrito Federal, Mexico: Plaza y Valdes, 2008.

"The INAH presents the digital editioin of the 'Codex Boturini' or 'Strip of the Pilgrimage'." Instituto Nacioinal de Antropología e Historia. http://www.inah.gob.mx/es/boletines/572-el-inah-presenta-la-edicion-digital-del-codice-boturini-o-tira-de-la-peregrinacion.

Kennedy, Diana. *Techniques and Ingredients*. New York: Clarkson Potter, 2003.

Krondl, Michael. *The Taste of Conquest: The Rise and Fall of the Three Great Cities of Spice*. New York: Ballantine Books, 2007.

Larousse de la Cocina Mexicana. Accessed April 10, 2018. www.laroussecocina.mx.

Lavín, Mónica, and Ana Benitez. *Sor Juana en la Cocina*. Mexico: Penguin Random House Grupo Editorial, 2016.

Limon D., G. Arturo. *Día de Muertos: Cultura e Identidad*. Torreón, Mexico: Carmona Impresores, 2015.

Malvido, Elsa. Radio INAH interview. January 24, 2013. https://youtu.be/ELOAEnUXQKA.

Mexico desconocido. Accessed April 10, 2018. www.mexicodesconocido.com.mx/recetas-dia-muertos-mexico.html.

Mexico Destinos. Accessed April 10, 2018. www.mexicodestinos.com/blog/2015/10/12-delicias-gastronomicas-para-el-dia-de-muertos/.

"Mictlan, el fascinante inframundo de los mexicas, explicado paso a paso." Accessed April 10, 2018. https://matadornetwork.com/es/mictlan-el-fascinante-inframundo-de-los-mexicas-explicado-paso-paso/.

Moreno, Manuel Aguilar. *Handbook to Life in the Aztec World*. New York: Facts on File, 2006.

Nulart, Jaime. *La Festividad Indigena Dedicada a los Muertos en Mexico: Obra maestra del patrimonio oral e intangible de la humanidad UNESCO*. Distrito Federal, Mexico: Conaculta, 2005.

Palazuelos, Susana. *México: The Beautiful Cookbook*. Mexico: HarperCollins, 1991.

Paz, Octavio. *The Labyrinth of Solitude*. New York: Grove Press, 1985.

Phillips, Charles. *The Illustrated Encyclopedia of Aztec and Maya: The History, Legend, Myth, and Culture of the Ancient Native Peoples of Mexico and Central America*. London: Hermes House, 2017.

Pinedo, Encarnación. *Encarnación's Kitchen: Mexican Recipes from Nineteenth-Century California, Selections from Encarnación Pinedo's el Cocinero Español*. Translated by Dan Strehl. Oakland, CA: University of California Press, 2003.

Pool, Christopher, and Barry Kidder. "A Glimpse into Ancient Mexico: Writings of the Aztecs, Mixtec and Maya." Accessed April 12, 2018. http://uknowledge.uky.edu/world_mexico_codices/9/.

Popol Vuh. *The Definitive Edition of the Mayan Book of the Dawn of Life and the Glories of Gods and Kings*. Translated by Dennis Tedlock. New York: Touchstone, 1985.

Presilla, Maricel E. *Peppers of the Americas: The Remarkable Capsicums That Forever Changed Flavor*. San Francisco: Lorena Jones Books, 2017.

Quintana, Patricia. *El Sabor de México*. New York: Harry N. Abrams, 1986.

"Rediscovering Amaranth, the Aztec Superfood." Forbes. www.forbes.com/sites/michellemaisto/2011/12/05/meet-amaranthquinoas-ancient-superfood-cousin/#219dad0d2581.

Romero Rojas, Óscar. *La Festividad Indigena Dedicada a los Muertos en Mexico: Obra maestra del patrimonio oral e intangible de la humanidad, UNESCO.* Mexico: Conaculta, 2005.

San Pelayo, Gerónimo de. *Libro de Cocina del Hermano Fray Gerónimo de San Pelayo México, siglo XVII.* México: Consejo Nacional para la Cultura y las Artes, 2010.

Tannahill, Reay. *Food in History.* New York: Stein and Day Publishers, 1973.

Toussaint-Samat, Maguelonne. *History of Food.* Translated by Anthea Bell. Cambridge, MA: Blackwell, 1992.

Townsend, Richard F. *The Aztecs.* Third Edition. New York: Thames, 2009.

Tsang, Mandy. "Natural Healing With Copal." Accessed April 10, 2018. www.belize.com/copal.

Villegas Daniel Cosío, Ignacio Bernal, Alejandra Moreno Toscano, Luis González, Eduardo Blanquel, and Lorenzo Meyer. *Historia Mínima de México.* México, D.F.: Colegio de México, 1997.

Wikipedia contributors. "Amaranth grain." Wikipedia, the Free Encyclopedia. Accessed April 10, 2018. https://en.wikipedia.org/w/index.php?title=Amaranth_grain&oldid=834375443.

Wikipedia contributors. "Anthropophagy." Wikipedia, the Free Encyclopedia. Accessed April 10, 2018. https://en.wikipedia.org/w/index.php?title=Anthropophagy&oldid=729846172.

Wikipedia contributors. "New Spain." Wikipedia, the Free Encyclopedia. Accessed April 10, 2018. https://en.wikipedia.org/w/index.php?title=New_Spain&oldid=832788345.

Wikipedia contributors. "Tamale," Wikipedia, The Free Encyclopedia, https://en.wikipedia.org/w/index.php?title=Tamale&oldid=835364415 (accessed April 10, 2018).

World Digital Library. "General History of the Things of New Spain by Fray Bernardino de Sahagún: The Florentine Codex," www.wdl.org/en/item/10096/ (accessed 2017).

World Digital Library. "General History of the Things of New Spain by Fray Bernardino de Sahagún: The Florentine Codex. Book X: The People, Their Virtues and Vices, and Other Nations," www.wdl.org/en/item/10621/ (accessed 2017).

Index

A

Abuelita, *10*
accompaniments, 177
   See also beans; rice
achiote paste, 46
aguamiel, 326
aguas frescas, *240–43*
   Agua Fresca de Avena, 245
   Agua Fresca de Chia con Limón y Hierbabuena, 245
   Agua Fresca de Guayaba, 245
   Agua Fresca de Jamaica con Canela, 244
   Agua Fresca de Mandarina, 244
   Agua Fresca de Melón Chino, 244
   Agua Fresca de Plátano, 245
   Agua Fresca de Sandía con Hierbabuena, 244
aguardiente, 310
   Calientitos, 34, 314
   Ponche de Granada, *332,* 333
   Ponche de Mandarina y Anís, 335
   Ponche de Membrillo, 331
   Ponche de Zarzamora, 334
   See also alcoholic beverages
ajo, 46, *47*
   Arroz al Ajo, 201
alcoholic beverages, 21, 310, 325–335
   Blackberry Punch, 334
   Citrus Tequila Jarritos, Jalisco Style, 330
   Mandarin and Anise Punch, 335
   Mexican Flags, 329
   Mezcal Shots with Worm Salt, 327
   Pomegranate Punch, *332,* 333
   Quince Punch, 331
Alegrías de Amaranto y Miel, *256,* 257
alfeñiques, 16
Alipuses y Chamucos, 325–335
All Saints' Day, 3–5, 9, *32,* 281
   See also Día de Muertos (Day of the Dead)
All Souls' Day, 3–5, 9, *32,* 281
   See also Día de Muertos (Day of the Dead)
allspice, 46
altars (altares)
   decorations for, 342–57
   elements of, 13, 33–34
   how to make, 339
   images of, *4, 27–30, 32, 35, 338, 340, 341*
   origins of, 31
   sizes of, 339
   for small souls, 292
   See also offerings (ofrendas)
amaranth
   Amaranth and Honey Skulls, *258,* 259
   Amaranth and Honey Treats, *256,* 257
   Amaranth Skull Cookies, 304–8

amate paper, 33
ancestor worship, 3
   See also altars (altares); Día de Muertos (Day of the Dead)
anchos, *54, 55,* 152, 164
animas (soul), 9
anise
   Mandarin and Anise Punch, 335
annatto seeds, 46, *47,* 138
antojitos Mexicanos, 7, 16, 81, 145
   Enchiladas de Plaza en Casa estilo Morelia, 88–91
   Sopes de Pollo, *82, 83*
   Tacos Dorados, 86, *87*
   Tostados de Pierna, *84, 85*
   See also street snacks
appliances, 41
árbol Yahualica, *54,* 55
arches (gateways), 33
arroz, 200
   Arroz al Ajo, 201
   Arroz a la Mantequilla con Rajas, Elote y Queso Adobera, *204,* 205
   Arroz a la Mexicana, 202, *203*
   Arroz Verde estilo Puebla, 206, *207*
ates (fruit pastes), 16, 252
atoles, 260, 316
   Atole Blanco, 248, 260, 317
   Atole de Calabaza, 317
   Atole de Canela, *318,* 319
   Atole de Guayaba, *318,* 319
   Atole de Nuez, 317
   Champurrado, 43, 320
   molinillos for making, 43
   See also hot drinks
avocado leaf, 50–51
Aztec culture and traditions
   cooking tools, 42
   Dame of Death. *See* Coatlicue
   Day of the Dead origins, 1, 3–8
   deities of, *8, 10–11*
   food, 109, 259, 304, 320, 322
   food preparation methods, 1, 37, 93, 132, 143
   rituals, 31, 326, 339

B

baby's breath, 13, 33
Banana Agua Fresca, 245
banana leaves, 138, 140, 145, 159–65
   Banana Leaf Tamales, Filled with Mole Negro or Mole Poblano, 161–63
   preparing, 159
Banderitas, *328,* 329
Basic Tamale Dough, 147
bay leaf, *50,* 51

beans, 179–81
    cooking frijoles de la olla, 183
    Pinto Bean Sauce Enchiladas, *196, 197, 198*
    pot beans, 183–84
    refried beans, *186*, 187, *188–89*
    refried black beans, *190, 191*
    spicy chorizo beans, *192, 193*
    Tarascan Bean Soup, 194, *195*
bean smashers, 43
beets, 277
bitter orange, 46, *47*, 138
biznaga and acitrón, 16
black beans, *180*
    refried black beans, *190, 191*
    See also beans
blackberries
    Blackberry Punch, 334
    Blackberry Tamales, *278*, 279
booze. *See* alcoholic beverages
bread. *See* pan dulce
Bread of the Dead, 5, 16, 281, 282–88, *309*
Bullfighting Chiles, 218, *219*
Buñuelos, 260, *262*, 263, *264*, 265, 316, 317
Buttered Rice with Roasted Poblanos, Corn, and Queso
    Adobera, *204*, 205

C

Cacahuates Chile-Ajo, 238
cacao, 31, 320, 322
    See also chocolate
Café de Olla, *309*, 314
cajeta quemada, 16
calabazas
    Atole de Calabaza, 317
    Calabaza en Tacha, 16, 248–49, *251*, 317
La Calavera Garbancera (Dapper Skeleton), *6, 7*, 8
Calaveras de Amaranto y Miel, *258*, 259
Calaveras de Azucar, 5, 16, *308, 342*, 343–47
calaveritas (literary verses), 34
Calaveritas de Galleta de Amaranto, 304–8
caldo de pollo
    Caldo de Pollo Casero, 65
    Caldo de Pollo para Deshebrar, 62
    See also chicken
Calientitos, 34, 314
calla lilies, 13, 33
Camotes Envinados, 253
canary beans, *180*
candied camote, 16
candies, 16
    See also desserts
candles, 5, 13, 21, 31, 33, 34
canela, *47, 48*, 319
Cantaloupe Agua Fresca, 244
Capula, Michoacán, Mexico, 8
Caramel Pumpkin Atole, 317
cardinal directions, 33
carnations, 13, 33

Carne de Cerdo para Deshebrar, 63
Carne de Pavo para Deshebrar, 63
Casa Blanca lilies, 13
Casa Crespo Chocolate, 320, 322
cascabel chiles, *54*, 55, 210
catarina chiles, *54*, 55
Catholicism, 3–5, 9, 21, 33
La Catrina, *2, 6, 8, 11*, 33
cazuelas, 41, 330
Cebollitas Desflemadas para Mole Poblano, 221
cemeteries and funerary rituals, *5, 14, 20*, 21, *22–29*
    See also altars (altares); Día de Muertos (Day of the Dead)
cempasúchil. *See* marigolds
cerdo. *See* pork
Ceylon cinnamon, 48
Champurrado, 43, 320, *321*
Charanda, 253, 310
Charred Street Corn, 235
charring chiles, 59
cheese, *47, 49*
cherubs, 292
Chia, Mint, and Lime Agua Fresca, 245
chicken
    Chicken Sopes, *82, 83*
    Coloradito Mole Tamales in Banana Leaves, 164, *165*
    Enchiladas de Plaza en Casa estilo Morelia, 88–91
    Green Guerrero-Style Pozole, 104, *105, 106*
    Mexican Homestyle Chicken Stock, 65, 94, 112
    Shredded Chicken and Stock, 62
Chicken Sopes, 83
chickpeas, 239
chile catarina, *54*, 55
chile de árbol, *54*, 55, *192, 193*, 210, 216
chiles
    Chile-Garlic Peanuts, 238
    Chile Para Papas, 234
    Chile Pasilla en Polvo, 234
    Chile Sauce for Potato Chips, 234
    chiles en escabeche, 51
    Chiles Manzanos (Perones), Zanahorias y Cebollas en
        Escabeche, 224, *225*
    Chiles Toreados, 218, *219*
    comal for, 41
    frescos, *52, 53*
    powder, 234
    preparing, 57–59
    secos, *54*, 55–56
    See also moles
chilhuacle negro, 55
Chilpancingo, Guerrero, 104
chiltepíns, *52, 53*, 55–56
chipotle meco, *54*, 56
chochoyotes, 123–124, *125*
chocolate, 31
    Champurrado, 43, 320, *321*
    chocolate caliente, 34
    chocolate tamales, *274, 275*
    Mexican Hot Cocoa, 43, 322, *323*

Chocolate Mexicano, 43, 322, *323*
Cholula, Great Pyramid of, 326
chorizo, *192*, *193*
Chunky, Mortar-style Manzano Chile Salsa, 212, 213
cilantro, 51
cinnamon, *47*, 48, 319
Cinnamon Atole, 319
citrus conchitas, 298
Citrus Tequila Jarritos, Jalisco Style, 330
clay dishes, 42
Clay Pot Coffee, *309*, *314*
clay pots, 41, 179
cleaning chiles, 57
Clemole, 136, *137*
Coatlicue (diety), 8, *8*, *10–11*
Cochinita Pibil, 53, 138–41
La Cocina Mexicana, origins of, 7, 37–38
Cocineras Tradicionales (Traditional Cooks of Michoacán) organization, 1, 173
cockscomb, 13, 33
cocoa, 34, 43, 275, 295, 322, *323*
coconut, 271
coffee, *309*, *314*
Coloradito Mole, 126, *127*
Coloradito Mole Tamales in Banana Leaves, 164, *165*
comal, 37, 41
Conchas de Pan Dulce, *294*, 295–98, *299*
Conchitas de Naranja y Limon Real, 298
cookies
    Amaranth Skull Cookies, 304–8
    Lil' Piglets, 300, *301*
    Rainbow Nonpareil Sprinkle Cookies, 302, *303*
    See also desserts; pan dulce
cooking oils, 46
Cooking with Rosalba, 173
copal, 34
Copper Pot Potato Chips, *231*, *232*, *233*
corn (maize), *13*, 66
    Buttered Rice with Corn, Roasted Poblanos, and Queso Adobera, *204*, 205
    Charred Street Corn, 235
    corn on the cob, 16
    Corn Smut Tamales with Oaxacan Cheese and Epazote, *156*, 157–58
    Fresh Corn Tamales, 148, *149*, *150*, *151*
    historical importance of, 37
    hominy, 68, 72, *73*
    masa, 1, 75, 147
    Mexican Street Corn Kernels, 16, 236, *237*
    nixtamal, 69, *70–71*
    nixtamalization process, 67, 68
    as ofrenda, 31
    See also atoles; tamales; tortillas
corn husk tamales, 145
corn husks, 66, 145
corn mills, 42
corn smut, 109, *156*, 157, *157–58*
corridos, 7

Cortés, Hernán, 3, *11*, *37*, 257
Corundas Tradicionales de Cinco Picos, *172*, *174*, 172–75
costeños, 56
cotija cheese, 49
crema, 46
cresta de gallo, *13*, 33
Curtido de Cebolla Morada, 221

D

dahlias, 33
Dapper Skeleton, *6*, *7*, 8
Dark Chocolate and Cacao Nib Tamales, *274*, *275*
Day of the Dead. *See* Día de Muertos
Day of the Dead—Party in the City (Rivera), 7
The Day of the Dead—the Dinner (Rivera), 7
Day of the Faithful Departed. *See* Día de Fieles Difuntos
deep-fried tacos, 86, *87*
de la Asunción, Andrea, 111
de Sánchez, LaViuda, 329
desserts, 247
    Amaranth and Honey Skulls, *258*, 259
    Amaranth and Honey Treats, *256*, *257*
    Guava Preserves, 252
    Marigold and Caramel Flan, *266*, 267
    Mexican Pecan and Pumpkin Seed Pralines, 254
    Mexican Wafers with Honey, Sea Salt, and Toasted Pumpkin Seeds, 255
    Rum and Orange Glazed Sweet Potatoes, 253
    Syrup and Cinnamon Braised Pumpkins, 248–49, *251*
    See also cookies; pan dulce; sweet tamales
Día de Fieles Difuntos, 3–5, 9, *32*, 281
Día de Muertos (Day of the Dead)
    altars and offerings, *4*, 13, 31–35
    celebrations in Mexico today of, 8, 9
    cemetery and funerary rituals, *5*, *20*, 21, *22–29*
    history of, 3–8
    market flowers for, 13
    market food for, 16
    origins of, 1, 3–8
    preparations for, 13
Díaz, Porfirio, 5, 7
dough windowpane test, 263
Dream of a Sunday Afternoon in the Alameda Central (Rivera), *6*, 7–8
dried chiles, *54*, 55–56
drinks. *See* agua frescas; alcoholic beverages; atoles; hot drinks

E

earth, as element, 33
Elotes Asados, 235
El Rey de los Moles, Mole Negro Oaxaqueño, *128*, 129–34, *135*
enamelware pots, 42, 179
enchiladas
    Enchiladas de Plaza en Casa estilo Morelia, 88–91
    Pinto Bean Sauce Enchiladas, *196*, *197*, 198

encurtidos, 209
    Encurtido de Cebolla Morada y Habaneros Tatemados, 222, *223*
Enfrijoladas, *196*, 197
epazote, *50*, 51
escabeches, 209
    chiles en escabeche, 51
    Escabeche of Manzano (Perón) Peppers, Carrots, and Onions, 224, *225*
    Escabeche-Pickled Vegetables, 226, *227*
    See also pickles
Esquites, 16, 236, *237*
Estado de Mexico, Mexico, 109

F
fire, as element, 33
Flan de Cempasúchil, *266*, 267
flor de mayo beans, *180*
flor de muerto. *See* marigolds
flor de obispo, 33
flor de terciopelo, 33
Florentine Codex, 93, 316
flores de muerto. *See* marigolds
flowers, 5, 13, *14–15*, 21, 33
    See also marigolds; tissue paper flowers
food offerings, 16, *17–19*, 34, 293
four cardinal directions, 33
four elements, 33
fresh chiles, 53
Fresh Corn Tamales, 148, *149*, 150, *151*
frijoles, 179–81
    Enfrijoladas, *196*, 197
    Frijoles Con Chorizo y Chile de Árbol, *192*, 193
    Frijoles de la Olla, 183–84
    Frijoles Negros Refritos, *190*, 191
    Frijoles Refritos, *186*, 187, *188–89*
    Sopa Tarasca, 194, *195*
fruit drinks, 329–35
    See also agua frescas
fruit preserves, 16, 252
    See also desserts
fruit punch, 34, 312, *313*, 314
funerary rituals. *See* cemeteries and funerary rituals; Día de Muertos (Day of the Dead)

G
Galleta de Grageitas (Pan de Chochitos), 302, *303*
La Garbancera, *6*, 7, 8
garbanzo bean skull lady, 8
garlands of paper flowers, 354–55
garlic, 46, *47*
    Garlic Rice, 201
garra de tigre, 33
gladiolas, 13, 33
Gran Mitla, 327
Green Guerrero-Style Pozole, 104, *105*, *106*
green jalapeños, *52*, 53
Green Mole, 46, *118*, 119–21

Green Pozolillo, 94, *95*
green sauce, 152
Green Tamales, 152, *153*, 154, *155*
Ground Chile de Árbol Salsa, 55, 56, 216, *217*
Guadalajara, Jalisco, 236, 260
guajillos, *54*, 56, *152*, 164
Guasanas al Vapor, 239
guava
    Guava Agua Fresca, 245
    Guava Atole, 319
    Guava Preserves, 252
Guayabate, 252
Guerrero, Mexico, 56, 104, 109

H
habanero chiles, *52*, *53*, 222
heirloom tomatoes, *47*, 49
herbs (hierbas), 50–51
    herb bundles, 34
Hibiscus & Canela Agua Fresca, 244
hierbabuena, *50*, 51
hierbas de olor, 51
hoja de aguacate, 50–51
hoja santa, *50*, 51
hojas de milpa, 173
Homestyle Morelia Plaza Enchiladas, 88
hominy, 72, *73*
    See also pozoles
hot drinks, 310–11
    Champurrado, 43, 320, *321*
    Clay Pot Coffee, *309*, 314
    hot chocolate, 43, 322, *323*
    Hot Spiced Punch, 34, 314
    Mexican Hot Cocoa, 43, 322, *323*
    Warm Fruit Punch, 312, *313*
    See also atoles
Hot Spiced Punch, 34, 314
huesos de santo (bones of the saint), 5, 281
huitlacoche, 109, *156*, *157–58*
Huitzilopochtli (diety), 143
hydrating chiles, 59

I
icing for sugar skulls, 346
Indigenism movement, 7
Inés de La Cruz, Juana, 136
ingredients, 47
    dried chiles, *54*, 55–56
    essential, 46–49
    fresh chiles, *52*, 53
    herbs, 50–51
    sourcing of, 45, 360–62
Intangible Cultural Heritage of Humanity designation (UNESCO), 1

J
jalapeños, *52*, 53
Jalisco-Style Red Pozole, *100*, 101–2

Jarritos de Tequila estilo Jalisco, 330
jitomates, *47, 49*
    Salsa de Jitomate, Oregano y Canela, 220
    Salsa de Jitomate Sencilla para Antojitos Mexicanos, 220
    See also salsas
Jobito, 310
Juarez, Benito, *10*

K
Kahlo, Frida, 8, *10*
kitchen equipment, 41–43

L
ladles, 43
Laguna de Pátzcuaro, Michoacán, Mexico, 1
La Lucha Chocolate, 322
lard, 46
Large Multilayer Tissue Paper Flowers, *350*, 351, *352*
las almas chiquitas. *See* little souls
laurel bay, *50, 51*
lemon
    Orange and Lemon Citrus Conchitas, 298
Leonardo Morales, Celeste, 173
La Leyenda de Popocatépetl e Iztaccíhuatl, 10
Like Water for Chocolate (Esquivel), 260
lilies, 13
Lil' Piglets, 300, *301*
literary verses as ofrendas, 34
little souls, 21, 292
longaniza, 136
long-stem paper marigolds, 356, *357*
"Los bebedores de Pulque" (mural painting), 326

M
machacadoras, 43
maguey plant, 37, 326
maíz. *See* corn (maize)
Maize Festival, The (Rivera), 7
La Malinche, *11*
Malvido, Elsa, *11*
Manchamanteles, 109
mandarin
    Mandarin and Anise Punch, 335
    Mandarin Orange Agua Fresca, 244
manzanos, *52, 53*
    manzano chile salsa, 212
marigolds, *12, 13, 14*
    on altars and cemetery arrangements, 7, 13, *14*, 21, 31, 33
    Marigold and Caramel Flan, *266*, 267
    of paper flowers, 354, 356–57
marjoram, *50, 51*
market food and flowers for Día de Muertos, 13, *16–19*
masa, 1, 75, 147
    See also corn (maize); tamales
masa harina, 66, 75, 147
Masa para Tamales, 147
Masienda Molinito, 42
Mayahuel (diety), 326

Mayan culture and traditions, 37, 42, 138, 143, 320
mayocoba beans, *180*
memorabilia of the departed, 31, 34
mestizo, 7, 38, 138
metates, 42
Mexican bay leaf, *50*, 51
Mexican crema, 46
Mexican cinnamon, *47*, 48, 319
Mexican cuisine, origins of, 7, 37–38
Mexican cultures and traditions, 1–8, 31, 37
    See also Día de Muertos (Day of the Dead)
Mexican cutout paper, 13, 33, 348, *349*
Mexican Flags (drink), *328*, 329
Mexican Homestyle Chicken Stock, 65, 94, 112
Mexican Hot Cocoa, 43, 322, *323*
Mexican independence, 5
Mexican marigolds. *See* marigolds
Mexican oregano, *50*, 51
Mexican Pecan and Pumpkin Seed Pralines, 254
Mexican Revolution, 7
Mexican spearmint, *50*, 51
Mexican Street Corn Kernels, 16, 236, *237*
Mexican street food. *See* antojitos Mexicanos
Mexican-Style Rice, 202, *203*
Mexican vanilla, 49
Mexican Wafers with Honey, Sea Salt, and Toasted Pumpkin Seeds, 255
Mexico City, Mexico, 145
Mexico City Cathedral, *11*
mezcal
    Mezcal con Sal de Gusano, 327
    Mezcal Shots with Worm Salt, 327
    Ponche de Granada, *332*, 333
    Ponche de Mandarina y Anís, 335
    Ponche de Membrillo, 331
    Ponche de Zarzamora, 334
Michoacán, Mexico, 1, 8, *32*, 109, *173*, 232
Mictlan, 339
mini conchitas, 298
Mixcoatl (diety), 143
molcajetes, 42, 109, 209, 212
moles, 109
    Clemole, 136, *137*
    Mole Amarillo, *122, 123–24, 125*
    Mole Coloradito, 126, *127, 164, 165*
    Mole Negro Oaxaqueño, *128, 129–34, 161–63*
    Mole Poblano, 111–15, 161–63, 221
    Mole Verde, 46, *118, 119–21*
    origins of, 37–38
    Piernas de Pavo Rostizadas bañadas en Mole Poblano, *116*, 117
    pots for, 42
    Tamales en Hoja de Plátano Rellenos de Mole Negro o Mole Poblano, 161–63
    See also chiles
molinillos, 43
Molinito, Masienda, 42
molli, 37

Morales Bartolo, Rosalba, *172, 173, 174*, 175
moras, *54*, 56
Morelos, Mexico, 109
moritas, *54*, 56
mortar and pestle, 42, 209
Moscos, 310
Mosquito, 310
Mukbil Pibipollo, Tamal Yucateco, 53, 168, *169*, 170, *171*
mulatos, *54*, 56
murals, *6, 7*–8
Museo de Artes e Industrias Populares, Pátzcuaro, *30*
Museum of the Old Franciscan Convent of Santa Ana, Michoacán, *32*
music, 7, 34

N
naranja
    agua de flor de naranja, 48–49
    Conchitas de Naranja y Limon Real, 298
    naranja agria, 46, *47*, 138
nixtamal, 42, 69, *70–71*
nixtamalization, 37, 67–68
Nixtamatic, 42
nubecita, *13*

O
Oat-chata Agua Fresca, 245
Oaxaca, Mexico, 55, 56, 109, 126, 281, 289
Oaxacan Egg Yolk Bread, 289–91
Oaxacan Egg Yolk Bread Cherubs, 292, *293*
Oaxacan Mole Negro, the King of Moles, *128, 129–34, 135*
Obleas con Miel, Sal de Mar y Pepitas, 255
Obregón, Álvaro, 7
offerings (ofrendas), 13, *27–29*, 31–35, 281, 282, 337
    See also altars (altares)
ofrendas. *See* offerings
Olmec culture and traditions, 143, 320
onions, 49
    Pickled White Onions for Mole Poblano, 221
    Quick-Pickled Red Onions and Charred Habaneros, 222, *223*
    Quick-Pickled Red Onions, 221
orange
    bitter orange, 46, *47*, 138
    Mandarin and Anise Punch, 335
    Orange and Lemon Citrus Conchitas, 298
    orange blossom water, 48–49
oregano, *50, 51*
Orujo, 310
Otomi culture and traditions, 281

P
Palanquetas de Nuez y Pepitas, 254
Pan de Chochitos (Galleta de Grageitas), 302–303
Pan de Muerto, 5, 16, 281, 282–88, *309*
Pan de Yema Oaxaqueño, 289–91
pan dulce, 34, *280*, 281
    Conchas de Pan Dulce, *294, 295–98, 299*

Conchitas de Naranja y Limon Real, 298
Galleta de Grageitas (Pan de Chochitos), 302, *303*
Pan de Muerto, 5, 16, 281, 282–88, *309*
Pan de Yema Oaxaqueño, 289–91
Puerquitos, 300, *301*
Querubines Oaxaqueños de Pan de Yema, 292, *293*
See also cookies; desserts
panela, *47, 49*
panocha, *47, 49*
Papas Fritas en Cazo de Cobre, *231, 232, 233*
Papel Picado Mexicano, 13, 33, 348, *349*
paper decorations
    papel picado, 13, 33, 348, *349*
    tissue paper flowers, *350*, 351–57
Paper Flower Making Party, 353
pasillas, *54, 56*
    Pasilla Chile Powder, 234, 235, 236
    pasilla negro chiles, *54*, 56, 173
pavo
    Carne de Pavo para Deshebrar, 62
    Piernas de Pavo Rostizadas bañadas en Mole Poblano, *116, 117*
    Tamales de Mole Coloradito en Hoja de Plátano, 164, *165*
peanuts, 238
pecans
    Pecan Atole, 317
    Pecan Palanqueta, 254
pepitorias, 255
peppers. *See* chiles
pequins, *52, 53*
perones, *52*, 53
peruano beans, *180*
pibipollo, 168
pickles, 209
    Pickled White Onions for Mole Poblano, 221
    Quick-Pickled Red Onions and Charred Habaneros, 222, *223*
    Quick-Pickled Red Onions, 221
    See also escabeches
Piernas de Pavo Rostizadas bañadas en Mole Poblano, *116*, 117
piglet-shaped cookie, 300, *301*
piloncillo, *47, 49, 246*
pimienta gorda, 46
Pineapple, Coconut, and Rum Raisin Tamales, *270, 271–73*
pineapples, 271
pinto beans, *180*
    Pinto Bean Sauce Enchiladas, *196, 197, 198*
    See also beans
piping, 346
piquetito, 314
Poblano Mole, 111–15, 221
poblanos, *52, 53*, 205
pollo. *See* chicken
Pomegranate Punch, *332, 333*
pom-poms, 354–55
ponches
    Calientitos, 34, 314

Ponche de Frutas, 312, *313*
Ponche de Granada, *332*, 333
Ponche de Mandarina y Anís, 335
Ponche de Membrillo, 331
Ponche de Zarzamora, 334
Porfiriato, 5
pork
    Clemole, 136, *137*
    Cochinita Pibil, 53, 138–41
    Coloradito Mole Tamales in Banana Leaves, 164, *165*
    Green Guerrero-Style Pozole, 104, *105, 106*
    Jalisco-Style Red Pozole, *100, 101–2*
    lard, 46, 147
    Shredded Pork, 63
    Shredded Pork Tostadas, *84, 85*
    White Pozole, 96, *97, 98*
portrait of the departed, 31, 33, 34
    See also altars (altares)
Posada, José Guadalupe, *6*, 7, *8, 11*
potato chips, 232
Pot Beans, 183–84
pots and pans, 41–42, 179
pozoles, 93
    pots for, 42
    Pozole Blanco, 96, *97, 98*
    Pozole Rojo, Estilo Jalisco, *100, 101–2*
    Pozole Verde Guerrerense, 104, *105, 106*
    Pozolillo Verde, 94, *95*
    Salsa Roja Pozolera, 103
    Serrano Sauce, 107
    See also hominy; soups
Pozolillo Verde, 94, *95*
preparing chiles, 57–59
preserves, 252
pressure cooker, 181
psychopomp symbols, 34
Puebla, Mexico, 109, 111, 206
Puebla-Style Green Rice, 206, *207*
Puerquitos, 300, *301*
pulque, 37, 326
pulquerias, 326
pumpkin, 248–49, *251*, 317
pumpkin seeds, 119, 255, 257
punch. *See* ponches
Purépecha culture and traditions, 1, *20*, 175, 253, 281

Q
Querubines Oaxaqueños de Pan de Yema, 292, *293*
queso blanco, *47*, 49
queso cotija, 49
queso fresco, *47*, 49
Quetzalcoatl, 8
Quick-Pickled Red Onions and Charred Habaneros, 222, *223*
Quick-Pickled Red Onions, 221
quince
    Quince Candies, 16
    Quince Punch, 331

R
Rainbow Nonpareil Sprinkle Cookies, 302, *303*
raisins, 271
Rancho Gordo New World Specialty Food, 179, 322
La Raza Cósmica (Vasconcelos), 7
rebosero beans, *180*
recipes, overview, 39
red jalapeños, *52, 53*
red onions, 221, 222
Red Pozole Hot Sauce, 103
red sauce, 152
Red Tamales, 152, *153*, 154, *155*
refried beans, *186–89*
    black beans, *190, 191*
    machacadoras for making, 43
    See also beans
Refried Black Beans, 191
religious objects on altars, 34
Rellenos de Mole Negro o Mole Poblano, 161–63
rice, 200
    Buttered Rice with Corn, Poblanos, and Queso Adobera, *204*, 205
    Garlic Rice, 201
    Mexican-Style Rice, 202, *203*
    Puebla-Style Green Rice, 206, *207*
Rivera, Diego, *6*, 7, *7–8, 10*
Roasted Red Salsa with Árbol and Cascabel Chiles, 55, 210, *211*
Roasted Tomatillo Salsa Verde, *214, 215*
Roasted Turkey Legs with Mole Poblano, *116*, 117
roasting chiles, 57
Roman Catholicism, 3–5, 9, 21, 33
roma tomatoes, *47*, 49
royal icing, 346
Rum and Orange Glazed Sweet Potatoes, 253

S
Sacrificial Offering—Day of the Dead, The (Rivera), 7
Sahagún, Bernardino de, *11*, 93, 316
sahumerio, 34
salbutes, 53
Sal Marina de Cuyutlán, Colima, 49
salsas, 209
    equipment for making, 42
    Salsa de Chile Serrano, 107
    Salsa "Espanta Rabitos," Salsa de Chile Serrano, 107
    Salsa de Jitomate, Oregano y Canela, 220
    Salsa de Jitomate Sencilla para Antojitos Mexicanos, 220
    Salsa Martajada de Chile Manzano en Molcajete, 212, *213*
    Salsa Mucha Muchacha (Salsa Macha), 55, 56, *216, 217*
    Salsa Roja Asada con Chile de Árbol y Chile Cascabel, 55, 210, *211*
    Salsa Roja Pozolera, 103
    Salsa Verde de Tomatillo Asada, 148, *149, 214, 215*
salt, 33, 49, 181, 327
Sando, Steve, 179

sangrita, 329
San Jerónimo Purenchécuaro, Michoacán, *173*
Santa Clara del Cobre, Michoacán, 232
La Santa Muerte, 34
Santiago Tulyehualco, Xochimilco, Mexico City, 257
sausage, 136, *192*, 193
sea salt, 49
serranos, *52, 53*
Serrano Salsa, 107
Shredded Chicken and Stock, 62
Shredded Pork, 63
Shredded Pork Tostadas, 85
Shredded Turkey, 62
shrines. *See* altars (altares)
Simple Tomato Sauce for Mexican Antojitos, 220
social inequality, 7
Sopa Tarasca, 194, *195*
sopeadito, 282, 289
Sopes de Pollo, *82, 83*
soups
    Mexican Homestyle Chicken Stock, 65, 94, 112
    Tarascan Bean Soup, 194, *195*
    See also pozoles
sourcing ingredients, 45, 360–62
    See also ingredients
Spanish conquest in Mexico, 3, 37–38
Spanish *verbenas*, 5
spearmint, *50, 51*
Spicy Chorizo Beans, *192*, 193
"Spooky Tail" Sauce, Serrano Salsa, 107
spoons, 43
stainless steel pots, 42
Steamed Fresh Young Chickpeas, 239
steamer pots, 41
strainers, 43
street snacks, 231
    accompaniments for, 234
    Charred Street Corn, 235
    Mexican Street Corn Kernels, 16, 236, *237*
    Papas Fritas en Cazo de Cobre, *231*, 232, *233*
    See also antojitos Mexicanos
Sueño de una Tarde Dominical en la Alameda Central (Rivera), *6, 7–8*
sugar cane cones, *47*, 49, 246
sugar skulls, 5, *16, 308, 342,* 343–47
    decorating, 345
    royal icing for, 346
sweet bread. *See* pan dulce
Sweet Bread Shells, *294,* 295–98, *299*
sweet potatoes, 253
sweets. *See* cookies; desserts; pan dulce
sweet tamales, 269
    Blackberry Tamales, *278,* 279
    Dark Chocolate and Cacao Nib Tamales, *274, 275*
    Pineapple, Coconut, and Rum Raisin Tamales, *270, 271–73*
    Sweet Red Beet Tamales, *276,* 277
    See also desserts; tamales

Swiss Chard and Queso Fresco Tamales, 166, *167*
Syrup and Cinnamon Braised Pumpkin, 248–49, *251*

T

Tacos Dorados, 86, *87*
tamalera, 41
tamales, 143
    basic dough for, 147
    considerations when making, 145
    fillings for, 62–63
    freezing, 145
    reheating, 145
    tamalera for, 41
    Tamales de Acelgas y Queso Fresco, 166, *167*
    Tamales de Elote, 148, *149, 150, 151*
    Tamales de Huitlacoche con Quesillo y Epazote, *156, 157–58*
    Tamales de Mole Coloradito en Hoja de Plátano, 164, *165*
    Tamales en Hoja de Plátano, Rellenos de Mole Negro o Mole Poblano, 161–63
    Tamales Tradicionales Rojos o Verdes, 152, *153,* 154, *155*
    wraps for, 145, 159
    Yucatecán Ceremonial Tamale, 168, *169,* 170, *171*
tamales dulces, 269
    Tamales de Chocolate Obscuro con Trocitos de Cacao, *274, 275*
    Tamales de Piña, Coco y Pasas al Ron, *270, 271–73*
    Tamales Dulces de Betabel, *276,* 277
    See also desserts; tamales
Tarascan Bean Soup, 194, *195*
Tarimbaro, Michoacán, 326
Taza Chocolate, 320
tejolote, 42
telera, 145
Tender Corn Tamales with Salsa Verde, 148, *149, 150, 151*
tequesquite, 143
tequila
    Banderitas, *328,* 329
    Jarritos de Tequila estilo Jalisco, 330
    Ponche de Granada, *332, 333*
    Ponche de Mandarina y Anís, 335
    Ponche de Membrillo, 331
    Ponche de Zarzamora, 334
thyme, *50, 51*
tissue paper flowers, *350,* 351–57
    See also flowers
Tlaxcala, Mexico, 109
toasting chiles, 57
Toltec culture and traditions, 143
tomatillo milpero, 49
tomatillos, *47,* 49, *152,* 215
tomatoes, *47,* 49
    Simple Tomato Sauce for Mexican Antojitos, 220
    Tomato, Oregano, and Cinnamon Salsa, 220
    See also salsas
tomillo, *50, 51*
Tonanzin. *See* Coatlicue (diety)

tongs, 43
toreados, 53, 218
tortilla press, 43
tortillas, 66, 77
    de maíz, *76, 77, 78–79*
    equipment for making, 41, 43
    See also corn (maize)
tostadas, 66
Tostadas de Pierna, *84, 85*
Traditional Cooks of Michoacán organization, 1
Traditional Five Peaks Corundas, *172, 174,* 172–75
Traditional Red or Green Sauce Tamales, 152, *153,* 154, *155*
turkey
    Coloradito Mole Tamales in Banana Leaves, 164, *165*
    Roasted Turkey Legs with Mole Poblano, *116,* 117
    Shredded Turkey, 62
tzompantli, 281

U
Uchepos, 148, *149, 150, 151*
UNESCO designation, 1
utensils, 43

V
vanilla, 49
Vasconcelos, José, 7, *10*
veneration of the dead, 3
    See also altars (altares); Día de Muertos (Day of the Dead)
Veracruz, Mexico, 109
verbenas, 5
Verduras en Escabeche, 226, *227*
Victoria Professional Manual Grain Grinder and Table Clamp Corn Mill, 42
Villa, Pancho, 7

W
wallflowers, 33
Warm Fruit Punch, 312, *313*
water, as element, 33
Watermelon and Mint Agua Fresca, 244
White Atole, 248, 260, 317
white onions, 49, 221
White Pozole, 96, *97, 98*
wind, as element, 33
wood paddles, 43
worm salt, 327

X
xocolatl, 322

Y
Yellow Mole, *122, 123–24, 125*
Yes, More Please! blog, 1
Yucatán, Mexico, 222
Yucatán Pibil Pork, 53, 138–41
Yucatecán Ceremonial Tamale, 168, *169,* 170, *171*

Z
Zacualpan, 310
Zapata, Emiliano, 7
zarzamoras
    Ponche de Zarzamora, 334
    Tamales de Zarzamora, *278,* 279

Viva la Vida!

About the Creators

MARIANA NUÑO RUIZ was born and raised in Guadalajara, Jalisco, Mexico, and comes from a long line of strong women. Margarita, her traditional grandma, kindled her passion for traditional Mexican cooking at an early age. Ana Fernanda, her modern grandma, inspired her to become a woman with a professional career and to see the world with wider eyes. The combination of their teachings ignited Mariana's love for cooking and her curiosity beyond the kitchen, to learn about ingredients, their origins, and the history of foods. Mariana earned an architecture degree from ITESO and after working as an architect for more than eight years, she followed her bliss to acquire a culinary arts degree from AWC in Arizona. Since then, she has cooked in restaurants, catered, baked, and sculpted and decorated cakes. She also likes to teach cooking classes and workshops. Mariana enjoys mambo, food history, creating recipes, and collecting new and rare cookbooks. She also loves chiles and worships tomato season. Her last supper would be frijolitos de la olla. When she is not cooking she is thinking about cooking.

IAN MCENROE was born in Michigan but grew up in Texas. His interest in photography started with a manual camera on which he learned to shoot film. Ian earned his Fine Arts degree from the University of Texas, which led to his award-winning photography and a long career as a photographic consultant and an instructor to hundreds of students at all levels of learning. When he's not taking photos, he enjoys painting, jazz, collecting records, reading, coffee, and, of course, good food.

In 2013 IAN and MARIANA co-created the cooking blog, *Yes, more please!*, where they combine their skills in creating recipes, photography, writing, design, and production. Driven by their motto, "An extra serving of cooking inspiration…," they work to inspire people to get into the kitchen and to cook from scratch. Together, they have since created more than 150 original and traditional recipes with step-by-step photos, showcasing Mariana's cooking and production design and Ian's photography. In 2014 the *Austin Chronicle* named their blog one of the top ten local cooking blogs, and a year later, their blog was invited to be an official participant and recipe contributor for Expo Milano 2015. They have developed recipes for national and local brands, and their work has been featured at *Huffpost*, *Food52*, James Beard Foundation Instagram feed, *The Kitchn*, *Country Living*, the Today Show website, and in the *Austin American Statesman*, to name a few. They have given food photography workshops and cooking and photography classes. Ian and Mariana are happily married and live in Austin, Texas. To see more of what they are up to, visit their website, www.yes-moreplease.com.